Organizational Stress Around the World

Stress is defined as a feeling experienced when a person perceives that demands exceed the personal and social resources the individual is able to mobilize. It can occur due to environmental issues, such as a looming work deadline, or psychological, for example, persistent worry about familial problems. While the acute response to life-threatening circumstances can be life-saving, research reveals that the body's stress response is largely similar when it reacts to less threatening but chronically present stressors such as work overload, deadline pressures, and family conflicts. It is proffered that chronic activation of stress response in the body can lead to several pathological changes such as elevated blood pressure, clogging of blood vessels, anxiety, depression, and addiction.

Organizational Stress Around the World: Research and Practice aims to present a sound theoretical and empirical basis for understanding the evolving and changing nature of stress in contemporary organizations. It presents research that expands theory and practice by addressing real-world issues across cultures and by providing multiple perspectives on organizational stress and research relevant to different occupational settings and cultures. Personal, occupational, organizational, and societal issues relevant to stress identification along with management techniques/approaches to confronting stress and its associated problems at the individual and organizational levels are also explored.

It will be of value to researchers, academics, practitioners, and students interested in stress management research.

Kajal A. Sharma is the Associate Head of the Organizational Studies and Human Resource Management Department in the Portsmouth Business School at the University of Portsmouth, United Kingdom.

Cary L. Cooper is a 50th anniversary Professor of Organizational Psychology and Health in Manchester Business School at the University of Manchester, United Kingdom.

D.M. Pestonjee is a GSPL Chair Professor in the School of Petroleum Management at Pandit Deendayal Petroleum University, Gandhinagar, India.

Routledge Studies in Management, Organizations, and Society

The Institutional Theory of the Firm
Embedded Autonomy
Alexander Styhre

Organizational Culture and Paradoxes in Management
Firms, Families, and Their Businesses
Saulo C. M. Ribeiro

The Democratic Organisation
Democracy and the Future of Work
Thomas Diefenbach

Management and the Sustainability Paradox
David M. Wasieleski, Paul Shrivastava, and Sandra Waddock

The Psychodynamics of Toxic Organizations
Howard Stein and Seth Allcorn

Organizational Reliability
Human Resources, Information Technology, and Management
Agnieszka Bieńkowska, Katarzyna Tworek, and Anna Zabłocka-Kluczka

Management, Organization, and Fear
Causes, Consequences, and Strategies
Marek Bugdol and Kazimierz Nagody-Mrozowicz

History in Management and Organization Studies
From Margin to Mainstream
Behlül Üsdiken and Matthias Kipping

Organizational Stress Around the World
Research and Practice
Edited by Kajal A. Sharma, Cary L. Cooper, and D.M. Pestonjee

Public Administration and Epistemology
Experience, Power, and Agency
Arthur J. Sementelli

Organizational Stress Around the World
Research and Practice

Edited by Kajal A. Sharma,
Cary L. Cooper,
and D.M. Pestonjee

NEW YORK AND LONDON

First published 2021
by Routledge
52 Vanderbilt Avenue, New York, NY 10017

and by Routledge
2 Park Square, Milton Park, Abingdon, Oxon, OX14 4RN

Routledge is an imprint of the Taylor & Francis Group, an informa business

© 2021 Taylor & Francis

The right of Kajal A. Sharma, Cary L. Cooper, and D.M. Pestonjee to be identified as the authors of the editorial material, and of the authors for their individual chapters, has been asserted in accordance with sections 77 and 78 of the Copyright, Designs, and Patents Act 1988.

All rights reserved. No part of this book may be reprinted, reproduced, or utilized in any form or by any electronic, mechanical, or other means, now known or hereafter invented, including photocopying and recording, or in any information storage or retrieval system, without permission in writing from the publishers.

Trademark notice: Product or corporate names may be trademarks or registered trademarks, and are used only for identification and explanation without intent to infringe.

Library of Congress Cataloging-in-Publication Data

Names: Sharma, Kajal Anurag, 1982- editor. | Cooper, Cary Lynn, 1940- editor. | Pestonjee, Dinyar Minocher, 1939- editor.
Title: Organizational stress around the world : research and practice / edited by Kajal A. Sharma, Cary L. Cooper and D.M. Pestonjee.
Description: 1 Edition. | New York : Routledge, 2021. | Series: Routledge studies in management, organizations and society | Includes bibliographical references and index.
Identifiers: LCCN 2020034948 (print) | LCCN 2020034949 (ebook) | ISBN 9780367263157 (hardback) | ISBN 9780429292538 (ebook)
Subjects: LCSH: Job stress.
Classification: LCC HF5548.85 .O747 2021 (print) | LCC HF5548.85 (ebook) | DDC 158.7/2--dc23
LC record available at https://lccn.loc.gov/2020034948
LC ebook record available at https://lccn.loc.gov/2020034949

ISBN: 978-0-367-26315-7 (hbk)
ISBN: 978-0-429-29253-8 (ebk)

Typeset in Sabon
by MPS Limited, Dehradun

Contents

Tables viii
Figures x
Contributors xi
Foreword xxi
Acknowledgments xxv

1 Introduction 1
  Kajal A. Sharma, Carry L. Cooper, and
  D.M. Pestonjee

2 "She'll Be Right, Mate!": Occupational Stress
  Research in Australia 7
  Paula Brough, Mitchell Raper, and
  Jason Spedding

3 Work Stress Research in Brazil 23
  Maria Cristina Ferreira, Helenides Mendonça,
  Ronald Fischer, and Leonardo Fernandes Martins

4 Job Stressors in Greater China: An Explorative
  Study Using the Qualitative and Quantitative
  Approaches 43
  Chang-qin Lu, Oi-ling Siu, Hai-Jiang Wang,
  and Luo Lu

5 The Causes and Consequences of Organizational
  Stress: The Case of Greece 62
  Ritsa Fotinatos-Ventouratos

vi Contents

6 Work Stress: A Systematic Review of Evidence from India 80
Kajal A. Sharma

7 Organizational Stress in Contemporary Japan 128
Tsuyoshi Ohira, Tetsushi Fujimoto, and Tomoki Sekiguchi

8 Organizational Stress: A Critical Review from Nigeria 145
Chianu H. Dibia, Emeka S. Oruh, Omotayo A. Osibanjo, and Ojebola Oluwatunmise

9 Increasing Work-Related Stress in the Netherlands and Belgium: How Do These Countries Cope? 167
Irene L.D. Houtman, Christophe Vanroelen, and Karolus O. Kraan

10 Occupational Stress, Coping Strategies, and the Impact of Culture in the Middle East: A Systematic Review of Evidence from Oman 194
Kaneez Fatima Sadriwala and Mustafa Malik

11 Occupational Stress, Health, and Well-Being Research in Portugal: A Qualitative Systematic Literature Review 221
Maria José Chambel, Vânia Sofia Carvalho, and Mariana Neto

12 Organizational Stress in Russia 268
Natalia Ermasova, Natalia Rekhter, and Sergey Ermasov

13 Occupational Stress in South Africa: From the Past to the Fourth Industrial Revolution 284
Claude-Hélène Mayer and Rudolf M. Oosthuizen

14 Organizational Stress in the United States of America Research and Practice 303
James C. Quick

15 **Key Issues and Future Research** 318
*Kajal A. Sharma, Carry L. Cooper, and
D.M. Pestonjee*

Index 330

Tables

3.1	Characterization of workers composing the samples	28
3.2	Stressors adopted in the studies	29
3.3	Work stress reactions adopted in the studies	30
4.1	Results of open-ended interviews in Study 1 (N = 91, total incidents = 88)	47
4.2	Results of descriptive statistics in Study 2 (N = 379)	49
4.3	Intercorrelations of Chinese stressors in Study 2 (N = 379)	50
4.4	Summary of fit statistics for measurements of Chinese job stressors in Study 2 (N = 379)	50
4.5	Intercorrelations of main variables in Study 3 (N = 1,032)	53
4.6	Results of regression analyses in Study 3 (N = 1,032)	54
6.1	Stressor identifies in studies	87
6.2	Consequences of stress	92
7.1	The average annual number of hours worked by individual workers and the proportion of workers working 49 hours or more weekly in developed counties	131
8.1	Summary of stressors/strains and coping mechanisms identified within reviewed studies on organizational stress in Nigeria	162
9.1	Trends in different demands and control indicators (percentages for high risk) for Belgium and the Netherlands	170
9.2	Evolution in the prevalence of "acute problematic" risk factors and workability outcomes among Flemish employees (2004–2016)	180
9.3	Psychosocial risk factors present in enterprises (% establishments)	180
9.4	Measures implemented to prevent psychosocial risks during the last three years (% establishments)	181
10.1	Reliability statistics	202

10.2	KMO and Bartlett's Test	203
10.3	Stress level	203
10.4	Gender	203
10.5	Education	204
10.6	Nationality	205
10.7	Occupation	205
10.8	Do you feel that your life is interesting?	205
10.9	Do you think that you have achieved the standard of living and the social status that you had expected?	206
10.10	Do you feel you can manage situations even when they do not turn out as expected?	206
10.11	Do you feel easily upset if things don't turn out as expected?	206
10.12	Do you feel disturbed by the feeling of anxiety and tension?	207
10.13	Do you consider your family as a source of help to you in finding solutions to most of the problems you have?	207
10.14	Do you sometimes worry about your health?	207
10.15	Are you troubled by disturbed sleep?	208
11.1	Summary of reviewed studies	224
11.2	Two-step cluster analysis	250

Figures

3.1	Flowchart of survey strategy and inclusion of studies	25
3.2	Temporal distribution of the articles reviewed	27
3.3	Distribution of articles by knowledge area	27
3.4	Research methodology adopted in the studies	28
6.1	Yearly distribution of articles reviewed	83
6.2	Type of organizations studied	84
6.3	Work sectors studied	85
6.4	Research methods used in studies	85
6.5	Research methodologies applied in studies	86
9.1	Mean levels of burnout in Europe (scale 1–5)	169
9.2	Psychosocial risks in the Netherlands and Belgium as compared to the rest of Europe	176
9.3	Trends in burnout complaints among a representative sample of Dutch employees	177
9.4	Relative evolution of disabled workers in Belgium 1999–2018	179
10.1	Low, moderate, and high-stress score	204
10.2	Behavioral changes	208
10.3	Coping strategies	209
11.1	Flow diagram of the systematic selection of studies	223

Contributors

Paula Brough is a Professor of Organizational Psychology in the School of Applied Psychology at Griffith University in Brisbane, Australia. Paula's primary research and teaching areas are occupational stress and coping, employee mental health and well-being, work engagement, work-life balance, workplace conflict (e.g., bullying, harassment, and toxic leadership), and the psychosocial work environment. Paula assesses how work environments can be improved via job redesign, supportive leadership practices, and enhanced equity to improve employee health, work commitment, and productivity. Paula has authored over 60 industry reports and over 100 journal articles and book chapters and has produced 9 scholarly books based on her research.

Jason Spedding is an organizational researcher currently completing his PhD at Griffith University. His key research areas are in shared and formal leadership processes, occupational stress, organizational climate, and team dynamics in complex workplaces. He also has an interest in advancing quantitative methodologies in occupational health research through the application of multilevel modeling, the Bayesian analysis, and the Monte Carlo simulation.

Mitchell Raper is a PhD candidate in organizational psychology at Griffith University, Australia. His research focuses on occupational stress and coping and how employee proactivity can reduce workplace stress. In particular, he is interested in the categorization of workplace stressors and how cognitive appraisals and future-oriented coping impact daily well-being at work.

Maria Cristina Ferreira is a Professor and the Psychology Graduate Program Coordinator at Universidade Salgado de Oliveira (Universo – Niterói), Brazil, where she has been teaching and advising master and doctoral students. Her work focuses on culture and positive organizational behavior, with a special interest in Brazilian cultural characteristics, well-being, engagement, and passion at work. She is a member of the Brazilian Society of Organizational and Work Psychology.

Helenides Mendonça is a Professor at Pontifícia Universidade Católica de Goiás (PUC Goiás), Brazil. She has been teaching and advising undergraduate, master, and doctoral students at PUC Goiás. She was a board member of the Brazilian Society of Organizational and Work Psychology and held the following positions at PUC Goiás: Director of Psychology Faculty and Dean of Institutional Development. Her research focuses on the field of culture and positive psychology. Particularly, she is interested in creativity, innovation in organizations, and psychological well-being at work.

Ronald Fischer is a Professor in Psychology at Victoria University of Wellington, New Zealand and is a Researcher at Instituto D'Or de Pesquisa e Ensino, Brazil. His work focuses on cultural and evolutionary dynamics, with a special interest in cultural similarities and differences in values, norms, prosociality, and well-being. His work on culture has been highly influential and he has been named as one of the top 10 most highly cited researchers in culture and psychology. His latest book entitled, "Personality, Values, Culture: An Evolutionary Perspective," appeared with Cambridge University Press.

Leonardo Fernandes Martins is a Professor at Universidade Salgado de Oliveira (Universo – Niterói), Brazil. He has been lecturing and advising undergraduate and master students at Universo – Niterói. His work focuses on training health professionals to reduce social stigma related to people who use alcohol and other drugs. He is a member of the Latin American Network about Drugs and Stigma and a member of the Association for Contextual Behavioral Science.

Chang-Qin Lu is a Research Professor at the School of Psychological and Cognitive Sciences, Peking University, China. He received his PhD in Industrial and Organizational Psychology from the Institute of Psychology, Chinese Academy of Sciences. His research focuses broadly on job insecurity, work stress, self-efficacy, spillover, and crossover effects of work-family conflict/balance. His work has been published in the Journal of Applied Psychology, the Journal of Organizational Behavior, the Journal of Vocational Behavior, Human Relations, and the Journal of Occupational and Organizational Psychology, among others. Prof. Lu is currently the Associate Editor of Applied Psychology: An International Review.

Professor Oi-ling Siu is Chair Professor of Applied Psychology and Dean of Faculty of Social Sciences, Lingnan University. Her research interests include occupational stress, work-life balance, and psychology of safety. Prof. Siu was the Editor of the International Journal of Stress

Management from 2015 to 2020 and Associate Editor of the Journal of Occupational Health Psychology since 2015. She has published 80 journal articles and 23 book chapters.

Hai-Jiang Wang is an Associate Professor in the School of Management at the Huazhong University of Science and Technology, Wuhan, China. He received his PhD in Industrial and Organizational Psychology from the Eindhoven University of Technology, Netherlands. His research areas include job insecurity, job crafting, leadership, and employee work engagement.

Professor Luo Lu received her PhD in Psychology from the University of Oxford, United Kingdom, and she is currently the Distinguished Professor in the Department of Business Administration, College of Management, National Taiwan University, Taiwan. Her major research interests are stress and adjustment, work stress and occupational health, subjective well-being, and culture and self. She has published more than 190 referred journal papers and authored over 30 books and book chapters. She is currently the Editor of the International Journal of Stress Management (SSCI, APA journals), the Senior Associate Editor of the Journal of Organizational Effectiveness: People and Performance (ESCI, Scopus), and the Editor-in-chief of Research in Applied Psychology(Taiwan).

Professor Ritsa Fotinatos-Ventouratos obtained her Doctorate Degree in Organizational Psychology from the University of Manchester Institute of Science & Technology (UMIST), United Kingdom. Her areas of research lie in the field of psychological well-being at work, occupational stress, gender differences, as well as investigating the social impact of the changing and diverse nature of the world of work. As a Professor employed at the Deree College, The American College of Greece, she lectures in the areas of Industrial-Organizational Psychology and Social Psychology. In addition to presenting her research at international congresses and publishing in the domains of work psychology, she serves as a member of the British Psychological Society, International Relations Committee, for the Division of Occupational Psychology.

Dr. Kajal A. Sharma is the Associate Head of Organisation Studies and Human Resource Management Group at the University of Portsmouth, United Kingdom. Prior to joining the University in 2010, she had seven years of work experience in India. Her research areas are evaluating and enhancing HR systems in healthcare, work stress, cross-culture management, and organizational culture. Her work in these areas has been published on various platforms. She has been a consultant to many private hospitals, delivering management development programs for medics and non-medics on stress management and has also steered Stress Audits Indian hospitals.

Professor Cary L. Cooper, CBE, is a 50th Anniversary Professor of Organizational Psychology and Health at the Manchester Business School, University of Manchester, United Kingdom. He is the Founding President of the British Academy of Management, President of the Chartered Institute of Personnel and Development (CIPD), former President of RELATE, and the President of the Institute of Welfare. He was the Founding Editor of the Journal of Organizational Behavior, the former Editor of the scholarly journal Stress and Health, and is the Editor-in-Chief of the Wiley-Blackwell Encyclopaedia of Management, now in its' 3rd Edition. He has been an advisor to the World Health Organization, ILO, and EU in the field of occupational health and well-being, and was Chair of the Global Agenda Council on Chronic Disease of the World Economic Forum (2009–2010) – then served for five years on the Global Agenda Council for mental health of the WEF – and was Chair of the Academy of Social Sciences 2009–2015. Professor Cooper is the Chair of the National Forum for Health and Well-Being at Work which is comprised of 40 global companies (e.g., BP, Microsoft, NHS Executive, UK government, Rolls Royce, John Lewis Partnership, etc.). Professor Cooper is the author/editor of over 250 books in the field of occupational health psychology, workplace well-being, women at work, and occupational stress. He was awarded the CBE by the Queen for his contributions to occupational health, and in 2014, he was awarded Knighthood for his contribution to the social sciences.

Professor D.M. Pestonjee, PhD, is currently associated with the School of Petroleum Management, Pandit Deendayal Petroleum University, Gandhinagar, as GSPL Chair Professor since July 2009. He is also associated with CEPT University, Ahmedabad, as Dean of the Faculty of Applied Management. He has served at eminent institutions like IIM, Ahmedabad, and Banaras Hindu University. He is a psychologist who has a PhD in Industrial Psychology from the Aligarh Muslim University, and he was conferred the DLitt (Honoris Causa) by the Banaras Hindu University in April 2003. In November 2000, he was conferred the title of Honorary Professor of the Albert Schweitzer International University, Geneva, Switzerland. He was awarded the Albert Schweitzer Medal for Science and Peace in April 2004. He has over four decades of teaching and research experience. Among his better-known works are: Organization Structure and Job Attitudes (1973), Behavioral Processes in Organization (1981), Second Handbook of Psychological and Social Instruments (1988), Third Handbook of Psychological and Social Instruments (1997), Studies in

Organizational Roles and Stress and Coping (1997), Studies in Stress and Its Management (1999), and the celebrated Stress and Coping: The Indian Experience (1992, 2002).

Tetsushi Fujimoto is a Professor of Sociology at the Graduate School of Policy and Management, Doshisha University, Kyoto, Japan. His research interests include the intersection of gender, work, and family. He is currently investigating the non-linear patterns of career development for Japanese women holding advanced degrees in science and engineering. His article, co-authored by Sayaka Shinohara and Tsuyoshi Oohira, entitled Work-Family Conflict and Depression for Employed Husbands and Wives in Japan: Moderating Roles of Self and Spousal Role Involvement received the 2015 Outstanding Author Contribution award in Contemporary Perspectives in Family Research from the Emerald Group Publishing.

Tsuyoshi Ohira is a Postdoctoral Fellow of Organizational Behavior at the Organization for Research Initiatives and Development and the Department of Policy Studies, Doshisha University, Kyoto, Japan. His research focuses on the effects of aging, technology, and social interaction on organizational effectiveness including efficiency, service quality, and employee retention.

Tomoki Sekiguchi is a Professor at the Graduate School of Management, Kyoto University, Japan. His research interests include employee behaviors, person-environment fit, cross-cultural organizational behavior, and international human resource management. His work has been published in such journals as Personnel Psychology, Organizational Behavior, and Human Decision Processes, the Journal of World Business, Management International Review, and the International Journal of Human Resource Management. He currently serves as the Co-Editor-in-Chief of Applied Psychology: An International Review, the Vice President (Asia) of the Euro-Asia Management Studies Association (EAMSA), and the Vice President of the Association of Japanese Business Studies (AJBS), among many other positions.

Chianu Harmony Dibia (BSc, MSc, PhD) teaches Organizational Studies and Human Resource Management at the University of Portsmouth, United Kingdom. His research focuses on human resource management, lean manufacturing, and employee working conditions in organizations operating in Nigeria.

Emeka Smart Oruh is a Lecturer in Organizational Studies and Human Resource Management at the University of Portsmouth Faculty of Business and Law, United Kingdom. He obtained his PhD in Employment Relations (ER) and Human Resource Management

(HRM) at Brunel University London, United Kingdom. His key research examines ER, OB, and HRM issues within international business, particularly in emerging markets. Dr. Smart has authored several publications – some of which have appeared in reputable international journals such as the International Journal of Human Resource Management and Employee Relations.

Omotayo Adewale Osibanjo is an Associate Professor in the Department of Business Management at Covenant University, Nigeria. He obtained a Doctorate degree of Philosophy in Management at Babes Bolyai University, Cluj-Napoca, Romania under the scholarship of the Romanian Government in the year 2008. His research focuses on human resource management, industrial relations, communication, and management.

Ojebola Oluwatunmise is a doctoral student in the Department of Business Management at Covenant University, Nigeria. He obtained his first degree in Business Administration at Ambrose Alli University, Nigeria, and his second degree in Project Management at Virginia International University, United States. His research focuses on human resource management, organization behavior, industrial relations, and management.

Irene Houtman has been working at TNO since 1990. After her PhD on Stress and Coping in Lecturing at the Free University in Amsterdam in 1990, she was involved in many large-scale projects at TNO on occupational risks at work, often with particular emphasis on psychosocial risks, mental health, and prevention of occupational risks as well as stimulating return to work. These projects are financed by national and international funds. From 1995 onwards, she has been working at TNO as a senior researcher.

Christophe Vanroelen is an Associate Professor and the Director of Interface Demography – a research center connected to the Department of Sociology of the Vrije Universiteit Brussel. He holds a PhD in Social Health Sciences and Master's Degrees in Sociology and Applied Social Science Statistics. He collaborated in several scientific research projects regarding socioeconomic health inequalities, work-related health, and job quality. His current research focuses predominantly on the quality of work and employment as determinants of health and well-being among workers.

Karolus Kraan has been working at TNO since 1998 as a Research Scientist. During these years, he has conducted a large number of studies on working conditions, work organization, and technology, in relation to health and well-being outcomes. He is well familiar with many large-scale surveys among employees and employers – both national and international. He has also conducted a lot of cross-country studies – for instance, on behalf of the Dutch Ministry of Employment and Social Affairs, the European Commission, and European agencies.

Kaneez Fatima Sadriwala is an Associate Professor in Accounting, Acting Head of the Department of Accounting. Dr. Kaneez Fatima works in the field of accounting, business statistics, marketing, and management. Her research span is multidisciplinary, ranging from financial analysis, accounting for SMEs, e-Learning, entrepreneurship, stress management, work-life balance, students' learning process, and measurement of learning outcome to accounting ontology, etc. She, along with her student team, won TRC FURAP awards twice for Best Research Project, one in the year 2015, and followed by another in the year 2018. She has published two books, Marketing Management and Mall Management from Himalaya Publishers, with several research papers on national and international platforms. She is a renowned orator and has represented the university on various international platforms. Dr. Kaneez Fatima received her Master's Degree in Commerce (Accounting and Business Statistics) in 1991 and her PhD degree in Commerce (Business Administration) from Mohanlal Sukhadia University, Udaipur, India in 2004, and FDP from Indian Institute of Management (IIMA), India in 2009 and served as Professor cum Director at Aravali Institute of Management, Udaipur, India prior to joining the University of Nizwa in February 2010.

Mustafa Malik has been teaching in the areas of tourism and sustainable development, tourist consumer behavior, and marketing of tourism services. He has been teaching Tourism Management courses for the past seven years. Dr. Mustafa received his PhD degree in Commerce (Tourism Management) from Aligarh Muslim University, India in 2004 and his Master's degree in Tourism Administration (MTA) from Aligarh Muslim University, India in 2001. He has also qualified at the UGC-NET examination in Tourism Management in 2004. He is a two-time recipient of the University Medal from Aligarh Muslim University (AMU) for securing 1st position in B.Sc (Hon's) 1999 and in MTA 2001.

Maria José Chambel is an Associate Professor at the Faculty of Psychology, the University of Lisbon in Lisbon, Portugal. She has a PhD in Social Psychology and teaches work and organizational psychology and occupational health psychology. She is a member of the Research Center of Psychology Science of the University of Lisbon (CicPsi), where she coordinates the group of Adaptation Process in Context (Applied Psychology) and has participated in several research projects. Her main research interests include subjects such as employment relations and stress and well-being at work.

Vânia Sofia Carvalho is an Assistant Professor at the Faculty of Psychology, University of Lisbon, Portugal. She has a PhD in Human Resources, Work and Organizational Psychology and teaches in the field of work and organizational psychology. She is a member of the Research Centre of Psychology Science of the University of Lisbon (CicPsi) and the Institute of Cognitive Psychology (IPCDHS/FPCE, University of Coimbra). Her research focuses on work-life intersectionality with boundary management, job design, and organizational supportive cultures to advance employees' well-being.

Mariana Neto is a Public Health Doctor and an Occupational Medicine Specialist working at the National Institute of Health Doutor Ricardo Jorge, Portugal, where she is the Coordinator of the Health Observation and Epidemiological Surveillance Unit of the Epidemiology Department. She has Master of Science degrees in Public Health and Organizational Behavior. She has also a PhD in Environmental Health. She is directly responsible for the National Health Interview Survey at the Ministry of Health and for the health household panel survey (ECOS) among others. Her research interests are mainly related to the fields of mental health, social determinants of health, occupational health, and the effects of environmental risks on health.

Natalia Ermasova is an Associate Professor at Governors State University, Illinois, United States. She received a PhD for Public Affairs at the Indiana University, United States and a PhD for Economics at the Saratov State Technical University, Russia. Her primary research interests are strategic management, business ethics, public finance, risk management, innovation management, and the state capital budgeting. Before starting her work in the United States, she worked as a Professor of Finance in the Volga Region Academy for Civil Services in Russia for 12 years and as a Professor of Saratov State University for 2 years. She was a Visiting Professor in the Ludwigsburg Academy for Civil Services, Germany, a Fulbright Visiting Professor at the SPEA, Indiana University in Indiana and the Corvinus University in Hungary. She has published more than 30 articles in the United States and more than 45 books and articles in Russia. Her articles were published in the Journal of Management Development, State and Local Government Review, Public Organization Review, World Review of Business Research, Post-Communist Economies, and the SAM Advanced Management Journal.

Natalia Rekhter obtained her Master's Degree in Health Services Administration from the University of Michigan, Ann Arbor and her PhD in Higher Education from Indiana University, Bloomington. Currently, she is an Assistant Professor and a Director of the

Undergraduate Health Administration program at the Governors State University. Natalia's research interests include the use of social media for education and health maintenance. She is a recipient of ten grants, two Fulbright Specialist awards, and an author of several research articles. She also has over a decade's worth of healthcare industry experience.

Sergey Ermasov has a PhD in Economics, Russia. He is a teacher at the Russian School of Indiana. He has worked as a Professor of the Finance Department at Saratov State University, Russia since 2007. He worked as an Associate Professor of Finance at the Saratov Economic University from 1992 to 2007. His primary research interests are innovation management, risk management, project management, and insurance. Dr. Ermasov is the author of several books on insurance, innovation management, and financial management. He has published more than 50 articles in Russia.

Claude-Hélène Mayer (Dr. Habil., PhD) is a Professor in Industrial and Organizational Psychology at the Department of Industrial Psychology and People Management at the University of Johannesburg, an Adjunct Professor at the European University Viadrina in Frankfurt (Oder), Germany, and a Senior Research Associate at Rhodes University, Grahamstown, South Africa. She holds Master's degrees in MA Cultural Anthropology (MA) and Crime Sciences (MSc), PhD's in Psychology and Management, a Doctorate in Political Sciences and a Habilitation in Psychology with focus on work, organizational, and cultural psychology. She has published work on transcultural mental health and well-being, a sense of coherence, shame, transcultural conflict management and mediation, women in leadership, the Fourth Industrial Revolution, and psychobiography.

Rudolf M Oosthuizen received a BA degree (cum laude) from the University of Pretoria, South Africa in 1992 and obtained a B.A. Honors in Psychology at the same university in 1993. In 1999, he received an MA degree in Industrial and Personnel Psychology from the Potchefstroom University for Christian Higher Education. In 1999, he registered as an Industrial Psychologist with the Health Professions Council of South Africa. In 2005, he completed a DLitt et Phil in Industrial and Organizational Psychology at the University of South Africa (Unisa). Currently, Rudolf is an Associate Professor in the Department of Industrial and Organizational Psychology at the University of South Africa. Rudolf's fields of interest are career psychology, positive psychology, employment relations, and the Fourth Industrial Revolution.

James Campbell Quick is a Distinguished University Professor and Professor Emeritus at the University of Texas at Arlington and a

Professor at the Alliance Manchester Business School, The University of Manchester, United Kingdom. Dr. Quick and his brother Jonathan's signature work is the Theory of Preventive Stress Management (TPSM). His awards include the 2016 Regents Outstanding Teaching Award (The University of Texas System) and the Maroon Citation (Colgate University). Dr. Quick is a Fellow of the American Psychological Association. Colonel Quick retired from the United States Air Force. His highest military award is the Legion of Merit. Dr. Quick is married to the former Sheri Grimes Schember.

Foreword

"Organizational stress" is commonly defined as an emotional, cognitive, behavioral, and physiological response to noxious aspects of work, work environment, and organizational climate. As amply documented in this highly important and timely volume, there is no doubt that occupational stressors have been – and still remain – major determinants of human morbidity and mortality worldwide. The World Economic Forum (2020) publishes annual reports on "Global Risks" facing mankind and our planet, however, without including working-life related risks – except "unemployment" – in its graph. One of the many complex, powerful and interacting risks included (see Figure 1) is "Infectious diseases," such as the Covid-19 pandemic. This pandemic's direct and indirect impacts on productive employment, unemployment, and occupational and public health are likely to become both severe and long-lasting.

To counteract such global risks – as well as the present mounting disaffection and disruption across the world partly due to short-term and silo thinking by many elites – all 193 member states of the United Nations have agreed on Agenda 2030, comprising 17 very ambitious Sustainable Development Goals (SDGs) and 169 targets (United Nations, 2015).

The SDGs are concerned with a wide multitude of stressors, and accordingly intend to reach an entire "package" of interacting goals: end poverty, end hunger, encourage good health and well-being, provide quality education, promote gender equality, provide clean water and sanitation, promote affordable and clean energy, provide decent work and economic growth, address industry, innovation, and infrastructure, reduce inequalities, develop sustainable cities and communities, encourage responsible consumption and production, take action on climate change, promote life below water, promote life on land, work towards peace, justice, and strong institutions, and create partnerships to achieve these goals (United Nations, 2015).

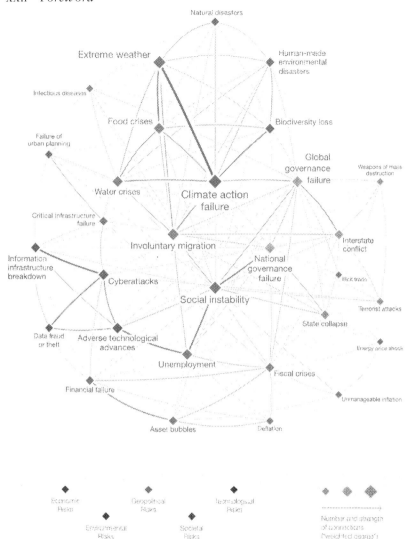

Figure 1 Global risks.

However, recent political changes put this hope at risk. To increase the likelihood of success for these 17 SDGs, higher education institutions worldwide must teach and train today's students – tomorrow's decision-makers – to think both critically and ethically, to learn to cope with ethical dilemmas, and to apply systems-thinking approaches to serious and complex societal problems (Levi & Rothstein, 2018; Levi, 2020).

Needless to say, the resulting stress and/or otherwise pathogenic effects of noxious exposures also depend on our resilience and coping ability. Such aspects remain important targets for disease prevention and health promotion.

However, they can never replace the situational factors focused on in this Foreword.

Students need to be made aware of the local, regional, and global contexts in which they live and make decisions. Many of today's students do not grasp their role in, and their responsibility to, the world – and a large number do not seem to care.

A single course at college can only be the beginning. Families, media, religious bodies, primary and secondary schools, and workplaces as well as higher education institutions must be educated and recruited to play their part.

The 2030 Agenda for Sustainable Development aims to promote the entire cluster of 17 SDGs and 169 targets. The critical-ethical analytic skills and systems-based approach mentioned above are indispensable prerequisites to achieving this.

By "critical" we may refer to "the application of careful, exact evaluation and judgment" (cf. Paul & Elder, 2013). By "ethical" we may refer to "a set of principles about the right way to behave" (cf. United Nations, 1948). By "systems" we may refer to "a group of interacting, interrelated, or interdependent elements forming a complex whole" (OECD, 2017). Accordingly, systems-thinking is based on the recognition of interconnectedness and systems processes.

The International Association of Universities (IAU) – with more than 640 member universities world-wide – has designated 16 lead universities, each taking on one of the SDGs and each in collaboration with a cluster of allies for its specific purpose – combing economic, social, and environmental sustainability. Integrating all of this (SDG # 17) remains a task for IAU.

Similarly, the European Branch of the World Health Organization (WHO), has requested its Regional Director to "take the leading exploring ways to bring together policymakers from other sectors responsible for the determinants of health, including education, housing, employment, the environment, and poverty reduction, in order to develop a systematic approach to taking action."

But as a Chinese proverb formulates it, "words do not cook rice." There exists a very considerable gap between what we know and what we implement (Levi, 2017).

Recognizing the university sector's potential and responsibility to help shape the moral contours of society for the better and given the societal benefits from increased social capital, they should endorse a cross-faculty approach to broaden the curricula to include components of critical-ethical analysis and systems thinking to implement Agenda 2030, with, for example, Hedenus *et al.* (2019) as required reading.

But do we have a mandate? The answer is yes, from the United Nations and from all 193 Member States (Target # 4.7): "Ensure that all participants acquire by 2030 the knowledge and skills needed to promote sustainable development and lifestyles, including education in human rights, gender equality, peace, nonviolence, global citizenship, appreciation of diversity, and respect for the role of culture."

As wisely put by Harari (2015), "starvation, war, and disease have been transformed from incomprehensible forces of nature – to problems that can actually be solved." So, dear Reader, please, just start doing it!

Lennart Levi; MD, PhD
Emeritus Professor of Psychosocial Medicine (Karolinska Institutet)

References

World Economic Forum. (2020). *The Global Risks*. Insight Report. 15th Edition.

Levi, L., & Rothstein, B. (2018). To cope with present and future catastrophic risks – Higher education must train future decision makers to think critically, ethically and in systems. *World Academy of Art and Sciences Rome conference proceedings* 13–15. http://worldacademy.org/files/rome2017/papers/RCP-compiled-papers.pd.

Levi, L. (2019/2020). *Stressors at work and elsewhere – A global survival approach*. The American Institute of Stress: *Contentment Magazine*, Winter, pp. 46–51.

United Nations. (1948). *Universal Declaration of Human Rights*. General Assembly Resolution 217 A.

OECD. (2017). *Systems approach to public sector challenges: Working with change*. Paris: OECD Publishing. https://doi.org/10.1787/9789264279865-en.

Levi, L. (2017). Bridging the science-policy and policy-implementation gaps. In Cooper, C. L. & Campbell Quick, J. (Eds.). *The handbook of stress and health – A guide to research and practice*. Wiley.

Paul, R. & Elder, L. (2013). *Critical thinking*. FT Press.

European Commission. (2020). *The EU Budget Powering the Recovery Plan for Europe*. COM, 442 Final.

WHO. (2019). Regional Office for Europe: Resolution EUR/RC69/R5.

Acknowledgments

The current health and well-being scenario in our globalized world calls for a collective and thoughtful approach by multiple stakeholders to prevent and manage negative health outcomes for the world population. Although there is voluminous literature on work stress and its significant impact on the workforce, there are glaring national differences in stress research and practice. In developed countries, we see a close collaboration between policymakers and other stakeholders at all levels – working on defining health priorities, identifying action plans, recognizing drivers and barriers to change, and implementing strategic interventions at national, regional, organizational, and individual levels. However, in most of the developing countries, policymakers have only recently come to recognize the full-scale of the impact of work stress on society. Hence we are seeing increasing discussions on issues related to the rights of workers, improving working conditions, introducing new legislation, the challenges of formal and informal workforce, the need for public-private partnership, discourse with other social partners, international research collaborations, raising stress awareness in workers, responsible and responsive organizations, and the implementation of effective stress management initiatives. Such dissimilarities in identification, prevention, management, and treatment of stress in societies mean that there is a considerable research gap.

We hope that, by providing an overview of organizational stress research and stress management initiatives from different countries, this volume will prove useful to academics, students, and practitioners alike. With this book, we aim to facilitate the development of stress management research and education, while also developing practitioner knowledge on the importance of stress and stress management in a global environment.

We extend our thankfulness to all our international contributors for sharing their latest thinking with us and making this effort successful. We would like to say a special thank you to Professor Lennart Levi for graciously writing the foreword for our book. We are also grateful to publishing team who helped in preparing the final versions of the manuscript.

Cary would also like to thank all his international students who contributed to his research over the years.

Dinyar would also like to thank all his colleagues, students, and family for their support.

Finally, I would like to thank my Dad, who gave me the best things in life – his time, his care, and his love and to my husband, Anurag, for his unconditional love and motivation.

Kajal A. Sharma
Cary L. Cooper
D.M. Pestonjee

1 Introduction

Kajal A. Sharma, Cary L. Cooper, and D.M. Pestonjee

Stress has been accepted as a reality of modern work life. It is not a new problem but has aggravated in recent years and reached epidemic proportions. Today it is recognized as a massive health and safety challenge, and all countries are attempting to establish various strategies to overcome it. In a survey conducted by the International Labour Organization (2016), over 90% of participants acknowledged that work stress was a concern in their country, and nearly 70% of respondents reported that it was a source of higher concern in specific sectors like healthcare, education, services, finance, retail trade, transport, construction, and the public sector in general. The World Health Organisation's report (2017a, 2017b) states that work-related health problems result in an economic loss of 4–6% of GDP for most countries. Hence, work stress is now recognized as an issue with global impact.

The modern, dynamic, complex, and stressful world of work has its roots in many old and new developments around the world. The developed economies, like the United States, United Kingdom, and other European countries, are currently facing economic uncertainty and minimal growth whereas emerging economies, like China, India, Russia, and Brazil, are expanding but have regional concerns resulting in challenges. Moreover, factors like rapid globalization, technological advancement, the rise of consumerist society, and climate change, to name a few, are also influencing the world of work. Such changes test the sustainability of organizations and drive their strategic choices like mergers, acquisitions, downsizing, restructuring, offshoring, outsourcing, the use of a temporary workforce, and many others. These circumstances have a profound impact on employees who face financial concerns, fewer choices, less control, job insecurity, unrealistic and multiple job demands, constant competition, and the continually changing nature of work and the work environment. All this translates into pressure at work for employees. Additionally, such employees receive little support from their managers and colleagues, and their fundamental needs, like recognition and respect at work, are not met due to work intensification (Semmer, 2007). Many work stressors like workload, family-work conflict, increasing work intensity, leadership styles, workplace conflict, organizational downsizing, restructuring, and organizational mergers have been identified across cultures and outcomes have typically considered job satisfaction, commitment, psychological health, work-family balance, and withdrawal behaviors (Burke, 2010). Results reveal that as increased work demands exceed employees' capacity and ability to cope, it often leads to distress.

Painful experiences at work lead to various emotional, cognitive, behavioral, and physiological fallouts (Kompier & Marcelissen, 1990) in employees. The effects of stress on employees are well documented in literature. Ailments like frequent headaches, hypertension, obesity, increased heart rate, blood pressure, and cardiac arrest are linked to stress. Moreover, many health problems like anxiety, emotional disorders, musculoskeletal disorders, depression, burnout, and work-life imbalance in employees are also caused due to stress experienced at work. Belief in optimal levels of stress has been exploited, on various occasions by the organizations to justify poor management practices, but stress also has far-reaching consequences on the organization in terms of low motivation and productivity, an increase in health cost, and employee turnover (Sharma & Cooper, 2016). A report by the Health and Safety Executive (2019) suggested that in 2018/2019 stress, depression, or anxiety accounted for 44% of all work-related ill health cases, and 54% of all working days are lost due to employee ill health in the United Kingdom. Research in Malaysia concluded that the cost of absenteeism and presenteeism equated to 4.5% of the GDP in 2015 (Wee *et al.*, 2019), and according to the Japanese Ministry of Health, Labor, and Welfare, work-related suicide (known as K*aro-Jisatsu* – suicide due to overwork and stressful working conditions) has become a social concern. Depression, sickness absence and presenteeism problems cost Australian employers approximately AU$8 billion per year, and of that figure, AU$693 million is due to job strain and bullying (Dollard *et al.*, 2012). A Canadian study (Anderssen, 2011) estimated that mental health problems cost employers about CA$20 billion annually. These results reflect that work stress leads to human distress and diminished economic performance globally.

Organizations have realized that they cannot eliminate stress from employees' work life, but, at the same time, they cannot afford to be passive - as a decline in employee mental and physical health invariably leads to a decline in the organization's productivity and competitiveness. According to the WHO (2019), negative working environment in organizations may lead to physical and mental health problems, use of harmful substances or alcohol, absenteeism, and lost productivity in employees; whereas, workplaces that promote employee mental health are more likely to reduce absenteeism, increase productivity, and benefit from associated economic gains. Hence, organizations have now concentrated energies toward creating a healthier work environment where there is a balance of job demands, resources, control, and support for employees to thrive. Emphasis is on handling stress by limiting the harmful conditions at work and endorsing health-promoting initiatives by managing issues like work-life balance, developing social support structures, mental health issues, diversity, and gender management. Research by Spreitzer and Porath (2012) suggests that thriving employees are highly energized as they know how to avoid burnout. Organizations can integrate the key components of a thriving environment-vitality and learning as suggested by Spreitzer and Porath (2012) in their culture to create healthy and creative work organizations.

Additionally, organizations can address this problem with a three-tier approach of primary, secondary, and tertiary prevention strategies as suggested by Cartwright and Cooper (2011). In the primary prevention stage, organizations identify and minimize or eliminate the source of employee stress. The secondary prevention stage consists of learning and training related to stress management for employees. Lastly, the tertiary prevention stage is comprised of rehabilitation of employees affected by stress through various support mechanisms in the role and organization. Organizations can select any intervention strategy; however, their key initiatives should embrace elements like changing poor business practices, building healthy culture, acknowledging stress, and providing appropriate support to employees experiencing stress caused by factors both inside and outside the workplace. Organizational culture and practices should focus on the physical and psychological safety of employees considering a whole-person approach. It is also important for contemporary organizations to build a trusting and healthy work culture wherein all employee groups – including women, BAME, and LGBT – achieve physical and psychological safety. It is important to emphasize that all employees should be trained on how to deal with stress at work, but it is equally important to train managers so that they can be sensitized to stress and mental health issues and illness at work, develop critical skills like empathy to break down the employee stigma and build trust, and effectively support employee well-being and welfare through engagement, performance, resilience, and general happiness. The right support received at the right time from the organization can help employees overcome stress, succeed, and thrive at work. Therefore, it should be the organization's prime responsibility to devise proactive systems and strategies to support employees.

The current globally unfolding emergency caused by Covid-19 has once again highlighted the social relevance of work stress and employee health issues and has put the organization's role in supporting employee health at the forefront. As businesses struggle to survive during the current pandemic, employers are also starting to realize the impact it has had on the mental and physical health of employees. According to CIPD (2020), early research on Covid-19 effects on employee health indicates an increase in fatigue, musculoskeletal conditions, poor work-life balance, reduced exercise, increased alcohol consumption, reduced motivation, loss of purpose and motivation, anxiety, and isolation. Such health implications have the potential to significantly impact the ability of many organizations to survive and cope during and post Covid-19 work and economic scenarios. However, timely and effective organizational policies and interventions to support employees achieve better health and work-life balance can make a real difference under the current circumstances. Recognizing workplace stress as a priority issue, this volume presents chapters representing the work of authors from several countries that offer an understanding of the evolving and changing nature of work stress in contemporary organizations across different countries. All contributors have reviewed country-specific organizational stress literature and drawn comparisons with international literature trends. We believe that issues raised concerning the nature of stress and its management in the following chapters are thought-provoking and can help organizations mitigate the barriers to creating healthy organizations around the world that offer safe, empowering, enterprising, and satisfying work environments for employees.

The second chapter in this volume offers insights on common international trends and unique stress topics like the impact of geographic distance, extreme heat, and threat from wildlife related to occupational stress research in Australia. It also provides an understanding of the primary flavors of contemporary occupational stress research conducted in Australia. The third chapter is on Brazil, which presents a literature review based on 118 studies published in the last decade. The discussion uncovers stress issues exclusive to the social, cultural, and economic contexts in Brazil. It climaxes with the discussion on future research which highlights the need to consider more explicitly the specific work conditions in the country, evolving more powerful methodological procedures, as well as more sophisticated analysis strategies, to provide a more holistic understanding of work stress in Brazil. Chapter Four investigates main job stressors and its consequences in Greater China (covering Beijing, Hong Kong, and Taipei) using a two-tier mixed-method study. A Six-factor model of job stressors was developed, tested, and found suitable in the contemporary Chinese work environment. The discussion also covers the investigation of local and international trends in literature. The fifth chapter on Greece scientifically exhibits how the occupational stressors and strains in Greece are unique, ever-changing, severe, and chronic as a result of economic and political instability associated with turbulent recessionary times. The sixth chapter is India-centric. It offers a systematic review of Indian stress studies published in the last decade encompassing descriptive and thematic analysis. Distinctive theoretical and methodological challenges and concerns are examined while comparing Indian research trends with international literature.

Chapter Seven offers a review of organizational stress research in Japan. Devastating stress problems unique to Japanese work culture – like long work hours, nonregular employment, workplace harassment, *Karoshi* (death from overwork), and *Karo-Jisatsu* (suicide caused by work stress) – are assessed in detail. Government policies and organizational responses to manage stress are also scrutinized. Chapter Eight investigates the status of organizational stress in different work sectors in Nigeria. Unique stressors and strains experienced by the Nigerian worker and their coping approaches are reviewed. The conclusion explores the mediating roles of state and culture on organizational stress in Nigeria. The Ninth chapter studies the increasing trend associated with psychosocial risks and work-related mental health risks in the Netherlands and Belgium. Consequences of these risks, challenges associated with their management, and effective strategies to prevent such risks are deliberated in the chapter. Chapter Ten offers a literature review on occupational stress research in Oman. The analysis explains culture-specific stressors and demonstrates that Oman is undergoing a rapid demographic, educational, and economic transition, but religion and culture have an immense influence on society. The Eleventh chapter summarizes the literature on occupational stress, health, and well-being research in Portugal. A qualitative systematic review and the two-step cluster analysis was undertaken based on 75 published papers. Critical observations on trends in Portuguese literature are presented in the conclusions.

Organizational stress in the Russian context is investigated in the Twelfth chapter. Stressors unique to Russian society are discussed at length; simultaneously, prevalent unhealthy coping approaches have been highlighted. The Thirteenth chapter is based on the South African occupational stress context. It offers an overview of South African stress studies and highlights specific work and living contexts from historical and contemporary perspectives of the Fourth Industrial Revolution. Contemporary stressors, its consequences, and stress management strategies at individual, organizational, and societal levels have been researched in depth. The Fourteenth chapter provides coverage of salient concepts and measures relevant to organizational stress in the United States. The chapter explores the influence of the cultural context on organizational stress and concludes with a discussion of contemporary practices in physical fitness, positive stress, organizational clinical psychology, and healthy work organization. Lastly, in the Fifteenth chapter, editors have identified and discussed the common themes emerging from all the contributions in this volume. Directions for future research are explored in light of these popular themes.

References

Anderssen, E. (2011, June 17). *Ottawa to fund mental-health strategy: First-ever Canadian-wide standards to tackle problem estimated to cost $20-billion a year in workplace losses alone*. The Globe and Mail, A3.

Burke, R. J. (2010). Workplace stress and well-being across cultures: Research and practice. *Cross Cultural Management: An International Journal*, 17(1), 5–9.

Cartwright, S., & Cooper, C. (2011). *Innovations in stress and health*. Basingstoke, UK: Palgrave Macmillan.

CIPD (20 May, 2020). Coronavirus (Covid-19): Mental health and returning to the workplace. https://www.cipd.co.uk/knowledge/culture/well-being/supporting-mental-health-workplace-return.

Dollard, M. F., Bailey, T., McLinton, S., Richards, P., McTernan, W., Taylor, A., & Bond, S. (2012). *The Australian Workplace Barometer: Report on psychosocial safety climate and worker health in Australia*. Centre for Applied Psychological Research, University of South Australia.

International Labour Organization. (2016). Workplace stress: A collective challenge. https://www.ilo.org/wcmsp5/groups/public/---ed_protect/---protrav/---safework/documents/publication/wcms_466547.pdf.

Kompier, M. A. J., & Marcelissen, F. H. G. (1990). *Handboek werkstress [Handbook of work stress]* (Vol. 6, pp. 681–703). Amsterdam, The Netherlands: NIA.

Sharma, R. R., & Cooper, C. L. (2016). *Executive burnout: Eastern and western concepts, models and approaches for mitigation*. Emerald Group Publishing.

Spreitzer, G., & Porath, C. (2012). Creating sustainable performance. *Harvard Business Review*, 90(1), 92–99.

Semmer, K. N. (2007). *Recognition and respect (or lack thereof) as predictors of occupational health and well-being*. Conference Presentation. WHO, Geneva: Universität Bern, 14, February.

Wee, L. H., Yeap, L. L. L., Chan, C. M. H., Wong, J. E., Jamil, N. A., Nantha, Y. S., & Siau, C. S. (2019). Anteceding factors predicting absenteeism and presenteeism in urban area in Malaysia. *BMC Public Health*, 19(4), 540.

World Health Organisation. (2017a). Occupational health: Stress at the workplace. https://www.who.int/occupational_health/topics/stressatwp/en.

World Health Organisation. (2017b). Protecting workers health (Fact sheet). https://www.who.int/news-room/fact-sheets/detail/protecting-workers'-health.

World Health Organisation. (2019, May). *Mental health in the workplace*. https://www.who.int/mental_health/in_the_workplace/en/.

Health and Safety Executive. (2019). Annual Statistics. Work-related stress, anxiety or depression statistics in Great Britain. https://www.hse.gov.uk/statistics/causdis/stress.pdf.

2 "She'll Be Right, Mate!"
Occupational Stress Research in Australia

Paula Brough, Mitchell Raper, and Jason Spedding

Introduction

In this chapter, we discuss key occupational stress empirical research conducted within Australia. First some context: Australia is the planet's sixth-largest country after Russia, Canada, China, the United States of America, and Brazil – accounting for 5% of the world's land area. Australia has a continental landmass of 7.692 million square kilometers and is the smallest continental landmass but the world's largest island. Australia is about 32 times larger than the United Kingdom, 21 times larger than Japan, 14 times larger than France, and 2.5 times larger than India. Australia has a relatively small total population of approximately 26 million people and is ranked at 55th place in national population totals. Approximately half of the Australian population (13 million people) is of working age. The Gross Domestic Product (GDP) in Australia was approximately US$1,432 billion in 2018, representing approximately 2.3% of the world economy.

Similar to many developed countries, occupational stress is a major public health problem in Australia, costing the economy up to AU$15 billion per annum (Safe Work Australia, 2013). The physical and mental health of Australian employees is protected by the 2011 Work Health and Safety Act. Each of the eight Australian states and territories implements this Act with compensation legislation to support all workers' who experience any work-related physical or psychological injury or illness. Approximately 7,800 Australians are compensated for work-related mental health conditions each year, and the vast majority (90%) of these mental disorder claims are attributed to mental stress (Safe Work Australia, 2015). These claims total approximately AU$543 million and equate to approximately 6% of the annual number of workers' compensation claims submitted. Thus, the number of submitted work-related mental health claims is relatively small, but their combined costs are substantial. Lost productivity specifically attributable to employee absenteeism, caused by the physical and mental health impacts of occupational stress, costs Australian organizations a total of approximately $5 billion per annum (Price Waterhouse Coopers, 2014).

8 *Paula Brough et al.*

The primary causes of occupational stress within Australia are unambiguous and are common to antecedents reported internationally, namely: excessive work demands, inadequate work resources, and exposure to psychologically unhealthy work environments predominately marked by interpersonal conflicts including "toxic leadership" (Brough, Drummond, & Biggs, 2018; Brough, O'Driscoll, Kalliath, Cooper, & Poelmans, 2009; Webster, Brough, & Daly, 2016). The occupations in Australia which report the highest levels of occupational stress, also reflect those in international reports, namely: public service occupations characterized by hierarchical, bureaucratic structures, involving high levels of interactions with the public, and which may also include experience with a high frequency of physical dangers. These occupations consist of military and emergency services workers, school teachers, and health and social welfare workers (Brough, Brown, & Biggs, 2016). Later in this chapter, we discuss the occupational stress antecedents which are unique to Australian workers – including indigenous culture, geographic distance, climate, and threats from wildlife. Next, we discuss the primary "flavors" of occupational stress research currently being conducted in Australia and represented in the scholarly international literature.

Key Areas of Australian Occupational Stress Research

Similar to research being conducted internationally, in Australia, there are several researchers and their teams spread throughout the country focusing on specific areas of occupational stress research. Here, we provide an overview of four of these occupational stress research topics.

Occupational Stress Interventions

How best to manage, reduce, and recover from occupational stress experiences underpins occupational stress intervention research. Professor Paula Brough and her team at Griffith University in Brisbane have worked with numerous "high-risk of stress" occupations to develop evidence-based stress management interventions (SMIs). For example, Biggs, Brough, and Barbour (2014a) described the implementation of a quasi-experimental SMI with police managers, focusing on improving their confidence in their personal people management skills. This SMI program was based on the theoretical framework of the job demands-resources model (Demerouti, Bakker, Nachreiner, & Schaufeli, 2001), contained multiple components including both group and individual coaching sessions, and linked the police leaders' skills to the well-being and performance of their direct reports (subordinates). Importantly, Biggs, Brough, and Barbour (2014a) noted how improving leadership abilities "produces significant improvements in some aspects of the psychosocial work environment for the leader's direct subordinates" (p. 60). Thus, how an employee's experience of stress can be reduced by enhancing their leader's behaviors. This research also demonstrated that high-quality SMI research could be conducted within a quasi-experimental research design, including both control and experimental groups and multiple pre- and post-assessments individually tracked over time (see also: Biggs, Brough, & Barbour, 2014c, 2014d; Brough & Biggs, 2015b). An extension of this work was also described by Webster et al. (2016) who demonstrated how the chronic experiences of a "toxic" manager can have serious health and performance consequences for their subordinates.

Professor Angela Martin and her team in Tasmania have also conducted pertinent SMI research focused on reducing levels of occupational stress experienced by small to medium-sized enterprise (SMEs) owners. Martin, Sanderson, Scott, and Brough (2009) also conducted their SMI via a quasi-experimental research design – comparing the impact of a self-administered versus telephone-coaching intervention, with a control group of SMEs managers. Martin and colleagues demonstrated the success of the telephone-coaching SMI component in reducing levels of psychological distress experiences reported by the SME managers (see also: Martin et al., 2015).

Job Demands, Job Resources, and Stressor Appraisals

A second key area of occupational stress research in Australia focuses on the assessment of stress caused by different types of job demands. Australian occupational stress research has been instrumental in expanding our understanding of job demands, the categorization of these demands, and the employees' interpretation (i.e., appraisal) of these demands. Research led by both Peter Hart in Melbourne and Paula Brough in Brisbane has demonstrated the importance of assessing both generic (global) job demands and occupational-specific job demands in order to provide accurate estimates of stress. Hart and his colleagues, for example, developed and validated measures of negative stressors (work hassles) and positive experiences (work uplifts) experienced by police officers (Hart, Wearing, & Headey, 1995). Hart and colleagues' (Hart *et al.*, 1995) research is important for two reasons. First, this work demonstrated that both positive and negative "minor" work experiences independently contribute to an officer's perceived quality of life. Second, Hart *et al.* (1995) demonstrated that organizational work demands, rather than operational experiences were more important in estimates of police officers' well-being. Thus, organizational work demands such as managing bureaucratic red tape and correctly completing paperwork were rated as more onerous for the police officers' long-term well-being, as compared to operational demands such as going on a raid or making an arrest.

Hart's work was also validated by Brough (Brough, 2004; Brough & Biggs, 2015a) who demonstrated that organizational work demands were stronger predictors of a police officer's mental ill-health levels over time, as compared to either generic job demands or traumatic work experiences. Brough (Brough & Biggs, 2010; Brough & Williams, 2007) also extended this work by developing a measure of occupational-specific job demands experienced by correctional (prison) officers. Brough and Williams (2007) recommended that assessing common work experiences of correctional officers, such as violence from offenders and offenders' deaths or escapes, in combination with generic measures of job demands were necessary to produce accurate estimates of correctional officers' mental health. In similar more recent work, Brough and Boase (2019), found that relaxing and cognitive restructuring were the two common stress management techniques employed by lawyers, reflecting international findings and relating to these two methods of stress management. Of particular interest, was how the use of cognitive restructuring had a similar impact upon levels of job satisfaction and work engagement, compared to the generic job demands experienced by this sample of lawyers. As seen above, Brough and Boase recommended the inclusion of lawyer-specific measures of occupational stress in addition to generic job demands, to better explore this reported use of cognitive restructuring within the stress process.

Research conducted by Brough and colleagues also considered the distinction between generic and specific job resources. One investigation assessed whether specific organizational resources (i.e., strategic alignment) assisted in promoting work engagement and reducing stress experiences for police officers, in comparison with generic job resources (i.e., social support and job control). Strategic alignment refers to an employee's perception and awareness of their organization's strategic priorities and how their daily tasks contribute to these priorities. Biggs *et al.* (2014d) not only found strategic alignment increased work engagement across multiple time lags, but these associations were stronger compared to the equivalent associations with both job control and social support. Raper, Brough, and Biggs (2019) extended this research and investigated the impact of strategic alignment with both work engagement and psychological strain over time. The results also indicated strategic alignment reduced psychological strain compared to generic job resources and highlighted the importance of assessing both specific and broad work resources

Similar research was conducted by Michelle Tuckey and colleagues in Adelaide. Tuckey and Hayward (2011) argued that occupational-specific emotional resources (i.e., camaraderie) may be more effective in reducing the negative outcomes of emotional demands experienced by firefighters, as compared to generic emotional resources. They demonstrated that camaraderie did indeed significantly reduce – moderated – levels of burnout and psychological distress when emotional demands were high. This impact of camaraderie was stronger than the impact of generic emotional resources. These findings are also consistent with other Australian stress research calling for inclusions of organizational level resources in promoting positive workplace environments (e.g., Albrecht, 2012; Albrecht, Breidahl, & Marty, 2018).

Research conducted by Tuckey and colleagues has also focused on a different typology of job demands. Tuckey, Searle, Boyd, Winefield, and Winefield (2015) argued the challenge-hindrance framework (Cavanaugh, Boswell, Roehling, & Boudreau, 2000) does not adequately account for threat demands or cognitive appraisals. Instead, Tuckey *et al.* (2015) proposed the typology of a challenge-hindrance-threat framework and argued that employees' exposure to these different demands impacts specific emotional outcomes including positive affect, anger, anxiety, and dedication. Furthermore, Searle and Auton (2015) noted the presence of inconsistent results reported in the challenge-hindrance framework literature and argued the same job demands can be appraised as a challenge or a hindrance, or indeed as both, by employees. Their findings also indicated that challenge and hindrance cognitive appraisals accounted for significant proportions of unique variance in positive affect, anger, and venting (see also: Espedido & Searle, 2018; Espedido, Searle, & Griffin, 2019; Searle & Tuckey, 2017).

Psychosocial Safety Climate

Recent research in occupational health has advanced knowledge regarding the organizational climates in which the stress-strain processes are nested. Maureen Dollard in Adelaide has advanced one such climate construct, the Psychosocial Safety Climate (PSC). PSC refers to the shared perceptions of policies, practices, and procedures endorsed by senior leaders within an organization designed to protect the psychological health of employees (Dollard & Bakker, 2010). Heightened levels of PSC have been directly linked to a range of organizational and individual benefits such as reduced bullying and exhaustion (Bond, Tuckey, & Dollard, 2010; Law, Dollard, Tuckey, & Dormann, 2011) and enhanced employee engagement (Dollard & Bakker, 2010). In addition, the direct benefits of maintaining positive PSC offer pertinent implications for extending existing theory, namely as a distal antecedent (an "upstream resource") within the job demands-resources model (Demerouti *et al.*, 2001).

In many organizations it is the remit of senior leaders to design and enact macro-level policies that balance both employee productivity and well-being, this balance is largely captured via the measurement of PSC. The PSC-12 (Hall, Dollard, & Coward, 2010) collates four subscales of PSC into an aggregate climate construct. As organizational climates are inherently multilevel phenomena, this process of conceptualization and measurement is rife with difficulties (cf. Schneider, González-Morales, Ostroff, & West, 2017); however, contemporary research has begun to explore the benefits of maintaining supportive PSCs within organizations. One large scale population study explored the potential psychological risk factors facing Australian workplaces (Dollard *et al.*, 2012). Data collected from over 5,000 participants demonstrated the positive relationship between PSC and perceptions of organizational resources, productivity, and health outcomes, and negatively predicted job demands. PSC explained 13% of the variance in employee work engagement and up to 9% of the variance in employee self-reported health outcomes. The impacts of rural versus urban workplace demands were also assessed. Urban employees reported heightened job demands compared to their rural counterparts, albeit with less physical demands, less work-family conflict, and reported less mental and physical health issues.

In another investigation of the impact of PSC, Afsharian, Zadow, Dollard, Dormann, and Ziaian (2018) operationalized the standard deviation of PSC, to quantify the strength of climate exhibited within organizational work units. This technique of dispersion modeling (Chan, 1998), investigated the effects of aligned perceptions of climate. Afsharian *et al.* (2018) reported the direct effects of PSC were moderated by the perceived strength of the climate, such that employees in high PSC work units were more engaged in their work roles. Research exploring how climate strength may impact other group-level workplace dynamics remains a pertinent avenue for future scholars.

Bullying and Workplace Incivility

While workplace bullying and incivility are global workplace issues, Australian research has assisted researchers and practitioners to better understand these complex issues and has developed interventions to reduce these incidents. Approximately 10% of Australian employees experience these forms of workplace mistreatment (Safe Work Australia, 2016), corresponding with international estimations of between 10% and 15% (Zapf, Escartin, Einarsen, Hoel, & Vartia, 2011). Brough, Brown, and Biggs (2016) provided an overview of negative workplace behaviors commonly experienced within the criminal justice systems. They noted criminal justice (military, police, corrections, and law) organizations that contain strong hierarchical structures are more likely to adopt toxic work environments, as compared to organizations with lateral or flatter structures. Webster *et al.* (2016) also highlighted the issues of toxic management styles in creating unsafe workplaces by providing key recommendations for organizations and employees to be more proactive in reporting and reducing these negative workplace behaviors.

Australian research has also focused on the job characteristics and personal resources which may precipitate bullying and harassment in the workplace. Tuckey, Chrisopoulos, and Dollard (2012) found hindrance job demands (organizational constraints, role conflict, ambiguity, and overload) resulted in aggressive behaviors when the demands outweighed the buffering effects of job resources. These findings were validated by Li, Chen, Tuckey, McLinton, and Dollard (2019), who argued that job design is one of the key prevention mechanisms to reduce workplace bullying. Job characteristics – including irregular work schedules and conflictual contact – increase job demands which, in turn, increase workplace bullying. Re-designing occupations to reduce stressful job characteristics and to enhance beneficial job characteristics is recommended to prevent the propagation of bullying work environments (Tuckey & Neall, 2014).

Australian research has also highlighted the influence of PSC on the occurrence of workplace bullying. Law *et al.* (2011), for example, demonstrated that the associations between bullying, employee psychological distress, and work engagement were reduced – moderated – by high levels of PSC. Similarly, Bond *et al.* (2010) demonstrated that high levels of PSC in police stations reduces the positive association between bullying and post-traumatic stress experienced by the police officers over time.

Australian-Specific Occupational Stress Research

Australia's isolation, size, climate, and proliferation of dangerous wildlife have also generated more nuanced fields of occupational stress research. In this section, we highlight three areas of stress research that are more specific to the Australian context.

Distance

Australia has a very centralized population with approximately 68% of its population living within or close to a capital city, particularly along the eastern coast of Australia (Australian Bureau of Statistics, 2019). For those who live and work in rural inland areas of Australia, the vast distances involved can be a significant stressor. These remote communities also commonly contain fewer healthcare professionals per capita, resulting in poorer health outcomes as compared to Australia's urban populations (Opie *et al.*, 2010). Consequently, the remote area nurses (RANs) working in these rural communities report high levels of occupational stress – characterized by high workloads, high turnover, less access to medical resources, and high levels of workplace violence (Opie *et al.*, 2010). Lenthall *et al.* (2009) also found that the isolation reduced the social resources accessible to these RANs, resulting in reduced professional and personal boundaries (see also Opie, Dollard, Lenthall, & Knight, 2013).

A specific pattern of work referred to as fly-in fly-out (FIFO) employment, involves mining and construction workers commuting long distances to rural inland work sites by airplane, living and working on-site for several weeks and then taking another one or two weeks of leave when they commute back to their homes and families. These elongated work-rest cycles represent new challenges to occupational health research and theory, with recent work building our understanding of how these processes impact both employee well-being and their family outcomes. Considine *et al.* (2017), for example, conducted a multisite study of FIFO coal workers and found these employees experienced additional stressors. Considine and colleagues reported that 39% of the FIFO workers in their sample reported moderate to very high levels of psychological distress, which is significantly higher than the 26% prevalence within a comparable community sample. They also reported that 46% of male FIFO workers had hazardous levels of alcohol use, which is almost twice as high as comparable community samples (Tynan *et al.*, 2017). Job-specific stressors for these FIFO workers included high levels of job insecurity and pursuing mining work purely for extrinsic financial reasons (Considine *et al.*, 2017).

Other research with FIFO workers has identified how misalignment between employee's needs and the organizational culture can attenuate workers' negative mental health outcomes (Morrow & Brough, 2019). Finally, utilizing ecological momentary assessment, Gardner, Alfrey, Vandelanotte, and Rebar (2018) found that during work trips, both the FIFO workers and their spouses/partners who remained at home reported reduced sleep quality, reduced exercise, and consumed more cigarettes, compared to when FIFO workers remained at home. Reducing the occupational stress experienced by these workers employed in remote communities is also a focus of other Australian research (e.g., Rickard *et al.*, 2012; Robinson, Peetz, Murray, Griffin, & Muurlink, 2017; Vojnovic, Michelson, Jackson, & Bahn, 2014).

Heat

Australia is renowned for its extreme heat. Indeed, heat is the most dangerous environmental hazard in Australia, accounting for 55% of natural hazard-related deaths each year (Coates, Haynes, O'Brien, McAneney, & De Oliveira, 2014). Australia's hot and humid climates cause considerable risk and additional stress for employees who work outside – particularly in construction, mining, farming, and emergency services. The impact of climate change has caused the Australian climate to recently become even warmer, with more frequent occurrences of extreme heat events across the country (Hanna, Kjellstrom, Bennett, & Dear, 2011). Rising numbers of very hot days (i.e., above 35 °C) places increasing strain on outdoor workers (Hanna et al., 2011; Xiang, Bi, Pisaniello, Hansen, & Sullivan, 2013). Estimated costs to the Australian economy due to workers' experiences of heat-related stress are approximately AU$9 billion per annum, and this cost is increasing annually (Zander, Botzen, Oppermann, Kjellstrom, & Garnett, 2015). These costs have negative consequences for economic output. For example, during the 2002–2003 drought, GDP in Australia dropped by 1.0 percentage point (Australian Bureau of Statistics, 2006). As such, increasing research is focused on how to best relieve heat stress among the workforces, especially for workers who must work outside (Maté & Oosthuizen, 2012; Zander, Mathew, & Garnett, 2018).

Employers are very much aware of the occurrence of heat stress and commonly provide a variety of heat prevention measures to protect employees – including the provisions of cool drinking water on worksites, heat stress training, shaded rest areas, protective hats, and cooling fans. However, Xiang, Hansen, Pisaniello, and Bi (2015) reported common barriers to the prevention of heat stress-related injuries, namely a lack of adequate training and awareness for employees, lack of management commitment, and low compliance rates (see also Jia, Rowlinson, & Ciccarelli, 2016; Singh, Hanna, & Kjellstrom, 2015). The negative impact of heat on the productivity and well-being of office employees has also been identified (Lamb & Kwok, 2016). Finally, Australia's increasing prevalence of heatwaves and other extreme weather conditions (e.g., cyclones, floods, and bushfires) emphasize the importance of the appropriate provisions of work resources for both emergency and volunteer workers during their management of these natural disasters (Biggs et al., 2014d).

Dangerous Wildlife

A discussion of Australian-specific stressors would not be complete without some mention of rather dangerous wildlife residents in this country. While visitors of the Australia commonly anticipate encountering snakes, spiders, crocodiles, and sharks at every turn, most Australians actually experience relatively few encounters with these animals, and, indeed, typically experience more frequent encounters with the "cuddlier" part of Australian wildlife: koalas, kangaroos, wallabies, etc. Nevertheless, unique and considerable stress can be experienced by workers who do interact with dangerous Australian wildlife, although published research on this topic is scarce.

Whether the Australian animal encountered is cuddly or dangerous, risks arise from its capture and handling. Clearly, physical risks (e.g., being bitten) are the most prevalent and for animal professionals, these risks can be considered as a specific job demand. Thompson and Thompson (2007), for example, described the necessity of using appropriate types of traps for capturing snakes, spiders, and small mammals in Western Australia – for the physical safety of both the animal and the human worker. Mirtschin (2006) provided more details of the dangers for herpetologists with the enviable task of extracting venom from Australia's deadly snakes. Snake venom is required for the production of antivenoms. Mirtschin (2006) reported that most herpetologists' deaths are caused by the highly venomous tiger snake and that, bizarrely, many herpetologists died after willingly being bitten – in order to demonstrate the effectiveness (or lack thereof) of the antivenom that they had produced.

Stevenson, Gowardman, Tozer, and Woods (2015) reported on the physical dangers for Australian park rangers from wildlife encounters – specifically via the transmission of Q-fever from both live and dead animals – including the disposal of deceased "road-kill" kangaroos and wallabies. Similarly, seal handlers may also be exposed to an arthritis infection called "*spaek* finger" arising from seal bites or the handling of seal skins (Dendle & Looke, 2008). While Australia is free of rabies, people working with bats may be exposed to a similar unpleasant and potentially fatal disease – the Australian bat lyssavirus – caused by bat bites (Dendle & Looke, 2008). Finally, Baynes-Rock (2019) provided an interesting account of the social connections occurring between crocodiles and their handlers at a Queensland crocodile farm. The physical safety of these farmworkers is a paramount concern; however, the strong attachments formed between the workers and their reptilian charges were surprising, and care is taken to ensure these attachments do not override the physical risks to these workers.

Final Thoughts

Australian researchers collaborate with numerous international colleagues based in Europe and the United States. However, increasing collaboration is also occurring with researchers based in the Asia-Pacific region and this more "local" collaboration is likely to intensify in the future. The establishment of the multidisciplinary Asia Pacific Academy for Psychosocial Factors at Work in 2012 (www.apapfaw.org), is a significant boost to formalizing research collaborations between Australian researchers and equivalent scholars in Japan, China, Malaysia, South Korea, Indonesia, Hong Kong, Taiwan, and neighboring countries. Similar to its European and United States counterparts, this academy hosts annual conferences and workshops to encourage research discussions and collaborations and has produced output highlighting research collaborations occurring in this region (Brough,

Dollard, & Tuckey, 2014; Dollard, Shimazu, Bin Nordin, Brough, & Tuckey, 2014). Both the membership of this Academy and the collaboration it fosters continue to grow.

Occupational stress research in Australia remains a productive and pertinent growth area of organizational psychology and is unlikely to diminish in the near future. Indeed, with continual technological advances, it is likely that increased interest will be placed on web-based and smartphone application-based stress management developments. Such developments will be of significant value to workers particularly based in rural areas, where vast distances isolate them from readily accessing other forms of assistance (e.g., Brew, Inder, Allen, Thomas, & Kelly, 2016). The concentration of the majority of the Australian population in coastal cities and towns is also predicted to increase, with Australian projected population estimates of up to 42.5 million people by 2056 and 62.2 million people by 2101 (Treasury, 2010). This population growth will require more public services and thus, more public servants. Unless working conditions for these workers are significantly changed, we can anticipate a steady increase in occupational stress experiences reported by these workers.

To conclude, in this chapter, we have discussed the key foci of occupational stress research being conducted in Australia and identified the common stressors experienced by Australian workers, including stressors that are somewhat unique to Australia – such as dangerous wildlife encounters, the heat, and the vast distances. We have highlighted the growth of research collaborations with our Asia-Pacific neighbors, and how the projected population growth will ensure a continuing need for innovative and impactful Australian occupational stress research.

References

Afsharian, A., Zadow, A., Dollard, M. F., Dormann, C. & Ziaian, T. (2018). Should psychosocial safety climate theory be extended to include climate strength? *Journal of Occupational Health Psychology, 23*(4), 496–507. 10.1037/ocp0000101.

Albrecht, S. L. (2012). The influence of job, team and organizational level resources on employee well-being, engagement, commitment and extra-role performance. *International Journal of Manpower, 33*(7), 840–853. 10.1108/01437721211268357.

Albrecht, S. L., Breidahl, E. & Marty, A. (2018). Organizational resources, organizational engagement climate, and employee engagement. *Career Development International, 23*(1), 67–85. 10.1108/CDI-04-2017-0064.

Australian Bureau of Statistics. (2006). *Impact of the Drought on Australian Production in 2002–03.* Retrieved from https://www.abs.gov.au/AUSSTATS/abs@.nsf/featurearticlesbyReleaseDate/3039D9149F3FDB73CA257129007E7E78?OpenDocument.

Australian Bureau of Statistics. (2019). *Regional Population Growth, Australia, 2017–18*. Retrieved from https://www.abs.gov.au/AUSSTATS/abs@.nsf/mf/3218.0.

Baynes-Rock, M. (2019). Precious reptiles: Social engagement and placemaking with saltwater crocodiles. *Area*, *51*(3), 578–585.

Biggs, A., Brough, P. & Barbour, J. P. (2014a). Enhancing work-related attitudes and work engagement: A quasi-experimental study of the impact of an organizational intervention. *International Journal of Stress Management*, *21*, 43–68. 10.1037/a0034508.

Biggs, A., Brough, P. & Barbour, J. (2014b). Exposure to extraorganizational stressors: Impact on mental health and organizational perceptions for police workers. *International Journal of Stress Management*, *21*(3), 255–282.10.1037/a0037297.

Biggs, A., Brough, P. & Barbour, J. (2014c). Relationships of individual and organizational support with engagement: Examining various types of causality in a three-wave study. *Work & Stress*, *28*(3), 236–254. 10.1080/02678373.2014.934316.

Biggs, A., Brough, P. & Barbour, J. (2014d). Strategic alignment with organizational priorities and work engagement: A multi-wave analysis. *Journal of Organizational Behavior*, *35*, 301–317. 10.1002/job.1866.

Bond, S. A., Tuckey, M. R. & Dollard, M. F. (2010). Psychosocial safety climate, workplace bullying, and symptoms of posttraumatic stress. *Organization Development Journal*, *28*(1), 37–56.

Brew, B., Inder, K., Allen, J., Thomas, M. & Kelly, B. (2016). The health and wellbeing of Australian farmers: A longitudinal cohort study. *BMC Public Health*, *16*(1), 988.

Brough, P. (2004). Comparing the influence of traumatic and organisational stressors upon the psychological health of police, fire and ambulance officers. *International Journal of Stress Management*, *11*, 227–244. 10.1037/1072-5245.11.3.227.

Brough, P. & Biggs, A. (2010). Occupational stress in police and prison staff. In J. Brown & E. Campbell (Eds.), *The Cambridge handbook of forensic psychology* (pp. 707–718). Cambridge, UK: Cambridge University Press.

Brough, P. & Biggs, A. (2015a). Job demands x job control interaction effects: Do occupation-specific job demands increase their occurrence? *Stress & Health*, *31*(2), 138–149. 10.1002/smi.2537.

Brough, P. & Biggs, A. (2015b). The highs and lows of occupational stress intervention research: Lessons learnt from collaborations with high-risk industries. In M. Karanika-Murray & C. Biron (Eds.), *Derailed organizational stress and well-being interventions: Confessions of failure and solutions for success* (pp. 263–270). UK: Springer.

Brough, P. & Boase, A. (2019). *Occupational stress management in the legal profession: Development, validation, and assessment of a stress-management instrument*. Australian Journal of Psychology, *71*, 273–284. 10.1111/ajpy.12244.

Brough, P., Brown, J. & Biggs, A. (2016). *Improving criminal justice workplaces: Translating theory and research into evidenced-based practice*. London: Routledge.

Brough, P., Dollard, M. & Tuckey, M. (2014). Theory and methods to prevent and manage occupational stress: Innovations from around the globe. *International Journal of Stress Management, 21*, 1–6. 10.1037/a0035903.

Brough, P., Drummond, S. & Biggs, A. (2018). Job support, coping and control: Assessment of simultaneous impacts within the occupational stress process. *Journal of Occupational Health Psychology, 23*(2), 188–197. 1037/ocp0000074.

Brough, P., O'Driscoll, M., Kalliath, T., Cooper, C. L. & Poelmans, S. (2009). *Workplace psychological health: Current research and practice.* Cheltenham, UK: Edward Elgar.

Brough, P. & Williams, J. (2007). Managing occupational stress in a high-risk industry: Measuring the job demands of correctional officers. *Criminal Justice and Behavior, 34*, 555–567. 10.1177/0093854806294147.

Cavanaugh, M. A., Boswell, W. R., Roehling, M. V. & Boudreau, J. W. (2000). An empirical examination of self-reported work stress among U.S. managers. *Journal of Applied Psychology, 85*(1), 65–74. 10.1037/0021-9010.85.1.65.

Chan, D. (1998). Functional relations among constructs in the same content domain at different levels of analysis: A typology of composition models. *Journal of Applied Psychology, 83*(2), 234–246. 10.1037/0021-9010.83.2.234.

Coates, L., Haynes, K., O'Brien, J., McAneney, J. & De Oliveira, F. D. (2014). Exploring 167 years of vulnerability: An examination of extreme heat events in Australia 1844–2010. *Environmental Science & Policy, 42*, 33–44.

Considine, R., Tynan, R. J., James, C., Wiggers, J., Lewin, T. J., Inder, K. & Kelly, B. J. (2017). The contribution of individual, social and work characteristics to employee mental health in a coal mining industry population. *PLoS One, 12*(1), e0168445. 10.1371/journal.pone.0168445.

Demerouti, E., Bakker, A. B., Nachreiner, F. & Schaufeli, W. B. (2001). The job demands-resources model of burnout. *Journal of Applied Psychology, 86*(3), 499–512. 10.1037//0021-9010.86.3.499.

Dendle, C. & Looke, D. (2008). Animal bites: An update for management with a focus on infections. *Emergency Medicine Australasia, 20*(6), 458–467.

Dollard, M., Shimazu, A., Bin Nordin, R., Brough, P. & Tuckey, M. (Eds.). (2014). *Psychosocial factors at work in the Asia Pacific.* London, UK: Springer.

Dollard, M. F., Bailey, T. S., McLinton, S. S., Richards, P., McTernan, W. P., Taylor & Bond, S. (2012). *The Australian Workplace Barometer: Report on psychosocial safety climate and worker health in Australia.* Retrieved from Centre for Applied Psychological Research, University of South Australia.

Dollard, M. F. & Bakker, A. B. (2010). Psychosocial safety climate as a precursor to conducive work environments, psychological health problems, and employee engagement. *Journal of Occupational and Organizational Psychology, 83*(3), 579–599. 10.1348/096317909x470690.

Espedido, A. & Searle, B. J. (2018). Goal difficulty and creative performance: The mediating role of stress appraisal. *Human Performance, 31*(3), 179–196. 10.1080/08959285.2018.1499024.

Espedido, A., Searle, B. J. & Griffin, B. (2019). *Peers, proactivity, and problem-solving: A multilevel study of team impacts on stress appraisals of problem-solving demands. Work & Stress, 34* (3), 1–19. 10.1080/02678373.2019.1579767.

Gardner, B., Alfrey, K. L., Vandelanotte, C. & Rebar, A. L. (2018). Mental health and well-being concerns of fly-in fly-out workers and their partners in Australia: A qualitative study. *BMJ Open, 8*(3), e019516.

Hall, G. B., Dollard, M. F. & Coward, J. (2010). Psychosocial safety climate: Development of the PSC-12. *International Journal of Stress Management, 17*(4), 353–383. 10.103/a0021320.

Hanna, E. G., Kjellstrom, T., Bennett, C. & Dear, K. (2011). Climate change and rising heat: Population health implications for working people in Australia. *Asia-Pacific Journal of Public Health, 23*(2), 14S–26S. 10.1177/1010539510391457.

Hart, P. M., Wearing, A. J. & Headey, B. (1995). Police stress and well-being: Integrating personality, coping and daily work experiences. *Journal of Occupational & Organisational Psychology, 68,* 133–156.

Jia, Y. A., Rowlinson, S. & Ciccarelli, M. (2016). Climatic and psychosocial risks of heat illness incidents on construction site. *Applied Ergonomics, 53,* 25–35. 10.1016/j.apergo.2015.08.008.

Lamb, S. & Kwok, K. C. (2016). A longitudinal investigation of work environment stressors on the performance and wellbeing of office workers. *Applied Ergonomics, 52,* 104–111. 10.1016/j.apergo.2015.07.010.

Law, R., Dollard, M. F., Tuckey, M. R. & Dormann, C. (2011). Psychosocial safety climate as a lead indicator of workplace bullying and harassment, job resources, psychological health and employee engagement. *Accident Analysis & Prevention, 43*(5), 1782–1793. doi: 10.1016/j.aap.2011.04.010.

Lenthall, S., Wakerman, J., Opie, T., Dollard, M., Dunn, S., Knight, S. & Watson, C. (2009). What stresses remote area nurses? Current knowledge and future action. *Australian Journal of Rural Health, 17*(4), 208–213. doi: 10.1111/j.1440-1584.2009.01073.x.

Li, Y., Chen, P. Y., Tuckey, M. R., McLinton, S. S. & Dollard, M. F. (2019). Prevention through job design: Identifying high-risk job characteristics associated with workplace bullying. *Journal of Occupational Health Psychology, 24*(2), 297–306. 10.1037/ocp0000133.

Martin, A., Kilpatrick, M., Cocker, F., Sanderson, K., Scott, J. & Brough, P. (2015). Challenges in the evaluation of a mental health promotion intervention targeting small-to-medium enterprises. In M. Karanika-Murray & C. Biron (Eds.), *Derailed organizational stress and well-being interventions: Confessions of failure and solutions for success* (pp. 191–200). UK: Springer.

Martin, A., Sanderson, K., Scott, J. & Brough, P. (2009). Promoting mental health in small-medium enterprises: An evaluation of the "Business in Mind" program. *Public Health, 9,* 239–247. 10.1186/1471-2458-9-239

Maté, J. & Oosthuizen, J. (2012). Global warming and heat stress among Western Australian mine, oil and gas workers. *Environmental health–Emerging issues and practice* (pp. 289–305). Croatia: InTech.

Mirtschin, P. (2006). The pioneers of venom production for Australian antivenoms. *Toxicon, 48*(7), 899–918.

Morrow, R. & Brough, P. (2019). 'It's off to work we go!' Person-environment fit and turnover intentions in managerial and administrative mining personnel. *International Journal of Occupational Safety and Ergonomics, 25*(3), 467–475. 10.1080/10803548.2017.1396028.

Opie, T., Dollard, M., Lenthall, S. & Knight, S. (2013). Occupational Stress in

Remote Area Nursing: Development of the Remote Area Nursing Stress Scale (RANSS). *Journal of Nursing Measurement*, 21(2), 246–263. 10.1891/1061-3749.21.2.246.

Opie, T., Lenthall, S., Dollard, M. F., Wakerman, J., MacLeod, M. & Knight, S. (2010). Trends in workplace violence in the remote area nursing workforce. *Australian Journal of Advanced Nursing*, 27(4), 18–23.

Price Waterhouse Coopers. (2014). *Creating a mentally health workplace: Return on investment analysis*. Retrieved from Beyond Blue: http://www.headsup.org.au.

Raper, M. J., Brough, P. & Biggs, A. (2019). Evidence for the impact of organisational resources versus job characteristics in assessments of occupational stress over time. *Applied Psychology: An International Review*, 69(3), 715–740. 10.1111/apps.12201.

Rickard, G., Lenthall, S., Dollard, M., Opie, T., Knight, S., Dunn, S. & Brewster-Webb, D. (2012). Organisational intervention to reduce occupational stress and turnover in hospital nurses in the Northern Territory, Australia. *Collegian*, 19(4), 211–221. 10.1016/j.colegn.2012.07.001.

Robinson, K., Peetz, D., Murray, G., Griffin, S. & Muurlink, O. (2017). Relationships between children's behaviour and parents' work within families of mining and energy workers. *Journal of Sociology*, 53(3), 557–576.

Safe Work Australia. (2013). *The incidence of accepted workers compensation claims for mental stress in Australia (Publication No. 978-0-642-78719-4)*. Retrieved from http://www.safeworkaustralia.gov.au.

Safe Work Australia. (2015). *Work-related mental disorder profile*. Retrieved from https://www.safeworkaustralia.gov.au/system/files/documents/1702/work-related-mental-disorders-profile.pdf.

Safe Work Australia. (2016). *Psychosocial health and safety and bullying in Australian workplaces: Inidcators from accepted workers' compensation claims*. Retrieved from https://www.safeworkaustralia.gov.au/collection/psychosocial-health-and-safety-and-bullying-australian-workplaces.

Schneider, B., González-Morales, M. G., Ostroff, C. & West, M. A. (2017). Organizational climate and culture: Reflections on the history of the constructs in the Journal of Applied Psychology. *Journal of Applied Psychology*, 102(3), 468–482. doi: 10.1037/apl0000090.

Searle, B. J. & Auton, J. C. (2015). The merits of measuring challenge and hindrance appraisals. *Anxiety, Stress, and Coping*, 28(2), 121–143. 10.1080/10615806.2014.931378.

Searle, B. J. & Tuckey, M. R. (2017). Differentiating challenge, hindrance, and threat in the stress process. In C. L. Cooper & M. P. Leiter (Eds.), *The Routledge companion to wellbeing at work* (pp. 25–36). London: Routledge, Taylor and Francis Group.

Singh, S., Hanna, E. G. & Kjellstrom, T. (2015). Working in Australia's heat: Health promotion concerns for health and productivity. *Health Promotion International*, 30(2), 239–250. https://doi.org/10.1093/heapro/dat027.

Stevenson, S., Gowardman, J., Tozer, S. & Woods, M. (2015). Life-threatening Q fever infection following exposure to kangaroos and wallabies. *BMJ Case Reports*, 2015, 1–3. 10.1136/bcr-2015-210808.

Thompson, G. G. & Thompson, S. A. (2007). Usefulness of funnel traps in catching small reptiles and mammals, with comments on the effectiveness of the alternatives. *Wildlife Research, 34*(6), 491–497.

Treasury. (2010). *Australia to 2050: Future challenges*. Canberra Retrieved from http://www.treasury.gov.au/igr/igr2010/report/pdf/IGR_2010.pdf.

Tuckey, M. R., Chrisopoulos, S. & Dollard, M. F. (2012). Job Demands, Resource Deficiencies, and Workplace Harassment: Evidence for Micro-Level Effects. *International Journal of Stress Management, 19*(4), 292–310. 10.1037/a0030317.

Tuckey, M. R. & Hayward, R. (2011). Global and Occupation-Specific Emotional Resources as Buffers against the Emotional Demands of Fire-Fighting. *Applied Psychology: An International Review, 60*(1), 1–23. 10.1111/j.1464-0597.2010.00424.x.

Tuckey, M. R. & Neall, A. M. (2014). Workplace bullying erodes job and personal resources: Between- and within-person perspectives. *Journal of Occupational Health Psychology, 19*(4), 413–424. 10.1037/a0037728.

Tuckey, M. R., Searle, B. J., Boyd, C. M., Winefield, A. H. & Winefield, H. R. (2015). Hindrances are not threats: Advancing the multidimensionality of work stress. *Journal of Occupational Health Psychology, 20*(2), 131–147. 10.1037/a0038280.

Tynan, R. J., Considine, R., Wiggers, J., Lewin, T. J., James, C., Inder, K. & Kelly, B. J. (2017). Alcohol consumption in the Australian coal mining industry. *Occupational and Environmental Medicine, 74*(4), 259–267. 10.1136/oemed-2016-103602

Vojnovic, P., Michelson, G., Jackson, D. & Bahn, S. (2014). Adjustment, well-being and help-seeking: Among Australian FIFO mining employees. *Australian Bulletin of Labour, 40*(2), 242–261.

Webster, V., Brough, P. & Daly, K. (2016). Fight, flight or freeze: Common responses for follower coping with toxic leadership. *Stress & Health, 32*, 346–354. 10.1002/smi.2626.

Xiang, J., Bi, P., Pisaniello, D., Hansen, A. & Sullivan, T. (2013). Association between high temperature and work-related injuries in Adelaide, South Australia, 2001-2010. *Occupational and Environmental Medicine, 71*(4), 246–252. 10.1136/oemed-2013-101584.

Xiang, J., Hansen, A., Pisaniello, D. & Bi, P. (2015). Perceptions of workplace heat exposure and controls among occupational hygienists and relevant specialists in Australia. *PLoS One, 10*(8), e0135040. 10.1371/journal.pone.0135040

Zander, K. K., Botzen, W. J. W., Oppermann, E., Kjellstrom, T. & Garnett, S. T. (2015). Heat stress causes subtantial labour productivity loss in Australia. *Nature Climate Change, 5*, 647–652. 10.1038/nclimate2623.

Zander, K. K., Mathew, S. & Garnett, S. T. (2018). Exploring heat stress relief measures among the Australian labour force. *International Journal of Environmental Research and Public Health, 15*(3), 401–415. 10.3390/ijerph15030401.

Zapf, D., Escartin, J., Einarsen, S., Hoel, H. & Vartia, M. (2011). Empirical findings on prevalene and risk groups of bullying in the workplace. In S. Einarsen, H. Hoel, D. Zapf & C. Cooper (Eds.), *Bullying and harassment in the workplace: Developments in theory, research, and practice* (2nd ed., pp. 75–105). Boca Raton, FL: CRC Press.

3 Work Stress Research in Brazil

Maria Cristina Ferreira, Helenides Mendonça, Ronald Fischer, and Leonardo Fernandes Martins

Introduction

This chapter presents a systematic review of Brazilian literature on work stress over the last decade. Similar to international trends, the labor market situation has deteriorated significantly. This further exacerbated an already precarious working context characterized by high unemployment, low labor rights, and endemic levels of corruption. The combination of poor pre-existing labor conditions with increasing market pressures helped to shape a profound economic, financial, and political crisis that continues to affect the country.

Brazilian corporate organizations have sought to restructure their production and work processes, as well as their management models to increase competitiveness, leading to the adoption of technical and organizational innovations designed to reduce costs, making companies more efficient and competitive nationally and internationally. The outcome has been a dramatic reduction in staffing in some sectors of the economy, large-scale privatizations, and outsourcing of a number of support services.

In the wake of this process, employment instability has further risen, there has been a progressive expansion of temporary labor contracts and self-employment, as well as an increase in outsourcing services to external consultancies and service providers. These processes have led to an increase in the number of workers entering the informal labor market. These trends have had negative repercussions throughout the working population and increased work stress.

Statistics on workers' psychological health problems are alarming. In Brazil, 70% of the active population report being stressed (Silva & Salles, 2016) with an unknown but potentially harmful impact on workers, organizations, and society. As indicated by international literature, stress at work can trigger depressive conditions, hypertension, and heart problems, as well as medical insurance costs, loss of staff productivity, and absenteeism, among other problems. How has the Brazilian academic community responded to these conditions? Our review aims to describe the Brazilian literature on the topic of work stress, which has been conducted and reported over the last 10 years.

Method

This systematic review followed the Transparent Reporting of Systematic Reviews and Meta-Analysis (PRISMA, http://www.prisma-statement.org/). Our review covers Brazilian literature on work stress for the period of 2009 to 2018.

Survey Strategy and Inclusion of Studies

The database search was performed in June 2019, covering research published from January 2009 to December 2018. We focused on the last 10 years to capture the most recent literature on work stress in Brazil and to describe the most current work conditions. The search was done using Scielo Brasil, a Brazilian database that gathers the full articles published in the most peer-reviewed journals in Brazil. The following keywords were used: "stress at work," "occupational stress," "professional stress," "work stress," "psychosocial stress in the workplace," "psychosocial stress at work," "job stressors," "occupational stressors," "professional stressors," "labor stressors," "psychosocial job stressors," and "psychosocial stressors in the workplace."

This initial search yielded 235 publications. No additional records were identified through other sources. We first examined titles and abstracts and used the following criteria for inclusion in our database: (a) published in a peer-reviewed Brazilian journal, (b) having "stress at work" as the core theme of the publication, which led to the exclusion of articles that focused on workers' health, mental illness at work or psychological illness,[1] (c) including empirical data, both qualitative or quantitative data collection, and (d) involving samples composed of Brazilian workers. From the original list, 87 publications were excluded for the following reasons: theoretical or conceptual papers (4), literature reviews on work stress (22), student samples (2), samples of non-Brazilian workers (9), and articles that did not focus on job stress (50). This list of 148 articles was read in detail. Another 30 articles were excluded due to any of the above reasons. The final literature review was based on a total of 118 publications (see Figure 3.1).

Coding Scheme

The articles were analyzed and coded in a spreadsheet by the first author. The following information were coded: year of publication, author/s, journal area, theoretical models adopted, type of empirical research, sample size, workers surveyed, job stressors considered, stressor

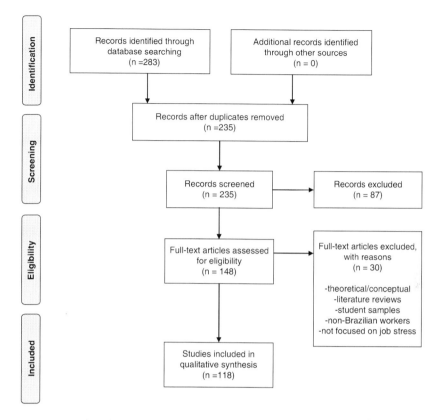

Figure 3.1 Flowchart of survey strategy and inclusion of studies.

measurement instruments, stress reactions considered, stress reaction measurement instruments, and the main results obtained. Afterward, the second author independently coded 33% of the studies, and 28 studies randomly selected, to ensure consistency and accuracy of the adopted classification. Cohen's Kappa Coefficients of rater agreement were all above 0.75, indicating sufficient levels of agreement.

Results

We present the results in four main sections. First, we present a review of the theoretical and conceptual foundations of the investigations. In the second section, we review temporal trends, research areas, and methodological characteristics of the studies. Third, we describe the different work stressors and stress reactions included in the studies. The final section discusses the main findings observed in the studies that were reviewed separately based on their methodological features.

Theoretical Grounds of the Studies Reviewed

The most commonly cited theoretical model (n = 81; 67%) was the Demand-Control-Social Support Model (JDCS; Karasek & Theörell, 1990). It describes the interplay between job demands that a worker faces, the degree of control that a worker has to make decisions and influence results, and social support that a worker receives.

Psychological demand and control are characterized as independent dimensions, both ranging from low to high levels, generating four possibilities for psychosocial work experiences. A high-demand or high-stress job combines high demand with low control; active work is characterized by high demand and high control; passive work features low demand and low control; and finally, low-demand or low-stress work is encountered in situations of low demand and high control (Karasek & Theörell, 1990).

The second most common theoretical model (n = 11; 14%) was the Effort-Reward Imbalance model (ERI; Siegrist, 1996), although it was considerably less prevalent compared to the JDCS. Effort concerns the demands and obligations arising from the labor organization, while rewards relate to financial gains and occupational status. The imbalance between a lot of effort and little recognition can lead to stressful situations. A third and novel dimension of the model refers to overcommitment to garner approval and esteem, which can interact with the effort-reward imbalance and increase the risks of work stress. The remaining studies adopted different theoretical approaches or did not explicitly report their theoretical basis.

Temporal, Geographical, and Methodological Characteristics

From 2009 to 2018, the number of published empirical articles ranged from 7 to 19 per year, with the lowest number of publications (7) in 2012 and the largest number (19) in 2015. The average number in other years was relatively stable, ranging between 9 to 12 articles. Thus, the publications within the ten-year time frame have been relatively stable (see Figure 3.2).

The articles were published in journals across different fields, with the highest concentration occurring in nursing journals (n = 52; 44%), followed by journals in other health areas, such as public health, or medicine (n = 35; 30%), and by psychology journals (n = 16; 14%) (see Figure 3.3). This distribution reflects the multidisciplinarity work stress research in Brazil.

Regarding the research methodology adopted in the studies, more studies used quantitative (n = 104; 88%) compared to qualitative methods (n = 14, 11%). Among the quantitative studies, cross-sectional

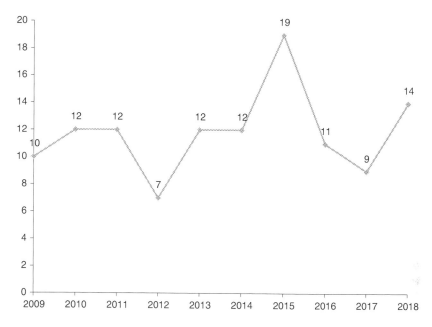

Figure 3.2 Temporal distribution of the articles reviewed.

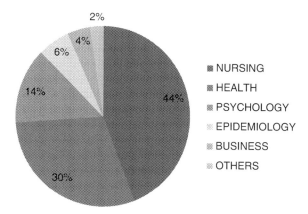

Figure 3.3 Distribution of articles by knowledge area.

investigations prevailed (n = 76; 73%), while other types of research showed much lower percentages (see Figure 3.4).

In the qualitative studies, sample sizes ranged from 1 to 62 participants (*M* = 20.14). In contrast, quantitative studies reported data from samples ranging from 18 to 3,253 participants (*M* = 380.91), with the highest concentration observed in the range of up to 100 participants

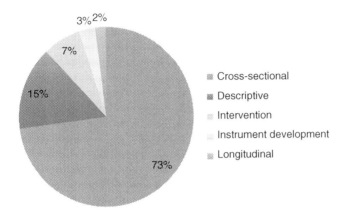

Figure 3.4 Research methodology adopted in the studies.

(n = 28; 30%), followed by the range of up to 200 participants (n = 16; 17%). Finally, among the intervention studies, samples ranged from 20 to 105 participants (*M* = 43.42).

The majority of the studies were conducted with workers of a specific sector (health institutions, educational institutions, etc.), although some of them involved heterogeneous samples of individuals from different labor sectors. Most studies (n = 64; 54%) were carried out with health professionals – especially nursing professionals, followed by education professionals (n = 23; 19%) – especially teachers (Table 3.1). These data are in line with previous reviews carried out in Brazil (Rodrigues & Faiad, 2019) and abroad (Havermans *et al.*, 2016).

Stressors and Reactions to Work Stress

Out of the 118 articles reviewed, only 81 (67%) explicitly measured some stressors. The remaining articles typically focused on sociodemographic relationships and work organization with different

Table 3.1 Characterization of workers composing the samples

Work Sectors	Frequency	Percentage
Health	64	54
Education	23	19
Safety	8	7
Industry	8	7
Service renderers	8	7
Workers in general	7	6
Total	118	100

reactions to work stress. Considering that the JDCS model is the main theoretical reference adopted in Brazilian work stress research, the most frequently investigated job stressors were demands at work and the degree of work control (n = 47; 58%). The job stressors advocated by the ERI model – such as effort, reward, and overcommitment – are less frequently reported in the literature (n = 11; 14%). Six studies combined the two theoretical models mentioned, thus using the six job stressors together. Interpersonal relationships, overload and conflict, and role ambiguity have been measured in a smaller number of studies (Table 3.2).

For measuring the job stressors included in the JDCS, the most frequently adopted instruments (n = 6) were the Job-Content Questionnaire (JCQ; Karasek, 1985) and its reduced version (Job Stress Scale-JSS; Theörell et al., 1988; n = 41). For measuring the ERI, the only scale used was the Effort-Reward Imbalance Questionnaire (ERIQ; n = 11) – both in its complete and reduced versions (Siegrist et al., 2004). A few studies (n = 10) included scales originally developed in Brazil, among which the Work Stress Scale (EET; Paschoal & Tamayo, 2004; n = 3) and the Nurses' Stress Inventory (IEE; Stacciarini & Tróccoli, 2000; n = 4) stand out.

The specific work stress reactions were explicitly mentioned in 96 (81%) of the reviewed articles. Table 3.3 summarizes the different categories of work stress reactions used in those studies. The most frequent reaction was burnout (n = 22; 23%), followed by self-perceived stress (n = 14; 15%), work ability (n = 10; 11%), and psychophysiological indicators such as hypertension, salivary cortisol, and low back pain (n = 10; 11%).

The main scale adopted to measure burnout was the Maslach Burnout Inventory (Maslach, Jackson, & Leiter, 1996; n = 15). As for the other reactions to work stress, the main measurement instruments used were the Self Reporting Questionnaire (Harding et al., 1980; n = 6) – already validated in Brazil (Mari & Williams, 1985) – and the Lipp's Inventory of Symptoms of Stress for Adults (ISSL; Lipp, 2000; n = 5) – originally developed in Brazil.

Table 3.2 Stressors adopted in the studies

Stressors	Frequency	Percentage
Demands, control, social support	47	58
Effort, reward, overcommitment	11	14
Interpersonal relationships	9	10
Overload	7	9
Conflict and role ambiguity	7	9
Total	81	100

Table 3.3 Work stress reactions adopted in the studies

Work Stress Reactions	Frequency	Percentage
Burnout	22	23
Self-perceived stress	14	15
Ability to work	10	11
Psychophysiological indicators	10	11
Coping	9	9
Self-perceived health	6	6
Depression	5	5
Vocal condition	5	5
Minor psychic disorders	4	4
Work satisfaction	3	3
Common mental disorders	3	3
Patient care	2	2
Alcohol consumption	1	1
Anxiety	1	1
Negative affects at work	1	1
Total	96	100

Main Results Observed in the Reviewed Studies

There were six qualitative studies that were generally conducted through interviews and subsequently subjected to content analysis. The outcome of these analyses indicated that the identified main categories of job stressors mentioned by workers were similar to those reported in non-Brazilian contexts: work overload, pressure at work, repetition of tasks, lack of autonomy at work, difficulties in interpersonal relationships, and the lack of resources for work (Cardoso, Padovani, & Tucci, 2014). Similarly, among the qualitatively reported: stress symptoms, changes in sleep patterns, psychosomatic complaints, and the reduced ability to concentrate were generally mentioned in the studies (Mininel, Baptista, & Felli, 2011).

Quantitative descriptive studies focused mainly on the percentages of different stressors. Focusing on job stressors, high percentages of demand, control, effort-reward imbalance and overcommitment, as well as low percentages of social support, were reported (Silva-Junior & Fischer, 2015). Other studies reported a high percentage of work overload, negative aspects related to work organization – such as night work, and the lack of resources to perform the job (Martins, Enumo, & Paula, 2016). It is noteworthy that these patterns do not concord with the general perception of Brazilian workplaces that were outlined in the introduction. Regarding the incidence of stress indicators, stress percentages on the average (Maffia & Pereira, 2014), and low burnout percentages (Padilha et al., 2017) were found in general in the samples considered.

The studies testing the JDCS model mainly analyzed associations via correlation coefficients and regression analyzes. The general pattern we found is in line with international findings: the higher the demands and the lower the degree of control over work, the higher the rates of depression (Lima, Assunção, & Barreto, 2015), of job dissatisfaction (Costa & Ferreira, 2014), of back pain occurrence (Fernandes, Carvalho, Assunção, & Silvany Neto, 2009), the more negative assessments on working conditions (Pelegrini, Cardoso, Claumann, Pinto, & Felden, 2018), the lower quality of life (Fogaça, Carvalho, Nogueira, & Martins, 2009), of lower self-perceived health (Griep, Rotenberg, Landsbergis, & Vasconcellos-Silva, 2011), of lower ability to work (Martinez, Latorre, & Fischer, 2017), and the lower job satisfaction. Regarding social support, in line with international patterns, it was found that lower social support is associated with worse self-rated health (Theme Filha, Costa, & Guilam, 2013), more precarious working conditions (Pelegrini *et al.*, 2018), lower quality of life (Fogaça *et al.*, 2009), less ability to work (Martinez *et al.*, 2017), job dissatisfaction (Costa & Ferreira, 2014), depression (Costa & Ferreira, 2014), psychosomatic complaints (Costa & Ferreira, 2014), and burnout (Vidotti, Ribeiro, Galdino, & Martins, 2018). In other words, the higher the social support, the lower the stress at work (Lopes & Silva, 2018). However, it is also noteworthy that, in contrast to previous international studies, some studies have not found significant correlations between the typically reported job stressors and either burnout (Mota, Dosea, & Nunes, 2014) or work ability (Negeliskii & Lautert, 2011).

Focusing on the categories of work conditions proposed by the JDCS model, Brazilian studies have shown similar patterns to international studies. These studies demonstrated that high-demand work (high demand and low control) is associated with more illness (Pinhatti *et al.*, 2018), higher prevalence of common mental disorders (Araújo, Mattos, Almeida, & Santos, 2016), higher occurrence of minor psychological disorders (Urbanetto *et al.*, 2013), higher rates of psychosomatic complaints (Pereira, Kothe, Bleyer, & Teixeira, 2014), greater voice disorders (Giannini, Latorre, & Ferreira, 2012), higher blood pressure rates (Pimenta & Assunção, 2016), worse health self-assessment (Theme Filha *et al.*, 2013), worse self-reported mouth health (Scalco, Abegg, Celeste, Hökerberg, & Faerstein, 2013), lower work capacity (Sampaio, Coelho, Barbosa, Mancini, & Parreira, 2009), and worse quality of life (Azevedo, Nery, & Cardoso, 2017). In contrast, active work (high demand and high control) was correlated with a lower incidence of burnout (Silva *et al.*, 2015), but also with a higher occurrence of minor psychological disorders (Urbanetto *et al.*, 2013) and psychosomatic complaints (Pereira *et al.*, 2014). This is somewhat contrary to international trends. Passive work (low demand and low control) conditions were correlated with a lower incidence of burnout (Silva *et al.*, 2015). Some studies did not observe significant associations between the different categories of work stress (high demand, passive work, and active work) and hypertension (Alves, Chor, Faerstein, Werneck, & Lopes, 2009).

Studies testing the Effort-Reward Imbalance Model generally showed similar patterns as international literature. The greater imbalance between efforts and rewards, which indicates higher degrees of stress, was associated with a greater prevalence of common mental disorders (Marcelino Filho & Araújo, 2015), minor psychological disorders (Marconato et al., 2017), lower mental health (Silva, Souza, Borges, & Fischer, 2010), more illness indicators (Pinhatti et al., 2018), lower self-reported health indexes (Griep et al., 2011), quality of life at work (Fogaça et al., 2009), and work ability (Martinez et al., 2017).

Other studies also reported significant associations of job stress with work overload (Meneghini, Paz, & Lautert, 2011), conflicts between personal and organizational values (Meneghini et al., 2011), lack of adequate resources for proper work performance (Andolhe, Barbosa, Oliveira, Costa, & Padilha, 2015), task conflicts (Costa & Martins, 2011), and teacher-student relationship issues (Rodrigues, Paula, Silveira, & Silveira, 2017). Focusing on possible factors for protection, the organizational values of autonomy, well-being, ethics, and community concern (Canova & Porto, 2010), the possibilities of professional development and advancement (Meneghini et al., 2011), and receiving rewards (Meneghini et al., 2011) have been considered protective factors for work stress.

Correlations and consequences of work stress were increased levels of depression (Pozzebon, Piccin, Silva, & Corrêa, 2016), anxiety (Pozzebon et al., 2016), self-perceived deterioration of health (Guido, Linch, Pitthan, & Umann, 2011), decreased productivity (Umann, Guido, & Silva, 2014), self-reported voice disorders (Valente, Botelho, & Silva, 2015), work ability index (Martinez & Latorre, 2009), alcohol consumption (Maffia & Pereira, 2014), and lower job satisfaction (Andolhe et al., 2015). These patterns are, again, generally in line with international trends.

Investigating burnout as a chronic consequence of stress, some studies found that younger workers (Trindade, Lautert, Beck, Amestoy, & Pires, 2010) with less work experience (Guedes & Gaspar, 2016), who experience greater relationship problems with their students (Dalagasperina & Monteiro, 2014), and who have a greater workload (Guedes & Gaspar, 2016) are those who are most likely to be affected by burnout. Burnout was also associated with lower job satisfaction (Ferreira & Lucca, 2015).

There were seven intervention studies – four of which used quasi-experimental pre- and posttest designs with a single group. The interventions adopted in these studies consisted of: a set of stress-related lectures (Dalcin & Carlotto, 2018), workplace exercises sessions (Freitas-Swerts & Robazzi, 2014), a physical activity program (Freitas,

Carneseca, Paiva, & Paiva, 2014), and a wellness program (Jacques et al., 2018). Only the study by Dalcin and Carlotto (2018) found a significant reduction in stress indices between the post- and pretest. Among the three studies with control groups, Damásio, Habigzang, Freitas, and Koller (2014) showed reduced burnout among participants in an intervention group using cognitive behavioral therapy compared to a nonrandomized control group. Freitas, Calais, and Cardoso (2018) reported reduced stress symptoms in a progressive relaxation intervention compared with two nonrandomized control groups. Montibeler et al. (2018) conducted a completely randomized experiment testing the effectiveness of aromatherapy massage. The results showed a reduction in blood pressure and heart rate indicators between the posttest and the pretest of the experimental group, but there were no significant differences between the self-reported stress symptoms pre and post.

Finally, only three studies reported new development or refinement of instruments. One of them concerns the construction of a Brazilian scale for the evaluation of psychosocial stressors in the workplace, but with a specific focus on measuring the theoretical model of Cooper, Dewe, and O'Driscoll (2001). The instrument is composed of seven factors – role conflict and ambiguity, role overload, interpersonal difficulties, career insecurity, lack of autonomy, work/family conflict, and pressure on the degree of responsibility – and the final scale showed good psychometric characteristics (Ferreira et al., 2015). Tamayo and Tróccoli (2009) developed a Brazilian Burnout Inventory which is based on the burnout syndrome model proposed by Maslach et al. (1996). Similar to the United States scale, it is composed of three factors – emotional exhaustion, dehumanization, and job disappointment – and has shown adequate psychometric characteristics. Aguiar, Fonseca, and Valente (2010) conducted a test-retest reliability analysis of the Job Stress Scale (Theörell et al., 1988). The results of that investigation suggested high stability of the three dimensions of the scale – psychological demands, work control, and social support.

Discussion

Our review found that there has been a steady rate of publication of stress-related work in Brazilian journals. The work conducted in Brazil is largely influenced by international models, instruments, and trends. We discuss some suggestions for future development.

The first observation is the prevalence of Western theories, models, and instruments in the context of Brazilian research. As outlined in our introduction, the economic context in Brazil is characterized by more precarious labor market conditions compared to many other Western countries. Furthermore, the social and cultural environment in Brazil is more complex with a large number of different ethnic and racial groups that are socially and economically stratified. Overall, the Brazilian context is characterized by a greater emphasis on traditional in-groups – most notably extended family networks and correspondingly much lower levels of individualism and self-orientation – as well as higher hierarchies and power distance, but with greater informality in social interactions than would be indicated by those marked by hierarchy differences and higher levels of uncertainty avoidance, which is highly relevant for understanding stress processes (Hofstede, 2001). Recent research suggested that there are a number of cultural problem-solving strategies such as Jeitinho Brasileiro (Ferreira, Fischer, Porto, Pilati, & Milfont, 2012) that emerged in a highly bureaucratic and unequal societal context, which in turn is likely to affect social health and well-being. We would encourage more specific consideration of the social, cultural, and economic conditions in Brazil when studying work stress.

It is also noteworthy that there was little to no consideration of the specific macroeconomic conditions that Brazilian workers and companies are facing and how these processes may diverge from international trends, typically reported in the United States or European contexts. It is also worrisome that the large majority of studies used instruments developed elsewhere with little consideration of cultural, economic, or social conditions that may render results open to alternative interpretations. Simply reporting reliability or factor analyses is not sufficient for an adequate adaption of instruments, since it may miss important locally relevant indicators and information and may not adequately cover the domain of interest.

In line with these trends, the most frequently adopted theoretical models have been the Demand-Control-Social Support Model and the Effort-Reward Imbalance Model. These models have been developed in the United States and Western Europe, and it would be useful to more critically question their relevance and appropriateness for Brazilian contexts.

Another important avenue for future studies would be the development of novel theoretical models that jointly consider stress and well-being processes in the workplace – such as, the Job Demands and Resources Theory (JD-R) (Bakker & Demerouti, 2017). Such models allow the joint analysis of the illness processes that are thought to cause job stress and of motivational processes that are assumed to lead to well-being at work. When adopting these models, it would be important to conduct investigations that broaden the scope of the job stressors usually adopted in research by considering the role played by broader contextual factors – such as leadership style and organizational culture – since both types of variables are organizational characteristics capable of causing work stress (Cooper et al., 2001).

The majority of studies tested relatively simple designs, with not a single study in our review testing mediators and moderators in the stress process. Such models have made a significant contribution to our understanding of the stress process in the international arena. We would encourage more sophisticated models and more longitudinal research that can adequately test the presence of possible mediators between stressors and stress reactions, as well as their impact on work performance outcomes. In addition, individual-difference variables – such as personality characteristics (e.g., proactive personality, extroversion, etc.) and organizational context dimensions (e.g., leadership styles, organizational culture, etc.) should be investigated and included as potential causes and/or moderators of the work stress process.

Our review also showed a preoccupation with stress in health professionals – especially nurses – followed by studies conducted with education professionals. On one hand, we would encourage more research in diverse occupations and work environments to get a better perspective on occupations and sectors that were underrepresented and to provide a more holistic understanding of work stress in Brazil. In this regard, the category of security professionals deserves special mention, as it is considered a high-risk category in the current Brazilian reality (Calazans, 2010). At the same time, we would also encourage more focused research on those occupations where work stress is likely to have significant negative consequences. For example, medical doctors are likely to show high levels of burnout (Rosa, Falavigna, & Silva, 2019), which is likely to impact their ability to perform medical procedures and jeopardizes the health and physical well-being of both doctors and patients. These effects of stress on the larger society – beyond the immediate respondent of a survey – need to be documented. Similarly, more high-quality intervention studies that can be used to address these stress-related effects are needed.

Methodologically, cross-sectional correlational studies were most prevalent. We found a single study that adopted a more state-of-the-art structural equation modeling. Structural equation modeling is a more robust statistical technique for testing complex multivariate relationships between job stressors and reactions to work stress. Similarly, only two longitudinal studies were found in this review, which also contrasts with the international literature on work stress – in which longitudinal studies are more prevalent. We strongly encourage longitudinal studies as they allow a more detailed understanding of the pattern and evolution of stress conditions over time. Also, no preregistered studies were found and the null-hypothesis significance testing framework was dominant. This is a concern, given the current replication crisis within the social and medical sciences, and concerns the null-hypothesis testing framework.

We had already mentioned that experimental and quasi-experimental studies designed to test the effectiveness of different interventions in reducing stress at work were scarce. This contrasts with international literature, in which publications focusing on interventions have steadily increased and systematic reviews on the subject have become available (Havermans *et al.*, 2016). Moreover, Brazilian studies lack methodological rigor. Among the seven intervention articles included in our review, four reported quasi-experimental interventions involving a single pre- and posttest group and three used an experimental group and a control group, but without randomization. Thus, only one study actually met the criteria needed to establish causal relationships between the type of stress reduction intervention adopted and the stress reactions measured. We strongly recommend more randomized control trials with control groups, preferably with active control groups to show the effectiveness of the assumed theoretical process in the experimental group. This is necessary to more reliably test the effectiveness of different intervention strategies in reducing work stress.

In summary, it is important for future research on work stress in Brazil to more explicitly consider the economic, social, and cultural conditions of workplaces in the country and to evolve toward more powerful methodological procedures, such as longitudinal and experimental studies, as well as more sophisticated analysis strategies, such as structural equation modeling and multilevel analysis. Such studies can undoubtedly contribute to a better understanding of this phenomenon within the Brazilian reality.

Note

1 Job stress might have been measured or included in these articles.

References

Aguiar, O. B., Fonseca, M. J. M. & Valente, J. G. (2010). Reliability (test-retest) of the Swedish "Demand-Control-Support Questionnaire" scale among industrial restaurants workers, state of Rio de Janeiro, Brazil. *Revista Brasileira de Epidemiologia*, *13*, 212–222. 10.1590/s1415-790x2010000200004.

Alves, M. G. M., Chor, D., Faerstein, E., Werneck, G. L. & Lopes, C. S. (2009). Job strain and hypertension in women: Estudo Pró-Saúde (Pro-Health Study). *Revista de saúde pública*, *43*, 893–896. 10.1590/s0034-89102009000500019.

Andolhe, R., Barbosa, R. L., Oliveira, E. M., Costa, A. L. S. & Padilha, K. G. (2015). Stress, coping and burnout among Intensive Care Unit nursing staff: Associated factors. *Revista da Escola de Enfermagem da USP*, *49*(spe), 58–64. 10.1590/s0080-623420150000700009.

Araújo, T. M., Mattos, A. I. S., Almeida, M. M. G. & Santos, K. O. B. (2016). Psychosocial aspects of work and common mental disorders among health workers: Contributions of combined models. *Revista Brasileira de Epidemiologia*, *19*, 645–657. 10.1590/1980-5497201600030014.

Azevedo, B. D. S., Nery, A. A. & Cardoso, J. P. (2017). Occupational stress and dissatisfaction with quality of work life in nursing. *Texto & Contexto - Enfermagem*, *26*, e3940015. 10.1590/0104-07072017003940015.

Bakker, A. B. & Demerouti, E. (2017). Job Demands–Resources theory: Taking stock and looking forward. *Journal of Occupational Health Psychology, 22,* 273–285. 10.1037/ocp0000056.
Calazans, M. E. (2010). Resenha [Review]. *Cadernos de Saúde Pública, 26,* 206–211. 10.1590/s0102-311x2010000100022.
Canova, K. R. & Porto, J. B. (2010). O impacto dos valores organizacionais no estresse ocupacional: Um estudo com professores de ensino médio [The impact of organizational values on occupational stress: A study with secondary school teachers]. *RAM. Revista de Administração Mackenzie, 11,* 4–31. 10.1590/s1678-69712010000500002.
Cardoso, P. Q., Padovani, R. C. & Tucci, A. M. (2014). Análise dos agentes estressores e a expressão do estresse entre trabalhadores portuários avulsos [Analysis of stressors agents and stress expression among temporary dock workers]. *Estudos de Psicologia, 31,* 507–516. https://doi.org/10.1590/0103-166x2014000400005.
Cooper, C. L., Dewe, P. J. & O'Driscoll, M. P. (2001). *Organizational stress: A review and critique of theory, research, and applications.* Thousand Oaks, CA: Sage.
Costa, D. T. & Martins, M. C. F. (2011). Stress among nursing professionals: Effects of the conflict on the group and on the physician's power. *Revista da Escola de Enfermagem da USP, 45,* 1191–1198. 10.1590/s0080-62342011000500023.
Costa, M. F. A. A. & Ferreira, M. C. (2014). Sources and reactions to stress in Brazilian lawyers. *Paidéia, 24,* 49–56. 10.1590/1982-43272457201407.
Dalagasperina, P. & Monteiro, J. K. (2014). Preditores da síndrome de burnout em docentes do ensino privado [Predictors of burnout syndrome for teachers in private education]. *Psico-USF, 19,* 263–275. 10.1590/1413-82712014019002011.
Dalcin, L. & Carlotto, M. S. (2018). Avaliação de efeito de uma intervenção para a Síndrome de Burnout em professores [Evaluation of the effect of an intervention for Burnout Syndrome in teachers]. *Psicologia Escolar e Educacional, 22,* 141–150. 10.1590/2175-35392018013718.
Damásio, B. F., Habigzang, L. F., Freitas, C. P. P. & Koller, S. H. (2014). Can a Cognitive-Behavioral Group-Therapy Training Program for the treatment of child sexual abuse reduce levels of burnout and job-strain in trainees? Initial evidence of a Brazilian model. *Paidéia, 24,* 233–242. 10.1590/1982-43272458201411.
Fernandes, R. C. P., Carvalho, F. M., Assunção, A. Á. & Silvany Neto, A. M. (2009). Interactions between physical and psychosocial demands of work associated to low back pain. *Revista de saúde pública, 43,* 326–334. 10.1590/S0034-89102009000200014.
Ferreira, M. C., Fischer, R., Porto, J. B., Pilati, R. & Milfont, T. L. (2012). Unraveling the mystery of Brazilian jeitinho: A cultural exploration of social norms. *Personality and Social Psychology Bulletin, 38,* 331–344. 10.1177/0146167211427148.
Ferreira, M. C., Milfont, T. L., Silva, A. P. C., Fernandes, H. A., Almeida, S. P. & Mendonça, H. (2015). Escala para avaliação de estressores psicossociais no contexto laboral: Construção e evidências de validade [Evaluation of psychosocial stressors in the labor context scale: Development and psychometric

evidence]. *Psicologia: Reflexão e Crítica, 28,* 340–349. 10.1590/1678-7153. 201528214.

Ferreira, N. N. & Lucca, S. R. (2015). Burnout syndrome in nursing assistants of a public hospital in the state of São Paulo. *Revista Brasileira de Epidemiologia, 18,* 68–79. 10.1590/1980-5497201500010006.

Fogaça, M. C., Carvalho, W. B., Nogueira, P. C. K. & Martins, L. A. N. (2009). Occupational stress and repercussions on the quality of life of pediatric and neonatal intensivist physicians and nurses. *Revista Brasileira de Terapia Intensiva, 21,* 299–305. 10.1590/s0103-507x2009000300010.

Freitas, G. R., Calais, S. L. & Cardoso, H. F. (2018). Estresse, ansiedade e qualidade de vida em professores: Efeitos do relaxamento progressivo [Stress, anxiety and quality of life in teachers: Effects of progressive relaxation]. *Psicologia Escolar e Educacional, 22,* 319–326. 10.1590/2175-35392018018180.

Freitas, A. R., Carneseca, E. C., Paiva, C. E. & Paiva, B. S. R. (2014). Impact of a physical activity program on the anxiety, depression, occupational stress and burnout syndrome of nursing professionals. *Revista Latino-Americana de Enfermagem, 22,* 332–336. 10.1590/0104-1169.3307.2420.

Freitas-Swerts, F. C. T. & Robazzi, M. L. C. C. (2014). The effects of compensatory workplace exercises to reduce work-related stress and musculoskeletal pain. *Revista Latino-Americana de Enfermagem, 22,* 629–636. 10.1590/0104-1169.3222.2461.

Giannini, S. P. P., Latorre, M. R. D. O. & Ferreira, L. P. (2012). Distúrbio de voz e estresse no trabalho docente: Um estudo caso-controle [Voice disorders related to job stress in teaching: A case-control study]. *Cadernos de Saúde Pública, 28,* 2115–2124. 10.1590/s0102-311x2012001100011.

Griep, R. H., Rotenberg, L., Landsbergis, P. & Vasconcellos-Silva, P. R. (2011). Combined use of job stress models and self-rated health in nursing. *Revista de saúde pública, 45,* 145–152. 10.1590/s0034-89102011000100017.

Guedes, D. & Gaspar, E. (2016). Burnout in a sample of Brazilian Physical Education professional. *Revista Brasileira de Educação Física e Esporte, 30,* 999–1010. 10.1590/1807-55092016000400999.

Guido, L. A., Linch, G. F. C., Pitthan, L. O. & Umann, J. (2011). Stress, coping and health conditions of hospital nurses. *Revista da Escola de Enfermagem da USP, 45,* 1434–1439. 10.1590/s0080-62342011000600022.

Harding, T. W., Arango, M. V., Baltazar, J., Climent, C. E., Ibrahim, H. H. A., Ladrido-Ignacio, L. & Wig, N. N. (1980). Mental disorders in primary health care: A study of their frequency and diagnosis in four developing countries. *Psychological Medicine, 10,* 231–241. 10.1017/s0033291700043993.

Havermans, B. M., Schelvis, R. M. C., Boot, C. R. L., Brouwers, E. P. M., Anema, J. R. & Beek, A. J. (2016). Process variables in organizational stress management intervention evaluation research: A systematic review. *Scandinavian Journal of Work, Environment & Health, 42,* 371–381. 10.5271/sjweh.3570.

Hofstede, G. (2001). *Culture's consequences: Comparing values, behaviors, institutions and organizations across nations.* Thousand Oaks, CA: Sage.

Jacques, J. P. B., Ribeiro, R. P., Scholze, A. R., Galdino, M. J. Q., Martins, J. T., & Ribeiro, B. G. A. (2018). Wellness room as a strategy to reduce occupational stress: Quasi-experimental study. *Revista Brasileira de Enfermagem, 71,* 483–489. 10.1590/0034-7167-2017-0572.

Karasek, R. A. (1985). *Job content questionnaire and user's guide*. Lowell, MA: University of Massachusetts.

Karasek, R. A. & Theörell, T. (1990). *Healthy work: Stress, productivity, and the reconstruction of working life*. New York: Basic Books.

Lima, E. P., Assunção, A. A. & Barreto, S. M. (2015). Prevalência de depressão em bombeiros [Prevalence of depression among firefighters]. *Cadernos de Saúde Pública, 31*, 733–743. 10.1590/0102-311x00053414.

Lipp, M. E. N. (2000). *Manual do inventário de sintomas de stress para adultos de Lipp (ISSL)[Lipp's inventory of symptoms of stress for adults manual]*. São Paulo: Casa do Psicólogo.

Lopes, S. V. & Silva, M. C. (2018). Estresse ocupacional e fatores associados em servidores públicos de uma universidade federal do sul do Brasil [Occupational stress and associated factors among civil servants of a federal university in the south of Brazil]. *Ciência & Saúde Coletiva, 23*, 3869–3880. 10.1590/1413-812320182311.28682015.

Maffia, L. N. & Pereira, L. Z. (2014). Estresse no trabalho: Estudo com gestores públicos do estado de Minas Gerais [Stress at work: A study with public managers of state of Minas Gerais]. *Revista Eletrônica de Administração, 20*, 658–680. 10.1590/1413-2311.0052014.47163.

Marcelino Filho, A. & Araújo, T. M. (2015). Estresse ocupacional e saúde mental dos profissionais do centro de especialidades médicas de Aracaju [Occupational stress and the mental health of the professionals of the medical specialties center of Aracaju, Sergipe, Brazil]. *Trabalho, Educação e Saúde, 13*, 177–199. 10.1590/1981-7746-sip00016.

Marconato, C. S., Magnago, A. C. S., Magnago, T. S. B. S., Dalmolin, G. L., Andolhe, R. & Tavares, J. P. (2017). Prevalence and factors associated with minor psychiatric disorders in hospital housekeeping workers. *Revista da Escola de Enfermagem da USP, 51*, e03239. 10.1590/s1980-220x2016026303239.

Mari, J. J. & Williams, P. A. (1985). Comparison of the validity of two psychiatric screening questionnaires (GHQ-12 and SRQ-20) in Brazil, using relative operating characteristic (ROC) analysis. *Psychological Medicine, 15*, 651–659. 10.1017/s0033291700031500.

Martinez, M. C. & Latorre, M. R. D. O. (2009). Fatores associados à capacidade para o trabalho de trabalhadores do Setor Elétrico [Factors associated with labor capacity in electric industry workers]. *Cadernos de Saúde Pública, 25*, 761–772. 10.1590/s0102-311x2009000400007.

Martinez, M. C., Latorre, M. R. D. O. & Fischer, F. M. (2017). Stressors influence work ability in different age groups of nursing professionals: 2-year follow-up. *Ciência & Saúde Coletiva, 22*, 1589–1600. 10.1590/1413-81232017225.09682015.

Martins, S. W., Enumo, S. R. F. & Paula, K. M. P. (2016). Manejo da dor neonatal: Influência de fatores psicológicos e organizacionais [Neonatal pain management: Influence of psychological and organizational factors]. *Estudos de Psicologia, 33*, 633–644. 10.1590/1982-02752016000400007.

Maslach, C., Jackson, S. E. & Leiter, M. P. (1996). *The Maslach Burnout Inventory: Test manual* (3rd ed.). Palo Alto, CA: Consulting Psychologist Press.

Meneghini, F., Paz, A. A. & Lautert, L. (2011). Fatores ocupacionais associados aos componentes da síndrome de Burnout em trabalhadores de enfermagem

[Occupational factors related to Burnout syndrome components among nursing personnel]. *Texto & Contexto - Enfermagem, 20*, 225–233. 10.1590/s0104-07072011000200002.

Mininel, V. A., Baptista, P. C. P. & Felli, V. E. A. (2011). Psychic workloads and strain processes in nursing workers of Brazilian university hospitals. *Revista Latino-Americana de Enfermagem, 19*, 340–347. 10.1590/s0104-11692011000200016.

Montibeler, J., Domingos, T. S., Braga, E. M., Gnatta, J. R., Kurebayashi, L. F. S. & Kurebayashi, A. K. (2018). Effectiveness of aromatherapy massage on the stress of the surgical center nursing team: A pilot study. *Revista da Escola de Enfermagem da USP, 52*, 03348. 10.1590/s1980-220x2017038303348.

Mota, C. M., Dosea, G. S. & Nunes, P. S. (2014). Avaliação da presença da Síndrome de Burnout em Agentes Comunitários de Saúde no município de Aracaju, Sergipe, Brasil [Assessment of the prevalence of burnout syndrome in community health agents of the city of Aracaju in the state of Sergipe, Brazil]. *Ciência & Saúde Coletiva, 19*, 4719–4726. 10.1590/1413-812320141912.02512013.

Negeliskii, C. & Lautert, L. (2011). Occupational stress and work capacity of nurses of a hospital group. *Revista Latino-Americana de Enfermagem, 19*, 606–613. 10.1590/s0104-11692011000300021.

Padilha, K. G., Barbosa, R. L., Andolhe, R., Oliveira, E. M., Ducci, A. J., Bregalda, R. S. & Secco, L. M. D. (2017). . Nursing workload, stress/burnout, satisfaction and incidents in a trauma intensive care units. *Texto & Contexto - Enfermagem, 26*, e1720016. 10.1590/0104-07072017001720016.

Paschoal, T. & Tamayo, A. (2004). Validação da escala de estresse no trabalho [Validation of the work stress scale]. *Estudos de Psicologia, 9*, 45–52. 10.1590/s1413-294x2004000100006.

Pelegrini, A., Cardoso, T. E., Claumann, G. S., Pinto, A. A. & Felden, E. P. G. (2018). Percepção das condições de trabalho e estresse ocupacional em policiais civis e militares de unidades de operações especiais [Perception of work conditions and occupational stress among civil and military police officers of special operations units]. *Cadernos Brasileiros de Terapia Ocupacional, 26*, 423–430. 10.4322/2526-8910.ctoao1160.

Pereira, E. F., Kothe, F., Bleyer, F. T. S. & Teixeira, C. S. (2014). Work-related stress and musculoskeletal complaints of orchestra musicians. *Revista Dor, 15*(2), 112–116. https://doi.org/10.5935/1806-0013.20140025.

Pimenta, A. M. & Assunção, A. A. (2016). Job strain and arterial hypertension in nursing professionals from the municipal healthcare network in Belo Horizonte, Minas Gerais, Brazil. *Revista Brasileira de Saúde Ocupacional, 41*, e6. 10.1590/2317-6369000113515.

Pinhatti, E. D. G., Ribeiro, R. P., Soares, M. H., Martins, J. T., Lacerda, M. R. & Galdino, M. J. Q. (2018). Psychosocial aspects of work and minor psychic disorders in nursing: Use of combined models. *Revista Latino-Americana de Enfermagem, 26*, e3068. 10.1590/1518-8345.2769.3068.

Pozzebon, D., Piccin, C. F., Silva, A. M. T. & Corrêa, E. C. R. (2016). Relationship among perceived stress, anxiety, depression and craniocervical pain in nursing professionals under stress at work. *Fisioterapia em Movimento, 29*, 377–385. 10.1590/0103-5150.029.002.ao17.

Rodrigues, C. M. L. & Faiad, C. (2019). Pesquisa sobre riscos psicossociais no trabalho: Estudo bibliométrico da produção nacional de 2008 a 2017 [Research on psychosocial risks at work: A bibliometric study of Brazilian national production from 2008 to 2017]. *Revista Psicologia: Organizações e Trabalho, 19*, 571–579.

Rodrigues, F. A. F. C., Paula, K. M. P., Silveira, K. A. & Silveira, K. A. (2017). Concepções sobre mediação da aprendizagem e relações com indicadores de estresse ocupacional [Conceptions on mediated learning and relations with indicators of occupational stress]. *Psicologia Escolar e Educacional, 21*, 253–263. 10.1590/2175-3539201702121112.

Rosa, R. G., Falavigna, M. & Silva, D. B. (2019). Effect of flexible family visitation on delirium among patients in the intensive care unit: The ICU visits randomized clinical trial. *Journal of the American Medical Association, 322*, 216–228. 10.1001/jama.2019.8766.

Sampaio, R. F., Coelho, C. M., Barbosa, F. B., Mancini, M. C. & Parreira, V. F. (2009). Work ability and stress in a bus transportation company in Belo Horizonte, Brazil. *Ciência & Saúde Coletiva, 14*, 287–296. 10.1590/s1413-81232009000100035.

Scalco, G. P. C., Abegg, C., Celeste, R. K., Hökerberg, Y. H. M. & Faerstein, E. (2013). Occupational stress and self-perceived oral health in Brazilian adults: A Pro-Saude study. *Ciência & Saúde Coletiva, 18*, 2069–2074. 10.1590/s1413-81232013000700022.

Siegrist, J. (1996). Adverse health effects of high-effort/low-reward conditions. *Journal of Occupational Health Psychology, 1*, 27–41. 10.1037/1076-8998.1.1.27.

Siegrist, J., Starke, D., Chandola, T., Godin, I., Marmot, M., Niedhammer, I. & Peter, R. (2004). The measurement of effort-reward imbalance at work: European comparisons. *Social Science Medicine, 58*, 1483–1499. 10.1016/s0277-9536(03)00351-4.

Silva, J. L. L., Soares, R. S., Costa, F. S., Ramos, D. S., Lima, F. B. & Teixeira, L. R. (2015). Psychosocial factors and prevalence of burnout syndrome among nursing workers in intensive care units. *Revista Brasileira de Terapia Intensiva, 27*, 125–133. 10.5935/0103-507x.20150023.

Silva, A. A., Souza, J. M. P., Borges, F. N. S. & Fischer, F. M. (2010). Health-related quality of life and working conditions among nursing providers. *Revista de saúde pública, 44*, 718–725. 10.1590/s0034-89102010000400016.

Silva, L. C. & Salles, T. L. A. (2016). O estresse ocupacional e as formas alternativas de tratamento [Occupational stress and forms treatment alternatives]. *Revista de Carreiras e Pessoas, 6*, 234–247. 10.20503/recape.v6i2.29361.

Silva-Junior, J. S. & Fischer, F. M. (2015). Sickness absence due to mental disorders and psychosocial stressors at work. *Revista Brasileira de Epidemiologia, 18*, 735–744. 10.1590/1980-5497201500040005.

Stacciarini, J. M. R. & Tróccoli, B. T. (2000). Instrumento para mensurar o estresse ocupacional: Inventário de Estresse em Enfermeiros (IEE) [An instrument to measure occupational stress: A nurses' stress inventory]. *Revista Latino-Americana de Enfermagem, 8*(6), 40–49. https://doi.org/10.1590/s0104-11692000000600007.

Tamayo, M. R. & Tróccoli, B. T. (2009). Construção e validação fatorial da Escala de Caracterização do Burnout (ECB) [Construction and factorial validation of the Burnout Characterization Scale (ECB)]. *Estudos de Psicologia, 14*, 213–221. 10.1590/s1413-294x2009000300005.

Theme Filha, M. M., Costa, M. A. S. & Guilam, M. C. R. (2013). Occupational stress and self-rated health among nurses. *Revista Latino-Americana de Enfermagem, 21*, 475–483. 10.1590/s0104-11692013000200002.

Theörell, T., Perski, A., Akersdedt, T., Sigala, F., Ahlberg-Hultén, G., Svensson, J. & Eneroth, P. (1988). Changes in job strain in relation to changes in physiological state. A longitudinal study. *Scandinavian Journal of Work, Environment and Health, 14*, 189–196. 10.5271/sjweh.1932.

Trindade, L. L., Lautert, L., Beck, C. L. C., Amestoy, S. C. & Pires, D. E. P. (2010). Stress and burnout syndrome among workers of the Family Health team. *Acta Paulista de Enfermagem, 23*, 684–689. 10.1590/s0103-21002010000500016.

Umann, J., Guido, L. A. & Silva, R. M. (2014). Stress, coping and presenteeism in nurses assisting critical and potentially critical patients. *Revista da Escola de Enfermagem da USP, 48*, 891–898. 10.1590/s0080-6234201400005000016.

Urbanetto, J. S., Magalhaes, M. C. C., Maciel, V. O., SantAnna, V. M., Gustavo, A. S., Poli-de-Figueiredo, C. E. & Magnago, T. S. B. S. (2013). Work-related stress according to the demand-control model and minor psychic disorders in nursing workers. *Revista da Escola de Enfermagem da USP, 47*, 1180–1186. 10.1590/s0080-623420130000500024.

Valente, A. M. S. L., Botelho, C. & Silva, A. M. C. (2015). Distúrbio de voz e fatores associados em professores da rede pública [Voice disorder and associated factors among public schools teachers]. *Revista Brasileira de Saúde Ocupacional, 40*, 183–195. 10.1590/0303-7657000093814.

Vidotti, V., Ribeiro, R. P., Galdino, M. J. Q. & Martins, J. T. (2018). Burnout Syndrome and shift work among the nursing staff. *Revista Latino-Americana de Enfermagem, 26*, e3022. 10.1590/1518-8345.2550.3022.

4 Job Stressors in Greater China

An Explorative Study Using the Qualitative and Quantitative Approaches

Chang-qin Lu, Oi-ling Siu, Hai-Jiang Wang, and Luo Lu

Introduction

Job stress is becoming one of the most prevalent health issues nowadays, especially for the Greater China regions. These regions are undergoing fundamental transformations of industrial structures, as well as rapid social modernization in both work and lifestyles (e.g., Siu, Spector, Cooper, Lu, & Yu, 2002; Wang, Lu, & Siu, 2015; Xie, Schaubroeck, & Lam, 2008). Moreover, with the globalization of the world economy and Mainland China joining the World Trade Organization (WTO), many multinational companies are attracted to put more investments in these regions. In the spirit of free competition, employees in Mainland China, Hong Kong, and Taiwan are becoming more exposed to stressful Western and industrialized work situations. Recently, scholars and practitioners (e.g., Bliese, Edwards, & Sonnentag, 2017; Houtman, Jettinghoff, & Cediollo, 2007) call for more job stress research in developing countries. Therefore, Greater China offers one of the most important contexts for job stress research.

The majority of job stress models have been developed in Western societies, which demonstrated that stressors at the workplace lead to job strains – such as low level of job satisfaction, poor physical and psychological well-being, and poor performance (e.g., Bliese *et al.*, 2017; Chang & Baard, 2011; Ganster & Rosen, 2013). The sources of job stress have been well-documented since the late 1970s (Cooper, Sloan, & Williams, 1988). Although researchers developed or adopted different schemes of categorization, there are also considerable commonalities. For instance, Burke (1988) provided a summary of findings for six categories of stressors – physical environment, role stressors, organizational structure and job characteristics, relationships with others, career development, and work-family conflict. Cooper, Sloan, and Williams (1988) identified six sources of job stress at the workplace – job-intrinsic sources of stress, management roles, relationships with others, career and achievement, organizational structure and climate, and work-to-home interface. These scales were also adapted in a variety of languages for use in non-English-speaking countries. Moreover, the British-originated Occupational Stress Indicator (OSI) (Cooper et al., 1988) was developed into the Chinese version and used for job stress-related studies (e.g., Lu, Cooper, Chen, Hsu, Li, Wu, & Shih, 1995; Lu, Kao, Cooper, & Spector, 2000; Lu, Siu, Au, & Leung, 2009; Lu, Siu, & Cooper, 2005; Siu, Donald, & Cooper, 1997; Yu, Sparks, & Cooper, 1998), which has broadened our understandings of job stress in Chinese society.

However, it has been argued that almost all of the job stress models and stress theories were developed and empirically tested in Western, industrialized countries, which are based on the experiences of the employees there (Chang & Baard, 2011; Xie, 1996). Moreover, the environments among these countries seem more stable compared with Chinese society. One of the major limitations in using these models is their global approach, assuming that the people experience the same stressor under the different social and cultural contexts. Although the negative impacts and damages of job stress on individuals and organizations in different cultural societies may be the same, the types of stressors may not be so. Stress is influenced by cultural and social variables such as values, attitudes, and appraisals (Chang & Baard, 2011; Liu, Spector, & Shi, 2007; Xie et al., 2008). From the transactional approach, Lazarus (1991) reiterated that "stress is not a property of the person, or of the environment, but arises when there is a conjunction between a particular kind of environment and a particular kind of person that leads to a threat appraisal" (p.3). Moreover, culture is one of the fundamental aspects of society that influences both the environment and the person. Culture can set the tone for the characteristics of the environmental system, and for the dominant aspects of the social system, which both largely determine the pressures on a person – stressors – and the available resources to cope with these stressors. Culture offers individuals very different views about their nature and the way in which they themselves are related to the environments (Kitayama & Park, 2007). Therefore, stress implies a process rather than a static arrangement, mostly resulting from the interactions of the person with his/her environment.

Cross-cultural differences are also reported in several studies on job stressors. For instance, in an open-ended study comparing stressors in India – one of the collectivistic societies – and the United States, Narayanan, Menon, and Spector (1999) found that lack of structure was a major stressor in India but not in the United States. Spector, Sanchez, Siu, Salgado, and Ma (2004) found differences in perceived job stressors between the employees in the United States and Greater China. Role ambiguity was significantly higher in those from Hong Kong than in those from the United States, but it was significantly higher in the United States than in Mainland China. For interpersonal conflict, Hong Kong employees reported the highest level, Mainland

China employees scored in the middle, and the United States employees were the lowest. Recently, Hirst et al.'s (2008) cross-cultural study also found that climates for autonomy (or lack of autonomy) benefited and enhanced employees' well-being in the United Kingdom, but did harm to Chinese employees' well-being. Probst and Lawler (2006) found that Chinese employees suffered from the threat of job insecurity more than United States employees.

In addition, most studies about work stress – including those conducted in Greater China – have relied on the traditional approach, where the structured scales with close-ended measurements were adopted to investigate an individual's job stress over an unspecified time period. This was helpful to job stress researchers because they could use similar scales to tap the same set of job stressors – such as role overload and interpersonal conflict. However, it may be insufficient to identify the prominent stressors resulting from social and environmental changes. Moreover, cross-cultural researchers have questioned the extent to which such a way can be used to explore the prominent culture-specific stressors (Chang & Baard, 2011; Xie, 1996). A few researchers (e.g., Glowinkowski & Cooper, 1985; Liu et al., 2007; Liu, Spector, & Shi, 2008) have expressed concern about exclusive reliance on such traditional quantitative methods. Moreover, with the significant changing of work, the perceived stressors in the workplace seem to be changing. It is necessary and reasonable to explore the stressors associated with these changes, especially in a transitional society such as Greater China. Thus, some researchers (e.g., Cox, 1985; Mazzola, Schonfeld, & Spector, 2011; Schonfeld & Mazzola, 2015) have suggested using alternative approaches, such as qualitative methods, to examine stress at work. One qualitative approach is the open-ended method developed by Newton and Keenan (1985). Targeting professional engineers, they examined stress in an occupation-specific context, which was different from conventional approaches. We believe that open-ended methodology works better in capturing culture-specific stressors which may be obscured by using structured quantitative scales. Later on, Liu Spector and Shi (2007) used both quantitative and qualitative ways to explore cross-national (China versus the United States) job stress and found some interesting results. However, their study had two limitations. One is the representation of the samples. Their samples were from employees in universities which are in the public sector, and their job characteristics are very different from other professions. Another limitation is the research procedure. They did quantitative and qualitative studies all at once, and used quantitative scales in advance, which might have prevented them from exploring certain sensitive and contextual job stressors under the Chinese context. Therefore, the generalizability of their findings might be doubtful.

The above limitations provide the impetus for our study. The present study extended Liu and colleagues' study (2007) by using diverse group samples from three regions of Greater China, which were representatives of the Chinese working population. Moreover, we used a qualitative method to explore those serious job stressors inherent in the changing Chinese society and then combined the quantitative survey method to validate the measurement of the job stressors. To provide strong evidence, we also included job performance rated by supervisors as one of the outcomes. The whole study consisted of three studies. In Study 1, an open-ended method was used to collect qualitative data on employees' job stressors experienced at the workplace to be able to derive the most common job stressors. In Study 2, scales were adapted or modified to measure the stressors identified in Study 1. In Study 3, a quantitative survey study was conducted to investigate the relationships between job stressors and outcomes and to provide valid evidence for these measures as well. Using both qualitative and quantitative methods allowed us to explore and to identity those job stressors in contemporary Chinese society that are associated with employees' well-being, work attitudes, and performance during the transition process.

Study 1

Method

An open-ended qualitative methodology was used, asking respondents to describe a stressful critical incident at work using a modified version of the Stress Incident Record designed by Newton and Keenan (1985). A protocol was developed where a structured list of questions was constructed to explore the stressors reported by employees in Greater China. Specific questions were: "Think of a stressful event that occurred in the past month and describe it in detail, including what led up to it and what happened" and "How did it make you feel at that time." It aimed to obtain qualitative data on respondents' concerns with the job stressors they experienced at their current workplace. The qualitative data were analyzed by content to develop an exhaustive set of job stressors categories. Relative frequencies corresponding to each category were reported.

Sample and Procedure

A total of 91 employees from the public and private sectors in equal proportions of gender and rank – from line employees to top managers – in Hong Kong ($N = 36$), Beijing ($N = 25$), and Taipei ($N = 30$) were invited to participate in the study. Participants in Hong Kong were interviewed and tape-recorded, whereas those in Beijing and Taipei were asked to complete the same open-ended questionnaires. Each interview lasted for 30 to 45 minutes. The average age ranged from 31 to

36 years, and the average tenure ranged from three to six years across the three samples.

The responses generated from both the interviews and questionnaires were analyzed by content analysis, and coded by two independent raters – the first author (Dr. Chang-qin Lu) and a graduate student – to derive the most frequent stressors faced by Chinese employees. The first rater listened to tapes and read the open-ended materials, and the incidents were placed into as many categories as they fit in. The second rater then independently created categories. Both raters specifically sought to sort incidents into only a single category area. There was a 94.5% agreement rate between the two independent raters in the placement of incidents into categories. The remaining 2% were discussed to reach consensus, and 3% were thrown away. A total of 88 incidents were collected.

Results and Discussion

Table 4.1 shows the six most reported stressors categories generated from content analysis. They included "Interpersonal conflict" (22.7%), "Quantitative workload" (19.4%), "Organizational constraints" (15.9%), "Organizational politics" (12.5%), "Job insecurity" (10.2%), and "Work-family conflict" (8.0%). Some examples of incidents are presented in Table 4.1.

The result of the open-ended interviews corroborates Liu *et al.*'s study (2007), in which quantitative workload, interpersonal conflict, and organizational constraints were found to be the most common job stressors faced by Chinese employees. These stressors were also experienced by Western employees (Spector & Jex, 1998). Like previous studies in collectivistic societies (e.g., Liu *et al.*, 2007; Narayanan *et al.*, 1999;

Table 4.1 Results of open-ended interviews in Study 1 ($N = 91$, total incidents = 88)

Stressors	Frequency	Percentages	Example
Interpersonal conflict	20	22.7%	"I don't find harmony with superiors."
Quantitative workload	17	19.4%	"Heavy workload or meeting deadlines."
Organizational constraints	14	15.9%	"Due to poor work supplies or training, it is hard to fulfill my task."
Organizational politics	11	12.5%	"Some persons in my department implicitly favor in-group, which makes me hard to deal with."
Job insecurity	9	10.2%	"I am afraid I will lose my job."
Work-family conflict	7	8.0%	"It's difficult for me to balance work and home life."

Xie, 1996), the lack of job control, which is a common job stressor in Western society, was not found to be a stressor in the current study of Chinese society. Moreover, job insecurity (e.g., Feng, Lu, & Siu, 2008; Wang, Lu, & Lu, 2014; Wang et al., 2015) and work-family conflict (e.g., Lu, Wang, Siu, Lu, & Du, 2015; Spector et al., 2004; Yang, Chen, & Zou, 2000) were discovered to be the major job stressors in the present Chinese workplace.

Study 2

Method

Study 2[1] aimed to develop a set of measures for these common job stressors explored in Study 1 and to test their reliabilities and validities.

Sample and Procedure

A purposive sampling method was adopted to select various types of enterprises in the public and private service sectors in Hong Kong, Beijing, and Taipei. A total of 610 questionnaires were distributed, with a valid number of 379 returned, making an average response rate of 62.1%. The sample from Hong Kong consisted of 105 – 54 males, 50 females, and 1 unidentified – with an average age of 35.64 years (SD = 6.68), and an average tenure of 7.11 years (SD = 6.43), respectively. The sample from Beijing consisted of 128 – 46 males, 82 females – with an average age of 35.78 years (SD = 6.82), and an average tenure of 7.55 years (SD = 7.44), respectively. The sample from Taiwan consisted of 146 – 102 males, 43 females, and 1 unidentified – with an average age of 35.78 years (SD = 6.82 years), and an average tenure of 7.55 years (SD = 7.54), respectively.

In order to identify each of the six job stressors, the existing scales or items which measure these job stressors were collected. The scales which have Chinese version were primarily important. If unavailable, the authors tried to select the items from the developed Western scales. Moreover, two items from the composite stress index (Motowidlo, Packard, & Manning, 1986) were included to measure total perceived stress, which was used to examine where the stressor item was retained or not.

All of these were administered in Chinese. The scales that were originally developed in English were not previously used in Chinese were translated into Chinese by a back-translation method to assure the accuracy (Brislin, 1986) (the same procedure in Study 3).

Results and Discussion

Among those items, 29 items that were correlated, and more than .30 items with the total perceived stress were retained. The two-item measure of total perceived stress (Motowidlo et al., 1986) was reliable ($\alpha = .86$). There are examples of incidents such as "I feel a great deal of stress because of my job" and "my job is extremely stressful." Each item was assessed using a six-point scale that ranged from strongly disagree (1) to strongly agree (6). High scores indicate a high level of total perceive stress.

These 29 items were intended to measure the six job stressors. They are interpersonal conflict (4 items) (Spector & Jex, 1998) (e.g., "How often are people rude to you at work?"), quantitative overload (5 items) (Spector & Jex, 1998) (e.g., "How often is there a great deal to be done?"), organizational constraints (11 items) (Spector & Jex, 1998) (e.g., "poor equipment or supplies"), job insecurity (3 items) (ASSET, Cartwright & Cooper, 2002) (e.,g. "Your job is likely to change in the future"), organizational politics (3 items) (one item from Cooper et al., 1988; two items from Kacmar & Carlson, 1997; e.g., "There has always been an influential group in your department that no one ever crosses"), and work-family conflict (3 items) (one item from ASSET, Cartwright, & Cooper, 2002; two items from OSI, Cooper et al., 1988) (e.g., "You are pursuing a career at the expense of home life"). Each item was rated by frequency ranged Less than once per month or never (1) to Several times per day (6). For the first four subscales, reliability and validity were provided by the study conducted in China (Siu, Spector, Cooper, & Lu, 2005).

Tables 4.2 and 4.3 showed the descriptive statistics of six job stressors and their intercorrelations. All of the six job stressors scales were reliable, with Cronbach's alphas ranging from .73 to .93. In order to test whether the six scales were adequately distinct from each other, the Confirmatory Factor Analysis (CFA) was conducted. The results of the CFA demonstrated that the six-factor model fitted better ($\chi^2/df = 4.99$, GFI = 0.89, NFI = 0.90, IFI = 0.92, CFI = 0.92, RMSEA = 0.06) than the one-factor model (see Table 4.4). Thus, the valid structures of Chinese job stressor scales were verified. This also implied that our measurements

Table 4.2 Results of Descriptive Statistics in Study 2 ($N = 379$)

Subscales	Number of Items	M	SD	Range	Coefficient a
Interpersonal conflict	4	7.27	3.37	4–24	.81
Quantitative workload	5	13.66	6.25	5–30	.93
Organizational constraints	11	27.73	11.37	4–24	.93
Organizational politics	3	7.23	3.49	3–18	.76
Job insecurity	3	5.87	3.17	3–18	.73
Work-family conflict	3	7.25	3.29	3–18	.80

Table 4.3 Intercorrelations of Chinese Stressors in Study 2 (N = 379)

Variables	1	2	3	4	5	6
1. Interpersonal conflict	1.00					
2. Organizational constraints	.52***	1.00				
3. Quantitative workload	.52***	.57***	1.00			
4. Organizational politics	.58***	.43***	.61***	1.00		
5. Job insecurity	.44***	.34***	.44***	.43***	1.00	
6. Work-Family Conflict	.54***	.60***	.54***	.57***	.40***	1.00

Note
*p < .05, **p < .01, ***p < .001

Table 4.4 Summary of Fit Statistics for Measurements of Chinese Job Stressors in Study 2 (N = 379)

Models	χ^2/df	GFI	AGFI	RMSEA	NFI	CFI	IFI
1. One-factor model	49.34/9	.963	.914	.109	.946	.955	.955
2. Six-factor model	360.86/174	.918	.891	.053	.929	.961	.962

Note
One-factor model – combining six job stressors; Six-factors model – hypothesized mode, including Interpersonal Conflict, Quantitative Workload, Organizational Constraints, Organizational Politics, Job Insecurity, Work-Family Conflict.

are not seriously affected by common method bias (Podsakoff, MacKenzie, Lee, & Podsakoff, 2003).

Based on the results above, it is reasonable for us to conclude that there were six major job stressors in the contemporary Chinese workplace.

Study 3

Method

Study 3 aimed to verify the results obtained in Study 2 by collecting samples from the three regions again. The Confirmatory Factor Analysis was conducted to provide pieces of evidence for the reliability and validity of Chinese job stressors scales. Furthermore, Study 3^2 was done to investigate the impact that these stressors have on employees' well-being, work attitude, and job performance.

Sample and Procedure

A multistage cluster random sampling method was used to recruit employees in Hong Kong, and a purposive sampling method was adopted to select employees in Beijing and Taipei. A total of 1,384 questionnaires were distributed with a valid number of 1,032 returned, making an average response rate of 74.6%. The Hong Kong sample consisted of 132 males and 192 females, with an average age of 32.07 years (SD = 9.40 years) and an average tenure of 6.27 years (SD = 6.12), respectively. The Beijing sample consists of 209 males and 182 females, and 11 unidentified participants, with an average age of 31.85 years (SD = 7.41 years) and an average tenure of 4.34 years (SD = 5.15), respectively. The Taipei sample consists of 134 males and 172 females, with an average age of 32.85 years (SD = 6.65 years) and an average tenure of 6.31 years (SD = 6.31), respectively.

A survey packet consisting of an employee and a supervisor questionnaire, each marked with the same code, was distributed to the employees and the supervisors. An addressed self-adhesive envelope was included for employees and supervisors to return completed questionnaires independently.

Measures

Job Stressors

For five stressor scales – quantitative overload, interpersonal conflict, organizational constraints, organizational politics, and work-family conflict – all items were retained except for three. The three items were somewhat modified because of the loading of two factors simultaneously. For the job insecurity scale, two new items measuring affective job insecurity (e.g., "The thought of getting fired really scares you") were added (Feng et al., 2008).

Job Satisfaction

Job satisfaction was assessed with the three-item Cammann, Fichman, Jenkins, and Klesh (1979) job satisfaction subscale from the Michigan Organizational Assessment Questionnaire, in which a higher score indicates a higher level of job satisfaction. The Chinese version had a coefficient alpha of .82 (Siu et al., 2005).

Strains

The psychological well-being scale of An Organizational Stress Screening Tool (ASSET) (Cartwright & Cooper, 2002) was used to measure physical and psychological strains (20 items). The items are symptoms of stress-induced strains such as panic attacks and constant tiredness, with a respective high score denoting more strains. The scales were developed into the Chinese version and had a coefficient alpha of .82 and .92, respectively (Siu et al., 2005).

Job Performance

Items of the scale were chosen from Visewsevaran, Ones, and Schmidt (1996) supervisory job performance rating, which includes the quantity of work, quality of work, and others. A summation of ratings of these items constitutes the total performance score. The Chinese version had a coefficient alpha of .78 (Siu, Lu, & Spector, 2013).

Results

Confirmatory Factor Analysis was used to verify the structure of Chinese job stressor scales. The results demonstrated that the six-factor model fitted well ($\chi^2/df = 4.99$, GFI = 0.89, NFI = 0.90, IFI = 0.92, CFI = 0.92, RMSEA = 0.06). The Cronbach's alpha for each subscale (ranging from .77 to .94) also provided support for the reliabilities of the job stressors measures.

Table 4.5 shows the intercorrelations among the main variables and the reliabilities. The results of a series of regression analyses demonstrated that the job stressors were positively related to strains and negatively related to job satisfaction and job performance rating by supervisors, and the coefficients were significant except for two (see Table 4.6).

These results provided support for the criterion validity of the Chinese job stressor measures.

One interesting and rather surprising result is that quantitative workload was positively associated with job performance rated by supervisors. It implied that employees with too much work might maintain good job performance. Recently, the challenge-hindrance stress framework suggests that the stressors could be categorized into challenge stressors and hindrance-stressors and that challenge-stressor related positively to performance, while hindrance-stressors associated negatively with job performance, despite the harm caused by both stressors to employees' well-being (LePine, Podsakoff, & LePine, 2005). Quantitative workload is usually perceived as one of the challenging stressors (LePine et al., 2005; Lu, Du, & Xu, 2016).

Discussion

The purpose of the present study is to investigate the common important job stressors in Chinese societies, and how to measure these job stressors. A three-phase study design was conducted using both qualitative and quantitative approaches. From the perspective of the interaction between

Table 4.5 Intercorrelations of Main Variables in Study 3 (N = 1032)

Variables	Mean	SD	1	2	3	4	5	6	7	8	9
1. Conflict	7.90	4.31	.91								
2. Constraints	13.20	6.22	.64***	.94							
3. Workload	26.12	12.12	.68***	.70***	.86						
4. Politics	6.39	3.50	.65***	.55***	.69***	.78					
5. Job insecurity	5.90	3.19	.57***	.45***	.56***	.60***	.86				
6. WFC	6.92	3.37	.56***	.63***	.62***	.62***	.57***	.80			
7. Strains	57.16	18.20	.49***	.47***	.50***	.45***	.42***	.51***	.94		
8. Job satisfaction	12.46	2.89	-.29***	-.24***	-.38***	-.38***	-.28***	-.24***	-.31***	.74	
9. Job performance	23.84	3.11	-.16***	-.02	-.06*	-.08*	-.10***	-.05	-.13***	.07*	.76

Notes
Conflict = Interpersonal Conflict; Workload = Quantitative Workload; Constraints = Organizational Constraints; Politics = Organizational Politics; WFC = Work-Family Conflict; Strains = Physical Strain + Psychological Strain; Job Performance = Job Performance Rated by Supervisor. Cronbach's reliabilities are in parentheses on the diagonal.
* $p < .05$, ** $p < .01$, *** $p < .001$.

Table 4.6 Results of Regression Analyses in Study 3 (N=1032)

	Independent Variables	Dependent Variables		
		Strains	Job Satisfaction	Job Performance
Step 1	Gender	.01	.03	-.04
	Age	-.12**	.12**	.05
	Tenure	.09*	-.08*	-.02
	Job level	.17***	.01	.03
	Type of organizations	-.02	.03	.01
		Adjusted R^2 .033	Adjusted R^2 .007	Adjusted R^2 .001
		$\Delta R^2 = .037$	$\Delta R^2 = .012$	$\Delta R^2 = .005$
		F change = 7.96***	F change = 2.44*	F change = 1.13
Step 3	Conflict	.10*	-.02	-.20***
	Workload	.10*	.06	.10*
	Constraints	.13**	-.28***	.05
	Politics	.01	-.25***	-.01
	Job insecurity	.15***	.02	-.09*
	WFC	.20***	.05	.01
		Adjusted R^2 .316	Adjusted R^2 .165	Adjusted R^2 .031
		$\Delta R^2 = .286$	$\Delta R^2 = .162$	$\Delta R^2 = .036$
		F change = 71.95***	F change = 33.40***	F change = 6.45***

Notes
Conflict = Interpersonal Conflict; Workload = Quantitative Workload; Constraints = Organizational Constraints; Politics = Organizational Politics; WFC = Work-Family Conflict; Strains = Physical Strain + Psychological Strain. Job Performance = Job Performance Rated by Supervisor.
* $p < .05$, ** $p < .01$, *** $p < .001$.

the person and the environment (Lazarus, 1991), the concept of stress is highly culture-specific. The present study intends to investigate job stressors in contemporary Chinese society. Previous studies (e.g., Liu *et al.*, 2007; Narayanan *et al.*, 1999; Spector *et al.*, 2004) reported cultural differences in the perception of job stressors. We have updated the knowledge by providing support for a more comprehensive approach in studying job stressors under the context of Greater China, because only a few related studies have been conducted across the three regions of Greater China. The necessity of such research is even more prominent because of huge differences between the Chinese and Western societies in terms of cultural beliefs, society, politics, and economic systems.

In terms of methodology, the three-phase study approach is comprehensive and structurally systematic. Qualitative studies are advantageous in identifying employees' subjective and specifically experienced stressors, while quantitative studies are advantageous in efficient administration, high objectivity, and amenability to highly-developed psychometric techniques (Mazzola *et al.*, 2011; Schonfeld & Mazzola, 2015). We combined both approaches to determine both advantages in developing culture-specific as well as valid job stressors measures.

The present study has found similar results as Liu *et al.*'s study (2007) in terms of the top three stressors – quantitative workload, interpersonal conflict, and organizational constraints – which were found to be common among both Chinese and Western employees. However, three other stressors were found distinctive in contemporary Chinese society – namely organizational politics, job insecurity, and work-family conflict.

As one of the specific social stressors in the workplace, organizational politics has recently attracted attention in many Western societies (Ferris, Frink, Galang, Zhou, Kacmar, & Howard 1996; Siu, Lu, & Spector, 2013). Organizational politics can be defined as "self-serving behavior not formally sanctioned by organizations that creates conflict or disharmony in the workplace" (Ferris *et al.*, 1996). It is a distinctive stressor from "interpersonal conflict" since the former is frequently used as an upward influence strategy to promote the self-interests, such as salary raise or promotion, while the latter mainly refers to conflicts among colleagues. Chinese employees might be more vulnerable to organizational politics stressors. Due to cultural emphasis on hierarchy, Chinese organizations are structured with higher "power distance" and "paternalistic leadership" (Cheng, Chou, Wu, Huang, & Farh, 2004). Such organizational structures provide ground for two important predictors for organizational politics perceptions: a high degree of centralization and a low degree of formalization (Ferris *et al.*, 1996). The former means the concentration of power and control at top levels while the latter means a lack of formal written rules and procedures. Low control and power as well as high uncertainty and ambiguity could increase the employees' perception of organizational politics. Meanwhile, Chinese people are culturally known for being relationship-oriented. The strong emphasis on "*Guanxi*" extends to the workplace. Good relationships between supervisors and subordinates are maintained by mutually beneficial transactions (Ling & Powell, 2001). Therefore, employees might inevitably be divided into in-group versus out-group. Supervisors usually treat the employees impersonally or play favorites based on the degree of their relationships, which makes these employees feel that they are second-class citizens in the organization (Deluga, 1994). As a result, the employee feels more stressed to deal with such issues. Moreover, with a strong preference for uncertainty avoidance (Hofstede, 1980), Chinese employees would find undercover political activities in the workplace particularly intolerable and stressful.

Another distinctive stressor is job insecurity, which refers to "the anticipation of a stressful event in such a way that the nature and continued existence of one's job are perceived to be at risk" (Sverke & Hellgren, 2002, p.27). Decades of economic restructuring have given rise to major shifts in employment policies and practices which can be attributed to recent economic transformations and fierce competition in the job market. In Mainland China, government policies of downsizing state-owned enterprises and supporting a competitive labor market indicated the end of the "iron rice bowl" era. Workers are no longer guaranteed an "iron bowl" (i.e., permanent jobs) and face the threat of job loss. Moreover, with globalization and further economic growth in Mainland China, employees have to face the serious threat of job loss or job insecurity (Price & Fang 2002; Wang *et al.*, 2015). Meanwhile, employees in the Taiwan area have also suffered from job security and the overall prevalence of job insecurity is nearly 50% (Cheng, Chen, Chen, & Chiang, 2005). A survey in Hong Kong showed that employees perceived a relatively high level of job insecurity (Ngo, Loi, & Foley, 2013). Job insecurity implies a great deal of uncertainty, which constitutes as a great source of stress for individuals (Lazarus, 1991). Thus, the salience of perceived job insecurity is probably attributed to Chinese culture with relatively more conservative or traditional values in which security and stability are more affected (Probst & Lawler, 2006; Wang *et al.*, 2014).

Work-family conflict is another common job stressor that has received increasing research attention. With reference to previous studies (Ling & Powell, 2001; Spector *et al.*, 2004; Yang *et al.*, 2000), we believe that employees in Greater China are vulnerable to this form of job stressor, which represents the inter-role conflict when incompatible role pressures are exerted from both work and family domains (Greenhaus & Powell, 2003). In Greater China, dual-earner families are common and people play simultaneous roles as employees and husbands/wives, or even fathers/mothers (Lu, Lu, Du, & Brough, 2016). In terms of the work context, with increasing competition in the workplace, employees face great job demands from long working hours and maintaining interpersonal relationships in the workplace. Workplace stress is further intensified by high job insecurity and high-performance pressure. In terms of family context, people face great demands from fulfilling roles and maintaining relationships. Thus, employees are vulnerable to open conflicts over issues of mutual fulfillment of duties and division of housework. With great demands from both work and family contexts, employees in Greater China are distinctively vulnerable to the job stressor of work-family conflict (Lu *et al.*, 2015; Siu *et al.*, 2005). Recently, Lu, Gilmour, Kao, and Huang (2006) also found that employees in the Taiwan area reported more work-family conflict than those in Britain.

The main contribution of the present study is to explore common serious job stressors and to further modify and develop the Chinese version of job stressors measures. Thus, our study steps toward the calling of more job stress research in the developing country (Bliese *et al.*, 2017; Houtman *et al.*, 2007). Moreover, we used both qualitative and quantitative approaches to explore the major job stressors in the changing Chinese society, since different cultures and social-economical environments should shape an individual's experience of job stress at the workplace. It would enrich job stress research literature by using such mixed methods – including both qualitative and quantitative approaches – to study the design (Liu *et al.*, 2008; Mazzola *et al.*, 2011; Schonfeld & Mazzola, 2015). In terms of practical implications, our study could provide reliable and valid measures of job stressors for conducting job stress research in Greater China and good tools for practitioners to implement certain job stress prevention or management programs.

It should be acknowledged that the current study has some limitations, although the merit of both qualitative and quantitative approaches exists. One limitation is that the data came from self-reported measures except for job performance. Future research could use objective measures of strains or health, such as levels of cortisol or recorded sick days to provide stronger evidence to support the validation of our job stressors measures. In addition, it should be noted that there are subcultural differences in social institutions, political systems, as well as regional development histories in these three regions of Greater China, which may exert different impacts on these six job stressors and the consequences of these stressors.

Notes

1 The data were part of a larger data set for job stress project (Lu, Kao, Siu, & Lu, 2010).
2 The data were part of a larger data set for job stress project (Siu, Lu, & Spector, 2013).

References

Bliese, P. D., Edwards, J. R., & Sonnentag, S. (2017). Stress and well-being at work: A century of empirical trends reflecting theoretical and societal influences. *Journal of Applied Psychology, 102*, 389–402.

Brislin, R. W. (1986). The wording and translation of research instruments. In W. J. Lonner & J. W. Berry (Eds.), *Field methods in cross-cultural research* (pp. 137–164). Beverly Hills, CA: Sage.

Burke, R. J. (1988). Sources of managerial and professional stress in large organizations. In C. L. Cooper & R. Payne (Eds), *Causes, coping and consequences of stress at work* (pp. 77–114). New York: Wiley.

Cammann, C., Fichman, M., Jenkins, D., & Klesh, J. (1979). *The Michigan Organizational Assessment Questionnaire.* Ann Arbor: Unpublished manuscript. University of Michigan.

Cartwright, S., & Cooper, C. L. (2002). *ASSET: An organizational stress screening tool, the management guide.* Manchester, UK: RCL Ltd.

Chang, C.-H., & Baard, S. K. (2011). Cross-cultural occupational stress: An individual differences perspective. In P. L. Perrewé & D. C. Ganster (Eds.), *Research in occupational stress and well-being* (Vol. 9, pp. 265–303). Bingley, UK: Emerald Group Publishing.

Cheng, B. S., Chou, L. F., Wu, T. Y., Huang, M. P., & Farh, F. L. (2004). Paternalistic leadership and subordinate responses: Establishing a leadership model in Chinese organizations. *Asian Journal of Social Psychology, 7*, 89–117.

Cheng, Y., Chen, C. W., Chen, C. J., & Chiang, T. L. (2005). Job insecurity and its association with health among employees in the Taiwanese general population. *Social Science and Medicine, 61*, 41–52.

Cooper, C. L., Sloan, S. J., & Williams, S. (1988). *Occupational stress indicator: management guide.* Windsor: NFER-Nelson.

Cox, T. (1985). The nature and measurement of stress. *Ergonomics, 28*(8), 1155–1163.

Deluga, R. (1994). Supervisor trust building, leader-member exchange and organizational citizen behavior. *Journal of Occupational and Organizational Psychology, 67*, 315–326.

Ganster, D. C., & Rosen, C. C. (2013). Work stress and employee health: A multidisciplinary review. *Journal of Management, 39*, 1085–1122.

Glowinkowski, S. P., & Cooper, C. L. (1985). Current issues in organizational implications. *Canadian Psychology, 32*, 562–574.

Greenhaus, J. H., & Powell, G. N. (2003). When work and family collide: Deciding between competing role demands. *Organizational Behavior and Human Decision Processes, 90*, 291–303.

Feng, D. D., Lu, C. Q., & Siu, Q. L. (2008). Job insecurity, well-being, and job performance: The role of general of self-efficacy. *Acta PsychologicaSinica, 40*, 448–455.

Ferris, G. R., Frink, D. D., Galang, M. C., Zhou, J., Kacmar, K. M., & Howard, J. L. (1996). Perceptions of organizational politics: Predictions, stress-related implications, and outcomes. *Human Relations, 49*, 233–266.

Hirst, G., Budhwar, P., Cooper, B., West, M., Long, C., Chongyuan, X., & Shipton, H. (2008). Cross-cultural variations in climate for autonomy, stress

and organizational productivity relationships: A comparison of Chinese and UK manufacturing organizations. *Journal of International Business Studies, 39*, 1343–1358.
Hofstede, G. (1980). *Culture's consequences: International differences in work-related values*. Beverly Hills, CA: Sage Publications.
Houtman, I., Jettinghoff, K., & Cediollo, L. (2007). *Raising awareness of stress at work in developing countries: A modern hazard in a traditional working environment*. World Health Organization Health Series No. 6. Geneva: WHO Press.
Kacmar, K. M., & Carlson, D. S. (1997). Further validation of the perceptions of politics scale (Pops): A multiple sample investigation. *Journal of Management, 23*, 627–658.
Kitayama, S., & Park, H. (2007). Cultural shaping of self. emotion, and well-being: How does it work? *Social and Personality Psychology Compass, 1*, 202–222.
Lazarus, R. S. (1991). Psychological stress in the workplace. *Journal of Social Behavior and Personality, 6*, 1–13.
LePine, J. A., Podsakoff, N. P., & LePine, M. A. (2005). A meta-analytic test of the challenge stressor-hindrance stressor framework: An explanation for inconsistent relationships among stressors and performance. *Academy of Management Journal, 48*, 764–775.
Ling, Y., & Powell, G. N. (2001). Work-family conflict in Contemporary China: Beyond an American-based model. *International Journal of Cross-cultural Management, 1*, 357–373.
Liu, C., Spector, P., & Shi, L. (2007). Cross-national job stress: A quantitative and qualitative study. *Journal of Organizational Behavior, 28*, 209–239.
Liu, C., Spector, P. E., & Shi, L. (2008). Use of both qualitative and quantitative approaches to study job stress in different gender and occupational groups. *Journal of Occupational Health Psychology, 13*, 357–370.
Lu, C. Q., Du, D. Y., & Xu, X. M. (2016). What differentiates employees' job performance under stressful situations: The role of general self-efficacy. *The Journal of Psychology, 150*, 837–848.
Lu, C. Q., Lu, J. J., Du, D. Y., & Brough, P. (2016). Crossover effects of work-family conflict among Chinese couples. *Journal of Managerial Psychology, 31*, 235–250.
Lu, C. Q., Siu, O. L., Au, W. T., & Leung, S. S. (2009). Manager's occupational stress in state-owned and private enterprises in the People's Republic of China. *International Journal of Human Resource Management, 20*, 1670–1682.
Lu, C. Q., Siu, O. L., & Cooper, C. L. (2005). Managers' occupational stress in China: The role of self-efficacy. *Personality and Individual Differences, 38*, 569–578.
Lu, C. Q., Wang, B., Siu, O. L., Lu, L., & Du, D. Y. (2015). Work-home interference and work values in Greater China. *Journal of Managerial Psychology, 30*, 801–814.
Lu, L., Cooper, C. L., Chen, Y. C., Hsu, C. H., Li, C. H., Wu, H. L., & Shih, J. B. (1995). Chinese version of the OSI: A study of reliability and factor structures. *Stress Medicine, 11*, 149–155.

Lu, L., Gilmour, R., Kao, S. F., & Huang, M. T. (2006). A cross-cultural study of work/family demands, work/family conflict and wellbeing: The Taiwanese vs British. *Career Development International*, 11, 9–27.

Lu, L., Kao, S. F., Cooper, C. L., & Spector, P. E. (2000). Managerial stress, locus of control, and job strain in Taiwan and UK: A comparative study. *International Journal of Stress Management*, 7, 209–226.

Lu, L., Kao, S. F., Siu, O. L., & Lu, C. Q. (2010). Work stressors, Chinese coping strategies, and job performance in Greater China. *International Journal of Psychology*, 45, 294–302.

Mazzola, J. J., Schonfeld, I. S., & Spector, P. E. (2011). What qualitative research has taught us about occupational stress. *Stress and Health*, 27, 93–110.

Motowidlo, S. J., Packard, J. S., & Manning, M. R. (1986). Occupational stress: Its causes and consequences for job performance. *Journal of Applied Psychology*, 71, 618–629.

Narayanan, L., Menon, S., & Spector., P. E. (1999). Stress in the workplace: A comparison of gender and occupations. *Journal of Organizational Behavior*, 20, 63–73.

Newton, T. J., & Keenan, A. (1985). Coping with work-related stress. *Human Relations*, 2, 107–126.

Ngo, H. Y., Loi, R., & Foley, S. (2013). Perceived job insecurity, psychological capital and job attitudes: An investigation in Hong Kong. *International Journal of Employment Studies*, 21, 58–79.

Price, R. H., & Fang, L. L. (2002). Unemployed Chinese workers: The survivors, the worried young and the discouraged old. *International Journal of Human Resource Management*, 13, 416–430.

Probst, T. M., & Lawler, J. (2006). Cultural values as moderators of employee reactions to job insecurity: The role of individualism and collectivism. *Applied Psychology*, 55, 234–254.

Podsakoff, P. M., MacKenzie, S. B., Lee, J. Y., & Podsakoff, N. P. (2003). Common method biases in behavioral research: A critical review of the literature and recommended remedies. *Journal of Applied Psychology*, 88, 879–903.

Schonfeld, I. S. & Mazzola, J. J. (2015). A qualitative study of stress in individuals self-employed in solo businesses. *Journal of Occupational Health Psychology*, 20, 501–513.

Siu, O. L., Cooper, C. L., & Donald, I. (1997). Occupational stress, job satisfaction and mental health among employees of an acquired TV company in Hong Kong. *Stress Medicine*, 13, 99–107.

Siu, O. L., Donald, I., & Cooper, C. L. (1997). The use of Occupational Stress Indicator (OSI) in factory workers in China. *International Journal of Stress Management*, 4, 171–182.

Siu, O. L., Lu, C. Q., & Spector, P. E. (2013). Direct and indirect relationship between social stressors and job performance in Greater China: The role of strain and social support. *European Journal of Work and Organizational Psychology*, 22, 520–531.

Siu, O. L., Spector, P. E., Cooper, C. L., & Lu, C. Q. (2005). Work stress, self-efficacy, Chinese work values and work well-being in Hong Kong and Beijing. *International Journal of Stress Management*, 12, 274–288.

Siu, O. L., Spector, P. E., Cooper, C. L., Lu, L., & Yu, S. (2002). Managerial stress in Greater China: The direct and moderator effects of coping strategies and work locus of control. *Applied Psychology, 51*, 608–632.

Spector, P. E., & Jex, S. M. (1998). Development of four self-report measures of job stressors and strains: Interpersonal Conflict at Work Scale, Organizational Constraints Scale, Quantitative Workload Inventory, and Physical Symptoms Inventory. *Journal of Occupational Health Psychology, 3*, 356–367.

Spector, P. E., Sanchez, J. I., Siu, O. L., Salgado, J., & Ma, J. (2004). Eastern versus Western control beliefs at work: An investigation of secondary control, socioinstrumental control, and work locus of control in China and the U.S. *Applied Psychology, 53*, 38–60.

Sverke, M., & Hellgren, J. (2002). The nature of job insecurity: Understanding employment uncertainty on the brink of a new millennium. *Applied Psychology, 51*, 23–42.

Visewsevaran, D., Ones, D. S., & Schmidt, F. L. (1996). Comparative analysis of the reliability of job performance ratings. *Journal of Applied Psychology, 81*, 557–574.

Wang, H. J., Lu, C. Q., & Lu, L. (2014). Do people with traditional values suffer more from job insecurity? The moderating effects of traditionality. *European Journal of Work and Organizational Psychology, 23*, 107–117.

Wang, H. J., Lu, C. Q., & Siu, O. L. (2015). Job insecurity and job performance: The moderating role of organizational justice and the mediating role of work engagement. *Journal of Applied Psychology, 100*, 1249–1258.

Xie, J. L. (1996). Karasek's model in the People's Republic of China: Effects of job demands, control, and individual differences. *Academy of Management Journal, 39*, 1594–1618.

Xie, J. L., Schaubroeck, J., & Lam, S. S. (2008). Theories of job stress and the role of traditional values: A longitudinal study in China. *Journal of Applied Psychology, 93*, 831–848.

Yang, N., Chen, C. C., & Zou, Y. (2000). Sources of work-family conflict: A Sino-U.S. comparison of the effects of work and family demands. *Academy of Management Journal, 43*, 113–123.

Yu, S., Sparks, K., & Cooper, C. L. (1998). Occupational stress in employees and managers in steelworks in China. *International Journal of Stress Management, 5*, 237–245.

5 The Causes and Consequences of Organizational Stress
The Case of Greece

Ritsa Fotinatos-Ventouratos

Introduction

Greece, officially known as the Hellenic Republic and also known as Hellas, is a relatively small country located in Southern Europe. As of 2018, it had a total population of approximately 10.8 million people, of which 3.4 million people live in the capital of Athens (Wikipedia). In 1981, Greece became a member of the European Union, and in 2001, it became a member of the Eurozone, forming a common European Monetary Currency. Confirming evidence (Fotinatos-Ventouratos & Cooper, 2015) suggests that this latter move did not prove to be a smooth transition, rather, it resulted in major upheavals for the country, and, therefore, for most citizens and organizations. This decision set the ball in motion for many unique organizational and societal stressors.

For a country that often relies on a few isolated and specialized industries (e.g., shipping and tourism) to generate income, Greece became a vulnerable target that was often unable to compete with stronger European Union Countries – such as Germany and France. These accumulating factors, followed by the Global Economic Crisis that unfolded in 2008, placed Greece as a forerunner and on the front stage of European economic misfortune (Fotinatos-Ventouratos & Cooper, 2015). This resulted in total destabilization of its economy, which sent major ripple effects across the nation-state, thus making Greece a country of high vulnerability and causing major disruption of labor market fragility. It was coupled with uncertainty and sensitivity for years to come. Consequently, the intensity and severity of organizational stress, with its multiple manifestations of strain, became evident throughout Greece. Simultaneously, one may suggest that Greece is no longer considered a collectivist culture, but rather a country in "transit" towards a highly individualistic culture. This factor of cultural re-adjustment, as well as the eruption of the economic crisis, provided a potent mixture of both societal and organizational problems in its extreme, and thus warrants assessment and evaluation by organizational psychologists and scientists at large.

However, before proceeding to assess the causes and consequences of occupational stress in relation to this specific country, it is deemed necessary to provide a suitable definition of the term "stress" for readers to encapsulate in a uniform manner. For most organizational psychologists and on an international scale, it is recognized that this term has a long history within our scientific field, and one may suggest that it is a debatable one too. Indeed, the term stress can be referred to in a host of ways, ranging from assessing it either as a dependent variable or an independent variable or by viewing the term from an interactionist perspective (Fotinatos, 1996). Beyond the scope of this chapter is to assess and to scrutinize the specific terminology, although for continuity reasons and to be in alignment with a European perspective, the following definitions and terminology are deemed appropriate and often utilized on a European platform. To that end, The European Foundation for the Improvement of Living and Working Conditions (2010), have utilized the 2004 EU social partners' agreement, which describes stress as:

Stress is a state, which is accompanied by physical, psychological, or social complaints or dysfunctions and which results from individuals feeling unable to bridge a gap with the requirements or expectations placed on them.

And, more specifically, under the guidance of Work-Related Stress, prepared by the European Commission (see European Foundation for the Improvement of Living and Working Conditions, 2010), work stress is defined as:

The emotional, cognitive, behavioural, and psychological reaction to aversive and noxious aspects of work, work environments and work organisations. It is a state characterized by high levels of arousal and distress and often by feelings of not coping.

Evaluation of Work-Related Stress: Placing Greece in the European Context

As mentioned above, work-related stress is often difficult to define and evaluate. Moreover, and as acknowledged by a plethora of literature in our specific field, there is an abundance of intervening factors, as well as various methodologies used in research. Furthermore, one may propose that in some countries, stress is widely recognized as a work-related issue, yet elsewhere, well-being in the workplace is promoted, while in other countries it may not have such a high profile. Thus, contextual factors play a pivotal role in the assessment and overall evaluation of work-related stress factors. Nonetheless and according to the European Foundation for the Improvement of Living and Working Conditions

(2010), some studies have shown that there are different stress levels among different countries, as well as by demographics, such as age. It is interesting to note, for example, that in Cyprus, a survey conducted by the Department of Labour Inspection in 2006 showed that those who have worked for 25 years report the greatest proportion of stress-related problems. This is backed up by data from the Czech Republic which showed that levels of stress at work tend to increase with age. In Germany, however, surveys showed that people aged between 30–39 were most affected by stress, listing work-related stress as the main source. Interestingly and on a relevant note for Greece, information released shows that stress levels fall away sharply after the age of 54; 8% of people up to age 54 said that they suffered from work-related stress, compared to 1.8% of those aged 55 over. Taken together, therefore, one may clearly speculate that a multitude of intervening factors plays a substantial role, as does the "perception of stress," in relation to cultural and contextual factors.

Taking such information into consideration, it is vitally important to state that when positioning Greece on the map for work-related stress, the European Foundation of Living and Working Conditions in 2010 has recently reported that "Work-related stress is a growing concern for employees and employers in the European Union. Accordingly, in 2005, 22% of European workers reported suffering from stress, lower backache, muscular pain, and fatigue. About a quarter of those employed in Europe is exposed to job strain – between 13% in Sweden and 43% in Greece."

Similarly, in 2009, EU-OSHA reported that there are significant differences in stress prevalence across Europe, and indeed, the highest levels of stress were reported in **Greece** (55%), in Slovenia (38%), Sweden (38%), and Latvia (37%). Given such an insight, therefore, and in summary, it does seem that work-related stress in this particular country is a worrying state of affairs, and it is a phenomenon that is operating at high strength and intensity in comparison to other European noted countries.

The Causes and Consequences of Organizational Stress: The Case of Greece

A Review of the Economic Crisis

Focusing foremost on this unique and severe stressor and placing it in the context of this specific culture, Greece received its first financial aid package in May 2010 when Greece's economic output fell by a quarter. Living standards collapsed when more than a million people lost their jobs in a very short period of time, pushing unemployment to a high 28% (OECD, cited CIPD The People's Program in 2018). This overall

The Causes and Consequences 65

distressed the debt market and weak economic demand explains in part – the huge upheaval and severe problems – that subsequently encroached in the working domain, and therefore touched on the lives of all employees both in the public and private sector. To that end, one can suggest that the severity of this problem, in relation to other specific European and International countries, is considered to be relatively high (Fotinatos-Ventouratos & Cooper, 2015). Indeed, and over the accumulating years, changes in market forces resulted in two factors:

First, great turmoil was felt in the economic and financial world, and second, such changes resulted in extreme turbulence at the individual, organizational, and societal levels – which subsequently manifested negatively in terms of the psychosocial well-being of most Greek citizens. Frankly, the organizational setting was subjected to massive changes in both content and context, reflecting highly constrained and competitive activities (Fotinatos-Ventouratos & Cooper, 2015). Moreover and as a spillover effect, it should be noted that in recent years, for example, youth unemployment in Greece reached an unprecedented level; whereby in 2013, Greece hit the highest-ever recorded figures of approximately 30% (see Fotinatos-Ventouratos & Cooper, 2015).

Today at almost a decade later, Greece is still on the tail end of the worst economic crisis experienced since the Great Depression of the 1930s (Burke, 2015). However, taking all of the above into consideration, it should be noted that reports by Eurostat did emerge in October 2013, suggesting that unemployment in economically starved Greece was anticipated to remain at a tremendous high of approximately 34% until the year 2016, and that is approximately how the economic and financial mappings unfolded. Indeed, and according to OECD Economic Surveys for Greece in April 2018, it was reported that "the economy is recovering, and fiscal credibility has improved." For instance, in 2017, the GDP expanded by 1.3% – the fastest pace since the onset of the crisis. Thus, according to such figures, one may suggest that the economic crisis in Greece has begun to fade; **however** – and to be further analyzed – **the true assessment** of the organizational and corresponding sociopsychological consequences of this world crisis still remains vague and under-assessed, although one may suggest that it is severely tarnished. In the same footprints, the OECD report of 2018 is quick to note that:

"Despite significant reforms, cumbersome regulation, and lack of finance hinder private investment." More worrying for organizational psychologists is the fact that

"Labour market reforms have boosted employment, but wages and productivity remain depressed.... Workers' skills often do not match workplace's needs, trapping workers in low-skill and low-wage jobs." Hence, and as stated by OECD (2018), is the fact that:

> "The long crisis in Greece, combined with an ineffective social protection system caused a surge in poverty, especially among young families with children, the young and the unemployed.... and... work poverty is also high."

What may be implied and partially acknowledged is that the economic crisis for Greece was immense and, in many aspects, is still ongoing. While human beings are resilient and able to change, how quickly and how successfully Greece and the Greek people are able to adapt to these global markets is still not known. It can be speculated that it may take decades for their physiological and psychological characteristics to adapt to the ever-changing and demanding organizational environment.

Restructuring of Organizations and Its Effects on the Well-Being of the Worker

In order to make any economic recovery feasible and for Greece to stay afloat, huge changes and restructuring at the macro and micro levels of the economy and subsequent organizational levels were necessary. In relation to the world of work, this meant an immense restructuring of the workforce, encapsulating both the public and private sector as well as including blue-collar and white-collar occupational groups: However, it should be acknowledged that Greece was not the only country to restructure and have such adjustments taken place with a relatively strong force at the whole European level. Indeed and as stated by Storrie (2006), "Restructuring is often an organization's response to the changing economic environment.... In other words, restructuring of organizations is driven by the need to maintain or enhance profitability, and, therefore, to ensure the survival of the company and jobs over the long term." In the case of Greece, the "Kallikratis Reform" or the "New Architecture of Local Government and Decentralization" (Law 3852/2010) immediately came into effect and was aimed at cutting down public spending through limitation in the number of Local Government Organisations (OTA). At the beginning of 2011, over 4,000 legal entities were abolished, resulting in some 20,000 to 25,000 employees made redundant. Such drastic measures sent huge ripple effects throughout Greece. At the organizational level, these negative manifestations spilled over and into the private lives of many Greek people and engulfed their families. To that end and in a very recent study by Koukoulaki et al. (2017), which evaluated the restructuring of the actual Kallikratis program throughout Greece, it was confirmed that higher levels of work intensification and stress arose. More analytically, increased work-related stress was found to be related to increased emotional and quantitative job demands, as well as with job insecurity. As the authors specifically note "higher levels of emotional exhaustion were found to be related to increased job demands, job insecurity, and unfair treatment during change."

Lack of Transparency and Perceived Level of Justice in the Organization

It is exactly in this last paragraph that one needs to shine the torch on. Significant factors that may regulate the stress-strain relationship at work are the perceived level of justice, trustworthiness, and fairness involved in any major or minor alteration of work. During the midst of the economic recession, Antoniou and Cooper (2013) were quick to note that the story of the recession is not only economic. Macroeconomic factors – including regional, national, or international economic situations – put pressure directly on the unemployed as well as employed people in terms of the individual's reactions to the economic situation and indirectly through organizational restructuring. More specifically "As the workplace has changed and the economic recession increased, researchers indicate high job insecurity, low job satisfaction, reduced involvement, as well as a decline in the ratings of the organizations as trustworthy" (Antoniou & Cooper, 2013).

In regard to the specific country of Greece, lack of transparency in the operation of an organization and unfair treatment appears to sometimes prevail. Novel research has confirmed that new reforms and unplanned organizational changes – as a result of the economic crisis – have had an effect on certain occupational groups, such as school teachers, and their stress levels. More specifically and in a study by Mouza and Souchamvali (2016), it was revealed that the foremost factors that increased perceived stress under unplanned organizational change are related to exogenous factors that teachers cannot control, which include: reduction of wages, job insecurity, and the assessments used for distribution methods. Hence, and it is important to note, the results showed that teachers' increased stress levels in Greece were not related to demographic variables such as sex or age, or even qualifications such as work experience and educational level, that one may consider. Rather, these are associated with external factors that organizational changes and reforms bring about.

Such manifestations should not come as a surprise; however, as literature is scattered with studies that demonstrate the overall downsizing of activities – including staff reduction – negatively affect employee well-being (see e.g., Bohle, Quinlan, & Mayhew, 2001). Indeed in a well-known study by Vahtera *et al.*, 2004, poorer health was reported among employees who were made redundant, in addition to those who remain in the organization after the changes took place.

In a similar vein with key elements in Greece, it has been noted that nonstandard and atypical employment arrangements have taken place, in tandem with the poor economic crisis. For example and according to data of Labor Inspectorate Authorities (SEPE) which is cited in Koukiadaki and Kretsos, 2012, undeclared work increased, and a more bleak picture revealed that one in four companies in the private sector had not paid its employees for three months or more (see Koukiadaki & Kretsos, 2012). One may suggest, however, that even if several years have passed since such information was brought to the forefront, one may still suspect that the consequences in terms of felt occupational stress are far from gone or forgotten by many Greek employees today. From the evidence noted, it seems that restructuring and any form of organizational change, which has been a fundamental and ongoing business practice in Greece, has manifested in a host of negativities and uncertainty. Along with this uncertainty are possible breached and/or shadowed operations that lack full transparency. It may be suggested, therefore, that in times of organizational changes and economic swings, all forms of justice should become critically important and placed as a top priority for the overall well-being of workers. The paradox appears, however, that some organizations are subdued in maintaining fairness and adhering to procedures of justice, and especially so during this exceptionally stressful time of change and reforms in Greece.

Physical and Psychological Well-Being of the Greek People

From the review of literature as stated above, one can solidly confirm that since the onset of the economic crisis, the stressors and strains in Greece have been unique and ever-changing. Consequently and due to the rugged economic, political, and organizational landscape that subsequently unfolded, the well-being of Greek citizens has been scarred. To that end, and noted by Fotinatos-Ventouratos and Cooper (2015), suicide rates began to rise in tandem with the economic crisis, and more analytically according to the APA, suicide rates increased by 45% during the first four years of Greece's financial crisis.

With more recent information and according to Stylianidis and Souliotis (2019), the long-lasting crisis with unemployment, financial hardship, and income loss has resulted in substantial consequences on the physical health and mental health of the population. To that end, the researchers confirm that converging evidence corroborates a deterioration of self-rated health, an alarming rise in suicide rates, and a gradual increase in the prevalence of major depression. Taking this issue one step further Stylianidis and Souliotis claim that:

> *Concomitantly, the healthcare system is incapable of addressing the emerging needs, and, therefore, a multifaceted and concerted effort is urgently needed to mitigate the mental health effects of the recession.*

The above statement does not come unwarranted, given the fact that previous studies (Karanikolos *et al.*, 2013) have also documented that the impact on health systems in Europe revealed a decrease in the extent of medical coverage. Specifically for Greece, an estimated 40% of cutbacks in hospital budgets have been evident – which reflect in understaffing in hospitals, medical supply shortages, as well as excessive patients' queues (Kentikeleris & Papanicolas, 2011). On the same note and again very recently, this matter has led several scholars to further investigate the adjustment levels in times of crisis in Greece from a psychosocial perspective. More analytically, Lahad, Cohen, Fanaras, and Apostolopoulou (2018) advocate from their study that the participants generally rated their psychological health lower than their physical health. Moreover, their findings showed significantly higher perceptions of financial uncertainty and difficulties in coping with economic commitments. Again and recently, Theofanidis (2017) is quick to note from his study entitled, "Greek Nursing Under Austerity," that the ongoing implications of austerity measures imposed on the Greek health care system have had a particular emphasis on its effects on nursing and care delivery. Furthermore, the prolonged poor working environment has resulted in emotional strain – leading to possible burnout and detachment in the nursing staff.

Taken together, one may say in the affirmative that the economic and organizational misfortune has had serious physical and psychological connotations for the Greek people, and current assessments and evaluations are showing poor overall welfare at a national level and across wide occupational spectrums.

Specific Organizational Stressors in Greece: Opening Pandora's Box

The harsh implications that the economic crisis brought with it, in addition to other unique stressors that Greece has been confronted with (e.g., the sudden influx of immigrants) (Fotinatos-Ventouratos, 2016), as well as political change and often with turmoil has led to the manifestations of unique and specific organizational stressors emerging in this country. However, and as previously mentioned, one of the most recent economic surveys of this country (OECD, April 2018) does indicate that Greece is on the road to recovery, and the economy is bearing fruit again. For instance, one notices that exports have led to expansion – from 24% of GDP in 2008 to 34% in 2017, although this is still below the European Union average of 46%. Certain labor market reforms have been installed, improved economic competitiveness has begun, and overall employment figures are rising, albeit slowly. As stated by the OECD in 2018, "rebuilding employment is essential for the recovery in activity for reducing poverty." More analytical and updated information states that the seasonally adjusted unemployment rate in Greece fell to 17.8% in April of 2019 from an upwardly revised 18.2% in the previous month and as compared with 19.8% in April 2018. It was the lowest unemployment rate since June of 2011, as the number of unemployed people dropped by 3.1% from the prior month while the number of employed went up by 0.7%. The unemployment rate in Greece averaged at 16.26% in July 2013 and hit a record low of 7.30% in May of 2008 (Trading Economics, July 2019). However, and as one can generically attest, there is still much to be done at the organizational level – to sustain well-being, productivity, job satisfaction, and stability. For instance and beginning with demographic data, one can concur that challenges exist – for example, improving female labor participation is still among the lowest across all the OECD countries (OECD Economic Surveys: Greece, 2018), which is a bleak fact to report on, especially since gender struggles at the European level still exist. For example, much has been assessed and documented on the embedded gender wage gap and the psychological and social implications that this brings (Fotinatos-Ventouratos, 2019).

Moreover in Greece, such problems are also hindered by the fact that reported skill mismatch is also high, irrespective of the fact that overall participation in education compares very well with other OECD countries. Indeed, completion rates for high school and tertiary education among younger cohorts are above most of the other European Union members, and Greece's top students "go one to perform well on a global stage" (OECD, April 2018). Despite the fact that Greek people appear to be well-equipped with appropriate education, sadly, an unusually large share of Greek workers report being over-skilled for their job – reflecting low demand for skills from workplaces and high skill mismatch. This may lead one to suggest that adults in Greece may also have fewer opportunities to reskill via job training and to participate in professional courses, which is a worrying state of affairs for organizational psychologists to contend with. Our science acknowledges, with a plethora of literature, that correct training, talent retention, and professional development act as a shield to enhance worker satisfaction, motivation, and overall well-being at work (Robbins & Judge, 2009; Greenberg, 2008).

Also, encapsulating the right skills for the right job and utilizing valid and reliable selection and training methods allow a worker to feel in control of their job and clearly lead to increased overall autonomy. As early as 1998, Fotinatos-Ventouratos and Cooper clearly demonstrated that there is a fundamental need for all workers – whether white-collar or blue-collar workers and male or female – to feel in control of their job and possess autonomy at work, and this is a necessary requirement for both job satisfaction and overall well-being to materialize. One may suggest, therefore, that it is vitally important that Greece swiftly addresses issues of any business inequality, and it is necessary more than ever before to effectively address these problems of labor market discrepancies.

Another important and associated issue in regard to the varying organizational stressors in Greece and the consequences in terms of manifested strain refers to the recent attitudes toward women mangers and female authority in a particular county. One recognizes that during the past decades, women's active participation in the labor market has increased tremendously at a global level (Drosos & Antoniou, 2019; Fotinatos-Ventouratos, 2019). Nevertheless, the level of gender equality is uneven across different countries and regions – including within the European Union. For example, in Greece, the employment rate for women was 46.8%, while for men the rate was 65.8% (see Drosos & Antoniou, 2019). Although the gender employment gap in 2016 was 11.9%, it was 19% in Greece. Furthermore, and despite the growing numbers of women in the workforce, their representation in specific managerial and leadership positions in the corporate sector is scarce. In 2016, only 23.3% of the board members of the largest publicly listed companies in the European Union were women, while in Greece the figure was just 9.4% (European Commission, 2016, cited in Drosos & Antoniou, 2019). However, working women tend to have a higher level of education than men, and according to Eurostat (2017), in 2016, 38.5% of women in employment had tertiary level education compared to 31.2% of men. As noted well by researchers, it is clear that the skills of highly qualified women are underutilized and, in economic terms, there is a lack of return on investment and a loss of economic growth potential – as marvelously commented on "It is remarkable that in times when the labor market faces shortages of skilled personnel, a large percentage of human capital is wasted."

In addition to the above comments and findings, one may also suggest that such an unbalanced seesaw in regard to gender differences in the Greek workplace may result in tremendous stressors and strain for working women of all socioeconomic classes, and such findings should not go undetected or under-assessed by our profession. Furthermore and shining the torch on this specific study conducted by Drosos and Antoniou (2019), a bold attempt was made to investigate Greek female managers' attitudes toward women managers and female authority and their correlation with various personal characteristics – such as age, family status, educational level, work experience, and managerial success – on a sample of over 360 female managers who are employed in Greek private companies. The sample consisted of 26.9% high-level managers and 73.1% middle level managers. It is noteworthy that the average age was 34.42 years old, while the average years of working experience were 12.61. The shocking findings showed that female managers reported having several disturbing beliefs regarding the role of gender in career advancement. That is, the vast majority (63.1%)

stated that gender plays a very important role in career advancement, while 92% felt that women's family status is taken into account in recruitment and hiring procedures! Moreover, almost one-third of the participants responded with the view that discrimination again women exists within their company, and there are no women-friendly policies regarding promotion.

Given such bleak findings reported in this study, one may suggest that it would be highly beneficial if future research investigates the exact underpinnings of women's career paths in Greece and further explores the stress-strain relationship that may exist in the working environment for female professional occupational groups, in comparison to men. Given what has already been established, it may indeed be found that there are unprecedented consequences in terms of occupational stress among female managerial occupational groups, and the price tag in terms of psycho-social well-being may indeed be significant.

Intervention Strategies and Coping Mechanisms for Greece and Its Workforce

It is suggested that – in order to assess any possible intervention strategies to combat organizational stress and to promote well-being at work – firstly, a full assessment of this particular country with its corresponding culture, organizational structures, and economic performance needs to be taken into account. Therefore and essentially, one should recognize that the Greek economy is not only trying to recover from a huge recessionary period as discussed above but, it is often overcast by an economy that is made up of many small, traditional, and often family-run businesses. In fact, this issue has been well-documented in literature (see e.g., Zambarloukos & Constantelou, 2002). Given such a spectrum, it should be further noted that Greece is often overrepresented by small and medium-sized enterprises (SMEs) – classified with less than 250 employees (Makrydakis, Papagiannakis, & Caloghirou, 1996). If this is the case, it may not be surprising to find out that any attempt to install nationwide interventions and policies may be stalled by virtue of the organizational setup, and financial liquidity is available. Furthermore, it may indeed be the case that small companies have limited resources, often do not hire adequately trained personnel, and do not – or cannot – invest in innovative training methods for their employees. In Greece, thus, it may also be anticipated that firms which are often family-run, may lack professional management that would even enable them to undertake organizational changes and use new technologies (Zambarloukos & Constantelou, 2002). Such underlying factors surely impede organizational success and certainly play a crucial role in the manifestation of stress, with their corresponding risk factors. Thus the causes and consequences of occupational stress in Greece are far from a simple cause-effect relationship, but these appear to be a multitude of important variables all interwoven together.

A further obstacle for organizational psychologists to contend with is that evidence of current organizational stress prevention measures in Greece is somewhat limited, not often visible, and is rather scattered in literature. However, some evidence does appear to be picking up the pace. For instance, it does seem to be that large organizations have in part attempted to install work-related stress management interventions, with Piraeus Bank Group being an example (see European Foundation for the Improvement of Living and Working Conditions, 2010). Here for example, and in collaboration with Hellas Employee Assistance Programs (Hellas EAP), the large bank provides a program to support and to actively manage workers' health and well-being. The program provides information and support on preventative measures and traumatic events management – with an emphasis on prevention as well as support in cases such as bank robberies to critical family and work-related stress issues. It also offers guidance and support for workers on issues of career advancement and is aimed at realizing the full potential of workers' skills. Therefore, the attempt is being made, and one is positive that further strong and conscientious developments will abide in the not too distant future.

Concerning any structural reforms, one could also state, that a consequence of the financial crisis also resulted in the installation of severe and drastic austerity policies that were imposed in this country, and encapsulated many organizational effects too. On a political and economic front, this may be considered an advantage for some, while for others not so. While any political connotation is beyond the scope of this chapter, it is noteworthy to point out that this severe debt crisis did allow insight to take place in regard to employment protection in Greece; and for many governing bodies, employment protection came to be regarded as a major obstacle to structural change and the liberalization of domestic markets. Indeed, and as stated by La Spina and Sciortino (see Koukiadaki & Kretsos, 2012):

> *Greece suffered from the "Mediterranean Syndrome," a low administrative capacity for policy implementation – linking noncompliance with particular institutional and cultural deficiencies.*

If this is the case, then ripple effects in terms of employment regulations and best work practices may become more apparent, as one may suggest that any interventions must always address possible inequalities arising from weak welfare state policies and impediments. As one recognizes, in the absence of any correct social dialogue, correct procedures at the organizational level may be difficult to implement. Hence, it is suggested that individual labor laws must be scrutinized to assist the worker and enhance well-being at all times: For instance and according to Koukiadaki and Kretsos (2012), until recently, the termination of employment under Greek Labor Law has been permitted without the employer having to justify the action or invoke a potentially fair reason. For us, as organizational psychologists, we recognize and understand that such obstacles inherent in the "Greek system" must surely result in ripple effects with Greek employees feeling highly insecure in already insecure and turbulent economic times. For example, and in recent research by Anagnostopoulos and Siebert (2015) conducted in Central Greece (Thessaly, Greece), they, unfortunately, found that high temporary work contracts are evident especially among workplaces that pay low wages. In particular, it was noted that managers prefer temporary contracts because they are less protected by any form of employment rights and regulations. Additionally, the recent Troika (2012) (cited in Kathimerini, 2012) allowed freezing of wage increments, reduction of the minimum wage (especially among unskilled workers), as well as the abolition of the 13th and 14th salaries (i.e., payment of an extra month or two's salary). While such issues are currently being readdressed, it did, for a very long period of time, put immense psychological pressure on all Greek workers – who were abruptly faced with challenging conditions to work in and with apparently no safety net installed.

Forward Initiatives

It may be more proactive, therefore, if one encourages the individual worker to attempt to install interventions and best practices from an individual's perspective to enhance well-being and sustain prosperity as best as possible. For instance, practices to increase resilience and enhance personal adjustment may be more viable and are avenues that one should encourage and explore. Recently and as assessed by Petrou, Demerouti, and Xanthopoulou (2017), the role of employee job crafting may be advantageous. In their study, it was revealed that in times of Organizational Change Contexts, job crafting can relate to employee work-related well-being. More specifically, they confirmed that in times of threatening cutback-related change (i.e., due to the financial recession in Greece), seeking resources when job autonomy is low is associated with better well-being and greater engagement. Thus job crafting is proactive employee behavior that is targeted at seeking job resources and challenges and at limiting job demands. As Griffin, Neal, and Parker, 2007 propose (cited in Petrou *et al.*, 2017), job crafting strategies enable new work roles to emerge to help employees in dealing with changing situations. Thus for the case of Greece and the Greek worker, one may propose that this is a "hand in glove" proposal for the imminent Greek worker. Thus, more attention should be given to what employees can do themselves to deal effectively with stressful times and when turbulence sets in. Hence, an assessment in terms of promoting all types of interventions – ranging from primary interventions (i.e., aiming to prevent exposure to known risk factors and to increase resilience) to secondary interventions (i.e., aimed at reversing a progression, to finally assessing tertiary interventions, and to reduce severity may be advantageous) (WHO, 2008, cited in Leka & Jain, 2017).

More analytically and at all times, Greece with its corresponding organizations should bear in mind that organizational approaches to well-being at work involve a combination of organizational interventions which should provide a portfolio of employee-friendly options that simultaneously benefit the organization (Weinberg & Cooper, 2012; Robertson & Cooper, 2011). Specifically, therefore, the three-pronged approach to organizational health in this specific country may be warranted. As previously mentioned, it combines prevention, management, and treatment options to tackle the immediate concerns of the day as well as to lay the foundations for a longer-term strategy for employee well-being – which appears to be needed in this particular country, which is on the road to recovery from recessionary times. Specifically shown below, is this triangular approach (as cited in Fotinatos-Ventouratos & Cooper, 2015):

- Primary interventions are focused on the prevention of problems from arising in the first place. Examples are considerate and compassionate management with clear communication strategies which are essential during organizational change (which is apparent in Greece), participative job redesign, promoting organizational citizenship, and management coaching.
- Secondary interventions aim to manage the symptoms of strain and associated factors by targeting the individual in the workplace. Examples are stress management programs – such as relaxation techniques, stress management techniques, assertiveness training, interview skills, job-seeking workshops, and coaching initiatives.
- Tertiary interventions are designed to help the individual who may need more specialized input to deal with strain. An example is an employee assistance program offering counseling.

Therefore, and given the range of identified risk factors in Greece, reasonable intervention strategies can be proposed to modify such negativities as well as increase individual well-being at work. Furthermore and as previously discussed, most attempts to date appear to have been made by large organizations; understandably, they are most likely to have the available resources and financial leverage to carry out intervention strategies. Nonetheless, an attempt should be made in Greece to encourage ALL organizations to participate in stress intervention programs, thereby making good individual health benefits, as well as good organizational benefits – leading to possible increased profits. Furthermore, to promote intervention strategies in the workplace, it is necessary that management in Greece understands that there are multi-methods as well as multi-models. Utilizing more than one technique simultaneously will enhance effectiveness and maximize results, thereby producing a greater understanding of the multitude of demands currently being placed on the Greek worker. This way, both the organization and its corresponding workforce will understand that there are solutions and remedies available to assist the Greek people, and, especially so, after the tarnished and toxic environment that emerged as a consequence of the recession.

Conclusion

What is certain is that there are many causes of occupational stress in Greece, and the consequences are varied and complex; however, the principal stressors and strains in the occupational world in Greece are unique and ever-changing, primarily as a consequence of the economic and political instability found in global recessionary times (Fotinatos-Ventouratos & Cooper, 2015). It is evident that most organizations in both the public and private sector have been directly tarnished by turbulent times, making these occupational stressors both severe and chronic, while simultaneously touching on the lives of most employees in this particular country. Furthermore, and as observed in this chapter, accelerating the stress-strain relationship is a specific cultural issue that often hinders the Greek situation, making possible scientifically proven intervention strategies difficult to install and maintain. However, one does feel confident that if implemented correctly and conscientiously, then positive results will abide. Additionally, it may be beneficial if the Greek people have an eye on the past to provide a vision for the future, as indeed it was the Ancient Greeks that taught us many, many, years ago, that a "fool is a fool if they make the same mistake twice." It is important that all of us in Greece learn from the man-made mistakes that have engulfed this country and its people. Although and at the same time, the Greeks have been told from ancient times that "misfortunes and misdeeds will make a man stronger," and with this, one may suggest that despite the turmoil and challenges set upon the Greek people, that we will move forward ever more positively and strongly, taking us from sustainability to overall well-being and prosperity in the years to come.

References

Anagnostopoulos, A. & Siebert, W. (2015). The impact of Greek labour market regulations on temporary employment – evidence from a survey in Thessaly, Greece. *The International Journal of Human Resource Management*, 26(18), 2366–2393.

Antoniou, A. S. & Cooper, C. L. (2013). *The psychology of the recession on the workplace*. Cheltenham, UK and Northampton, MA. USA: Edward Elgar.

Burke, R. (2015). Book endorsement: The economic crisis and occupational stress. *Fotinatos-Ventouratos & Cooper (2015)*. Cheltenham, UK and Northampton, MA.USA: Edward Elgar Publishing.

Bohle, P., Quinlan, M. & Mayhew, C. (2001). The health and safety effects of job insecurity: An evaluation of the evidence. *Economic Labour Relations Review*, 12, 32–60.

Drosos, N. & Antoniou, A. S. (2019). Attitudes toward women managers and female authority: An empirical study among women mangers in Greece. In A. S. Antoniou, C. L. Cooper & C. Gatrell (2019), *Women, Business and Leadership*. Cheltenham, UK and Northampton, MA, USA: Edward Elgar Publishing.

EU-OSHA-European Agency for Safety and Health at Work. (2009). *OSH in figures: Stress at work – facts and figures*. Luxembourg: Office for Official publications of the European Communities.

European Foundation for the Improvement of Living and Working Conditions. Work-related stress. (2010). Retrieved from www.eurofound.europa.eu.

Eurostat Statistics. (2017, May). http://ec.europa.eu/eurostat/statistics-explained/index.php/Gender-statistics.

Fotinatos-Ventouratos, R. S. J. (2019). *The Psychological and Social Implications of the GenderWage Gap*, In. Women, Business and Leadership. A. S. Antoniou, C.L. Cooper & C. Gatrell (2019). Cheltenham, UK and Northampton, MA, USA: Edward Elgar Publishing.

Fotinatos-Ventouratos, R. S. J. (2016). *Integrating Refugees in the workplace: Multiple perspectives*. British Psychological Society (BPS) Journal, OP Matters, 32 (December).

Fotinatos-Ventouratos, R. S. J. & Cooper, C. L. (2015). *The Economic Crisis and Occupational Stress*. Cheltenham, UK and Northampton, MA, USA: Edward Elgar Publishing.

Fotinatos-Ventouratos, R. S. J. & Cooper, C. L. (2005). The role of gender and social class in work stress. *Journal of Managerial Psychology*, 20(1), 14–22.

Fotinatos-Ventouratos, R. S. J. & Cooper, C. L. (1998). Social class differences and occupational stress. *International Journal of Stress Management*, 5(4), 211–222.

Fotinatos, R. S. J. (1996). Doctoral thesis, *A Community Wide Survey of Occupational Stress*. Manchester: UMIST.

Greenberg, J. S. (2008). *Comprehensive stress management* (10th ed.). New York: Springer Publications.

Karanikolos, M., Mladovsky, P., Cylus, J., Thomson, S., Basu, S., Stuckler, D., Mackenbach, J. P. & McKee, M. (2013). Financial crisis, austerity, and health in Europe. Health in Europe 7 Series. www.thelancet.com. Published online March 7, 2013. http://dx.doi.org/10.1016/so140-6736(13)60102-6.

eKathimerini. (2012). Search for common ground continues. *International Herald Tribune* (English ed.), 13 September, available at: www.ekathimerini.com.

Kentikeleris, A. & Papanicolas, I. (2011). Economic crisis, austerity and the Greek public health system. *European Journal of Public Health*, 22(1), 4–5.

Koukiadaki, A. & Kretsos, L. (2012, September). Opening pandora's box: The sovereign debt crisis and labour market regulation in Greece. *Industrial Law Journal*, 41(3), 276–304.

Koukoulaki, T., Pinotsi, D., Georgiadou, P., Daikou, A., Zorba, K., Targoutzidis, A., Poulios, K., Panousi, P., Skoulatakis, Y., Drivas, S., Kapsali, K. & Pahkin, K. (2017). Restructuring seriously damages well-being of workers: The case of the restructuring programme in local administration in Greece. *Safety Science*, 100, 30–36. Elsevier Ltd.

Lahad, M., Cohen, R., Fanaras, D. L. & Apostolopoulou (2018). Resiliency and adjustment in times of crisis, the case of the Greek economic crisis from a psycho-social and community persepctive. *Social Indicators Research*, 135, 333–356. Springer. https://doi.org/10.1007/s11205-016-1472-5.

Leka, S. & Jain, A. (2017). *EU Compass for Action on Mental Health and Wellbeing: Mental Health in the Workplace in Europe - Consensus Paper*. Funded by the European Union in the fame of the 3rd EU Health Programme (2014–2020).

Makrydakis, S., Papagiannakis, L. & Caloghirou, Y. (1996). *Greek management developments, trends and prospects*. Athens: Association of Chief Executive Officers (in Greek).

Mouza, A. M. & Souchamvali, D. (2016). Effect of Greece's new reforms and unplanned organizational changes on the stress levels of primary school teachers. *Social Indicators Research*, 128, 981–994. Springer.

OECD Economic Surveys: Greece. (2018, April). Overview. www.oecd.org/eco/surveys/economic-survey-greece.htm.

Petrou, P., Demerouti, E. & Xanthopoulou, D. (2017). Regular versus cutback-related change: The role of employee job crafting in organizational change contexts of different. *International Journal of Stress Management*, 24(1), 62–85.

Robertson, I. & Cooper, C. L. (2011). *Wellbeing: Productivity and happiness at work*. Basingstoke: Palgrave Macmillan.

Robbins, S. P. & Judge, T. A. (2009). *Organizational behaviour*(13th ed.). Upper Saddle River, NJ: Pearson Prentice Hall.

Storrie, D. (2006). *Restructuring and employment in the EU: Concepts, measurement and evidence*. European Foundation for the Improvement of Living and Working Conditions.

STRATFOR (2013). Youth Unemployment in the European Union, 29 May, STRATFOR Global Intelligence, available at: www.stratfor.com.

Stylianidis, S. & Souliotis, K. (2019, February). The impact of the long-lasting socioeconomic crisis in Greece. *British Journal International*, 16(1), 16–18.

Theofanidis, D. (2017). Greek nursing under austerity. *International Journal of Caring Sciences*, 10(1), 601–606.

Trading Economics (July 2019). "Greece Unemployment Rate 2019." https://tradingeconomics.com/greece/unemployment-rate.

Vahtera, J., Kivimaki, M., Pentti, J., Linn, A., Virtanen, M., Virtanen, P. & Ferrie, J. E. (2004). Organisational downsizing, sickness absence and mortality: 10-town prospective cohort study. *British Medical Journal*, *328*(7439), 555.

Velonakis, E. & Lambropoulos, E. (1999). *Sources of Stress among Greek Workers*. New Health, *24(7)*.

Weinberg, A. & Cooper, C. L. (2012). *Stress in turbulent times*. Basingstoke: Palgrave Macmillan.

WHO–World Health Organisation. (2008). PRIMA-EF: Guidance on the European Framework for Psychosocial Risk Management: A Resource for Employers and Worker Representatives. Protecting workers' health series, no. 9. Geneva: World Health Organisation. Available at: http://www.who.int/occupational_health/publications/Protecting_Workers_Health_Series_No_9/en/index.html.

Zambarloukos, S. & Constantelou, A. (2002). Learning and skills formation in the new economy: Evidence from Greece. *International Journal of Training and Development*, 6, 4. ISSN 1360-3736. Blackwell Publishers.

6 Work Stress
A Systematic Review of Evidence from India

Kajal A. Sharma

Introduction

India is one of the most powerful and fastest emerging economies and is the country with the world's second-largest population. By International Monetary Fund (IMF) estimates, India already accounts for 15% of global growth (World Economic Forum, 2018). It has experienced a rapid social, cultural, and economic transition in recent years. The Indian economy has been predominantly rural, but, over the years, there has a steady decline in the rural population and workforce. This can be attributed to the push-pull forces of migration and the steady urbanization stemming from influences like an increase in education, social awareness, the mass proliferation of white-collar jobs, and the explosion of social media platforms, among others. Although contemporary Indian society has changed, family institutions and community ties continue to play a central role in the lives of people.

The Indian economy has some unique strengths and parallel challenges which makes it fascinating and complex at the same time. The Indian workforce has three distinct characteristics: (a) it is the biggest young workforce in the world; (b) the skills base of this workforce remains underdeveloped; and (c) most jobs are being created in the informal economy (Saran & Sharan, 2018). The biggest policy implications of these characteristics are the urgent response to value-adding job creation and the inclusion and welfare of the new workforce. To meet these policy implications, the state must regulate diversified sets of economic activities taking place in the formal (organized) and informal (unorganized) sectors. The unorganized sector employs 83% of the workforce and contributes to 50% of the GDP (National Statistical Office, 2019). Hence, the interest and rights of the majority of the Indian workforce in the unorganized sector are compromised as they work without a written contract, paid leave, health benefits, social security, and welfare protection. Secondly, the state needs to enhance its ability to form appropriate workforce welfare legislation and oversee its stricter statutory compliance. Such laws should principally consider providing the availability of income security (minimum wages), critical needs (health, retirement, and life insurance cover), and safe and congenial working conditions to its workforce (OECD, 2017). Although legislative action in recent years has been quite promising, more needs to be done.

This backdrop has given rise to a challenging and multifaceted work environment and culture in India. Factors like globalization, population, competition, migration to urban areas, scarcity of resources, limited opportunities, societal changes, technological advancements, family demands, multiple roles, and personal aspirations further complicate work dynamics. Employees face multiple, unrealistic, and uncertain demands at work. Due to these pressures, employees find themselves being pushed to limits by profit-focused organizations. The latest reports show that one in seven Indians were affected by mental disorders of varying severity in 2017, and the proportional contribution of mental disorders to the total disease burden in India has almost doubled since 1990 (Sagar et al., 2020). This signals that stress has become a constant feature of modern life. It is felt by most, irrespective of their status, occupation, position, gender, competence, education, and experience. Its causes, levels, assessment, consequences, and coping might vary on an individual basis. Some amount of stress is considered good for an individual to feel driven toward their goals, but the rigid rules and regulations and ever-changing and continuous work demands of modern work life make job commitments complex and unmanageable. It has become very difficult to switch off from work, and so work-life balance is difficult to achieve for an average Indian employee.

Stress has also become a significant challenge for Indian employers in recent years. It is a double-edged sword as it impacts employee well-being and also the organization's effectiveness and profitability. Research has shown that stress relates to an organization's problems – such as managerial ineffectiveness, poor job performance, turnover, absenteeism, accidents, and errors. It also leads to various psychological, physiological, and behavioral problems in employees. Therefore, employers are increasingly becoming sensitive and engaged in finding effective interventions through expert counseling assistance, career guidance, stress management sessions, or health awareness programs to help employees manage stress better. However, there are certain challenges in this process. A key issue around resource constraints is a test for small and medium-sized organizations. Another reason is that the Indian workforce is multigenerational. This makes the office space a ripe platform for intra-organizational disputes resulting from the lack of group conformity and group cohesion on one end of the spectrum and groupthink on the other, especially in orthodox Indian cultures wherein merely questioning elders or raising doubts is still considered akin to insulting them. Nevertheless, there has been a gradual shift from organizational performance orientation to focus on employee well-being.

Indian stress research has addressed different stress-related issues and has followed international trends. However, the literature highlights that a more proactive approach is needed by organizations for designing sustainable stress-inhibiting systems and cultures, in addition to stress management initiatives, to nurture employee happiness, health, and well-being to help them achieve work-life balance. This chapter presents a review of stress studies from the period of 2009–2018, highlighting unique trends in Indian stress literature and also identifying its commonalities with international literature. The areas for future research in the Indian context are also identified.

Methodology

This review adopted the systematic review methodology proposed by Tranfield, Denyer, and Smart (2003). There were three reasons for adopting this methodology. Firstly, compared to the traditionally used narrative method, this methodology has proved to be a more transparent, scientific, and reproducible procedure for literature search and analysis (Suarez-Barraza, Smith, & Dahlgaard-Park, 2012; Fisch & Block, 2018). Secondly, it provides extensive and clear guidance on how to conduct a literature review and present the findings. Lastly, this approach is widely adopted in different fields of management research (Rashman, Withers, & Hartley, 2009).

The systematic review consists of three stages: planning, conducting and dissemination. The author has adopted these stages while working on this chapter. In the first phase, a pool of all relevant journal and research articles was created through searching various search platforms like EBSCO, Emerald, JSTOR, Science Direct, Scopus, Taylor and Francis, Elsevier, and Google Scholar and by using keywords such as "work stress," "occupational stress," and "job stress." Papers generated from the search were then examined for their compatibility with this research by reviewing their titles, abstracts, and keywords. The sources – such as reports published by government and non-government organizations, eBooks, working papers, conference proceedings, and dissertations – were excluded from the search process.

All papers from 2009 to 2018 were searched and screened. Papers based on literature reviews add, cross-culture research and not written in the English language were excluded from the review. After reviewing all the papers, 158 relevant papers were screened out. The studies were then classified based on various characteristics – like the year of publication, author details, research methodology, industry/sector, gender, sampling process, sample characteristics, and results. An Excel spreadsheet was created to record all of the characteristics of these selected studies.

Tranfield *et al.* (2003) recommends that the reporting and dissemination stage should cover two parts: "descriptive analysis" and "thematic analysis." Following this, the data captured on the Excel spreadsheet was analyzed and used to identify and study the trends. The resulting descriptive analysis is presented in the next section through various graphs and pie charts. In the final phase, a detailed analysis of these papers was conducted to identify main literature themes, gaps in the literature, key findings, conclusions, and scope of future research. The analysis of the main thematic trends is presented in the Discussion section.

Descriptive Analysis

A total of 158 studies were examined for this review. These empirical studies covered a period of ten years, starting from 2009 to 2018 (see appendix for details). Figure 6.1 represents the number of empirical studies published each year from 2009 to 2018. The range of yearly publications has been between a minimum of ten studies in 2010 to a maximum of 27 studies in 2015. In other years, the number of published empirical studies has been between 12 and 19. The studies reviewed were published in several journals across multiple fields reflecting the multidisciplinary approach undertaken to understand the work stress phenomenon in the Indian context. The majority of the research studies were published in four types of journals – nursing-focused journals (38%), followed by medical and nonmedical healthcare journals (21%), psychology stream journals (20%), and business journals (17%).

As shown in Figure 6.2, the studies covered employees working in different types of organizations. There were 57 studies covering public sector employees, 54 studies focusing on the private sector, and 34 studies covering both private and public organizations, which offered

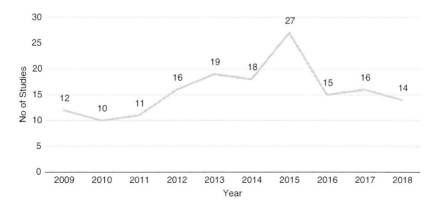

Figure 6.1 Yearly Distribution of Articles Reviewed.

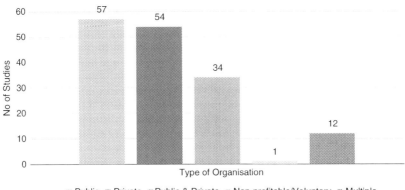

Figure 6.2 Type of Organizations Studied.

comparative insights about factors and consequences of stress. Public organizations included banks, insurance companies, universities, schools, healthcare institutions, the military, law enforcement, and railways. Private sector organizations included airlines, academic institutions, chemical/steel/mining/manufacturing industries, information and technology (IT), private healthcare providers, and automotive firms.

Figure 6.3 presents the percentage breakdown of studies undertaken in various work sectors. Out of the 158 studies, the maximum number of studies was undertaken in the health sector (35 or 22%) where samples consisted of various healthcare professionals like doctors, nurses, midwives, dentists, anesthetists, and pharmacists. The academic sector was the second most researched sector with 28 studies (18%) and included samples from various employee groups like school teachers, college teachers, university lecturers, non-academic staff, and research staff. There was an equal number of studies (n = 21, 13%) covering IT/BPO and law enforcement sectors. Overall 8% of studies (n = 13) had a heterogeneous sample. There were 12 studies (8%) that examined only male samples, 22 studies (14%) that collected only female samples, and the remaining 124 studies (78%) covered both genders in different work settings.

Figure 6.4 highlights that most studies examined (n = 133, 84%) followed a quantitative research approach. Questionnaires were extensively used in these studies. The quantitative analysis ranged from descriptive statistics on the data to more sophisticated analysis techniques like t-test, chi-square test, correlation, regression modeling, and factor analysis through the use of various statistical software. The Organizational Role Stress Scale (Pareek, 1983), Occupational, Stress Index (Srivastava & Singh, 1981), Perceived Stress Scale (Cohen, Kamarck, & Mermelstein,

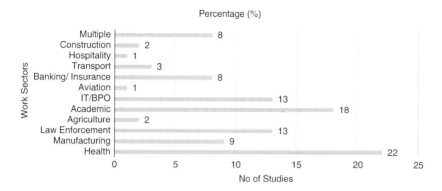

Figure 6.3 Work Sectors Studied.

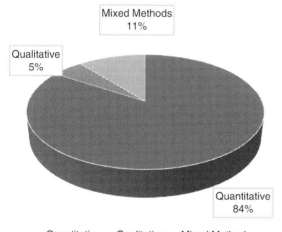

Figure 6.4 Research Methods Used in Studies.

1983), Coping Strategies Scale (Srivastava & Singh, 1988), General Health Questionnaire (Goldberg & Williams, 2000), and Burnout Inventory (Maslach & Jackson, 1981) have been widely used as tools to gather data in many studies. There were eight studies (5%) that adopted a qualitative approach and used methods like observation, interviews, case studies, and focus groups. Understandably, smaller samples were covered by such studies. There were 17 studies (11%) that applied mixed methods.

Stress research has been dominated by cross-sectional studies (Figure 6.5) which reveals a dearth of good longitudinal studies. Out of

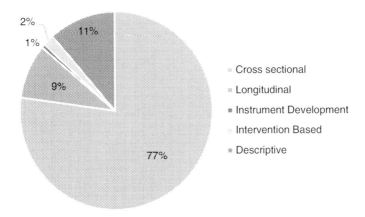

Figure 6.5 Research Methodologies Applied in Studies.

the 158 studies examined, there were only 14 (9%) longitudinal studies compared to 122 (77%) cross-sectional studies. The sample sizes varied in the studies. A maximum number of studies (n = 58, 37%) covered the sample size up to 100. Studies with sample sizes ranging from 101 to 200 were 24% (n = 38), 201 to 300 were 13% (n = 21), 301 to 400 were 6% (n = 10), 401 to 500 were 8% (n = 12), 501 to 1,000 were 9% (n = 14), and 1,001 and above were 3% (n = 5). The range of sample size in qualitative studies was from 9 to 150 employees/workers, whereas the range of sample size for quantitative studies was found to be from 50 to 4,500 employees/workers. Intervention studies were very few.

Thematic Analysis

Causes of Stress in Studies

Most studies covered in the review have not specifically tested any of the popular stress models from international literature. Only one study – Frank, Lambert, and Qureshi (2017) – has explicitly examined the Job Demands-Resources model (Karasek, 1979) in the policing context. Most studies have covered a few job demands, job resources, context, and support-related issues for various occupational groups in different sectors. However, there is much support in Indian literature that job demands are positively related, whereas resources are negatively related to work stress. Job demands are a major stress factor in the Indian context and are associated with higher levels of stress in employees from various occupational groups. Compared to this, job resources and support factors generate lower stress levels. Factors related to the Effort-

Reward Imbalance model (Siegrist,1996) – such as effort, rewards, and organizational justice – are less frequently reported in literature. Most studies in the review have focused on identifying the causes of stress in different occupational groups. The main stressors identified in the reviewed studies are presented in Table 6.1.

Reviewed studies examined different occupational groups like nurses (e.g., Oommen, Wright, & Maijala, 2010; Fernandes & Nirmala, 2015), the police (e.g., Joseph & Nagrajamurthy, 2014), and IT professionals (e.g., Dhar & Dhar, 2010; Kumari, Joshi, & Pandey, 2014; Babu, Sathyanarayana, Ketharam, Kar, & Detels, 2015). Most of these studies found high stress in employees due to various factors; the most common stressors that cut across all of the sectors were heavy workload, inadequate staff, role ambiguity, job control/autonomy, income, work culture, and interpersonal relationships. These studies also highlighted the behavioral, emotional, physical, and psychosomatic symptoms of stress on employees. Problem avoidance, mental disengagement, problem solving/planning, and social support were identified as the main coping strategies in such employees. The results were consistent with international literature.

Studies in healthcare have documented stressors like work overload (Sharma, Davey, Davey, Shukla, Shrivastava, & Bansal 2014; Gandhi, Sahni, Padhy, & Mathew, 2018; Dasgupta & Kumar, 2009), inter-role distance and resource inadequacy (Baba, 2012), low pay (Rajan, 2014), staff shortage (Fernandes & Nirmala, 2015), conflict with patient

Table 6.1 Stressor Identified in Studies

Main Stressors	No. of Studies	Percentage (%)
Factors associated with the role (overload, working hours, unrealistic role expectations, role ambiguity, role conflict, poor work conditions)	46	33
Relevance of the role in the organization (high responsibility/less autonomy, scarce resources)	19	15
Career and monetary aspects (lack of advancement and training opportunities, less or unequal pay, benefits, job insecurity)	23	19
Work relationships (role isolation, poor working relations, lack of social support)	14	11
Organizational factors (conflict, culture, unfair policies, poor communication, lack of transparency)	11	9
Personal issues (conflicting family commitments, work-life balance)	16	13
Total	124	100

relatives (Kane, 2009), staff attitude (Davey, Sharma, Davey, Shukla, Srivastava, & Vyas, 2016), conflict with supervisors and inadequate emotional preparation (Jathanna, Latha, & Prabhu, 2012), time pressure and personal issues (Bhatia, Kishore, Anand, & Jiloha, 2010), criticism, underappreciation and lack of personal time (Sharma et al., 2018), night shifts (Haldar & Sahu, 2015), and an inadequate amount of resources, facilities, and financial support (Purohit & Vasava, 2017) impacted the employees the most.

Studies undertaken on law enforcement personnel identified main stress factors like role ambiguity, role conflict, and role (Frank et al., 2017; Almale, Vankudre, Bansode-Gokhe, & Pawar, 2014), lack of basic amenities, long working hours, and privacy issues (Bora, Chatterjee, Rani, & Chakrabarti, 2016), tough working conditions, physical separation from the family, tight controls, and rigidly stratified hierarchies (Chhabra & Chhabra, 2013), staff shortage, limited time with family, overtime demand, fatigue, and health issues (Parsekar, Singh, & Bhumika, 2015; Kumar & Mohan, 2009), operational and organizational factors (Ragesh, Tharayil, Raj, Philip, & Hamza, 2017), and political pressure, negative public image, and low salary (Joseph & Nagrajamurthy, 2014) are associated with high levels of stress. Female personnel scored higher stress scores than their male counterparts in many of these studies (Suresh, Anantharaman, Angusamy, & Ganesan, 2013; Hunnur, Bagali, & Sudarshan, 2014).

Banking studies observed stress reasons like long working hours, conflict and political pressure (Kishori & Vinothini, 2016), highly intricate nature of the job, the lack of time for family and personal care, insufficient training, career uncertainties, performance constraints/pressures, surveillance required, unwanted criticism, traveling, transfers, and family obligations (Kang & Sandhu, 2012; Yadav & Dabhade, 2013; Neelamegam & Asrafi, 2010; Shukla &Garg, 2013). On the other hand, work stress was also a major concern for highly stressed Indian IT/BPO employees. Role stagnation, inter-role distance, and role erosion (Bhatt & Pathak, 2013), organizational climate, unequal pay, and no work-life balance (Gladies & Kennedy, 2011), relationships with others (Rao & Chandraiah, 2012), and long working hours, work pressure, and erratic working style (Mohan, Balaji, & Kumar, 2016) were some of the reasons of employee stress.

Academic sector studies also found medium to high stress levels in employees. Teachers showed stress due to reasons like high workload, noncooperation from colleagues, insufficient facilities, and unclear expectations from higher authorities (Singh, 2009; Nema, Nagar, & Mandhanya, 2010), unpleasant work conditions, poor quality students, lack of control (Kang & Sidhu, 2015; Aftab & Khatoon, 2015), poor work relationships (Banerjee & Mehta, 2016), location, administrative work and position (Dawn, Talukdar, Bhattacharje, & Singh,

2017), type of school (Hashmi, Hasan, & Khan, 2017), and the lack of organizational justice (Sehgal & Verma, 2017).

Heat stress was identified as an important occupational health risk/stressor in both formal and informal sector organizations. Various studies undertaken in different sectors (Ayyappan, Sankar, Rajkumar, & Balakrishnan, 2009; Lundgren, Kuklane, & Venugopal, 2014, Venugopal, Chinnadurai, Lucas, & Kjellstrom, 2016; Lundgren, Kuklane, & Venugopal 2014; Raval *et al.*, 2018) echo the effect of heat exposure on employees/workers.

Different Variables Explored in Studies

Stress and burnout relationship has been explored in the reviewed studies but was restricted to the health and academic sectors. A clear and positive relationship was established between occupational stress and professional burnout in groups like university teachers (Reddy & Poornima, 2012), cardiologists (Roz, Mondal, Podder, & Raval, 2016), nurses and support staff (Sihag & Bidlan, 2014), and anesthetists and surgeons (Gandhi *et al.*, 2018). These studies found high levels of stress and burnout in these professional groups which are identical to the trends in international literature. Results have also indicated that gender and occupation types have a significant role in determining stress and burnout levels (Bidlan & Sihag, 2014a). There was also an indication that emotional intelligence has a facilitative role in the relationship between stress and burnout (Bidlan & Sihag, 2014b).

Nine studies scrutinized work stress-related coping methods and styles adopted by employees. Most of the studies were in the IT and health sectors. Studies like Jathanna, Latha, and Prabhu (2012), Dhar and Dhar (2010), and Sihag and Bidlan (2014) concluded that employees resorted to healthier modes of coping – like resorting to humor, seeking social support, positive appraisal, and abstaining from using substances/drugs. However, other researchers like Ranta (2009), Bhatt and Pathak (2013), Chandramouleeswaran, Edwin, and Braganza (2014), and Fernandes and Nirmala (2015) established that employees also resorted to unhealthy coping mechanisms like adopting denial or avoidance tactics, mental disengagement, and the use of alcohol. Results also showed similar coping styles were adopted by the same professional groups in different types of organizations (Rao & Chandraiah, 2012), but there were significant differences in the coping styles adopted by different professional groups working in the same organizations (Sihag & Bidlan, 2014). More than one type of coping styles existed within professional groups, like doctors, which embraced avoidance coping, followed by approach coping (Rashid & Talib, 2015), whereas problem avoidance, mental disengagement, and religious coping were followed more by nurses (Fernandes & Nirmala, 2015).

Some studies have explored the relationship between stress and emotional intelligence. The results are mixed because few studies concluded that people with higher emotional intelligence (EI) will have lower occupational stress, and EI competencies can be used to improve physical and psychological health and overall efficiency of employees (Chhabra & Chhabra, 2013; Satija & Khan, 2013; Singh & Sharma, 2012); however, the level of EI and work stress varied significantly across different management ranks (Chhabra & Mohanty, 2013). On the contrary, Krishnakumar and Lalitha (2014) established the presence of high stress in employees with high EI in their study, and Mahmood and Yadav (2017) showed an insignificant relationship between the two variables.

Studies have also found that occupational stress affects the performance of employees in terms of efficiency and productivity. Prasad, Vaidya, and Anil Kumar (2018) suggested that there was a statistically significant association between occupational stress factors – like working hours, job insecurity, and social support – affecting performance. Findings by Singh and Prasad (2018) and Frank *et al.* (2017) showed that stress significantly affected job performance in relation to job demand and expectation, which had a deleterious effect on the physical and physiological health of professionals. Outcomes in the study by Banerjee and Mehta (2016) showed that overall workload, long working hours, negative behavior of the management, and the lack of communication with colleagues lead to work avoidance and job dissatisfaction, which affects performance. Finally, studies by Prasad, Vaidya, and Anil Kumar (2015) and Goswami (2015) found job-related factors like the nature of work, time pressure, insufficient information, lack of career prospects, and job security influenced performance. These results are similar to those found in international literature.

Job satisfaction was also linked to work stress. Davey *et al.* (2016) found job satisfaction linked to stress in government, semi-government, and private school teachers, and Goswami (2015) explained that stress largely increases the level of fear, anger, anxiety, and nervousness among employees and simultaneously reduces the level of job satisfaction – which causes behavioral and physiological consequences. Gandhi, Sangeetha, Ahmed, and Chaturvedi (2014) reported that, in nurses, somatic symptoms are positively correlated with stress perception and are negatively correlated with perceived job satisfaction. They also found that public hospital nurses had higher job satisfaction, which was probably due to higher financial benefits. This finding was surprising and contradicts other Indian studies on nursing. Other studies, like Rajan (2014), established that stress due to inconsistent practices of management leads to job dissatisfaction in employees were a powerful source of stress influencing job satisfaction. Lastly, studies like Madhura, Subramanya, and Balaram (2014), Jacob (2012) and Koshy, Ramesh, Khan, and

Sivaramakrishnan (2011) have observed that high levels of job satisfaction are negatively associated with stress but positively associated with job challenge, work commitment, and empowerment.

A smaller number of studies linked stress with workplace spirituality but the results were contradictory. Papers like Kumar and Kumar (2014) found that health was negatively correlated with stress and positively correlated with workplace spirituality; whereas, Chand and Koul (2012) reported a reduction in stress due to workplace spirituality practices among employees of public and private companies. Doraiswamy and Deshmukh (2015) concluded that workplace spirituality was negatively correlated to stress in nurses, and data analysis in Garg, Garg, and Prakash (2018) revealed that workplace spirituality emerged as the strongest mechanism to cope with job stress in insurance sector employees.

The review included three intervention-based studies that used the pre and post test design and carried out statistical analysis using repeated-measures analysis of variance. Ranta (2009) used multidimensional psychological interventions – like relaxation training, self-management, and mood management techniques – on police personnel to reduce their stress using a control group technique. Findings suggested that the interventions were significant in reducing job stress and enhanced the coping behavior of subjects. A different study on nurses (Sailaxmi & Lalitha, 2015) scrutinized the effect of the stress management program. The data was collected immediately after intervention and four weeks later, revealed that the stress management strategies positively impacted the nurses' stress levels. Lastly, Chitra and Karunanidhi (2018) examined the efficacy of a resilience training program in female police officers. Training included self-awareness, positive attitudes, emotional management, and interpersonal skills. Results revealed that resilience training was effective in enhancing resilience, job satisfaction, and the psychological well-being of female police officers and in reducing occupational stress. There was only one study (Lal & Singh, 2015) that worked on proposing a new stress model known as "a general model of workplace stress." This model proposed six stages of stress – job stressors, job reactions, mental reactions, the need for counseling and help, body reactions, and extreme helplessness.

Main Consequences of Stress in Studies

Several types of stress consequences were reported as presented in Table 6.2. Stress was found to be linked to emotional consequences like depression (Vimala & Madhavi, 2009), burnout (Reddy & Poornima, 2012; Amin, Vankar, Nimbalkar, & Phatak, 2015), and hypertension (Babu, Mahapatra, & Detels, 2013). Behavioral outcomes like smoking/drinking habits and substance abuse (Ragesh et al., 2017), negative attitude toward superiors and work in general (Neelamegam & Asrafi, 2010), diurnal bruxism (Rao, Bhat, & David, 2011), deprivation of general well-being, high absenteeism, and high attrition (Bhatt and Pathak, 2013), reduced levels of satisfaction (Bora et al., 2016; Mishra et al., 2011), loss of productivity (Lundgren et al., 2014), social dysfunction (Davey et al., 2016), and negative effects on personal life (Nema et al., 2010) were observed by various researchers. Physical concerns like work-related musculoskeletal disorder (Sharan & Ajeesh, 2012; Sethi, Sandhu, & Imbanathan, 2011) and other occupational disorders like pain in the neck, shoulder, wrist, and lower back and also eye problems like irritation and burning sensations and bad work postures (Ghosh, Das, & Gangopadhyay, 2010), oral problems (Acharya & Pentapati, 2012), knee pain (Anap, Iyer, & Rao, 2013), high systolic and diastolic blood pressure and heart rate (Das, Ghosh, & Gangopadhyay, 2013), perceived exertion, alertness, and uneven sleep patterns (Haldar & Sahu, 2015) were detected in various employee groups.

Discussion

The review reveals that there has been more concentration of studies in the health and academic sectors. The workforce in other sectors has not been researched as much, so there is less understanding of employees' encounters with stress in these work environments. Some of the less-studied sectors, like the service and manufacturing are key contributors to the Indian economy. Hence, future research should focus on such sector organizations. Researching the unexplored work sectors will generate further insights on stressors, their consequences and coping mechanisms adopted by employees. This will enable organizations to develop specific interventions to manage stress and promote beneficial coping styles in their specific work settings.

This review highlights that most stress research has been concentrated on examining the types of stressors faced by different occupational groups. There has been less focus on exploring the full impact of stress on the mental, physical, emotional, and behavioral state of an individual. It is strongly suggested that future research should focus more attention

Table 6.2 Consequences of Stress

Consequences of Stress	No. of Studies	Percentage (%)
Physical	18	16
Mental	44	37
Emotional	24	21
Behavioral	30	26
Total	116	100

on examining the impact of stressors on the health of employees, as extensively captured in Western literature (Cooper & Quick, 2017). This is not only important for managing and treating stress, but also for preventing stress at the workplace. Another related observation is that there is less research undertaken on the subject of involving the physiological measurement of stress. This review found only 18 (16%) studies that discussed the physiological consequences of stress on workers/employees. Hence, future research should focus on these areas.

International literature has explored issues related to gender differences in experiencing stress, its consequences and coping mechanisms in much depth. However, this review highlights the need for generating more data related to gender differences on stress-related parameters in the Indian context, which is similar to conclusions found in studies like Doble and Supriya (2010), Gaur and Jain (2013), Jain and Osmany (2019), and Tripathy, Tripathy, Gupta and Kar (2020). Further studies should explore issues like the involvement of women in different sectors and professions in the Indian workforce and a comparison of stressors, their consequences, and coping styles in males and females. Based on such data, more informed and beneficial interventions can be designed by organizations.

It has been observed that most of the studies in the Indian context have used quantitative methods over qualitative methods. There has been a debate on the usefulness of both types of methods in conducting stress research. Some researchers have highlighted the importance of qualitative studies in generating insights on the undercurrents related to the concept of stress (Mazzola, Schonfeld, & Spector, 2011; Hasan, Dollard, & Winefield, 2010). However, in recent years, there has been a growing focus on applying a mixed methods strategy (qualitative-quantitative) which is considered as a balanced approach to carry out stress research in international literature. Researchers like Cooper, DeweDewe, and O'Driscoll (2001), Liu, Spector, and Shi (2007, 2008), Skakon, Nielsen, Borg, and Guzman (2010), Barley, Meyerson, and Grodal (2011), and many others have endorsed that both designs can complement each other. We can see the use of the mixed methods strategy as a slow but growing trend in Indian studies. More studies based on mixed methods should be undertaken to eliminate the limitations of qualitative and quantitative methods and produce a more holistic understanding of the stress phenomenon.

This review, as many others carried out in international literature – for example, Lambert and Lambert (2001), Burke (2010), Skakon *et al.* (2010), Mäkikangas, Kinnunen, Feldt, and Schaufeli (2016), and Burman and Goswami (2018) – observes that stress research has been dominated by cross-sectional studies which reveals a dearth of good longitudinal studies in overall literature. Longitudinal studies require more commitment of time, resources, and effort, which may not be realistic for most individual researchers due to the lack of institutional and financial support. Accordingly, future research can focus on developing a larger assortment of longitudinal stress studies as its potential remains underrealized in literature.

This investigation has shown that Western tools of measurement have been extensively used in Indian studies. There was only one study on tool development in the review. It has also been noted that researchers have not actively attempted to revalidate or revise any of the popular scales in the Indian context. It needs to be stressed that these tools were developed years ago and since then, the landscape of work and work environment has changed drastically due to several global trends. Considering contemporary dynamics, most of such tools used for generating data may have become less effective. Thus, there is a critical need for the revision of current scales and the development of new culture-specific, purpose-specific, and well-designed scales that can help capture relevant data and enhance our understanding of the stress phenomenon in the Indian culture and context. This issue has been highlighted in both Indian and international literature (Cooper *et al.*, 2001; Pandey, Gaur, & Pestonjee, 2013; Burman & Goswami, 2018).

Culture has a significant influence on stress research. Aldwin (2004) suggested that culture can affect stress and coping processes in different ways. Several researchers have been able to establish a significant influence of culture on stress-coping (Laungani, 2007; Bhagat *et al.*, 2010; Behera & Hasan, 2018). Most of the stress models, theories, and measures utilized by Indian researchers to study and understand stress have been developed in Western cultures. Such research may not give an accurate and complete understanding of stress-related issues in the Indian context, as the cultural characteristics differ between countries. Though few of these measuring tools have been translated in regional Indian languages and sufficient standardization methods were applied before using them, deriving culture-specific interpretations from the data is challenging for researchers – as highlighted by various studies in literature (Bhagat *et al.*, 2010; Behera & Hasan, 2018). There might be commonalities in work settings due to the globalized nature of the world, but the cultural dimensions within societies can affect the dynamics of the stress-coping process significantly. Future studies should try to work on the development of culture-specific stress models and tools to develop understanding of important cultural characteristics that influence individual and organizational stress process.

In conclusion, work stress was and remains to be an important concern for employees and organizations alike. Research highlights the acknowledgment and awareness of various individual and organizational stressors, which have changed over the years. This knowledge has changed the outlook of organizations toward continuous and effective management of stress to some extent but more needs to be done. Future research in the areas emphasized in the discussion will expand understanding of stress and its implications on different groups of the population, especially in the Indian context. Given the dynamic and complex nature of stress and the ever-changing external environment, it will also enable organizations to become proactive in stress identification, diagnosis, and treatment.

References

Abhyankar, S., & Pujari, U. (2012). Occupational stress and work-life imbalance among industrial employees. *Journal of Psychosocial Research*, 7(1), 17–24.

Acharya, S., & Pentapati, K. C. (2012). Work stress and oral health-related quality of life among Indian information technology workers: An exploratory study. *International Dental Journal*, 62(3), 132–136.

Aftab, M., & Khatoon, T. (2015). Occupational stress and job satisfaction among Indian secondary school teachers. *Cypriot. Journal of Educational Sciences*, 10(2), 94–107.

Ahmad, A. (2017). Prevalence and predictors of occupational stress among quarry workers in rural Rajasthan, India. *Journal of Public Mental Health*, 16(4), 132–143.

Ahmed, A. (2013). Job stressors towards organizational change: A study of textile industries of Northern India. *IOSR Journal of Humanities and Social Science (IOSR-JHSS)*, 16(1), 10–19.

Almale, B. D., Vankudre, A. J., Bansode-Gokhe, S. S., & Pawar, V. K. (2014). An epidemiologic study of occupational stress factors in Mumbai police personnel. *Indian Journal of Occupational and Environmental Medicine*, 18(3), 109.

Aldwin, C. M. (2004, February). Culture, coping and resilience to stress. *Paper presented at the Proceedings of the first international conference on operationalization of gross national happiness*, Thimphu (pp. 563–573). Abstract retrieved from http://www.bhutanstudies.org.bt/gross-national-happiness-and-development/.

Amte, R., Munta, K., & Gopal, P. B. (2015). Stress levels of critical care doctors in India: A national survey. *Indian Journal of Critical Care Medicine: Peer-rEviewed, Official Publication of Indian Society of Critical Care Medicine*, 19(5), 257.

Amin, A. A., Vankar, J. R., Nimbalkar, S. M., & Phatak, A. G. (2015). Perceived stress and professional quality of life in neonatal intensive care unit nurses in Gujarat, India. *The Indian Journal of Pediatrics*, 82(11), 1001–1005.

Anap, D., Iyer, C., & Rao, K. (2013). Work related musculoskeletal disorders among hospital nurses in rural Maharashtra, India: A multi centre survey. *International Journal of Research in Medical Sciences*, 1(2), 101–107.

Ayyappan, R., Sankar, S., Rajkumar, P., & Balakrishnan, K. (2009). Work-related heat stress concerns in automotive industries: A case study from Chennai, India. *Global Health Action*, 2(1), 20.

Baba, I. (2012). Workplace stress among doctors in government hospitals: An empirical study. *ZENITH International Journal of Multidisciplinary Research*, 2(5), 208–220.

Babu, G. R., Mahapatra, T., & Detels, R. (2013). Job stress and hypertension in younger software professionals in India. *Indian Journal of Occupational and Environmental Medicine*, 17(3), 101.

Babu, G. R., Sathyanarayana, T. N., Ketharam, A., Kar, S. B., & Detels, R. (2015). Perceived occupational stressors and the health software professionals in Bengaluru, India. *The Qualitative Report*, 20(3), 314–335.

Balakrishnan, K., Ramalingam, A., Dasu, V., Chinnadurai Stephen, J., Raj Sivaperumal, M., Kumarasamy, D., & Sambandam, S. (2010). Case studies on heat stress related perceptions in different industrial sectors in southern India. *Global Health Action*, 3(1), 5635.

Bano, B., & Talib, P. (2011). Occupational stress among government employees. *Amity Global Business Review*, 6(1), 151–162.

Banerjee, S., & Mehta, P. (2016). Determining the antecedents of job stress and their impact on job performance: A study among faculty members. *IUP Journal of Organizational Behavior*, 15(2), 7–24.

Barley, S. R., Meyerson, D. E., & Grodal, S. (2011). E-mail as a source and symbol of stress. *Organization Science*, 22(4), 887–906.

Batham, C., & Yasobant, S. (2016). A risk assessment study on work-related musculoskeletal disorders among dentists in Bhopal, India. *Indian Journal of Dental Research*, 27(3), 236.

Behera, J., & Hasan, B. (2018). Cultural identity and acculturative stress: A systematic review. *Indian Journal of Health and Wellbeing*, 9(3), 454–458.

Benedict, J. N., Gayatridevi, S., & Velayudhan, A. (2009). Perceived overqualification, job satisfaction, somatization and job stress of MNC executives. *Journal of the Indian Academy of Applied Psychology*, 35(2), 283–289.

Bhagat, R., Krishnan, B., Nelson, T. A., Leonard, K. M., Ford, D. L., & Billing, T. K. (2010). Organizational stress, psychological strain, and work outcomes in six national contexts: A closer look at the moderating influences of coping styles and decision latitude. *Cross-Cultural Management: An International Journal*, 17(1), 10–29.

Bhatt, S., & Pathak, P. (2013). Organizational role stress: A comparison between professionals in IT and ITES Sectors. *South Asian. Journal of Management*, 20(2), 64.

Bhatia, N., Kishore, J., Anand, T., & Jiloha, R. C. (2010). Occupational stress amongst nurses from two tertiary care hospitals in Delhi. *Australasian Medical Journal (Online)*, 3(11), 731.

Bidlan, J. S., & Sihag, A. (2014a). Occupational stress, burnout, coping and emotional intelligence: Exploring gender differences among different occupational groups of healthcare professionals. *Indian Journal of Health & Wellbeing*, 5(3), 299–304.

Bidlan, J. S., & Sihag, A. (2014b). Emotional intelligence among healthcare professionals: Exploring its moderating effect in occupational stress and burnout relationship. *Indian. Journal of Positive Psychology*, 5(1), 37.

Bora, S., Chatterjee, A., Rani, P., & Chakrabarti, D. (2016). On-the-job stress: Interventions to improve the occupational well-being of policewomen in Assam, India. *Journal of International Women's Studies*, 18(1), 260–272.

Borkakoty, A., Baruah, M., & Nath, A. S. (2013). Occupational stress in organizations with special reference to gender, sector and income. *The Clarion-International Multidisciplinary Journal*, 2(1), 64–73.

Burke, R. J. (2010). *Workplace stress and well-being across cultures: Research and practice*. Cross Cultural Management: An International Journal, 17(1), 5–9.

Burman, R., & Goswami, T. G. (2018). A systematic literature review of work stress. *International. Journal of Management Studies*, 5(3), 9.

Chand, P., & Koul, H. (2012). Workplace spirituality, organizational emotional ownership and job satisfaction as moderators in coping with job stress. *Decision Making*, 9(10), 225–229.

Chandra, A., & Sharma, B. R. (2010). *Predictors of occupational stress: An exploratory study*. Indian Journal of Industrial Relations, 46, 300–312.

Chandramouleeswaran, S., Edwin, N. C., & Braganza, D. (2014). Job stress, satisfaction, and coping strategies among medical interns in a South Indian tertiary hospital. *Indian Journal of Psychological Medicine*, 36(3), 308–311.

Chandel, K., & Kaur, R. (2015). Exploring various contributors of work-life balance as a panacea for occupational stress. *Prabandhan: Indian. Journal of Management*, 8(1), 9–20.

Chitra, T., & Karunanidhi, S. (2018). *The impact of resilience training on occupational stress, resilience, job satisfaction, and psychological well-being of female police officers*. Journal of Police and Criminal Psychology, 1–16. Available on https://doi.org/10.1007/s11896-018-9294-9.

Chhabra, M., & Chhabra, B. (2013). Emotional intelligence and occupational stress: A study of Indian Border Security Force personnel. *Police Practice and Research*, 14(5), 355–370.

Chhabra, B., & Mohanty, R. P. (2013). Effect of emotional intelligence on work stress–a study of Indian managers. *International Journal of Indian Culture and Business Management*, 6(3), 300–313.

Cooper, C. L., Dewe, P. J., & O'Driscoll, M. P. (2001). *Organizational stress: A review and critique of theory, research, and applications*. Sage.

Cooper, C., & Quick, J. C. (Eds.). (2017). *The handbook of stress and health: A guide to research and practice*. John Wiley & Sons.

Cohen, S., Kamarck, T., & Mermelstein, R. (1983). A global measure of perceived stress. *Journal of Health and Social Behavior*, 24, 385–396.

Dasgupta, H., & Kumar, S. (2009). Role stress among doctors working in a government hospital in Shimla (India). *European Journal of Social Sciences*, 9(3), 356–370.

Davey, A., Sharma, P., Davey, S., Shukla, A., Srivastava, K., & Vyas, S. (2016). Are the adverse psychiatric outcomes reflection of occupational stress among nurses: An exploratory study. *Asian. Journal of Medical Sciences*, 7(1), 96–100.

Dawn, S., Talukdar, P., Bhattacharje, S., & Singh, O. P. (2017). A study on job related stress among school teachers in different schools of West Bengal, India. *Eastern Journal of Psychiatry*, 19(1), 12–17.

Das, B., Ghosh, T., & Gangopadhyay, S. (2013). Prevalence of musculoskeletal disorders and occupational health problems among groundnut farmers of West Bengal, India. *Journal of Human Ergology*, 42(12), 1–12.

Dey, N. C., Dey, S. C., & Sharma, G. D. (2017). Importance of ergonomic application for the improvement of coal productivity in mines. *Proceedings of the 17th coal operators' conference (pp. 306–313).*

Dey, S. C., Dey, N. C., & Sharma, G. D. (2018). Occupational Malfunctioning and Fatigue Related Work Stress Disorders (FRWSDs): An Emerging Issue in Indian Underground Mine (UGM) Operations. *Journal of the Institution of Engineers (India): Series D*, 99(1), 103–108.

Dhar, R. L., & Dhar, M. (2010). Job stress, coping process and intentions to leave: A study of information technology professionals working in India. *The Social Science Journal*, 47(3), 560–577.

Doraiswamy, I. R., & Deshmukh, M. (2015). Meaningful Work And Role Stress International. *Journal of Management & Organizational Studies*, 4(4), 174–177.

Doble, N., & Supriya, M. V. (2010). Gender differences in the perception of work-life balance. *Managing Global Transitions: International Research Journal*, 8(4), 331–342.

Fernandes, W. N., & Nirmala, R. (2017). Workplace stress and coping strategies among Indian nurses: Literature review. *Asian Journal of Nursing Education and Research*, 7(3), 449–454.

Fernandes, W. N., & Nirmala, R. (2015). Work stress, coping and expectations of nurses. *IOSR Journal of Nursing and Health Science*, 4(5), 49–56.

Fisch, C., & Block, J. (2018). Six tips for your (systematic) literature review in business and management research. *Management Review Quarterly*, 68(3), 103–106.

Frank, J., Lambert, E. G., & Qureshi, H. (2017). Examining police officer work stress using the job demands–resources model. *Journal of Contemporary Criminal Justice*, 33(4), 348–367.

Gandhi, K., Sahni, N., Padhy, S. K., & Mathew, P. J. (2018). Comparison of stress and burnout among anesthesia and surgical residents in a tertiary care teaching hospital in North India. *Journal of Postgraduate Medicine*, 64(3), 145.

Gandhi, S., Sangeetha, G., Ahmed, N., & Chaturvedi, S. K. (2014). Somatic symptoms, perceived stress and perceived job satisfaction among nurses working in an Indian psychiatric hospital. *Asian Journal of Psychiatry*, 12, 77–81.

Garg, N., Garg, N., & Prakash, C. (2018). Workplace spirituality and stress management in Indian insurance industry. *The Journal of Insurance Institute of India* (July–September), 39–44.

Gaan, N. (2008). Stress, social support, job attitudes and job outcome across gender. *ICFAI Journal of Organizational Behavior*, 7(4), 34–44.

Gaur, S. P., & Jain, S. S. (2013). Gender issues in work and stress. In Pandey, S., & Pestonjee, D.M. (Eds.). *Stress and work: Perspectives on understanding and managing stress*(pp. 180–208). New Delhi: Sage Publications.

Ghosh, T., Das, B., & Gangopadhyay, S. (2010). Work-related musculoskeletal disorder: An occupational disorder of the goldsmiths in India. *Indian Journal of Community Medicine: Official Publication of Indian Association of Preventive & Social Medicine*, 35(2), 321–325.

Gladies, J. J., & Kennedy, V. (2011). Impact of organisational climate on job stress for women employees in information technology sector in India. *Asia Pacific Journal of Research in Business Management*, 2(6), 66–76.

Goswami, T. G. (2015). Job stress and its effect on employee performance in banking sector. *Indian Journal of Commerce and Management Studies*, 6(2), 51.

Goldberg, D., & Williams, P. (2000). *General health questionnaire (GHQ)*. Swindon, Wiltshire, UK: nferNelson.

Gupta, B., & Tyagi, A. (2009). Employees' perception of workplace stressors and their attitude towards work and organisation: A study of Indian managers. *International Journal of Indian Culture and Business Management*, 2(6), 686–706.

Harikiran, A., Srinagesh, J., Nagesh, K. S., & Sajudeen, N. (2012). Perceived sources of stress amongst final year dental under graduate students in a dental teaching institution at Bangalore, India: A cross sectional study. *Indian Journal of Dental Research*, 23(3), 331.

Haldar, P., & Sahu, S. (2015). Occupational stress and work efficiency of nursing staff engaged in rotating shift work. *Biological Rhythm Research*, 46(4), 511–522.

Hashmi, K., Hasan, B., & Khan, K. A. (2017). Occupational stress as a function of type of school and gender. *Indian Journal of Positive Psychology*, 8(1), 1.

Hasan, Z., Dollard, M.F., & Winefield, A.H. (2010). Work-family conflict in east vs western countries. *Cross-Cultural Management: An International Journal*, 17(1), 30–49.

Hunnur, R. R., Bagali, M. M., & Sudarshan, S. (2014). Cause and effect of workplace stress among police personnel: An empirical study. *International Journal of Management Research and Business Strategy*, 3, 198–208.

Jain, N., & Osmany, M. (2019). Gender identity, perceived gender discrimination and stress among working professionals. In Prasad, P. M. & Nagar, R. (Eds.). *Law and economics: Market, non-market and network transactions* (p. 67). Vernon Press.

Jacob, D. K. (2012). Occupational stress and job satisfaction among working women in banks. *Paradigm*, *16*(1), 29–38.

Jathanna, P. N. R., Latha, K. S., & Prabhu, S. (2012). Occupational stress and coping among nurses in a super specialty hospital. *Journal of Health Management*, *14*(4), 467–479.

Jayakumar, D. (2017). Occupational stress and hypertension among railway loco pilots and section controllers. *Indian Journal of Occupational and Environmental Medicine*, *21*(1), 23.

Jose, T. T., & Bhat, S. M. (2013). A descriptive study on stress and coping of nurses working in selected hospitals of Udupi and Mangalore districts Karnataka, India. *IOSR Journal of Nursing and Health Science*, *3*(1), 10–18.

Joseph, J. K., & Nagrajamurthy, B. (2014). Stress in police officers. *IOSR Journal of Humanities and Social Science*, *19*(10), 39–40.

Joy, P. J., & Radhakrishnan, R. (2013). A study on occupational stress experienced by tile industry employees in Kannur and Calicut District of Kerala state. *International Journal of Research in Commerce & Management*, *4*(8), 17–19.

Kala, K., Jan, N. A., Subramani, A. K., & Banureka, R. (2017). Upshot of occupational stress on work life balance of employees working in information technology organizations in Chennai. *Prabandhan: Indian. Journal of Management*, *10*(7), 50–59.

Kane, P. P. (2009). Stress causing psychosomatic illness among nurses. *Indian Journal of Occupational and Environmental Medicine*, *13*(1), 28–32.

Kang, L. S., & Sandhu, R. S. (2012). Impact of stress on health: A study of bank branch managers in India. *Global Business Review*, *13*(2), 285–296.

Kang, L. S., & Sidhu, H. (2015). Identification of stressors at work: A study of university teachers in India. *Global Business Review*, *16*(2), 303–320.

Karunanidhi, S., & Chitra, T. (2015). Job attitude in relation to perceived occupational stress, interrole-conflict and psychological well-being of women police. *Indian Journal of Positive Psychology*, *6*(1), 19.

Kashyap, S. P., Kumar, S., & Byadwal, V. (2016). Positive affectivity as a moderator of occupational stress and ill-health. *Indian Journal of Health and Wellbeing*, *7*(1), 121.

Kashyap, S. P., Kumar, S., & Krishna, A. (2014). Role of resilience as a moderator between the relationship of occupational stress and psychological health. *Indian Journal of Health and Wellbeing*, *5*(9), 1023.

Karasek, R. A. (1979). Job demands, job decision latitude, and mental strain: Implications for job redesign. *Administrative Science Quarterly*, *24*, 285–308.

Kishori, B., & Vinothini, B. (2016). A study on work stress among bank employees in State Bank of India with reference to Tiruchirappalli. *IJIRST–International Journal for Innovative Research in Science & Technology*, *2*, 12.

Koshy, R. C., Ramesh, B., Khan, S., & Sivaramakrishnan, A. (2011). Job satisfaction and stress levels among anaesthesiologists of south India. *Indian Journal of Anaesthesia*, *55*(5), 513.

Krishnakumar, R., & Lalitha, S. (2014). A study on emotional intelligence and occupational stress. *International Journal of Multidisciplinary and Current Research*, 2, 21–24.

Kumar, V. K., Kumar, S. P., & Baliga, M. R. (2013). Prevalence of work-related musculoskeletal complaints among dentists in India: A national cross-sectional survey. *Indian Journal of Dental Research*, 24(4), 428.

Kumar, G. R., & Mohan, S. R. (2009). Work stress for traffic police in Chennai city. *Journal of Contemporary Research in Management*, 4(2), 107–115.

Kumar, D., Singh, J. V., & Kharwar, P. S. (2011). Study of occupational stress among railway engine pilots. *Indian Journal of Occupational and Environmental Medicine*, 15(1), 25.

Kumar, V., & Kumar, S. (2014). Workplace spirituality as a moderator in relation between stress and health: An exploratory empirical assessment. *International Review of Psychiatry*, 26(3), 344–351.

Kumar, U., Parkash, V., & Mandal, M. K. (2013). Stress in extreme conditions: A military perspective. In Pestonjee, M. & Pandey, S.(Eds.). *Stress and work: Perspectives on understanding and managing stress* (pp. 101–126). New Delhi, India: Sage.

Kumar, V., & Kamalanabhan, T. J. (2017). Moderating role of work support in stressor–burnout relationship: An empirical investigation among police personnel in India. *Psychological Studies*, 62(1), 85–97.

Kumar, V., & Kamalanabhan, T. J. (2017). Stress and health among the Indian police. In Hyde, M. (Ed.). *Work and health in India* (pp. 153–176). Bristol, UK; Chicago, IL, USA: Bristol University Press.

Kumari, G., Joshi, G., & Pandey, K. (2014). Job stress in software companies: A case study of HCL Bangalore, India. *Global Journal of Computer Science and Technology*, 14(7).

Lal, R. S., & Singh, A. P. (2015). Employee's work stress: Review and presenting a comprehensive model. *Journal of Psychosocial Research*, 10(2), 409.

Laungani, P. D. (2007). *Uogynderstanding cross-cultural psychol*. New Delhi: SAGE (South Asia).

Lambert, V. A., & Lambert, C. E. (2001). Literature review of role stress/strain on nurses: An international perspective. *Nursing & Health Sciences*, 3(3), 161–172.

Liu, C., Spector, P. E., & Shi, L. (2007). Cross-national job stress: A quantitative and qualitative study. *Journal of Organizational Behavior: The International Journal of Industrial, Occupational and Organizational Psychology and Behavior*, 28(2), 209–239.

Liu, C., Spector, P. E., & Shi, L. (2008). Use of both qualitative and quantitative approaches to study job stress in different gender and occupational groups. *Journal of Occupational Health Psychology*, 13(4), 357.

Lundgren, K., Kuklane, K., & Venugopal, V. (2014). Occupational heat stress and associated productivity loss estimation using the PHS model (ISO 7933): A case study from workplaces in Chennai, India. *Global Health Action*, 7(1), 25283.

Mahmood, A., & Yadav, L. K. (2017). Occupational Stress, Emotional Intelligence and Demography: A study among working professionals. *International Journal of Business Insights & Transformation*, 10(2), 72–79.

Maslach, C., & Jackson, S. E. (1981). The measurement of experienced burnout. *Journal of Organizational Behavior*, 2(2), 99–113.

Manjunatha, M. K., & Renukamurthy, T. P. (2017). Stress among banking employee – A literature review. *International Journal of Research - GRANTHAALAYAH*, 5(1), 206–213.

Madhura, S., Subramanya, P., & Balaram, P. (2014). Job satisfaction, job stress and psychosomatic health problems in software professionals in India. *Indian Journal of Occupational and Environmental Medicine*, 18(3), 153.

Malamardi, S. N., Kamath, R., Tiwari, R., Nair, B. V. S., Chandrasekaran, V., & Phadnis, S. (2015). Occupational stress and health-related quality of life among public sector bank employees: A cross-sectional study in Mysore, Karnataka, India. *Indian Journal of Occupational and Environmental Medicine*, 19(3), 134.

Mazzola, J. J., Schonfeld, I. S., & Spector, P. E. (2011). What qualitative research has taught us about occupational stress. *Stress and Health*, 27(2), 93–110.

Mäkikangas, A., Kinnunen, U., Feldt, T., & Schaufeli, W. (2016). The longitudinal development of employee well-being: A systematic review. *Work & Stress*, 30(1), 46–70.

Mishra, B., Mehta, S. C., Sinha, N. D., Shukla, S. K., Ahmed, N., & Kawatra, A. (2011). Evaluation of work place stress in health university workers: A study from rural India. *Indian Journal of Community Medicine: Official Publication of Indian Association of Preventive & Social. Medicine*, 36(1), 39.

Mitra, S., Sarkar, A. P., Haldar, D., Saren, A. B., Lo, S., & Sarkar, G. N. (2018). Correlation among perceived stress, emotional intelligence, and burnout of resident doctors in a medical college of West Bengal: A mediation analysis. *Indian Journal of Public Health*, 62(1), 27.

Modekurti-Mahato, M., Kumar, P., & Raju, P. G. (2014). Impact of emotional labor on organizational role stress–a study in the services sector in India. *Procedia Economics and Finance*, 11(14), 110–121.

Moom, R. K., Sing, L. P., & Moom, N. (2015). Prevalence of musculoskeletal disorder among computer bank office employees in Punjab (India): A case study. *Procedia Manufacturing*, 3, 6624–6631.

Mohanty, S. P. (2017). Organizational role stress of secondary school teachers with reference to gender and management. *Journal on School Educational Technology*, 13(2), 14–19.

Mohanraj, C., & Natesan, M. (2015). Stress and job satisfaction: An empirical study among the women police constables in Coimbatore, Tamil Nadu, India. *International Journal of Interdisciplinary and Multidisciplinary Studies (IJIMS)*, 2(5), 153–157.

Mohan, D. A. C., Balaji, K. D., & Kumar, T. K. (2016). An empirical study on stress levels among software professionals in the city of Chennai, India. *Abhinav Journal of Research in Commerce and Management*, 2(5), 33–40.

Nema, G., Nagar, D., & Mandhanya, Y. (2010). *A study on the causes of work related stress among the college teachers*. Pacific Business Review International, 3(2), 1–7.

Neelamegam, R., & Asrafi, S. (2010). Work stress among employees of Dindigul

district central cooperative bank, Tamil Nadu: A study. *IUP Journal of Management Research, 9*(5), 57.
Nidhikakkar, D., & Jyothi, M. A. (2013). Stress among women lecturer working in government and private college – A comparative study. *Advanced International Journal on Teachers Education, 1*, 11.
National Statistical Office. (2019). *Periodic Labour Force Survey (PLFS) – Annual report, July 2017 –June 2018, unit-level records*, Ministry of Statistics and Programme Implementation, Government of India, May 2019, New Delhi.
NSSO. (2014). *Employment and unemployment in India, 2011–2012, NSS 68th round—Key indicators of employment–unemployment in India, 2011–2012* (Report No. 554). New Delhi: Ministry of Statistics and Programme Implementation, Government of India.
OECD (2017). Beyond Shifting Wealth: Perspectives on Development Risks and Opportunities from the Global South. https://doi.org/10.1787/9789264273153-en.
Onkari, D., & Itagi, S. (2018). Occupational stress of women police. *Indian Journal of Health & Wellbeing, 9*(1), 38–42.
Oommen, H., Wright, M., & Maijala, H. (2010). Stress-promoting and stress-relieving factors among nurses in rural India: A case study. *Diversity in Health & Care, 7*(3), 189–200.
Padmini, D., & Venmathi, A. (2012). Unsafe work environment in garment industries, Tirupur, India. *Journal of Environmental Research And Development, 7*, 569–575.
Parsekar, S. S., Singh, M. M., & Bhumika, T. V. (2015). Occupation-related psychological distress among police constables of Udupi taluk, Karnataka: A cross-sectional study. *Indian Journal of Occupational and Environmental Medicine, 19*(2), 80.
Pandey, S., Gaur, S. P., & Pestonjee, D.M. (2013). Methodological issues in stress research: Challenges, concerns, and directions (p. 323). In Pandey, S., &Pestonjee, D.M. (Eds.). *Stress and work: Perspectives on understanding and managing stress.* New Delhi: Sage Publications.
Pareek, U. (1983). Organizational roles stress. In L.D. Goodstein & J.W. Pfeiffer (Eds.), *The 1983 Annual* (pp. 115–123). San Diego: California: University Associates.
Prasad, K. D. V., Vaidya, R., & Anil Kumar, V. (2015). A study on causes of stress among the employees and its effect on the employee performance at the workplace in an International Agricultural Research Institute, Hyderabad, Telangana, India. *International Journal of Management Research and Business Strategy, 4*(4), 68–82.
Prasad, K. D. V., Vaidya, R., & Anil Kumar, V. (2018). Association among occupational stress factors and performance at workplace among agricultural research sector employees at hyderabad, India. *Pacific Business Review International (TSI), 10*(7), 27–36.
Purohit, B., & Vasava, P. (2017). Role stress among auxiliary nurses midwives in Gujarat, India. *BMC Health Services Research, 17*(1), 69.
Ramesh, A. S., & Madhavi, C. (2009). Occupational stress among farming people. *Journal of Agriculture Sciences, 4*(3), 115–125.

Raval, A., Dutta, P., Tiwari, A., Ganguly, P. S., Sathish, L. M., Mavalankar, D., & Hess, J. (2018). Effects of occupational heat exposure on traffic police workers in Ahmedabad, Gujarat. *Indian Journal of Occupational and Environmental Medicine*, 22(3), 144.

Ragesh, G., Tharayil, H. M., Raj, M. T., Philip, M., & Hamza, A. (2017). Occupational stress among police personnel in India. *Open Journal of Psychiatry & Alled Sciencesi*, 8(2), 148–152.

Rajan, D. (2014). Work stress among pharmacists: A comparative analysis. *Global Management Review*, 8(2), 1–18.

Rajan, P., & Bellare, B. (2011). Work related stress and its anticipated solutions among post-graduate medical resident doctors: A cross-sectional survey conducted at a tertiary municipal hospital in Mumbai, India. *Indian Journal of Medical Sciences*, 65(3), 100.

Rao, S., & Ramesh, N. (2015). Depression, anxiety and stress levels in industrial workers: A pilot study in Bangalore, India. *Industrial Psychiatry Journal*, 24(1), 23.

Rao, S. K., Bhat, M., & David, J. (2011). *Work, stress, and diurnal bruxism: A pilot study among information technology professionals in Bangalore City, India*. International Journal of Dentistry, 2011, 650489. 10.1155/2011/650489.

Rashid, I., & Talib, P. (2013). Modelling a relationship between role stress and locus of control. *The Indian Journal Relations*, 48(4), 726–738.

Rashid, I., & Talib, P. (2015). Occupational stress and coping styles among doctors: Role of demographic and environment variables. *Vision*, 19(3), 263–275.

Rajeswari, M. B., & Chalam, G. V. (2018). A Review of Literature on Stress in Police Personnel. *Journal of Business and Management (IOSR-JBM)*, 20(7), 52–56.

Ravi, R., Gunjawate, D., & Ayas, M. (2015). Audiology occupational stress experienced by audiologists practicing in India. *International Journal of Audiology*, 54(2), 131–135.

Ranta, R. S. (2009). Management of stress and coping behaviour of police personnel through Indian psychological techniques. *Journal of the Indian Academy of Applied Psychology*, 35(1), 47–53.

Rashman, L., Withers, E., & Hartley, J. (2009). Organizational learning and knowledge in public service organizations: A systematic review of the literature. *International Journal of Management Reviews*, 11(4), 463–494.

Rao, J. V., & Chandraiah, K. (2012). Occupational stress, mental health and coping among information technology professionals. *Indian Journal of Occupational and Environmental Medicine*, 16(1), 22.

Reddy, G. L., & Poornima, R. (2012). Occupational stress and professional burnout of University teachers in South India. *International Journal of Educational Planning & Administration*, 2(2), 109–124.

Roz, H. K. B., Mondal, S., Podder, P., & Raval, D. T. (2016). A study on occupational stress and burnout among cardiologists: A cross-cultural perspective. *Indian Journal of Health & Wellbeing*, 7(3), 282–288.

Satija, S., & Khan, W. (2013). Emotional Intelligence as Predictor of

Occupational Stress among Working Professionals. *Aweshkar Research Journal*, *15*(1), 79–97.

Saran, S. & Sharan, V. (2018). The future of the Indian workforce: A new approach for the new economy, ORF occasional paper, March 2018. https://www.orfonline.org/research/the-future-of-the-indian-workforce-a-new-approach-for-the-new-economy/.

Saini, R., Kaur, S., & Das, K. (2016). Stress, stress reactions, job stressors and coping among nurses working in intensive care units and general wards of a tertiary care hospital: A comparative study. *Journal of Postgraduate Medicine, Education and Research*, *50*(1), 9–17.

Sailaxmi, G., & Lalitha, K. (2015). Impact of a stress management program on stress perception of nurses working with psychiatric patients. *Asian Journal of Psychiatry*, *14*, 42–45.

Sayeed, O. B., & Kumar, S. C. (2010). Role, work perception & stress in a high reliability work environment. *Indian Journal of Industrial Relations*, *46*(2), 287–299.

Sagar, R., Dandona, R., Gururaj, G., Dhaliwal, R. S., Singh, A., Ferrari, A., & Kumar, G. A. (2020). The burden of mental disorders across the states of India: The Global Burden of Disease Study 1990–2017. *The Lancet. Psychiatry*, *7*(2), 148–161.

Sehgal, M., & Verma, J. (2017). A study of perception of organizational justice in relation to organizational commitment and occupational stress in female school teachers. *Journal of Psychosocial Research*, *12*(2), 521–529.

Sethi, J., Sandhu, J. S., & Imbanathan, V. (2011). Effect of body mass index on work related musculoskeletal discomfort and occupational stress of computer workers in a developed ergonomic setup. *Sports Medicine, Arthroscopy, Rehabilitation, Therapy &. Technology*, *3*(1), 22.

Selokar, D., Nimbarte, S., Ahana, S., Gaidhane, A., & Wagh, V. (2011). Occupational stress among police personnel of Wardha city, India. *Australas Medical Journal*, *4*(11), 4–7.

Shirotriya, A. K., & Quraishi, M. I. (2015). Reliability, validity and factorial structure of the occupational stress scale for physical education teachers. *Medicina Sportiva: Journal of Romanian Sports Medicine Society*, *11*(3), 2609.

Sharma, S. (2015). Do demographic variables affect the stress levels of Indian soldiers? *Vision*, *19*(4), 324–335.

Sharma, N., Takkar, P., Purkayastha, A., Jaiswal, P., Taneja, S., Lohia, N., & Augustine, A. R. (2018). Occupational stress in the Indian army oncology nursing workforce: A cross-sectional study. *Asia-Pacific Journal of Oncology Nursing*, *5*(2), 237.

Sharma, M., & Kaur, G. (2013). Occupational self-efficiency and procrastination as predictors of occupational stress among female lecturers. *Journal of Psychosocial Research*, *8*(2), 275–285.

Sharma, E. (2015). A study of the factors that cause occupational stress among blue-collar employees. *IUP Journal of Organizational Behavior*, *14*(4), 52.

Sharma, P., Davey, A., Davey, S., Shukla, A., Shrivastava, K., & Bansal, R. (2014). Occupational stress among staff nurses: Controlling the risk to health. *Indian Journal of Occupational and Environmental Medicine*, 18(2), 52.

Shukla, H., & Garg, R. (2013). A study on stress management among the employees of nationalised banks. *Voice of Research*, 2(3), 72–75.

Sharan, D., & Ajeesh, P. S. (2012). Effect of ergonomic and workstyle risk factors on work related musculoskeletal disorders among IT professionals in India. *Work*, 41(Supplement 1), 2872–2875.

Shiji, P., Sequera, S., & Mathew, S. (2016). Perceived stress and coping strategies among the married staff nurses working in ward setting of selected hospitals in Mangalore, India. *Muller Journal of Medical Sciences and Research*, 7(1), 84–84.

Shivendra, D., & Kumar, M. M. (2016). A study of job satisfaction and job stress among physical education teachers working in government, semi-government and private schools. *International Journal of Sports Sciences & Fitness*, 6(1), 89–99.

Sivan, M. S., & Sathyamoorthy, K. (2014). Management of occupational stress and work life balance among women managers in Indian Industries – A contemporary issue. *Indian Journal of Applied Research*, 4(12), 144–146.

Singh, M. (2009). Factors causing occupational stress among senior secondary school teachers of Amritsar District. *Journal of Physical Education & Sport/Citius Altius Fortius*, 25(4), 100–104.

Singh, S., & Sharma, T. (2017). Affect of Adversity Quotient on the occupational stress of IT managers in India. *Procedia Computer Science*, 122, 86–93.

Singh, P., & Rani, S. (2015). Work stress among college teachers in self-financing college: An explorative study. *International Journal of Innovations in Engineering and Teaching*, 5(2), 443–448.

Singh, V., & Prasad, H. N. (2018). Impact of stress on the work performance of professional library employees: A study of selected Indian University Libraries. *International Journal of Information Library and Society*, 7 (2), 82–93.

Singh, N., & Srivastava, D. R. (2018). A study on qualification as a factor effecting stress on faculties of private universities in the state of Uttar Pradesh, India. *Pacific Business Review International*, 10(9), 145–153.

Singh, Y., & Sharma, R. (2012). Relationship between general intelligence, emotional intelligence, stress levels and stress reactivity. *Annals of Neurosciences*, 19(3), 107.

Singh, A. P. (2017). Coping with work stress in police employees. *Journal of Police and Criminal Psychology*, 32(3), 225–235.

Sihag, A., & Bidlan, J. S. (2014). Coping with occupational stress and burnout in healthcare. *Indian Journal of Positive Psychology*, 5(3), 325.

Siegrist, J. (1996). Adverse health effects of high-effort/low-reward conditions. *Journal of Occupational Health Psychology*, 1, 27–41. doi:10.1037/1076-8998.1.1.27.

Siegrist, J., Starke, D., Chandola, T., Godin, I., Marmot, M., Niedhammer, I., & Peter, R. (2004). The measurement of effort-reward imbalance at work:

European comparisons. *Social Science. Medicine*, 58, 1483–1499. doi:10.1016/s0277-9536(03)00351-4.

Skakon, J., Nielsen, K., Borg, V., & Guzman, J. (2010). Are leaders' well-being, behaviours and style associated with the affective well-being of their employees? A systematic review of three decades of research. *Work & Stress*, 24(2), 107–139.

Srivastava, A. K., & Singh, A. P. (1981). *Construction and standardization of an occupational stress index: A pilot study*. Indian Journal of Clinical Psychology, 8, 133–136.

Stanley, S., Buvaneswari, G. M., & Arumugam, M. (2018). *Resilience as a moderator of stress and burnout: A study of women social workers in India*. International Social Work. Epub ahead of print 23 October. 10.1177/0020872818804298.

Srivastava, A. K., & Singh, H. S. (1988). Modifying effects of coping strategies on the relation of organizational role stress and mental health. *Psychological Reports*, 62(3), 1007–1009.

Suri, S., & Arora, N. (2009). Work culture and occupational stress in Indian organisations. *ASBM. Journal of Management*, 2(1), 80.

Suresh, R. S., Anantharaman, R.N., Angusamy, A., & Ganesan, J. (2013). Sources of job stress in police work in a developing country. *International Journal of Business and Management*, 8(13), 102–110.

Suarez-Barraza, M. F., Smith, T., & Dahlgaard-Park, S. M. (2012). Lean Service: A literature analysis and classification. *Total Quality Management*, 23(4), 359–380.

Tabassum, S. (2013). *Occupational stress among employees of public and private insurance sector: A comparative study*. Amity Global Business Review, 8, 80–91.

Tabassum, S. (2012). A study of stress among employees in public and private insurance sector in Aligarh – A comparative study of LIC and ICICI Prudential. *Amity Global Business Review*, 7, 68–75.

2019 The burden of mental disorders across the states of India: The Global Burden of Disease Study 1990–2017. Published: December 20, 2019. Published Online December 23, 2019. https://doi.org/10.1016/S2215-0366(19)30475-4.

Tranfield, D., Denyer, D., & Smart, P. (2003). Towards a methodology for developing evidence-informed management knowledge by means of systematic review. *British Journal of Management*, 14(3), 207–222.

Venugopal, V., Chinnadurai, J. S., Lucas, R. A., & Kjellstrom, T. (2016). Occupational heat stress profiles in selected workplaces in India. *International Journal of Environmental Research and Public Health*, 13(1), 89.

Vijayadurai, D. J., & Venkatesh, S. (2012). A study on stress management among women college teachers in Tamil Nadu, India. *Pacific Business Review International*, 5(2), 50–61.

Vimala, B., & Madhavi, C. (2009). A study on stress and depression experienced by women IT professionals in Chennai, India. *Psychology Research and Behavior Management*, 2, 81.

World Economic Forum. (2018). As a rising global power, what is India's vision for the world? https://www.weforum.org/agenda/2018/08/what-is-indias-vision-for-the-world-modi/.

Yadav, R. K., & Dabhade, N. (2013). Work-life balance amongst the working women in public sector banks-A case study of State Bank of India. *International Letters of Social and Humanistic Sciences*, 7(1), 1–22.

Zaheer, A., Islam, J. U., & Darakhshan, N. (2016). Occupational stress and work-life balance: A study of female faculties of central universities in Delhi, India. *Journal of Human Resource Management*, 4(1), 1–5.

APPENDIX Table: Summary of studies reviewed

Work Stress 109

Year	Authors	Methodology	Design	Sample	Sample Size	Sector	Type of Organisation	Male/Female
2009	Dasgupta, H. and Kumar, S.	Quantitative	Cross-sectional	Doctors and nurses	150	Health	Public	Both
2009	Kane, P.P.	Quantitative	Cross-sectional	Nurses	106	Health	Public	Both
2009	Ayyappan, R., Sankar, S., Rajkumar, P. & Balakrishnan, K.	Quantitative	Longitudinal	Automotive, glass, and textile workers	3300	Manufacturing	Private	Both
2009	Kumar, G.R., & Mohan, S.R.	Quantitative	Cross-sectional	Traffic police officers	100	Law Enforcement	Public	Both
2009	Ramesh, A. S., & Madhavi, C.	Quantitative	Cross-sectional	Farmers	200	Agriculture	Public	Both
2009	Suri, S., & Arora, N.	Quantitative	Cross-sectional	Managers	80	Multiple	Multiple	Both
2009	Benedict, J. N., Gayatridevi, S., & Velayudhan, A.	Quantitative	Cross-sectional	Employees	52	Multiple	Private	Both
2009	Gupta, B., & Tyagi, A.	Quantitative	Cross-sectional	Managers	221	Multiple	Private	Both
2009	Scott, J., Evans, D., & Verma, A.	Quantitative	Cross-sectional	Police personnel	1300	Law Enforcement	Public	Both
2009	Singh, M.	Quantitative	Cross-sectional	School teachers	100	Academic	Multiple	Both

(Continued)

Year	Authors	Methodology	Design	Sample	Sample Size	Sector	Type of Organisation	Male/Female
2009	Ranta, R. S.	Quantitative	Cross-sectional	Police personnel	280	Law Enforcement	Public	Male
2009	Vimala, B., & Madhavi, C.	Quantitative	Cross-sectional	IT employees	500	IT/BPO	Private	Female
2010	Bhatt, S., & Pathak, P.	Quantitative	Cross-sectional	IT employees	241	IT/BPO	Private	Both
2010	Chandra, A., & Sharma, B. R.	Quantitative	Cross-sectional	Managers	53	Manufacturing	Public	Both
2010	Sayeed, O. B., & Kumar, S. C	Quantitative	Cross-sectional	Air traffic controllers	52	Aviation	Public	Both
2010	Nema, G., Nagar, D., & Mandhanya, Y.	Quantitative	Cross-sectional	College teachers	50	Academic	Private	Both
2010	Dhar, R. L., & Dhar, M.	Qualitative	Cross-sectional	IT employees	26	IT/BPO	Private	Both
2010	Bhatia N, Kishore J, Anand T, Jiloha RC.	Quantitative	Cross-sectional	Nurses	87	Health	Public	Both
2010	Neelamegam, R.; Asrafi, S.	Quantitative	Cross-sectional	Cooperative bank employees	74	Banking/Insurance	Non-profitable/Voluntary	Both
2010	Oommen, H., Wright, M., & Maijala, H.	Qualitative	Longitudinal	Nurses	9	Health	Public	Female

(Continued)

Work Stress 111

Year	Authors	Methodology	Design	Sample	Sample Size	Sector	Type of Organisation	Male/Female
2010	Balakrishnan, K., Ramalingam, A., Dasu, V., Chinnadurai Stephen, J., Raj Sivaperumal, M., Kumarasamy, D.,... & Sambandam, S.	Mixed Methods	Cross-sectional	Manufacturing employees	242	Manufacturing	Public & Private	Both
2010	Ghosh, T; Das, B; Gangopadhyay, S.	Quantitative	Cross-sectional	Goldsmiths	120	Manufacturing	Private	Male
2011	Rajan, P., & Bellare, B.	Quantitative	Cross-sectional	Doctors	71	Health	Private	Female
2011	Rao, S.K., Bhat, M., and David, J.	Mixed Methods	Cross-sectional	IT employees	147	IT/BPO	Private	Both
2011	Sethi, J., Sandhu, J. S., & Imbanathan, V.	Quantitative	Cross-sectional	BPO employees	100	IT/BPO	Private	Both
2011	Selokar, D., Nimbarte, S., Ahana, S., Gaidhane, A., Wagh, V.	Quantitative	Cross-sectional	Police personnel	102	Law Enforcement	Public	Both

(Continued)

Year	Authors	Methodology	Design	Sample	Sample Size	Sector	Type of Organisation	Male/Female
2011	Mishra, B., Mehta, S.C., Sinha, N., Shukla, S. K., & Ahmed, N.	Quantitative	Cross-sectional	University employees	406	Academic	Public	Both
2011	Bano, B., & Talib, P.	Quantitative	Cross-sectional	Government Employees	35	Multiple	Multiple	Both
2011	Sharan, D., Parijat, P., Sasidharan, A. P., Ranganathan, R., Mohandoss, M., & Jose, J.	Quantitative	Longitudinal	IT employees	4500	IT/BPO	Private	Both
2011	Koshy, R. C., Ramesh, B., Khan, S., & Sivaramakrishnan, A.	Quantitative	Cross-sectional	Anaesthesiologists	115	Health	Public & Private	Both
2011	Gladies, J. J., Kennedy, V.	Quantitative	Cross-sectional	IT employees	450	IT/BPO	Private	Female
2011	Kumar, D., Singh, J. V., & Kharwar, P. S.	Quantitative	Cross-sectional	Railway employees	185	Transport	Public	Both

(*Continued*)

Year	Authors	Methodology	Design	Sample	Sample Size	Sector	Type of Organisation	Male/Female
2011	Kumari, G., & Pandey, K. M.	Quantitative	Cross-sectional	Steelworkers	100	Manufacturing	Public & Private	Both
2012	Kumar, K, S. & Madhu, G.	Quantitative	Cross-sectional	Workers	860	Manufacturing	Public & Private	Both
2012	Reddy, G, L. and Poornima, R.	Quantitative	Longitudinal	University teachers	955	Academic	Public & Private	Both
2012	Sett, M and Sahu, S.	Mixed Methods	Cross-sectional	Jute mill workers	219	Manufacturing	Public	Male
2012	Vijayadurai, J and Venkatesh, S	Quantitative	Cross-sectional	College teachers	50	Academic	Private	Female
2012	Abhyankar, S., & Pujari, U.	Mixed Methods	Cross-sectional	Employees	210	Manufacturing	Private	Both
2012	Kumar, K, S. & Madhu, G.	Quantitative	Cross-sectional	Chemical industry workers	860	Manufacturing	Public	Both
2012	Acharya, S. &Pentapati KC,	Quantitative	Cross-sectional	IT employees	134	IT/BPO	Public & Private	Both
2012	Rao, J.V. & Chandraiah, K.	Quantitative	Cross-sectional	IT employees	200	IT/BPO	Public & Private	Both
2012	Sharan,D. & Ajeesh, A.P.	Quantitative	Cross-sectional	IT employees	200	IT/BPO	Private	Both
2012	Jacob, D. K.	Quantitative	Cross-sectional	Banking employees	100	Banking/Insurance	Public & Private	Both

(Continued)

Year	Authors	Methodology	Design	Sample	Sample Size	Sector	Type of Organisation	Male/ Female
2012	Lakshmi, K.S., Ramachandran, T. & Boohene, D.	Quantitative	Cross-sectional	Nurses	200	Health	Public & Private	Female
2012	Tabassum, S.	Quantitative	Cross-sectional	Insurance employees	100	Banking/ Insurance	Public & Private	Both
2012	Kang, L. S., & Sandhu, R. S.	Quantitative	Cross-sectional	Bank managers	316	Banking/ Insurance	Public & Private	Both
2012	Jathanna, P. N. R., Latha, K. S., & Prabhu, S.	Quantitative	Cross-sectional	Nurses	329	Health	Private	Both
2012	Baba, I.	Quantitative	Cross-sectional	Doctors	73	Health	Public	Both
2012	Rao, J. V., & Chandraiah, K.	Quantitative	Cross-sectional	IT employees	180	IT/BPO	Private	Male
2013	Das, B., Ghosh, T., & Gangopadhyay, S.	Mixed Methods	Cross-sectional	Farmers	170	Agriculture	Public	Male
2013	Sharma, M., & Kaur, G.	Quantitative	Cross-sectional	Lecturers	120	Academic	Public & Private	Female
2013	Babu, G. R., Mahapatra, T., & Detels, R.	Mixed Methods	Cross-sectional	IT employees	1071	IT/BPO	Private	Both

(Continued)

Year	Authors	Methodology	Design	Sample	Sample Size	Sector	Type of Organisation	Male/Female
2013	Joy P, J. I. N. S., & Radhakrishnan, R.	Quantitative	Cross-sectional	Tile industry worker	200	Manufacturing	Private	Male
2013	Bhatt, S., & Pathak, P.	Quantitative	Cross-sectional	BPO employees	234	IT/BPO	Private	Both
2013	Borkakoty, A., Baruah, M., & Nath, A. S.	Quantitative	Cross-sectional	Employees	100	Multiple	Multiple	Both
2013	Jose, T. T., & Bhat, S. M.	Quantitative	Cross-sectional	Nurses	200	Health	Public & Private	Both
2013	Chhabra, B & Mohanty, R.P.	Quantitative	Cross-sectional	Managers	103	Multiple	Private	Both
2013	Rashid, I., & Talib, P	Quantitative	Longitudinal	Doctors	176	Health	Public	Both
2013	Tabassum, S.	Quantitative	Cross-sectional	Insurance employees	100	Banking/Insurance	Public & Private	Both
2013	Nidhikakkar, A and Jyothi, A.	Quantitative	Cross-sectional	Lecturers	100	Academic	Public & Private	Female
2013	Shukla, H. and Garg, R.	Quantitative	Cross-sectional	Bank employees	50	Banking/Insurance	Public	Both
2013	Anap, D., Iyer, C. and Rao, K.	Quantitative	Cross-sectional	Nurses	228	Health	Public & Private	Female
2013	Satija, S., & Khan, W.	Quantitative	Cross-sectional	Working Professional	150	Multiple	Multiple	Both

(Continued)

Year	Authors	Methodology	Design	Sample	Sample Size	Sector	Type of Organisation	Male/Female
2013	Kumar, V. K., Kumar, S. P., & Baliga, M. R.	Quantitative	Longitudinal	Dentists	646	Health	Public & Private	Both
2013	Ahmed, A.	Quantitative	Cross-sectional	Textile workers	450	Manufacturing	Public	Both
2013	Chhabra, M., & Chhabra, B.	Quantitative	Cross-sectional	BSF personnel	161	Law Enforcement	Public	Male
2013	Rathi, N., Bhatnagar, D., & Mishra, S.K.	Quantitative	Cross-sectional	Hotel employees	204	Hospitality	Private	Both
2013	Yadav, R. K., & Dabhade, N.	Quantitative	Cross-sectional	Bank employees	100	Banking/Insurance	Public	Female
2014	Kumar, V., & Kumar, S.	Quantitative	Cross-sectional	Bank employees	150	Banking/Insurance	Public & Private	Both
2014	Chandramouleeswaran, S., Natasha C Edwin, N,C., and Braganza, D.	Quantitative	Cross-sectional	Doctors	93	Health	Public	Both
2014	Jolly, L.	Quantitative	Cross-sectional	College teachers	30	Academic	Private	Both
2014	Rajan, D.	Mixed Methods	Cross-sectional	Nurses	120	Health	Private	Female

(Continued)

Year	Authors	Methodology	Design	Sample	Sample Size	Sector	Type of Organisation	Male/Female
2014	Joseph, J.K. and Nagarajamurthy, B.	Qualitative	Cross-sectional	Police officers	118	Law Enforcement	Public	Both
2014	Modekurti-Mahato, M., Kumar, P., & Raju, P. G.	Quantitative	Longitudinal	Employees	411	Multiple	Public & Private	Both
2014	Rajan, D.	Quantitative	Cross-sectional	Pharmacists	60	Health	Private	Both
2014	Manjula, C.	Quantitative	Cross-sectional	School teachers	70	Academic	Private	Both
2014	Gandhi, S., Sangeetha, G., Ahmed, N., & Chaturvedi, S. K.	Quantitative	Cross-sectional	Nurses	150	Health	Multiple	Both
2014	Almale, B. D., Vankudre, A. J., Bansode-Gokhe, S. S., & Pawar, V. K.	Quantitative	Cross-sectional	Police personnel	276	Law Enforcement	Public	Male
2014	Sihag, A., & Bidlan, J. S.	Quantitative	Cross-sectional	Health workers	600	Health	Public & Private	Both
2014	Sharma, P., Davey, A., Davey, S., Shukla, A.,	Quantitative	Cross-sectional	Nurses	100	Health	Private	Both

(*Continued*)

Year	Authors	Methodology	Design	Sample	Sample Size	Sector	Type of Organisation	Male/Female
2014	Shrivastava, K., & Bansal, R.							
2014	Kashyap, S. P., Kumar, S., & Krishna, A.	Quantitative	Cross-sectional	Manufacturing employees	315	Manufacturing	Private	Both
2014	Madhura, S., Subramanya, P., & Balaram, P.	Quantitative	Cross-sectional	IT employees	141	IT/BPO	Private	Both
2014	Das, B.	Quantitative	Cross-sectional	Brickfield workers	350	Construction	Private	Both
2014	Kumari, G., Joshi, G., & Pandey, K. M.	Mixed Methods	Cross-sectional	IT employees	100	IT/BPO	Private	Both
2014	Lundgren, K., Kuklane, K., & Venugopal, V.	Quantitative	Cross-sectional	Workers	77	Multiple	Multiple	Both
2014	Sharma, R., & Sharma, K.	Quantitative	Cross-sectional	BPO employees	250	IT/BPO	Private	Both
2015	Amte, R., Munta, K., & Gopal, P. B.	Quantitative	Cross-sectional	Doctors	242	Health	Private	Both
2015	Shirotriya, A. K., & Quraishi, M. I.	Quantitative	Cross-sectional	Teachers	369	Academic	Public	Both

(Continued)

Work Stress 119

Year	Authors	Methodology	Design	Sample	Sample Size	Sector	Type of Organisation	Male/Female
2015	Babu, G. R., TN, S., Ketharam, A., Kar, S. B., & Detels, R.	Qualitative	Longitudinal	IT employees	32	IT/BPO	Private	Both
2015	Kang, L. S., & Sidhu, H.	Quantitative	Cross-sectional	University teachers	570	Academic	Public	Both
2015	Rao, S., & Ramesh, N.	Quantitative	Cross-sectional	Industrial workers	90	Manufacturing	Public	Male
2015	Karunanidhi, S., & Chitra, T.	Quantitative	Cross-sectional	Police personnel	72	Law Enforcement	Public	Female
2015	Amin, A. A., Vankar, J. R., Nimbalkar, S. M., & Phatak, A. G.	Quantitative	Longitudinal	Nurses	129	Health	Public	both
2015	Sailaxmi, G., et al	Quantitative	Longitudinal	Nurses	53	Health	Public	Both
2015	Rashid, I. and Talib, P.	Quantitative	Cross-sectional	Doctors	334	Health	Public	Both
2015	Singh, S. and Kar, S.K.	Mixed Methods	Cross-sectional	Police Personnel	300	Law Enforcement	Public	Both
2015	Aftab, M., & Khatoon, T.	Quantitative	Cross-sectional	School teachers	608	Academic	Multiple	Both
2015	Padma V, Anand NN, Gurukul SS, Javid SS, Prasad A, Arun S.	Quantitative	Cross-sectional	IT employees	1000	IT/BPO	Private	Both

(Continued)

Year	Authors	Methodology	Design	Sample	Sample Size	Sector	Type of Organisation	Male/Female
2015	Prasad, K.D.V., Vaidya, R., and Kumar, V.A.	quantitative	Cross-sectional	Research employees	232	Academic	Public	Both
2015	Anuradha N., Swarna Latha, P., and Naidu, G.T.	Quantitative	Cross-sectional	School teachers	100	Academic	Public & Private	Both
2015	Pal, A., De, S., Sengupta, P., Maity, P., and Dhara, P. C.	Mixed Methods	Cross-sectional	Cultivators	155	Agriculture	Private	Female
2015	Singh, P. and Rani, S.	Quantitative	Cross-sectional	College teachers	120	Academic	Private	Female
2015	Malamardi, S. N., Kamath, R., Tiwari, R., Nair, B. V. S., Chandrasekaran, V., & Phadnis, S.	Quantitative	Cross-sectional	Bank employees	562	Banking/Insurance	Public	Both
2015	Ravi, R., Gunjawate, D., & Ayas, M.	Quantitative	Cross-sectional	Audiologists	100	Health	Private	Both
2015	Mohanraj, C., & Natesan, M.	Mixed Methods	Cross-sectional	Police constables	240	Law Enforcement	Public	Female

(Continued)

Work Stress 121

Year	Authors	Methodology	Design	Sample	Sample Size	Sector	Type of Organisation	Male/Female
2015	Jain, P., & Batra, A.	Quantitative	Cross-sectional	Employees	62	Multiple	Private	Both
2015	Parsekar, S. S., Singh, M. M., & Bhumika, T. V.	Quantitative	Cross-sectional	Police Personnel	76	Law Enforcement	Public	Both
2015	Moom, R. K., Sing, L. P., & Moom, N.	Quantitative	Cross-sectional	Employees	50	Banking/Insurance	Private	Both
2015	Haldar, P., & Sahu, S.	Quantitative	Cross-sectional	Nurses	122	Health	Public	Female
2015	Sharma, S.	Quantitative	Cross-sectional	Army personnel	415	Law Enforcement	Public	Male
2015	Dolai, D.	Quantitative	Cross-sectional	Employees	224	Banking/Insurance	Public & Private	Both
2015	Sharma, E.	Quantitative	Cross-sectional	Employees	750	Manufacturing	Private	Both
2015	Fernandes, W. N., & Nirmala, R.	Mixed Methods	Cross-sectional	Nurses	51	Health	Public & Private	Both
2016	Singh, A.	Quantitative	Cross-sectional	College teachers	250	Academic	Public & Private	Both
2016	Kishori, B. and Vinothini, B.	Quantitative	Cross-sectional	Banking employees	100	Banking/Insurance	Public	Both
2016	Shivendra, D., & Kumar, M. M.	Quantitative	Cross-sectional	School teachers	75	Academic	Multiple	Both
2016	Banerjee, S., & Mehta, P.	Quantitative	Cross-sectional	University employees	110	Academic	Multiple	Both

(Continued)

Year	Authors	Methodology	Design	Sample	Sample Size	Sector	Type of Organisation	Male/ Female
2016	Asma Zaheer, Jamid Ul Islam, Nahid Darakhshan	Quantitative	Cross-sectional	University employees	90	Academic	Public & Private	Female
2016	Davey, A., Sharma, P., Davey, S., Shukla, A., Srivastava, K., & Vyas, S.	Quantitative	Cross-sectional	Nurses	100	Health	Private	Both
2016	Priyanka, R., Rao, A., Rajesh, G., Shenoy, R., & Pai, B. M.	Quantitative	Cross-sectional	Law enforcement personnel	304	Law Enforcement	Public	Both
2016	Lambert, E.G., Qureshi, H. and Frank, J.	Quantitative	Cross-sectional	Police officers	827	Law Enforcement	Public	Both
2016	Batham, C., & Yasobant, S.	Quantitative	Cross-sectional	Dentists	93	Health	Public & Private	Both
2016	Mohan, D. A. C., Balaji, K. D., & Kumar, T. K.	Quantitative	Cross-sectional	IT Professionals	300	IT/BPO	Private	Both
2016	Qazi, S., & Nazneen, A.	Quantitative	Cross-sectional	University employees	155	Academic	Public & Private	Both

(*Continued*)

Year	Authors	Methodology	Design	Sample	Sample Size	Sector	Type of Organisation	Male/Female
2016	Kashyap, S. P., Kumar, S., & Byadwal, V.	Quantitative	Cross-sectional	Manufacturing employees	315	Manufacturing	Private	Both
2016	Roz, H. K. B., Mondal, S., Podder, P., & Raval, D. T.	Quantitative	Cross-sectional	Cardiologists	180	Health	Private	Both
2016	Venugopal, V., Chinnadurai, J. S., Lucas, R. A., & Kjellstrom, T.	Mixed Methods	Longitudinal	Workers	442	Multiple	Public & Private	Both
2016	Shiji, P., Sequera, S., & Mathew, S.	Quantitative	Cross-sectional	Nurses	40	Health	Public & Private	Female
2017	Dawn, S., Talukdar, P., Bhattacharje, S., & Singh, O. P.	Quantitative	Cross-sectional	School teachers	338	Academic	Private	Both
2017	Frank, J., Lambert, E.G. and Qureshi, H.	Quantitative	Cross-sectional	Police personnel	827	Law Enforcement	Public	Both
2017	Bakshi, S.G., Divetia, J.V.,	Quantitative	Cross-sectional	Anesthesiologists	1178	Health	Public & Private	Both

(*Continued*)

124　*Kajal A. Sharma*

Year	Authors	Methodology	Design	Sample	Sample Size	Sector	Type of Organisation	Male/Female
2017	Kannan, S. and Myatra, S.N.	Quantitative	Cross-sectional	Police personnel	406	Law Enforcement	Public	Both
2017	Ragesh, G., Tharayil, H. M., Raj, M. T., Philip, M., & Hamza, A.	Quantitative	Cross-sectional	IT employees	102	IT/BPO	Private	Both
2017	Singh, S., & Sharma, T.	Quantitative	Cross-sectional	Employees	470	Multiple	Multiple	Both
2017	Mahmood, A., & Yadav, L. K.	Quantitative	Cross-sectional	Police personnel	240	Law Enforcement	Public	Both
2017	Singh, A.	Quantitative	Cross-sectional	School teachers	100	Academic	Public & Private	Both
2017	Mohanty, S. P..	Quantitative	Longitudinal	Mineworkers	35	Transport	Public	Male
2017	Dey, S.C.; Dey, N.C.; Sharma, G.D.	Quantitative	Cross-sectional	School teachers	60	Academic	Private	Female
2017	Sehgal, M., & Verma, J.	Quantitative	Longitudinal	Working women	345	Multiple	Multiple	Female
2017	Parashar, M., Singh, M., Kishore, J., Pathak, R., & Panda, M.							

(*Continued*)

Year	Authors	Methodology	Design	Sample	Sample Size	Sector	Type of Organisation	Male/Female
2017	Kumar, V., & Kamalanabhan, T. J.	Quantitative	Cross-sectional	Police personnel	491	Law Enforcement	Public	Both
2017	Jayakumar, D.	Quantitative	Cross-sectional	Loco pilots	230	Transport	Public	Both
2017	Hashmi, K., Hasan, B., & Khan, K. A.	Quantitative	Cross-sectional	School teachers	120	Academic	Public	Both
2017	Ahmad, A.	Quantitative	Cross-sectional	Mineworkers	421	Construction	Public	Both
2017	Purohit, B., & Vasava, P.	Quantitative	Cross-sectional	Nurses	84	Health	Public	Both
2018	Garg, N., Garg, N. and Prakash, C.	Quantitative	Cross-sectional	Insurance employees	197	Banking/Insurance	Public & Private	Both
2018	Dey, S.C., Dey, N.C. & Sharma, G.D.	Quantitative	Cross-sectional	Mineworkers	20	Transport	Public	Male
2018	Bharathi, S.; Rajan, V. T.	Quantitative	Cross-sectional	IT employees	100	IT/BPO	Private	Both
2018	Gandhi, K., Sahni, N., Padhy, S. K., & Mathew, P. J.	Quantitative	Cross-sectional	Doctors	200	Health	Private	Both
2018	Prasad, K.D.V., Vaidya, R. and Kumar, V.A.	Quantitative	Cross-sectional	Research employees	756	Academic	Public	Both

(*Continued*)

Year	Authors	Methodology	Design	Sample	Sample Size	Sector	Type of Organisation	Male/Female
2018	Chitra, T., & Karunanidhi, S.	Mixed Methods	Longitudinal	Police personnel	63	Law Enforcement	Public	Both
2018	Agarwal, S., Sayal, A., & Mishra, A.	Quantitative	Cross-sectional	University employees	204	Academic	Public & Private	Both
2018	Sharma, N., Takkar, P., Purkayastha, A., Jaiswal, P., Taneja, S., Lohia, N., & Augustine, A. R.	Quantitative	Cross-sectional	Nurses	81	Health	Public	Female
2018	Mitra, S., Sarkar, A. P., Haldar, D., Saren, A. B., Lo, S., & Sarkar, G. N.	Quantitative	Cross-sectional	Doctors	63	Health	Private	Both
2018	Onkari, D., & Itagi, S.	Mixed Methods	Cross-sectional	Police personnel	60	Law Enforcement	Private Public	Both Female
2018	Raval, A., Dutta, P., Tiwari, A., Ganguly, P. S., Sathish, L. M.,	Quantitative	Cross-sectional	Traffic police officers	16	Law Enforcement	Public	Both

(Continued)

Year	Authors	Methodology	Design	Sample	Sample Size	Sector	Type of Organisation	Male/Female
2018	Mavalankar, D., & Hess, J. Singh, N., & Srivastava, D. R.	Mixed Methods	Cross-sectional	University employees	440	Academic	Private	Both
2018	Singh, V. & Prasad, H. N.	Quantitative	Cross-sectional	University librarians	550	Academic	Public & Private	Both

7 Organizational Stress in Contemporary Japan

Tsuyoshi Ohira, Tetsushi Fujimoto, and Tomoki Sekiguchi

Introduction

Organizational stress is a contemporary social problem that undermines workers' physical and mental health in Japan. The stress that Japanese workers experience is tightly connected to the ways in which employment is structured in society. Traditionally, Japanese employment has been characterized by things such as seniority wages, lifetime employment, and enterprise labor union (Hamaaki, Hori, Maeda, & Murata, 2012). Although this employment system was a powerful engine to prompt economic growth in postwar Japan (Hamaaki et al., 2012), it started changing after 1973 when an oil shock hit the economy, deteriorating the conditions of work and affecting the lives of employed men and women. The problem of organizational stress emerged and became increasingly serious as an inevitable consequence of this change.

In this chapter, we conduct a systematic review of existing studies of organizational stress in Japan, with particular focus on the following issues: (1) *Karoshi* (death from overwork) and *Karo-Jisatsu* (suicide caused by work stress), (2) long hours of work, (3) non-regular employment, and (4) workplace harassment. Since a number of earlier research in Japan examined the relationship between organizational stressors and physical and mental health for Japanese workers (Nagata, 2005), we investigate this relationship by exploring peer-reviewed articles written in both Japanese and English and were published after the year 2000. We searched two databases – CiNii Articles and Google Scholar – for articles by using keywords such as "*Karoshi*," "*Karo-Jisatsu*," "*Cho-Jikan Rodo*" (long hours of work), "*Zangyo*" (overtime work), "*Hiseiki Koyo*" (non-regular employment), and "*Harasumento*" (harassment). In addition to these keywords, we also used the word "Japan" when searching for articles written in English and the word "*Sutoresu*" (stress) to search for articles written in Japanese. After the search, we selected 38 articles – these included two articles on *Karoshi* and *Karo-Jisatsu*, 17 articles on long hours of work, 11 articles on non-regular employment, and 8 articles on workplace harassment. Each section consists of an outline of issues including definitions, statistics, and a summary of findings. We also conducted an overview of government policies in Japan and the ways that Japanese employers respond to the problem of organizational stress. We conclude this chapter by noting some limitations in this review and by offering directions for future research.

Karoshi and Organizational Stress

Karoshi

Karoshi, or death from overwork, is perhaps the worst worker outcome of organizational stress in Japan. Japan's Act of Promoting Measures to Prevent Death and Injury from Overwork defines *Karoshi* as "death due to cerebrovascular or heart disease brought on by an overload of work, or death by suicide related to mental disorder from the intense psychological burden at work" (Ministry of Health, Labour, and Welfare, 2019d). *Karo-jisatsu* is suicide caused by a work-related mental disorder, and it is usually separated from *Karoshi* (Iwata, 2009; Komorida, 2016). According to the 2018 Status Report of Industrial Accident Compensation for *Karoshi* (Ministry of Health, Labour and Welfare, 2019e), the number of *Karoshi* incidents, legally admitted as compensable by insurance, amounted to 82 in 2018 as compared to 160 incidents in 2002, while the number of *Karo-Jisatsu,* including attempted suicide, rose from 43 in 2002 to 76 incidents in 2018.

Similarities and Differences between Karoshi and Karo-Jisatsu

There are similarities and differences between *Karoshi* and *Karo-Jisatsu*. According to the Ministry of Health, Labour, and Welfare (2019e), one of the similarities is that most workers who died from *Karoshi* or *Karo-Jisatsu* are men in regular employment. As for differences, a vast majority of *Karoshi* victims are in their 40s and 50s; whereas, *Karo-Jisatsu* tends to occur in all age groups. Employees who died from *Karoshi* are concentrated in the mailing and transportation industry; whereas, those who died from *Karo-Jisatsu* are distributed across a wide variety of industries – such as manufacturing, retail, lodging, and wholesale. In addition, many of the workers who died from *Karoshi* put in more than 60 hours of work per week, although *Karo-Jisatsu* occurred even among those who worked only a few hours of overtime in a day.

Causes of Karoshi and Karo-Jisatsu

Previous studies suggest that working long hours is a significant cause of *Karoshi* (Kanai, 2008). Long hours generally reduce sleep time, while increasing the risk of cerebrovascular and heart disease (Iwasaki, 2008). In addition to long hours, the presence of an extremely heavy workload is required for death to be certified as *Karoshi* by the Industrial Accident Compensation Insurance (Ministry of Health, Labour, and Welfare, 2019d). On the other hand, a prerequisite for suicide to be insured as *Karo-Jisatsu* is an individual experience of strong psychological pressure from work (Ministry of Health, Labour, and Welfare, 2019d). For example, *Karo-Jisatsu* is associated with unreasonable changes in job assignments, overtime work exceeding 80 hours per week, workplace harassment, and interpersonal problems with supervisors (Ministry of Health, Labour, and Welfare, 2019e).

Karoshi, Karo-Jisatsu, and Organizational Stress in Japan

Although a variety of work stressors is relevant to *Karoshi* and *Karo-Jisatsu*, a limited number of studies have explored how they may be related to organizational stress. Iwata (2009) found that workers who died from *Karoshi* had experienced a sudden increase in workload, and their work conditions were more likely to be severe compared to those who committed *Karo-Jisatsu*. In contrast, unexpected job assignments and interpersonal problems with their supervisors were more likely to be observed in the cases of *Karo-Jisatsu*. Komorida (2016) showed that those who committed *Karo-Jisatsu*, compared to those who died from *Karoshi*, tend to have been assigned an unreasonable amount of work and have experienced harassment in their workplace.

Long Work Hours and Organizational Stress

Long Work Hours

A general consensus seems to be that Japanese workers work long hours (Ogura, 2008). According to the Monthly Labor Survey conducted by the Japanese Ministry of Health, Labor, and Welfare (Ministry of Health, Labour, and Welfare, 2019a), the average annual hours rendered by an individual worker in 2018 is 1,706. Due to the increase in non-regular employment, the overall hours of work for the Japanese have gradually decreased in recent years. However, the hours for regular workers have not noticeably changed (2,010 hours in 2018), and they still work nearly twice as long as non-regular workers (1,025 hours in 2018). Moreover, men in their 30s and 40s and those who work in the mailing, transportation, building, manufacturing, and information and communication industries are more likely to put long hours at work. Table 7.1 shows the average number of hours worked by individual workers annually, as well as the proportion of workers working 49 hours or more per week in developed countries. As shown in the table,

Table 7.1 The Average Annual Number of Hours Worked by Individual Workers and the Proportion of Workers Working 49 Hours or More Weekly in Developed Countries

	The Average Annual Number of Hours Worked by Individual Workers in 2017	The Proportion of Workers Working 49 Hours or More Weekly in 2017
Japan	1,709	20.6%
USA	1,780	19.3%
Canada	1,695	12.3%
UK	1,543	11.7%
Germany	1,360	8.5%
France	1,522	10.1%
South Korea	2,018	29.0%

Sources: OECD (2020); International Labour Organization (2020).

Japan (1,713 hours in 2016) is among the countries with the longest hours of work in 2016. Other countries include South Korea (2,069 hours) and the United States (1,783 hours). While Japan's work hours are decreasing, the average annual overtime hours have slowly increased after 2009 – reaching 129 hours in 2018. Note that the number of employees working for more than 60 hours per week, excluding those who work in agricultural industries, has decreased in recent years, yet 4.32 million workers (7.7% of all workers) are still at risk of *Karoshi*. As Table 7.1 shows, the proportion of Japanese workers working 49 hours or more per week was 20.8% in 2015, and this proportion is the second largest next to Korea (32.0%).

Long Hours of Work and Organizational Stress in Japan

A number of studies conducted in Japan attempted to examine the relationship between long work hours and workers' health, but the results remain unclear. Approximately half of the research reported that long hours made workers' physical and mental health deteriorate. For example, an increase in work hours and overtime was negatively related to mental health for women workers with children and workers in community services (Koizumi, Sugawara, Maekawa, & Kitamura, 2003; Suzumura et al., 2013; Yamaguchi, 2010). Long hours and overtime also exerted harmful influence on workers' physical health – such as back and neck pain, fatigue, sleep deprivation, and tinnitus (Koda et al., 2000; Kubo, Sasaki, & Matsumoto, 2010; Nakata et al., 2001). Furthermore, Umehara, Ohya, Kawakami, Tsutsumi, and Fujimura (2007) showed that psychosomatic symptoms were more likely to result when workers work long hours and overtime. Fukui, Haratani, Fukazawa, Nakata, Takahashi, and Fujioka

(2003) found a significantly higher level of psychological and physical strain among IT engineers who work long hours beyond 10 P.M. The remaining half of the research failed to confirm the presence of a significant relationship between long hours and individual health (Fukuyama & Inoue, 2017; Haoka et al., 2010; Kataoka, Kazuhiro, Masahito, Tetsuya, & Beth, 2014; Nakada et al., 2016; Nishikitani, Nakao, Karita, Nomura, & Yano, 2005; Nishitani & Sakakibara, 2010; Nozaki et al., 2012; Tarumi & Hagihara, 2002; Tominaga & Asakura, 2006). Rather than long hours and overtime, some research showed that having heavy workload was negatively associated with physical and mental health (Fukuyama & Inoue, 2017; Haoka et al., 2010; Nakada et al., 2016; Tominaga & Asakura, 2006).

Non-Regular Employment and Organizational Stress

Non-Regular Employment

Expansion of non-regular employment is one of the most significant changes that took place in Japanese labor markets during the past 20 years. While there is no solid agreement on the definition of non-regular employment (Kitagawa, Ohta, & Teruyama, 2018), a recent labor force survey conducted by the Japanese government has categorized non-regular employment based on the terms used in employment contracts and divided non-regular employment into six types (Fu, 2013). Part-time workers share a large proportion of non-regular employees, and they can be classified further into *paato* (part-time workers) and *arubaito* (fringe workers). On one hand, the vast majority of *paato* workers are married mothers with children, and they are likely to have fixed work schedules. On the other hand, many *arubaito* workers tend to consist of young people, including students, who often have flexible and short work schedules. Contract workers work in a fixed-term employment contract. *Haken* workers (dispatch workers) are hired by and sent from a staffing agency. Entrusted workers tend to consist of older workers who are reaching retirement. Others include seasonal, emergency, or daily workers who are employed for a designated period of time.

Increasing Non-Regular Employment

According to the 2018 Labor Force Survey conducted by the Ministry of Internal Affairs and Communications (Ministry of Internal Affairs and Communications, 2019), the number of non-regular workers has gradually increased over the years and has reached 21.2 million in 2018. This includes 10.35 million *paato*, 4.55 million *arubaito*, 2.94 million contract workers, 1.36 million *haken*, 1.2 million of entrusted workers, and 0.8 million others. Non-regular workers consist of approximately 38% of all employees in 2018. Why have non-regular workers increased in Japan? Asano, Ito, and Kawaguchi (2013) argue that a part of the reason why non-regular employment boomed in Japan is that a large number of young men and women had to reluctantly choose non-regular work due to employer reluctance of long-term hiring of employees. In addition, Japanese Ministry of Health, Labour, and Welfare (2019c) suggests that the increase in foreign-born part-time workers, including international students, may have contributed to the increase of non-regular workers.

Non-Regular Employment and Organizational Stress in Japan

Along with an increase in non-regular workers, researchers have come to focus on two topics relevant to non-regular employment. The first topic is the antecedents of non-regular workers' stress. Earlier studies showed that organizational stressors – such as a wide range of job assignments (Ozono, 2010), employment insecurity (Takahashi, Morita, & Ishidu, 2014), and heavy workload (Takahashi et al., 2014) – have a detrimental effect on non-regular workers' mental health. Furthermore, women in non-regular employment (Ozono, 2010) and economically challenged non-regular workers (Takahashi et al., 2014) experience higher levels of stress in their jobs. Previous research also found several antecedents that exert positive effects. For example, job autonomy (Ozono, 2010; Uehara, Kanbara, Shido, Nishi, & Miyake, 2014), supervisors' active listening, and the number of supportive co-workers are likely to ameliorate non-regular workers' mental health. Moreover, age (Morita, 2018), family satisfaction (Nakahara, 2007; Uehara et al., 2014), health satisfaction (Uehara et al., 2014), internal locus of control (Uehara et al., 2014), job satisfaction (Nakahara, 2007; Takahashi et al., 2014), perceived work-life balance (Uehara et al., 2014), and a sense of contributing to their work (Morita, 2018) are also positively related to non-regular workers' mental health.

The second relevant topic is the difference in mental health between regular workers and non-regular workers. Compared to regular employment, M. Inoue (2012) argued that non-regular work may negatively affect an individual's mental health due to employment insecurity, severe work conditions, and limited opportunities for job training and career development. Although previous research conducted in the United States and European Union countries showed that non-regular workers' mental health is worse than those in regular employment (Virtanen et al., 2005), many earlier Japanese studies failed to confirm the difference in mental health between regular and non-regular workers (Imai, 2018; Matsuyama, 2010; Mori, Iwata, & Tanaka, 2014; Morita, 2018; Nakahara, 2007; Takahashi et al., 2014; Uehara et al., 2014). Only A.

Inoue, Kawakami, Tsuchiya, Sakurai, and Hashimoto (2010) found that men in part-time work experience a higher level of psychological distress than men regular workers. Inoue *et al.* (2010) also showed that women in temporary/contract work are more likely to experience psychological distress than women regular workers. Some prior research, however, found better mental health among non-regular workers than among regular workers (Kamiya, Sugiyama, Toda, & Murayama, 2011; Komura & Ishitake, 2012). Thus, results are mixed when it comes to the difference in mental health between regular and non-regular workers in Japan.

Workplace Harassment and Organizational Stress

Workplace Harassment

In Japan, workplace harassment is a serious emergent social problem at work. Although workplace harassment includes various types of harassment and bullying, this section deals with two major types of harassment in Japan: power harassment and sexual harassment. Power harassment is the most common type of harassment at work (Ministry of Health, Labour, and Welfare, 2017), and it is defined as "the acts of a worker that cause his/her co-workers (usually subordinates) mental or physical pains, or cause their work environment to deteriorate, using his/her managerial or relational superiority in the workplace" (The Japan Institute for Labour Policy and Training, 2013). Sexual harassment is the second most common type of harassment at work (Ministry of Health, Labour, and Welfare, 2017). The Japanese government defines sexual harassment as "an incident when a worker suffers disadvantages such as dismissal, demotion, and a decrease in wages as a result of his/her responses to harassment, and such incident seriously causes the work environment to deteriorate, thus exerting serious and adverse effects on the worker's performance" (Ministry of Health, Labour, and Welfare, 2012).

Characteristics of Power Harassment and Sexual Harassment

The Workplace Power Harassment Survey conducted in 2016 by Japanese Ministry of Health, Labour, and Welfare (Ministry of Health, Labour, and Welfare, 2017) reported that approximately one-third of Japanese workers had experienced power harassment at work in the past. According to the survey results, power harassment mainly consists of psychological abuse (73.5%) and physical attack (14.6%) (Ministry of Health, Labour, and Welfare, 2017). In most cases, supervisors are the perpetrators who harass their subordinates, and some junior and non-regular workers are also among the victims. In addition, the lack of communication between supervisors and subordinates in the workplace tended to cause power harassment.

According to the Annual Health, Labor, and Welfare Report 2018 (Ministry of Health, Labour, and Welfare, 2019b), sexual harassment is a type of job discrimination that Japanese women experience most frequently. A survey conducted in 2015 reported that 34.7% of regular workers experienced sexual harassment in the past, while only 17.8% of non-regular workers experienced it (The Japan Institute for Labour Policy and Training, 2016). The survey also found that 53.9% of the victims experienced unwanted remarks about their age and physical appearance, and 40% were asked sexual questions and experienced nonconsensual bodily touch. In a large proportion of cases, men, – particularly men in supervisory positions – harassed women, and the vast majority of victims could do nothing but tolerate such harassment.

Workplace Harassment and Organizational Stress in Japan

Although no prior research has focused on the relationship between power harassment and organizational stress, some studies looked at how workplace harassment may be related to Japanese workers' health. First, sexual harassment exerts a negative influence on workers' physical and mental health. For example, sexual harassment induces anxiety and stress-related physical symptoms for women in care work (Taniguchi *et al.*, 2012; Taniguchi, Takaki, Hirokawa, Fujii, & Harano, 2016). Although Kakuyama, Matsui, and Tsuzuki (2003) showed that sexual harassment is not associated with psychological and physical stress responses, they found a moderating effect of the victim's vulnerability in the relationship between sexual harassment and physical stress responses for women. Furthermore, sexual harassment has a positive influence on burnout of research workers (Takeuchi *et al.*, 2018). Second, workplace bullying is negatively associated with workers' physical and mental health. Person-targeted bullying at work (e.g., malicious gossip and rumors) has a negative effect on vigor for women in care work (Taniguchi *et al.*, 2012) and has a positive effect on their psychological and physical stress responses (Taniguchi *et al.*, 2016). Work-related bullying (e.g., intentionally withholding necessary information to affect co-worker's or subordinate's work) is negatively related to men care workers' vigor and positively associated with women's depression (Taniguchi *et al.*, 2012), but it has no significant influence on psychological and physical stress responses for care workers (Taniguchi *et al.*, 2016). Moreover, workplace bullying not only increases depression, but also intensifies the relationship between job strain and depression (Takaki *et al.*, 2010).

Government Policies and Employer Responses to Organizational Stress in Japan

As reviewed above, there are various issues relevant to organizational stress in Japan. Now then, how do the Japanese government and employers attempt to tackle the problems? In this section, we briefly summarize Japanese government policies and employer responses to organizational stress.

Acts for Promoting Work Style Reform

The Japanese government set goals in 2018 to reduce the proportion of workers who were rendering more than 60 hours of work per week to no more than 5% while increasing the usage rate of paid vacation days by up to 70% in 2020 (Ministry of Health, Labour, and Welfare, 2019d). To promote the Japanese government's Work Style Reform wherein the Japanese government attempted to decrease long hours of work, regulations on overtime work were tightened by amending the Labor Standards Law (Ministry of Health, Labour, and Welfare, 2018). The new regulation caps overtime at 45 hours per month and 360 hours per year, and employers must agree that the number of overtime hours is within the limits of the law and their employees. Moreover, the government encourages employers to adopt a work time scheduling system for reducing hours of work. The system sets intervals between each day's work so that employees have enough time to recover from fatigue.

Fair Treatment of Non-Regular Employment

The government has implemented policies to improve the work conditions of non-regular workers. Although employers have increasingly hired non-regular employees to reduce labor costs and to adjust employment (Hirano, 2010), they will be required to provide fair treatment for regular and non-regular workers from 2020 – if non-regular workers have the same job assignments as regular workers (Ministry of Health, Labour, and Welfare, 2018). In addition, the government has raised the minimum wage, and this has increased the number of social insurance holders among non-regular workers (Ministry of Health, Labour, and Welfare, 2019b).

Preventing Harassment at Work

The Japanese government stipulates that employers should take active measures against workplace harassment. For example, an act that will become effective in 2020 requires that employers launch consultation services and training programs to tackle power harassment while penalizing perpetrators of power harassment in accordance with their employment rules (The Japan Institute for Labour Policy and Training, 2019). As revealed in the 2016 Workplace Power Harassment Survey (Ministry of Health, Labour, and Welfare, 2017), a large number of employers had already implemented preventive measures against power harassment. Although employers are likely to opt for verbal reprimands and job transfers as punitive measures for perpetrators of power harassment, they are much less likely to fire or cut salaries of perpetrators (Ministry of Health, Labour, and Welfare, 2017). The government also obliges employers to respond firmly to sexual harassment, while providing appropriate consultations and educational programs (Cabinet Office, 2019). Employers commonly investigate sexual harassment claims and give warnings to those who are accused, yet some employers force victims of harassment into resigning or ignore their claims without taking any action (The Japan Institute for Labour Policy and Training, 2016).

Stress Check Program

The Japanese government initiated the Stress Check Program in 2015 in order to screen workers experiencing high levels of psychosocial stress in the workplace (Kawakami & Tsutsumi, 2016; Tsutsumi, Shimazu, Eguchi, Inoue, & Kawakami, 2018). The program requires employers to do the following steps (Tsutsumi et al., 2018): First, employers are required to examine workers' stress every year by administering the Brief Job Stress Questionnaire (BJSQ), a survey developed in Japan in reference to the Job Content Questionnaire (JCQ) (Karasek, 1979) and the NIOSH Generic Job Stress Questionnaire (Enoki, Maeda, Iwata, & Murata, 2017; Inoue et al., 2014). Second, they must inform workers of their stress levels based on the questionnaire results. Third, it is stipulated that employers must arrange physician interviews for workers experiencing high levels of work stress. Fourth, employers are expected to improve their workers' job environment in accordance with the physician's advice. Although the BJSQ predicts future risks of employees' long-term sick leaves (Tsutsumi et al., 2018), there is little evidence as to why and how the physician interviews may be effective (Kawakami & Tsutsumi, 2016; Tsutsumi *et al.*, 2018). Moreover, it is indicated that employers are less likely to arrange interviews for highly stressed workers (Tsutsumi *et al.*, 2018). The program also urges employers to take advantage of the survey data for improving their workplace, and it is expected that data analyses are conducted by more than 60% of employers (Ministry of Health, Labour, and Welfare, 2019d).

Facilitating Health and Productivity Management

Health and productivity management is viewed as an effective measure to enhance organizational performance by improving workers' health (Morinaga, 2019). The government launched the Certified Health and Productivity Management Organization Recognition Program to recognize outstanding organizations engaging in health and productivity management (Ministry of Economy, Trade, and Industry, 2018). Although no more than 0.1% of all profit and non-profit organizations in Japan obtained this certification in 2019, there are many unique examples. For instance, an information systems company provided a lump sum of money based on the extent of workers' engagement in health practices and the results of medical examinations. Another power and telecommunications company installed monkey bars at work, so that employees may exercise at the office (Morinaga, 2019).

Limitations and Future Directions

In this chapter, we reviewed existing research on organizational stress in Japan, focusing on *Karoshi* and *Karo-Jisatsu*, long work hours, non-regular employment, and workplace harassment. We conclude this chapter by underscoring some limitations in our review and by showing directions for future research.

Limitations

First, we admit that some stressors (e.g., workload) and outcomes (e.g., job satisfaction and absenteeism) were not included in this chapter. Although we are fully aware of their importance in organizational stress research, we decided to limit the content of this chapter to keep it focused. Second, although articles published without peer reviews in in-house journals of Japanese universities report interesting findings, we only included the results from peer-reviewed articles in this chapter, so that we could keep our systematic review academically acceptable. Third, we used a limited number of keywords when searching databases, so we may have omitted possible searchable studies with other keywords – such as "medical research."

Directions for Future Research

First, researchers examining the relationship between long work hours and workers' health must look at the influence of workload. Some of the previous studies showed that the impact of long hours on physical and mental health disappears when workload is taken into consideration (Fukuyama & Inoue, 2017; Haoka et al., 2010; Nakada *et al.*, 2016; Tominaga & Asakura, 2006). The information on workload might tell us something about the root cause of the negative influence that long hours exert on workers. Second, researchers studying *Karoshi* and *Karo-Jisatsu* should look more carefully at the specific characteristics of workplaces and organizations. There are many studies investigating the cause of *Karoshi* and *Karo-Jisatsu* (e.g., Ministry of Health, Labour, and Welfare(2019d)), but few have focused on how those causes might be related to characteristics of workplaces and organizations in which *Karoshi* and *Karo-Jisatsu* take place. We believe it is valuable to integrate the contexts of workplaces and organizations in analyses of *Karoshi* and *Karo-Jisatsu*. Third, researchers comparing regular and non-regular employment would benefit by using all types of non-regular employment in their analyses. It may be possible that the unsubstantiated difference in mental health between regular and non-regular workers reflects a variety of backgrounds and work conditions associated with each type of non-regular employment. Fourth, researchers should pay more attention to power harassment. Despite the growing awareness about the devastating consequences of workplace harassment (Tsuno, 2016), there has been little research that focuses on power harassment (e.g., Nii, Tsuda, Tou, Yamahiro, and Irie (2018)). In particular, research examining the relationship between power harassment and mental health is important because *Karo-Jisatsu* is related to interpersonal problems with their supervisors (Iwata, 2009; Komorida, 2016). Fifth, it would be worth conducting intervention studies in order to confirm the effectiveness of certain policies and management strategies. Since the vast majority of reports highlight unique examples of workplace practices, it is important for policymakers and employers to expand their scope by engaging in a new endeavor, like intervention study, so that *Karoshi* and *Karo-Jisatsu* – as well as deterioration of workers' health – may better be prevented.

References

Asano, Hirokatsu, Ito, Takahiro, & Kawaguchi, Daiji (2013). Why has the fraction of nonstandard workers increased? A case study of Japan. *Scottish Journal of Political Economy*, 60(4), 360–389. 10.1111/sjpe.12015.

Cabinet Office. (2019). White paper on gender equality 2019. Retrieved from http://www.gender.go.jp/english_contents/about_danjo/whitepaper/index.html.

Enoki, Mamiko, Maeda, Eri, Iwata, Toyoto, & Murata, Katsuyuki (2017). The association between work-related stress and autonomic imbalance among call center employees in Japan. *The Tohoku Journal of Experimental Medicine*, 243(4), 321–328. 10.1620/tjem.243.321.

Fu, Huiyan (2013). *An emerging non-regular labour force in Japan: The dignity of dispatched workers*. London, U.K.: Routledge.

Fukui, Satoe, Haratani, Takashi, Fukazawa, Kenji, Nakata, Akinori, Takahashi,

Masaya, & Fujioka, Yosei (2003). Stress reactions and their correlates of engineers working in the information technology industry: Using the brief job stress questionnaire. *Job Stress Research*, 10(4), 273–279.

Fukuyama, Kazue, & Inoue, Nobutaka (2017). Relationship of work hour and mental stress: Focusing gender differences of stress vulnerability. *Japanese Journal of Occupational Medicine and Traumatology*, 65(3), 147–152.

Hamaaki, Junya, Hori, Masahiro, Maeda, Saeko, & Murata, Keiko (2012). Changes in the Japanese employment system in the two lost decades. *ILR Review*, 65(4), 810–846. 10.1177/001979391206500403.

Haoka, Takeshi, Sasahara, Shin-ichiro, Tomotsune, Yusuke, Yoshino, Satoshi, Maeno, Tetsuhiro, & Matsuzaki, Ichiyo (2010). The effect of stress-related factors on mental health status among resident doctors in Japan. *Medical Education*, 44(8), 826–834. 10.1111/j.1365-2923.2010.03725.x.

Hirano, Mitsutoshi (2010). Diversification of employment categories in Japanese firms and its functionality: A study based on the human resource portfolio system. In R. Bebenroth & T. Kanai (Eds.), *Challenges of human resource management in Japan* (pp. 202–223). London: Routledge.

Imai, Hironori (2018). An analysis of the association between functional limitation and distress among employees with chronic illness: Moderating roles of gender and employment status. *Doshisha Policy and Managemant Review*, 19(2), 135–146. 10.14988/pa.2017.0000017000.

Inoue, Akiomi, Kawakami, Norito, Shimomitsu, Teruichi, Tsutsumi, Akizumi, Haratani, Takashi, Yoshikawa, Toru, & Odagiri, Yuko (2014). Development of a short version of the new brief job stress questionnaire. *Industrial Health*, 52(6), 535–540. 10.2486/indhealth.2014-0114.

Inoue, Akiomi, Kawakami, Norito, Tsuchiya, Masao, Sakurai, Keiko, & Hashimoto, Hideki (2010). Association of occupation, employment contract, and company size with mental health in a national representative sample of employees in Japan. *Journal of Occupational Health*, 52(4), 227–240. 10.1539/joh.O10002.

Inoue, Mariko (2012). Association between precarious employment and stress. *The Japanese Journal of Stress Sciences*, 27(1), 91–97.

International Labour Organization. (2020). ILOSTAT database. Available from https://ilostat.ilo.org/data/.

Iwasaki, Kenji (2008). Long working hours and health problems. *The Japanese Journal of Labour Studies*, 575, 39–48.

Iwata, Ittetsu (2009). Relation among death or suicide due to overwork, mental factors, and the working environment. *Labor and Management Review*, 19, 151–164. 10.24502/jalm.19.0_151.

Kakuyama, Takashi, Matsui, Tamao, & Tsuzuki, Yukie (2003). Influence of organizational climate on sexual harassment: The validity of the integrated process model. *Japanese Association of Industrial/Organizational Psychology Journal*, 17(1), 25–33.

Kamiya, Tetsuji, Sugiyama, Ryuichi, Toda, Yuichi, & Murayama, Yuichi (2011). Stress response and employment situation of teachers in day-care centers with a focus on employment status and the ratio of part-timers. *The Japanese Journal of Labour Studies*, 608, 103–114.

Kanai, Atsuko. (2008). "Karoshi (work to death)" in Japan. *Journal of Business Ethics*, 84(2), 209–216. 10.1007/s10551-008-9701-8.

Karasek, Robert A. (1979). Job demands, job decision latitude, and mental strain: Implications for job redesign. *Administrative Science Quarterly*, 24(2), 285–308. 10.2307/2392498.

Kataoka, Mika, Kazuhiro, Ozawa, Masahito, Tomotake, Tetsuya, Tanioka, & Beth, King (2014). Occupational stress and its related factors among university teachers in Japan. *Health*, 6(5), 299–305. 10.4236/health.2014.65043.

Kawakami, Norito, & Tsutsumi, Akizumi (2016). The stress check program: A new national policy for monitoring and screening psychosocial stress in the workplace in Japan. *Journal of Occupational Health*, 58(1), 1–6. 10.1539/joh.15-0001-ER.

Kitagawa, Akiomi, Ohta, Souichi, & Teruyama, Hiroshi (2018). *The changing Japanese labor market: Theory and evidence* (Vol. 12). Singapore: Springer Nature.

Koda, Shigeki, Yasuda, Nobufumi, Sugihara, Yuki, Ohara, Hiroshi, Udo, Hiroshi, Otani, Toru, & Aoyama, Hideyasu (2000). Analyses of work-relatedness of health problems among truck drivers by questionnaire survey. *Sangyo Eiseigaku Zasshi*, 42(1), 6–16. 10.1539/sangyoeisei.KJ00002552185.

Koizumi, Tomoe, Sugawara, Masumi, Maekawa, Kyoko, & Kitamura, Toshinori (2003). Direct and indirect effects of negative spillover from work to family, on depressive symptoms of Japanese working mothers. *The Japanese Journal of Developmental Psychology*, 14(3), 272–283. 10.11201/jjdp.14.272.

Komorida, Tatsuo (2016). The causal condition that distinguishes "suicide by overwork" from "death by overwork": Qualitative comparative analyses (QCA) of judicial precedents. *Sociological Theory and Methods*, 31(2), 211–225. 10.11218/ojjams.31.211.

Komura, Mitsuyo, & Ishitake, Tatsuya (2012). The relationship between burnout, personal traits, and the work environment of caregivers in group homes. *Japanese Journal of Public Health*, 59(11), 822–832. 10.11236/jph.59.11_822.

Kubo, Tomohide, Sasaki, Tsukasa, & Matsumoto, Shun (2010). Relationship between emotional load and behavioral fatigue in simulation of long-time intensive work. *Journal of Occupational Safety and Health*, 3(1), 47–54. 10.2486/josh.3.47.

Matsuyama, Kazuki (2010). Job attitudes and mental health of nonpermanent employees. *Japanese Journal of Administrative Science*, 23(2), 107–121. 10.5651/jaas.23.107.

Ministry of Economy, Trade, and Industry. (2018). Enhancing health and productivity management. Retrieved from https://www.meti.go.jp/policy/mono_info_service/healthcare/downloadfiles/180717health-and-productivity-management.pdf.

Ministry of Health, Labour, and Welfare. (2012). Inquire at the equal employment office of your prefectural labour bureau. Retrieved from https://www.mhlw.go.jp/bunya/koyoukintou/pamphlet/pdf/funso_en.pdf.

Ministry of Health, Labour, and Welfare. (2017). Syokuba no pawaa harasumento ni kansuru jittai chosa hokokusyo.[Workplace power harassment survey in

FY2016.] Retrieved from https://www.mhlw.go.jp/file/04-Houdouhappyou-11208000-Roudoukijunkyoku-Kinroushaseikatsuka/0000164176.pdf.
Ministry of Health, Labour, and Welfare. (2018). Outline of the act on the arrangement of related acts to promote work style reform. Retrieved from https://www.mhlw.go.jp/english/policy/employ-labour/labour-standards/dl/201904kizyun.pdf.
Ministry of Health, Labour, and Welfare. (2019a). 2018 monthly labour survey. Retrieved from https://www.mhlw.go.jp/toukei/itiran/roudou/monthly/30/30r/30r.html.
Ministry of Health, Labour, and Welfare. (2019b). Annual health, labour and welfare report 2018. Retrieved from https://www.mhlw.go.jp/stf/wp/hakusyo/kousei/18/.
Ministry of Health, Labour, and Welfare. (2019c). Gaikokujin koyo jyokyo no todokede jyokyo matome (heisei 30 nen 10 gatsu matu genzai). [Status of reporting on the employment of foreign workers by employers (October 2018).] Retrieved from https://www.mhlw.go.jp/stf/newpage_03337.html.
Ministry of Health, Labour, and Welfare. (2019d). Heisei 30 nen ban karoshi tou boshi taisaku hakusyo. [White paper on prevention of karoshi 2018.] Retrieved from https://www.mhlw.go.jp/wp/hakusyo/karoushi/18/index.html.
Ministry of Health, Labour, and Welfare. (2019e). Heisei 30 nen do karoshi tou no rosai hosyo jyokyo. [Status of industrial accident compensation for karoshi, etc. In FY2018.] Retrieved from https://www.mhlw.go.jp/stf/newpage_05400.html.
Ministry of Internal Affairs and Communications. (2019). 2018 labor force survey. Retrieved from http://www.stat.go.jp/english/data/roudou/results/annual/ft/index.html.
Mori, Kohei, Iwata, Ruka, & Tanaka, Atsushi (2014). Study of factors affecting the mental health of teachers involved in special needs education: Analysis of work area and employment. *Asian Journal of Human Services*, 6, 111–124. 10.14391/ajhs.6.111.
Morinaga, Yuta. (2019). Uerubiingu keiei no kangaekata to susumekata: Kenko keiei no shintenkai [The theory and practice of well-being management: New developments in health and productivity management.] Tokyo, Japan: Rodo Simbunsya.
Morita, Shinichiro (2018). The relation between job satisfaction and mental health among white-collared regular workers and involuntary non-regular workers: Focus on the support provided by supervisors and co-workers. *Japanese Association of Industrial/Organizational Psychology Journal*, 31(2), 155–166.
Nagata, Shoji (2005). Sangyo sutoresu [occupational stress]. In Ishikawa, T. & Kawano, T. (Eds.), *Dictionary of stress*. Tokyo, Japan: Asakura Syoten.
Nakada, Akihiro, Iwasaki, Shinichi, Kanchika, Masaru, Nakao, Takehisa, Deguchi, Yasuhiko, Konishi, Akihito, & Inoue, Koki (2016). Relationship between depressive symptoms and perceived individual level occupational stress among Japanese schoolteachers. *Industrial Health*, 54(5), 396–402. 10.2486/indhealth.2015-0195.
Nakahara, Tomoko (2007). The gap between the employment system and stress: Focusing on the full-time non-regular employment of women with pre-schoolers. *Japanese Journal of Family Relations*, 26, 49–60.
Nakata, Akinori, Haratani, Takashi, Kawakami, Norito, Takahashi, Masaya, Shimizu, Hiroyuki, Miki, Akiko, & Araki, Shunichi (2001). Relationship

between perceived job stress and sleep habits in daytime female workers: An epidemiological study of employees in an electric equipment manufacturing company in Japan. *Japanese Journal of Behavioral Medicine*, 7(1), 39–46. 10.11331/jjbm.7.39.

Nii, Momoko, Tsuda, Akira, Tou, Ka, Yamahiro, Tomomi, & Irie, Masahiro (2018). Development of the power harassment questionnaire for workplaces. *Stress Management Research*, 14(2), 78–90.

Nishikitani, Mariko, Nakao, Mutsuhiro, Karita, Kanae, Nomura, Kyoko, & Yano, Eiji (2005). Influence of overtime work, sleep duration, and perceived job characteristics on the physical and mental status of software engineers. *Industrial Health*, 43(4), 623–629. 10.2486/indhealth.43.623.

Nishitani, Naoko, & Sakakibara, Hisataka (2010). Job stress factors, stress response, and social support in association with insomnia of Japanese male workers. *Industrial Health*, 48(2), 178–184. 10.2486/indhealth.48.178.

Nozaki, Takuro, Mafune, Kosuke, Inoue, Akiomi, Tanaka, Nobuaki, Hori, Chiemi, Masuda, Kazuyuki, & Hiro, Hisanori (2012). The relationship between job stressors and mental health in relation to overtime work hours. *Health Development*, 17(2), 57–62.

OECD. (2020). LFS - Average Annual Hours Worked. Retrieved from https://stats.oecd.org/Index.aspx?DatasetCode=ANHRS accessed on 22 Jun 2020.

Ogura, Kazuya (2008). Long working hours in Japan: International comparison and research subjects. *The Japanese Journal of Labour Studies*, 575, 4–16.

Ozono, yoko (2010). Non-regular employees' job stress and their status as key workforces. *Journal of Career Design Studies*, 6, 19–34.

Suzumura, Miwa, Fushiki, Yasuhiro, Kobayashi, Kota, Oura, Asae, Suzumura, Shigeo, Yamashita, Masafumi, & Mori, Mitsuru (2013). A cross-sectional study on association of work environment, coping style, and other risk factors with depression among caregivers in group homes in Japan. *Industrial Health*, 51(4), 417–423. 10.2486/indhealth.2012-0204.

Takahashi, Miho, Morita, Shinichiro, & Ishidu, Kazuko (2014). The comparison of the mental health of full-time workers, part-time workers and unemployed people: Focusing on the voluntariness of the employment situation and attitude towards work. *The Japanese Journal of Labour Studies*, 650, 82–96.

Takaki, Jiro, Taniguchi, Toshiyo, Fukuoka, Etsuko, Fujii, Yasuhito, Tsutsumi, Akizumi, Nakajima, Kazuo, & Hirokawa, Kumi (2010). Workplace bullying could play important roles in the relationships between job strain and symptoms of depression and sleep disturbance. *Journal of Occupational Health*, 52(6), 367–374. 10.1539/joh.L10081.

Takeuchi, Masumi, Nomura, Kyoko, Horie, Saki, Okinaga, Hiroko, Perumalswami, Chithra R., & Jagsi, Reshma. (2018). Direct and indirect harassment experiences and burnout among academic faculty in Japan. *The Tohoku Journal of Experimental Medicine*, 245(1), 37–44. 10.1620/tjem.245.37.

Taniguchi, Toshiyo, Takaki, Jiro, Harano, Kaori, Hirokawa, Kumi, Takahashi, Kazumi, & Fukuoka, Etsuko (2012). Associations between workplace bullying, harassment, and stress reactions of professional caregivers at welfare facilities for the elderly in Japan. *Journal of Occupational Health*, 54(1), 1–9.

Taniguchi, Toshiyo, Takaki, Jiro, Hirokawa, Kumi, Fujii, Yasuhito, & Harano, Kaori (2016). Associations of workplace bullying and harassment with stress reactions: A two-year follow-up study. *Industrial Health*, 54(2), 131–138. 10. 2486/indhealth.2014-0206.

Tarumi, Kimio, & Hagihara, Akihito (2002). The effects of working hours and vacations on distress: A study of white-collar workers in a Japanese manufacturing company. *Japanese Journal of Health Promotion*, 4(2), 87–99.

The Japan Institute for Labour Policy and Training. (2013). Workplace bullying and harassment. Retrieved from https://www.jil.go.jp/english/reports/documents/jilpt-reports/no.12.pdf.

The Japan Institute for Labour Policy and Training. (2016). Ninshin tou wo riyu to suru hurieki toriatsukai oyobi sekusyuaru harasumento ni kansuru jittai chosa kekka. [A survey of disadvantage handling and sexual harassment due to pregnancy etc.] Retrieved from https://www.jil.go.jp/institute/research/2016/150.html.

The Japan Institute for Labour Policy and Training. (2019). Syokuba no pawaa harasumento ni kansuru hiaringu chosa kekka. [Interview report on power harassment in workplace.] Retrieved from https://www.jil.go.jp/institute/siryo/2019/216.html.

Tominaga, Maki, & Asakura, Takashi (2006). The effect of perceived work and organizational characteristics on psychological distress and intention to quit of information technology professionals. *Japanese Journal of Public Health*, 53(3), 196–207. 10.11236/jph.53.3_196.

Tsuno, Kanami (2016). Recent evidence in terms of antecedents and health and organizational outcomes of workplace bullying. *The Japanese Journal of Stress Sciences*, 31(1), 37–50.

Tsutsumi, Akizumi, Shimazu, Akihito, Eguchi, Hisashi, Inoue, Akiomi, & Kawakami, Norito (2018). A Japanese stress check program screening tool predicts employee long-term sickness absence: A prospective study. *Journal of Occupational Health*, 60(1), 55–63. 10.1539/joh.17-0161-OA.

Uehara, Naohiro, Kanbara, Ryu, Shido, Koichi, Nishi, Motoi, & Miyake, Hirotsugu (2014). The relevant factors and depressive symptoms in male workers of hokkaido and tohoku: Study in by type of employment. *Bulletin of Social Medicine*, 31(1), 95–104.

Umehara, Katsura, Ohya, Yukihiro, Kawakami, Norito, Tsutsumi, Akizumi, & Fujimura, Masanori (2007). Association of work-related factors with psychosocial job stressors and psychosomatic symptoms among Japanese pediatricians. *Journal of Occupational Health*, 49(6), 467–481. 10.1539/joh.49.467.

Virtanen, Marianna, Kivimäki, Mika, Joensuu, Matti, Virtanen, Pekka, Elovainio, Marko, & Vahtera, Jussi (2005). Temporary employment and health: A review. *International Journal of Epidemiology*, 34(3), 610–622. 10.1093/ije/dyi024.

Yamaguchi, Yoshie. (2010). The current status of operations in community general support centers and the correlation of personal traits, work environment and occupational stress. *Sangyo Eiseigaku Zasshi*, 52(3), 111–122. 10.1539/sangyoeisei.B9010.

8 Organizational Stress
A Critical Review from Nigeria

Chianu H. Dibia, Emeka S. Oruh, Omotayo A. Osibanjo, and Ojebola Oluwatunmise

Introduction

Stress has become a global phenomenon that occurs in all facets of life – including the workplace. Stress is a contemporary and fundamental problem that reflects a sense of anxiety, tension, and depression that spans through human endeavor; it has become an unavoidable consequence of modern living (Okeke, Echo, & Oboreh, 2016). Stress is generally believed to be a state of the mind as well as the body and is created by specific biochemical reactions in the human body as well as psychological responses to situations caused by demands from the environmental or internal forces that cannot be met by the resources available to the individual (Suresh, 2008). Basically, it can be conceptualized as an unpleasant emotional reaction that a person has when he or she perceives an event either internally or from their environment to be threatening, and, when an individual faces such threatening events, he or she is vulnerable to anxiety, depression, anger, hostility, inadequacy, and low frustration tolerance (Halgin & Whitbourne, 2007).

However, Akinyele, Epetimehin, Ogbari, Adesola, and Akinyele (2014) suggest that a reasonable amount of stress is essential to foster enthusiasm and creativity for optimal productivity but observed that intense, or simply put, "too much" stress in the work environment could lead to considerable risk to workers' safety, health, and emotional stability. This is further corroborated by Okeke *et al.* (2016) who have argued that stress can either be positive (eustress) or negative (distress). Eustress results in stimulating an employee, thus enhancing work performance and positively encouraging workers to make efforts, while distress results in adverse effects on workers' health and performance. Greenberg and Baron (2008) however, added that, in respect of how stress is viewed, it is essential to note that stress on the job will have a negative outcome on the job and the worker at most times.

Work has become an essential part of our existence as human beings, and the quality of the workforce and the workplace significantly contribute to an organization's ability to deliver its goals and existence.

However, stress is prevalent in the Nigerian work environment, as a review of extant literature highlights that the stress phenomenon remains a fundamental problem plaguing organizations across several sectors – including healthcare and education (Okebukola & Jegede, 1989; Ofoegbu & Nwadiani, 2006; Dibia, 2017; Ezenwaji et al., 2019).

Organizational stress is of serious concern to organizations as a whole and to managers in particular, because, when employees feel helpless, desperate, and disappointed, they experience distress, which fosters a sense of loss of feelings of security and adequacy. In turn, this affects the effectiveness and productivity of organizations as well as the morale and health of the workers (Bewell, Yakubu, Owotunse, & Ojih, 2014). Workplace stress which is experienced by individuals working in Nigeria can be attributed to the desperate quest by organizations to reduce labor costs and the drive to maximize production within a difficult economic terrain (David, 2016; Dibia, 2017). In such instances, workers are engaged in a multiplicity of tasks and thereby face undue pressure. That said, when people experience work-related stress in other climes, especially in industrialized countries, they are encouraged to understand how they feel and to take advantage of the stress management measures put in place to help them cope. Unfortunately, this is not often the case in Nigeria (Bewell et al., 2014). In a more recent study by Nwokeoma et al. (2019), it was observed that, and despite significant exposure to stressors at work – such as high workloads and traumatic events on the job – workers in Nigeria are still deprived of basic stress management mechanisms (e.g., counseling) by their employers and ultimately the Nigerian state, thereby compounding the levels of stress experienced.

It is against this backdrop that a substantial review of systematically selected studies on organizational stress and the coping mechanisms employed by workers in Nigeria, as well as the role of culture and weak institutional framework as mediating factors for this phenomenon within the Nigerian context, is subsequently undertaken.

Organizational Stress in Nigeria versus Other Parts of the World

Stress in organizations is a widespread phenomenon globally, with varying consequences. Reviewed literature revealed that stress exists virtually everywhere. For instance, in 2018, 64% of Americans considered in a survey perceived "work" to be one of the significant causes of stress (American Psychological Association, 2018). Some of the leading causes of workplace stress in the United States are a lack of employee-decision freedom especially in high work demands with low control, uncertainty about workplace aspects such as job insecurity, and poorly managed conflicts at work (Quick & Henderson, 2016). In the United Kingdom (UK), a survey conducted in the Health and Safety

Executive (HSE) found that work-related stress accounts for 57% and ill-health for 44% of working days lost between 2017 and 2018 (HSE, 2018). This work-related stress in the UK was attributed to factors such as lack of managerial support, high workload, role uncertainty, and violence at work; these are somewhat similar to the identified workers' stressors in the United States.

In the context of emerging economies – which perhaps share a higher similarity with Nigeria – in India, inadequate workplaces were attributed to being a leading cause of organizational stress (Venugopal et al., 2016). In Brazil, Macedo, Junior, and Sant'Anna (2017) emphasize that the lack of organizational structure, work overload and monotonous job tasks, absence of recognition, lack of career development, unsupportive leadership style, and the lack of inter and intradepartmental communication all constitute as work stressors.

Unique Stressors and Strains in Nigeria

Nigeria is commonly referred to as the giant of Africa, and, in 2014 – following a change in the approach used in measuring her Gross Domestic Product (GDP), Nigeria was acclaimed to have the biggest economy in Africa (Nigerian Bureau of Statistic, 2014). Evidence of the Nigerian economy, when considered superficially, suggests a prosperous nation. However, a consideration of studies on workplace stress in the Nigerian context shows that the growth of the Nigerian economy could perhaps be at the expense of the welfare of the workforce, as there has been a significant rise in the stressful conditions which individuals working in Nigeria are exposed to (Nweke, 2015; Amazue & Onyishi, 2016). Specifically, in the Nigerian setting, causes of workplace stress are not only numerous, but also complex. In most instances, organizations cite the need to reduce costs (due to rising costs of production), which often results in increased fear, uncertainty, and higher levels of stress on the part of the workers (Nweke, 2015).

Other research in Nigeria, such as Ibem, Anosike, Azuh, and Mosaku (2011), also identify high workload, lack of feedback, bureaucracy, and inadequate on-the-job training as stressors facing workers in the Nigerian work environment. In addition, authoritarian leadership style, ineffective communication channels, excessive workload, pressure from families, conflicting demands of the three elements in the organization (i.e., the employer, the employee, and the customer) are all stressors that Nigerian workers are exposed to (Okeke et al., 2016).

More broadly, Nicholas, Obasi, and Anene (2017) contextualized stressors which Nigerian workers are exposed to into work content and work context. Work content that triggers stress experienced by workers in Nigeria includes tedious work repetition and meaningless tasks, workload and work pace (either too much or too little to do and working under time pressure), working hours (inflexible, long and unsocial, unpredictable, and ill-designed shift systems), participation and control (lack of participation in decision-making, lack of control over work processes, pace, hours, methods, and the work environment). Work context, however, includes lack of career development, job insecurity, lack of promotion opportunities, work of low social value, unclear or unfair performance evaluation systems, being over or underskilled for a job, poor interpersonal relationships with supervisors and colleagues, and work-life imbalance like conflicting demands of work and home (Nicholas et al., 2017). Other all so common stressors to workers in Nigeria are socioeconomic variables like family issues, high cost of living, and poor purchasing power (Olusegun, Oluwasayo, & Olawoyimn, 2014; Amazue & Onyishi, 2016).

The reasons for Nigeria's enormous numbers of strains and stressors are not farfetched. Nigeria as a society is regarded as a fecund ground in which stressors emanate due to factors such as unreliable electricity and water supply, inflation, bad roads, and armed banditry (Onoyase, 2015; Amazue & Onyishi, 2016). Also, it is obvious that the Nigerian economic environment is accompanied by occupational stress as a result of restructuring, downsizing, and re-engineering owing to the intense competition which organizations are contending with (David, 2016; Dibia, 2017). Workers in Nigeria are exposed to excessive and unpredictable work schedules and the absence of job security, as is evident in the frequent mass retrenchment of thousands of workers both in the public and private sectors due to the constant shifts in the Nigerian economy.

Furthermore, the present state of the Nigerian work environment has led authors such as Olusegun, Oluwasayo, and Olawoyim (2014) to state that more than half of all Nigerian workers feel the pressure of job-related stress – an assertion which is possibly not improbable when industry-specific studies are reviewed. The industry-specific studies included in this chapter follow from a systematic search of open access sources for studies about organizational stress in Nigeria (see Table 8.1 in the Appendix, for the summary of studies reviewed, their authors, context considered, stressors/strains identified, and coping mechanisms)[1]. 24 studies were found, and they have been evaluated in completing this chapter. 22 studies are included in Appendix 1, as they represent contemporary views on organizational stress in Nigeria; while the other two studies – Cooper (1984) and Okebukola and Jegede (1989) – found as part of the search, were excluded from the table and subsequent discussion, as they were published in 1984 and 1989. However, the sectors which they considered as part of their early studies in the Nigerian context are perhaps covered by more recent studies included in the subsequent section. The industries covered by most of the studies were education (7), healthcare (7), banking (3), and manufacturing (3). Other sectors considered by fewer studies are construction (1) and policing (1).

Stress in the Nigerian Education Sector

The education sector is one of the prominent sectors given considerable coverage by workplace stress studies in the Nigerian context (e.g., Salami, 2010; Onyishi & Ugwu, 2012; Ejue, 2013; Osibanjo, Salau, Falola, & Oyewunmi, 2016; Ogbuanya et al., 2017; Ugwoke et al., 2018). Sadly, evidence of significant levels of workplace stress can be found in all levels of the education sector in Nigeria – from primary to tertiary education. The effects of workplace stress on workers and on the educational institutions where they work are damning. Onyishi and Ugwu (2012) mention in their study involving administrative staff that, in one of the prominent public universities in Nigeria, workplace stress as a result of high workload, role conflict, and ambiguity led to a reduction in worker engagement and the excessive use of alcohol by workers, not just outside of work but notably during working hours.

In their study on the issue of workplace stress and organizational performance in another Nigerian public university, Osibanjo et al. (2016) report that, following the current high rates of student enrolment and massive expansion drives by higher education institutions in Nigeria, workplace stress is on the increase. Some of the stressors identified are role conflict or incongruence (inadequate match between the demands of work and worker's characteristics), inequity and unfair treatment of workers (topics regarding pay, recognition, and promotion), and the distance traveled by workers from their homes to work and back. Role conflict was also one of the causes of stress stated in the preceding study in this section by Onyishi and Ugwu (2012). Ejue (2013) supports these findings and points out that there are high levels of stress due to work experienced by university workers in Nigeria, and it is irrespective of whether individuals work for federal or state-owned universities.

There is also evidence that highlights that workers in privately owned universities in Nigeria are also plagued by stress at work. Akinyele et al. (2014), in their account of workplace stress experienced by academic staff in a private university located in Southwest Nigeria, identify similar stressors as those found by studies in public universities. Stressors – which include work overload and resource inadequacy and workload or work intensification – were linked to having an adverse impact on the quality of graduates produced by the university. According to Akinyele et al. (2014), contributory factors to the increase in workload include lack of time for adequate preparation of teaching materials, meetings, and research, large class sizes and students' diverse needs, and the implementation of new study programs that are not adequately resourced. Resource inadequacy was considered to harm the quality of research published by academics as well as academic excellence.

In a more recent study (Ugwoke et al., 2018) which centered on special education teachers in southeast Nigeria, it was shown that these teachers are highly vulnerable to workplace stress, which might result in individuals experiencing insomnia, fatigue, and engagement in substance abuse. This is besides a reduction of the quality of teaching delivered by these teachers, a decline in the tolerance of students' misbehavior, and the adoption of cruel disciplinary measures to students' misdeeds. Interestingly, the causes of stress which Ugwoke et al. (2018) focus on are work-related irrational beliefs rather than typical stressors such as workload, role conflict, and role ambiguity as mentioned by other studies in the sector. That said, the authors do not give examples as to what these work-related irrational beliefs could be. The study by Ugwoke et al. (2018) mirrors the study and findings of Ogbuanya et al. (2017) on workplace stress, albeit involving a different group of workers (i.e., electronics workshop instructors working in technical colleges in Southeast Nigeria). Ogbuanya et al. (2017) describe work-related irrational beliefs as "beliefs that result in stress due to unhelpful ways of thinking adopted by highly stressed teachers about themselves". These thoughts or beliefs are about the high demands of the work they experience and are associated with high stress which might considerably exacerbate stress.

In secondary schools, Salami (2010) points out that workplace stress could result in counterproductive work behaviors (CWB) by teachers in Southwest Nigeria. Negative affectivity, i.e., the extent that individuals experience distressing emotions – for example, fear, hostility, and anxiety (Salami, 2010), is considered to be a mediating factor. The CWBs include harming or an intent to harm the organization and its stakeholders, physical and verbal aggression, acts of theft and sabotage, and bullying. Besides this, it was discovered that, in the Nigerian context, workers with high negative affectivity are more prone to engage in CWBs when faced with high levels of work stress. However, job stress did not increase the tendency of workers with low negative affectivity to adopt CWBs.

Stress in the Nigerian Healthcare Sector

Organizational stress has been studied in the Nigerian healthcare sector by numerous scholars (e.g., Mojoyinola, 2008; Gandi, Wai, Karick, & Dagona, 2011; Abaraogu, Ezema, & Nwosu, 2016; Olusegun et al., 2014; Lawal & Idemudia, 2017; Ezenwaji et al., 2019). A significant number of these studies focus on nurses (e.g., Mojoyinola, 2008; Gandi et al., 2011; Lawal & Idemudia, 2017; Ezenwaji et al., 2019). Overall, the studies highlight the current high levels of stress experienced by workers within this sector.

In the study by Gandi et al. (2011) about the role of stress and the level of burnout as a result of work among 2,245 nurses working in Nigeria, it was found that the job demands on nurses were high. However, high levels of resources were provided to nurses to perform their jobs, and these serve as a buffer for the negative effects of job demands. That said, the authors go on to state that, in most instances, the resources provided to balance job demands are not sufficient to prevent the organizational stress faced by nurses. This is due to each nurse having many patients with different needs to attend to – such as the patients' need for empathy and connections. In addition, the authors state that nurses in Nigeria experience high levels of exhaustion that may reflect accumulated tiredness as a result of broader political and economic worries which nurses bear, and this spills over into work and results in work-related exhaustion.

In a parallel and more recent study about work-related stress, burnout, and associated sociodemographic factors – such as gender, age, and work experience and environment – that are affecting nurses in Southeast Nigeria by Ezenwaji et al. (2019), it was discovered that sociodemographic factors explained, to a minute extent, the variability in work stress and burnout experienced by nurses. Gender was identified to be the only sociodemographic factor with a significant correlation with work-related stress – with female nurses being more stressed than their male counterparts. However, this significant correlation does not extend to burnout. The findings on gender and susceptibility to work-related stress perhaps highlight the entrenchment of gender roles and reactions in the Nigerian context.

Other research, such as Olusegun et al. (2014), looks at a wider selection of workers in the Nigerian healthcare sector. They identify workload, career development, and work-family conflict as major causes of organizational stress experienced by healthcare workers. Other sources of job-related stress mentioned in the study are repetitive work, the lack of communication between superiors, subordinates, and co-workers, underloading (having little or no work to do), uncomfortable working conditions, and exposure to dangerous conditions on the job (unsuitable physical work environment). Following these stressors, 57% of healthcare workers who took part in the study by Olusegun et al. (2014) said that they have or have had one form of illness or another as a result of the stressful conditions of work. These illnesses include headaches, body pains, fevers, and malaria. In another study about healthcare workers in a hospital in the Oyo State, Southwest Nigeria by Owolabi, Owolabi, OlaOlorun, and Olofin (2012), continuous exposure to highly stressful conditions at work was linked to the development of hypertension in healthcare workers.

Stress in the Nigerian Banking Sector

The Nigerian banking sector, which is driven by a free market economy, places higher demands on workers because of today's competitive environment as well as global bank reforms. For instance, the introduction of the e-payment system into the banking industry demands that employees must get trained to acquire the needed skills associated with the new reform. However, Nigerian banks always want to achieve more with less input because profitability is always their focus, at the detriment of the workforce (Ogungbamila, Balogun, Ogungbamila, & Oladele, 2014; Okeke et al., 2016). The authors go on to state that workers in the Nigerian banking system always live in persistent fear as a result of work overload, risk of fraud, unrealistic targets, job insecurity, risk of kidnapping and armed robbery attacks on banks, as well as organizational restructurings like mergers and acquisition.

In another study (Olatona, Ezeobika, Okafor, & Owoeye, 2014) conducted in the Lagos State – a state with the largest population and industry in Nigeria – the level of knowledge, the prevalent associated factors of stress amongst bank staff (on permanent contracts), and their coping strategies (see coping mechanism section of this chapter for coping strategies) were investigated. In the study, it was found that the majority of bank workers who took part in the study had poor to fair knowledge of the causes of stress, despite the workers classifying themselves as experiencing significantly moderate to high levels of stress (91.5%). Indeed, it was acknowledged that there is an inverse association between poor levels of knowledge of stress by workers and the experience of stress. The causes of stress to Nigerian bankers identified by Olatona et al. (2014) included some of the stressors found by Okeke et al. (2016), such as high workload and job insecurity. However, other stressors such as long working hours (e.g., some workers in the Nigerian banking sector start work as early as 7:30 a.m. and might not leave work until 9:00 p.m. and, in most cases, with a commute of no less than an hour to-and-fro home to work), lack of time to relax, and impatient customers were also mentioned as significant causes of stress. These stressors caused workers to develop anxiety and hypertension and had an adverse impact on their overall health. Workers also reported a rise in job dissatisfaction, poor working relationships with colleagues and other stakeholders, and low productivity.

Stress in the Nigerian Manufacturing Sector

Workplace stress is also prevalent in the Nigerian manufacturing sector. Following a study of manufacturers in Nigeria, Babajide and Akintayo (2011) attribute organizational stress experienced by workers to a poor relationship with superiors, task structure, workload, and working environment and technology. The experience of high-level stress in the workplace affected workers' psychological well-being negatively – causing mental disorders, depression, and fatigue – and this was reflected in their behavior at work (e.g., difficulties in complying with rules and regulations at work and instruction given by superiors, as well as a refusal to identify with the organization). For demographic factors, it was pointed out that the effects of increased exposure to high levels of workplace stress were more pronounced in older workers, and they considered this to be more deleterious to work behavior when compared to younger workers in the manufacturing sector. However, there was no significant difference between genders.

It is important to state that both domestic and foreign-owned manufacturers operating in Nigeria are all culprits in subjecting workers to high levels of workplace stress – a conclusion reached by David (2016), following a study on work-related stress among workers of foreign-owned manufacturers operating in Nigeria. David (2016) identifies one of the stressors pointed out by Babajide and Akintayo (2011), i.e., unfavorable physical working conditions – excessive noise and heat, and insufficient space and crowding, in addition to other stressors such as poor career development, job insecurity, and long working hours. These stressors were found to harm workers' health and well-being as they cause restlessness, nervousness, indigestion, anxiety, neck pain, headache, and an inability to concentrate.

Beyond a mixture of discrete and process, product manufacturers considered by the previous authors (whose works have been reviewed in this section), it is essential to discuss the work of Umege (2014) who studies organizational stress in the Nigerian oil and gas industry – a critical sector in the Nigerian economy. The study compares the incidence of occupational stress-induced hypertension between onshore and offshore engineering workers in the Nigerian oil and gas manufacturing sector. It was found that there is an association between the prevalence of occupational stress-induced hypertension and job location, with onshore workers/professionals being more prone to this type of hypertension as compared to their offshore peers. Also, age and gender were found to be relevant factors. Male workers were found to be more susceptible to occupational stress-induced hypertension as compared to their female colleagues. Likewise, workers between the ages of 30–49 had an increased tendency of suffering from occupational stress-induced hypertension as compared to other age groups.

Other Sectors

Aside from the sectors already discussed in this chapter on workplace stress, other sectors in which studies about workplace stress have been conducted in Nigeria include construction (Ojo, Adeyeye, Opawole, & Kajimo-Shakantu, 2019) and policing (Nwokeoma et al., 2019). However, compared to the education, healthcare, banking, and manufacturing sectors, these sectors have been relatively underexplored. Despite the minimal levels of exploration into the occurrences and experiences of workplace stress in these sectors, the studies in construction and in policing paint almost similar pictures of the happenings in other sectors.

Ojo et al. (2019), in their study of quantity surveyors working for both public and private establishments in Southwest Nigeria, highlight that the significant stressors experienced by these quantity surveyors include: inadequate staffing, insufficient training on the job, poor planning, poor communication, lack of feedback, interpersonal conflicts, bullying and harassment, inadequate pay and poor work status, discrimination, and a lack of career progression. It is mentioned that discriminatory barriers between the genders over career and financial advancement is common in the construction industry – quantity surveying included – and this causes higher levels of stress experienced by women in the profession. These stressors lead to increased irritability, invasion of family life, loss of self-esteem, anger, and feelings of helplessness among quantity surveyors. It also affects the quantity surveying organizations adversely, as it was stated that workplace stress experienced by individuals might lead to delays in project completion (Ojo et al., 2019).

In the Nigerian Police Force, Nwokeoma et al. (2019) observe the incidence of high levels of workplace stress among police officers. It is stated that officers in the Nigerian Police Force are stressed not only as a result of low wages and high workloads, but also because of frequent exposure to traumatic situations. The situations are comprised of community clashes, killings as a result of oil licks, bombs, and flooding, which result in severe psychological trauma. Also, there have been significant cases of police officers being killed while discharging their duties, not to mention they are also faced with inadequate support from the Nigerian authorities if ever harmed during the discharge from their duties. Nwokeoma et al. (2019) further assert that cultural demands for professional excellence in policing make the experience of stress worse. There have also been instances when Nigerian police officers have attempted suicide while out on patrol, as a result of the stress-inducing traumatic events that they are exposed to as part of their jobs.

Coping Mechanisms

Following a discussion of the unique stressors or strains in the Nigerian organizational context, this section will consider the coping mechanisms used in managing workplace stress. Stress management refers to the strategies of coping, recovering, reinterpreting, refraining, and cognitive restructuring adopted by an individual which may be with the help of their organization to make changes that can reduce stress or to take actions that can alter the impacts of stress (Agwu & Tiemo, 2012). From the review of studies on stress in the Nigerian context, evidence suggests that there are limited organizational provisions of stress-coping strategies used to mitigate this contemporary issue (Salami, 2010; Olatona et al., 2014; Amazue & Onyishi, 2016; Ojo et al., 2019; Nwokeoma et al., 2019). In addition, workers are charged with the responsibility of developing their own mechanisms to cope with stress, which are often unhealthy or a mixture of both helpful and unhelpful practices – probably due to inadequate knowledge of stress-related issues and how to cope with them (Onyishi & Ugwu, 2012; Olatona et al., 2014; Amazue & Onyishi, 2016).

Olatona et al. (2014), in their study about workplace stress in Nigerian banks, identify some of the diverse coping mechanisms adopted by workers – such as listening to music, exercising, meditating, relaxing, drinking alcohol, smoking, crying, overeating, and doing nothing. They also highlight that most of the workers adopted healthy coping mechanisms (92.4%), although most (69.5%) combined the healthy practices with unhealthy ones – making a case for banks to implement stress management programs to help their workers in developing better coping mechanisms or in supplying them with the knowledge of healthy and unhealthy coping mechanisms. Amazue and Onyishi (2016) also allude to the latter point, following their study of organizational stress experienced by bank workers in Nigeria. They state that banks have a responsibility to develop programs involving professionals as part of their human resource policies to interact with their workers and to provide them with training on more effective approaches to managing organizational stress.

Beyond banks, the studies reviewed other sectors of work in the Nigerian context (e.g., Onyishi & Ugwu, 2012 – education and Nwokeoma et al., 2019 – policing) and provided similar accounts on coping with stress. However, other identified approaches to coping with stress include a flexible work schedule, break periods at work, exercise, and seeking clarification from colleagues and superiors. The use of rational emotive behavior coaching or intervention (REBC), was also put forward by several studies on workplace stress in Nigeria as a means for workers to develop effective ways of coping (Ogbuanya et al., 2017; Ugwoke et al., 2018; Nwokeoma et al., 2019). The approach promotes coaching workers to develop stress-coping skills such as goal setting, Socratic questioning, and relaxation training (see Table 8.1 in the appendix for extended list). That said, although the studies confirm the effectiveness of this approach in helping workers cope during the period of the studies/interventions, and following the completion of these studies, there has been no further evidence to suggest the long-term sustainability of the benefits or practices from this approach. At this point, it is safe to say that high levels of workplace stress are prevalent in Nigeria's contemporary organizations, and workers are predominately charged with the responsibility of coping with stress with little or no organizational support.

Culture and the Nigerian State as Culprits to the Organizational Stress Experience of Workers in Nigeria

It would be difficult, if not impossible, to consider the topic of contemporary organizational stress in Nigeria without accounting for the roles of institutions (i.e., the Nigerian government) and the national culture in contributing to the increasingly stressful nature of work and the difficulties faced by the Nigerian worker in coping with organizational stress.

The failure of the Nigerian government and its contribution to the current state of organizational stress in Nigeria is exemplified by inadequate infrastructural provisions and weak enforcement of labor legislation that pervades the Nigerian terrain, making it difficult for workers to go about their daily lives and to demand better conditions of employment from their employers. For instance, in the Lagos State, which is the commercial nerve center of the country, one of the studies reviewed (Amazue & Onyishi, 2016) has highlighted that workers have to commute on roads that are in a deplorable state. Also, workers face chaotic traffic on roads, which leaves workers held up on the road for several hours every day. Workers also have to put up with chronic water shortage and erratic power supply – a situation not just limited to the Lagos State but also the entire nation (Gandi et al., 2011; Osibanjo et al., 2016). The situation is in addition to the weak enforcement of labor legislation that pervades the Nigerian employment context and the inadequate provisions for the rights of a Nigerian worker (Atilola, 2012; Umege, 2014). For instance, although the Employee's Compensation Act of 2010 makes provisions for employees to be able to make claims against their employers and to be compensated when work leads to "mental stress" (Atilola, 2012, p. 33), the Act has been criticized for failing to explicitly define a framework in determining mental stress (Atilola, 2012). It has even been suggested that the inclusion of mental stress as a part of this Act may have well been an afterthought (Atilola, 2012).

Thus, given the deplorable state of affairs, which contributes to high levels of organizational stress experienced by workers in Nigeria, one might question why the Nigerian workers are not outrightly demanding for a better deal. While this might be a difficult and complex question to fully answer within this chapter, one of the probable explanations that could be put forward as the answer is the national culture – the collective programming of the mind of individuals within a nation-state (Hofstede, 2001).

The role of culture as a contributory factor to the current levels of organizational stress in Nigeria can be illuminated using one of Hofstede's cultural dimensions – "power distance". Nigeria is categorized as a high power distance culture (Hofstede Insights, 2019), and in a high power distance culture, it is common for individuals not to question the unequal distribution of power or the ill-treatment received from the executive. This provides a plausible explanation for the current conditions that propagate and entrench the present state of organizational stress that permeates the Nigerian context – where workers struggle to cope with stressful conditions of work yet fail to heighten their demands for better conditions of work.

Conclusions and Summary

This chapter has explored organizational stress in Nigeria, examining the stressors and strains experienced by workers, stress-coping mechanisms, and the roles of the Nigerian state and culture in contributing to the current experience of workplace stress. Within the chapter, it is observed that organizational stress is a topical phenomenon that exists globally. However, there is a variation in the response to this issue among different jurisdictions.

In the Nigerian context, significant levels of organizational stress are observed. Workers are exposed to a wide range of stressors and strains at work against which they are struggling to cope. Besides this, it is observed that workers in Nigeria are also faced with exogenous stressors like threats emanating from social vices – such as kidnapping, armed robbery, and inadequate public infrastructure – which compound their experience of stress. Not to mention, the role of a high power distance culture prevents workers from challenging the status quo, as both the Nigerian Government and the owners of organizations are complacent to the plights of workers.

Furthermore, from the account provided in this chapter, it can be observed that most of the stress-coping mechanisms employed by workers are developed by the individual worker with little or no organizational or state support. That said, it is crucial to assert that most of the studies reviewed on organizational stress focus on identifying the stressors and strains at work, and less on how workers cope with stress. In view of the current evidence, it is therefore recommended that pertinent organizations and the Nigerian Government do more in helping workers within Nigeria to cope more effectively with stress and, where possible, reduce the significant factors leading to distress. Also, a more detailed study of the stress coping mechanisms of workers in Nigeria would be desirable.

Note

1 The databases interrogated include Business Source Complete, Scopus, and Google Scholar - using search terms such as "stress", "work* stress", "organization stress", "job* stress", "occupational stress" AND "Nigeria*".

References

Abaraogu, U. O., Ezema, C. I., & Nwosu, C. K. (2016). Job Stress Dimension and Work-related Musculoskeletal Disorders among Southeast Nigeria Physiotherapists. *International Journal of Occupational Safety and Ergonomics*, 1–9. http://dx.doi.org/10.1080/10803548.2016.1219476.

Agwu, M. O., & Tiemo, J. A. (2012). Problems and prospects of stress management in the Nigeria Liquefied Natural Gas construction project Bonny. *Journal of Emerging Trends in Economics and Management Sciences*, 3(3), 266–271.

Akinyele, S. T., Epetimehin, S., Ogbari, M., Adesola, A. O., & Akinyele, F. E. (2014). Occupational stress among academic staff in private university: Empirical evidence from covenant university, Nigeria. *Journal of Contemporary Management Research*, 8(1), 1–23.

Amazue, L. O., & Onyishi, I. E. (2016). Stress coping strategies, perceived organizational support and marital status as predictors of work–life balance among Nigerian bank employees. *Social Indicators Research*, 128(1), 147–159. https://doi.org/10.1007/s11205-015-1023-5.

American Psychological Association. (2018). *Stress in America^{TM}: Generation Z*. Retrieved from https://www.apa.org/news/press/releases/stress/2018/stress-gen-z.pdf.

Atilola, O. (2012). The challenges of assessing and providing compensation for mental stress under Nigeria's 2010 Employee's Compensation Act. *International Social Security Review*, 65(4), 31–50. https://doi.org/10.1111/j.1468-246X.2012.01446.x.

Babajide, E. O., & Akintayo, I. (2011). Occupational stress, psychological well being and workers' behavior in manufacturing industries in South-West Nigeria. *International Journal of Management and Innovation*, 3(1), 32–42.

Bewell, H., Yakubu, I., Owotunse, D., & Ojih, E. E. (2014). Work-induced stress and its influence on organizational effectiveness and productivity among Nigerian workers. *African Research Review*, 8(1), 112–125. http://dx.doi.org/10.4314/afrrev.v8i1.9.

Cooper, C. L. (1984). Executive stress: A ten-country comparison. *Human Resource Management*, 23(4), 395–407. https://doi.org/10.1002/hrm.3930230406.

David, A. (2016). Sources and effects of work-related stress among employees in foreign-owned manufacturing companies in Ogun state, Nigeria. *Journal of Human Resource Management*, 19(2), 31–43.

Dibia, C. H. (2017). *Lean manufacturing and employee working conditions in organizations operating in Nigeria: The managers' and supervisors' perspective*(Unpublished doctoral thesis) Retrieved from https://researchportal.port.ac.uk/portal/files/11068479/Lean_Manufacturing_and_Employee_Working_Conditions_in_Orgnisations_Operating_in_Nigeria_The_managers_and_supervisors_perspective.pdf.

Ejue, J. B. (2013). Comparison of occupational stress among academics in federal and state universities in Nigeria. *Research in Education*, 89(1), 85–89.

Ezenwaji, I. O., Eseadi, C., Okide, C. C., Nwosu, N. C., Ugwoke, S. C., Ololo, K. O., & Oboegbulem, A. I. (2019). Work-related stress, burnout, and related sociodemographic factors among nurses: Implications for administrators, research, and policy. *Medicine, 98*(3), 1–6. http://dx.doi.org/10.1097/MD.0000000000013889.

Gandi, J. C., Wai, P. S., Karick, H., & Dagona, Z. K. (2011). The role of stress and level of burnout in job performance among nurses. *Mental Health in Family Medicine, 8*(3), 181–194.

Greenberg, J., & Baron, R. A. (2008). *Behavior in Organizations* (9th ed.). New Jersey: Pearson Prentice Hall.

Halgin, R. P., & Whitbourne, S. K. (2007). *Abnormal Psychology Clinical Perspectives on Psychological Disorders* (5th ed.). New York: McGraw-Hill.

Hofstede, G. (2001). *Culture's Consequences: Comparing Values, Behaviours, Institutions and Organisations Across Nations* (2nd ed.). London: Sage.

Hofstede Insights (2019). Country Comparison: Nigeria. Retrieved from: https://www.hofstede-insights.com/country-comparison/nigeria/.

HSE (2018). *Work-related stress depression or anxiety statistic in Great Britain*. Retrieved from http://www.hse.gov.uk/statistics/causdis/stress.pdf.

Ibem, E. O., Anosike, N. M., Azuh, D. E., & Mosaku, T. O. (2011). Work stress among professionals in the building construction industry in Nigeria. *Australasian Journal of Construction Economics and Building, 11*(3), 45–57.

Lawal, A. M., & Idemudia, E. S. (2017). The role of emotional intelligence and organisational support on work stress of nurses in Ibadan, Nigeria. *Curationis, 40*(1), 1–8. https://doi.org/10.4102/.

Macedo, V. A., Junior, P. L. D., & Sant'Anna, A. D. S. (2017). Occupational stress: A study with supermarket professionals in Brazil. *International Journal of Business Management and Economic Research, 8*(6), 1115–1119.

Mojoyinola, J. K. (2008). Effects of job stress on health, personal and work behaviour of nurses in public hospitals in Ibadan Metropolis, Nigeria. *Studies on Ethno-Medicine, 2*(2), 143–148. https://doi.org/10.1080/09735070.2008.11886326.

Nicholas, A. I., Obasi, N. J., & Anene, O. P. (2017). The influence of job stress, commitment, job experience and employees performance in selected banks in Enugu. *Asian Journal of Applied Science and Technology, 1*(9), 451–463.

Nigerian Bureau of Statistic. (2014). *Measuring better: Frequently asked questions on the Rebasing / re-benchmarking of Nigeria's Gross domestic product (GDP)*. Retrieved from https://nigerianstat.gov.ng/elibrary?queries[search]=rebasing.

Nweke, J. O. (2015). Causes of job stress in the banking industry: A study of Guaranty Trust Bank Plc, Abakaliki, Ebonyi State, Nigeria. *International Journal of Education and Research, 3*(6), 145–156.

Nweke, J. O. (2016). Coping with job stress in the banking sector: A study of Guaranty Trust Bank Plc in Abakaliki, Ebonyi State, Nigeria. *Annals of Humanities and Development Studies, 7*(1), 52–60.

Nwokeoma, B. N., Ede, M. O., Nwosu, N., Ikechukwu-Illomuanya, A., Ogba, F. N., Ugwoezuonu, A. U., & Nwadike, N. (2019). Impact of rational emotive occupational health coaching on work-related stress management among staff of Nigeria police force. *Medicine*, 98(37), 1–7. http://dx.doi.org/10.1097/MD.0000000000016724.

Ofoegbu, F., & Nwadiani, M. (2006). Level of perceived stress among lecturers in Nigerian Universities. *Journal of instructional psychology*, 33(1), 66–74.

Ogbuanya, T. C., Eseadi, C., Orji, C. T., Ohanu, I. B., Bakare, J., & Ede, M. O. (2017). Effects of rational emotive behavior coaching on occupational stress and work ability among electronics workshop instructors in Nigeria. *Medicine*, 96(19), 1–8. http://dx.doi.org/10.1097/MD.0000000000006891.

Ogungbamila, B., Balogun, A. G., Ogungbamila, A., & Oladele, R. S. (2014). Job stress, emotional labor, and emotional intelligence as predictors of turnover intention: Evidence from two service occupations. *Mediterranean Journal of Social Sciences*, 5(6), 351–357.

Ojo, G. K., Adeyeye, G. M., Opawole, A., & Kajimo-Shakantu, K. (2019). Gender differences in workplace stress response strategies of quantity surveyors in Southwestern Nigeria. *International Journal of Building Pathology and Adaptation*, 37(5), 718–732. https://doi.org/10.1108/IJBPA-10-2018-0084.

Okebukola, P. A., & Jegede, O. J. (1989). Determinants of occupational stress among teachers in Nigeria. *Educational Studies*, 15(1), 23–36. https://doi.org/10.1080/0305569890150103.

Okeke, M. N., Echo, O., & Oboreh, J. C. (2016). Effects of stress on employee productivity. *International Journal of Accounting Research*, 2(11), 38–49.

Olatona, F. A., Ezeobika, E. N., Okafor, I. P., & O.Owoeye, (2014). Work related stress and coping mechanisms among bankers in Lagos, Nigeria. *African Journal of Medicine and Medical Sciences*, 43(1), 59–65.

Olusegun, A. J., Oluwasayo, A. J., & Olawoyim, O. (2014). An overview of the effects of job stress on employees performance in Nigeria tertiary hospitals. *Ekonomika, Journal for Economic Theory and Practice and Social Issues*, 60(4), 139–154.

Olusegun, A.J., Oluwasayo, A.J., & Olawoyim, O. (2014). An overview of the effects of job stress on employees performance in Nigeria tertiary hospitals. *Ekonomika, Journal for Economic Theory and Practice and Social Issues*, 62(4), 139-153.

Onoyase, A. (2015). Stress coping strategies among guidance counsellors in the performance of their jobs in secondary schools Delta North Senatorial District. *Journal of Education and Practice*, 6(30), 111–116.

Onyishi, I. E., & Ugwu, F. O. (2012). Stress, alcohol use and work engagement among university workers in Nigeria. *African. Journal of Drug Alcohol Studies&*, 11(2), 77–85.

Osibanjo, O. A., Salau, O. P., Falola, H.O., & Oyewunmi, A. E. (2016). Workplace stress: implications for organizational performance in a Nigerian public university. *Business: Theory and Practice*, 17(3), 261–269. http://dx.doi.org/10.3846/btp.2016.668.

Owolabi, A. O., Owolabi, M. O., OlaOlorun, A. D., & Olofin, A. (2012). Work-related stress perception and hypertension amongst health workers of a mission hospital in Oyo State, south-western Nigeria, *African Journal of Primary Health Care & Family Medicine*, 4(1), 1–7. .https://doi.org/10.4102/phcfm.v4i1.307

Quick, J. C., & Henderson, D. F. (2016). Occupational stress: Preventing suffering, enhancing wellbeing. *International Journal of Environmental Research and Public Health*, 13(459), 1–11. https://doi.org/10.3390/ijerph13050459.

Salami, S. O. (2010). Job stress and counterproductive work behaviour: Negative affectivity as a moderator. *The Social Sciences*, 5(6), 486–492.

Suresh, S. (2008). Stress and coping strategies. *Management and Labour. Studies*, 33(4), 482–487.

Ugwoke, S. C., Eseadi, C., Onuigbo, L. N., Aye, E. N., Akaneme, I. N., Oboegbulem, A. I., & Ene, A. (2018). A rational-emotive stress management intervention for reducing job burnout and dysfunctional distress among special education teachers: An effect study. *Medicine*, 97(17), 1–8. http://dx.doi.org/10.1097/MD.0000000000010475.

Umege, D. C. *Occupational Stress and Hypertension in the Nigerian Oil and Gas Industry*, 2014, September 15–17, Paper presented at *the SPE African Health, Safety, Security, and Environment and Social Responsibility Conference and Exhibition: Society of Petroleum Engineers*, Maputo. Retrieved from, https://www.onepetro.org/conference-paper/SPE-170199-MS.

Venugopal, V., Rekha, S., Manikandan, K., Latha, P. K., Vennila, V., Ganesan, N., & Chinnadurai, S. J. (2016). Heat stress and inadequate sanitary facilities at workplaces–an occupational health concern for women? *Global Health Action*, 9(1), 1–9. https://doi.org/10.3402/gha.v9.31945.

Appendix

Table 8.1 Summary of Stressors/Strains and Coping Mechanisms identified within reviewed studies on organizational stress in Nigeria

Author and Year	Context	Stressors/Strains	Coping Mechanisms
Salami (2010)	Education	Workload, time pressure, interpersonal problems working conditions, inadequate facilities, personal problems, and leadership problems.	Counterproductive work behaviors such as: harming or an intention to harm the organization and its stakeholders, physical and verbal aggression, acts of theft and sabotage, and bullying
Onyishi and Ugwu (2012)	Education	High workload, role conflict and ambiguity, and boredom	Excessive alcohol use
Ejue (2013)	Education	Workload, job role, university structure and climate, and career development	None stated
Akinyele et al. (2014)	Education	Workload, and resource inadequacy, for example, teaching staff, quality books, computers, and internet services.	Counseling
Osibanjo et al. (2016)	Education	Role conflict or incongruence, inequity and unfair treatment of workers, noise, the distance between workers' home and work, poor ergonomics and inadequate office spaces, and lack of recognition and engagement.	None stated
Ogbuanya et al. (2017)	Education	Work-related irrational beliefs	Rational emotive behavior coaching (REBC) with practices such as sensory awareness training, Socratic questioning, future self-technique, REBC dating technique, wheel of life

(Continued)

Organizational Stress 163

Table 8.1 (Continued)

Author and Year	Context	Stressors/Strains	Coping Mechanisms
Ugwoke et al. (2018)	Education	Work-related irrational beliefs	technique, and relaxation training and rational emotive imagery Rational emotive stress-management intervention program with practices such as goal setting, relaxation, disputing, role play, direct teaching, use of rational self-talk, Socratic questioning, motivational interviewing techniques, imagery techniques, homework assignments, desensitization techniques, and cognitive rehearsals
Olatona et al. (2014)	Banking	Work overload, long working hours, impatient customers, lack of time to relax, and job insecurity	Exercise, meditation/yoga, refocusing/reflection on the positive, muscle relaxation, breathing relaxation, listening to music, sleeping, withdrawal/detachment, drinking alcohol, smoking, crying, over-eating, and doing nothing
Amazue and Onyishi (2016)	Banking	Poor work-life balance, long working hours	Positive thinking, feigning sickness
Ogungbamila et al. (2014)	Banking and healthcare	Long working hours, low pay, work pressure, excessive workload, high job target, and pressure from customers	Emotional intelligence (e.g., by adopting mood repair strategies like remembering the pleasures of life when upset)

(Continued)

Table 8.1 (Continued)

Author and Year	Context	Stressors/Strains	Coping Mechanisms
Gandi et al. (2011)	Healthcare	Workload, the demands of nurse empathy for and connection with patients, economic and political worries	Social support, distancing self from patients
Abaraogu et al. (2016)	Healthcare	High physical job demands	Job control, a high sense of job security, and social support
Ezenwaji et al. (2019)	Healthcare	Limited resources, workload, under-training, inadequate supervision, and feeling undervalued	None stated
Lawal and Idemudia (2017)	Healthcare	Workload, the risk posed by contact with patients (e.g., unpleasant sights and sounds), standing for long periods, time pressures, and failure of colleagues to complete their duties	Emotional intelligence (understating of one's emotions and that of others and the constructive use of this understanding in managing work stress), and organizational support
Mojoyinola (2008)	Healthcare	Excessive workload, poor working condition, inadequate pay, lack of promotion, inadequate staffing, and poor working relationships	Job control, and work-related social support, withdrawal, bullying, absenteeism, and resignation from jobs
Olusegun et al. (2014)	Healthcare	Workload, career development, work/family conflict, repetitive work, workers being under-loaded (having little or no work to do), and unsuitable physical work environment	Flexible work schedule, break periods at work, exercise, absence from work, leave from work, watching movies, smoking, excessive drinking, and sleeping.

(Continued)

Table 8.1 (Continued)

Author and Year	Context	Stressors/Strains	Coping Mechanisms
Owolabi et al. (2012)	Healthcare	High job demands, conflicting demands, time pressure, low control overwork, and limited job variety and possibilities to learn new skills.	None stated
Babajide and Akintayo (2011)	Manufacturing	Relationship with superiors, task structure, workload, and working environment and technology	None stated
David (2016)	Manufacturing	Unfavorable working conditions, poor career development, job insecurity, and long working hours	None stated
Umege (2014)	Manufacturing	None stated	None stated
Ojo et al. (2019)	Construction	Inadequate staffing, insufficient training on the job, poor planning, poor communication, lack of feedback, interpersonal conflicts, bullying and harassment, poor pay and work status, discrimination, and lack of career progression.	Seeking clarification with colleagues and superiors, belonging to professional associations, opportunity to discuss with manager/supervisor, prioritizing future workloads, clubbing or socializing, offloading/delegating work, self-control, continuous professional development, coffee break, smoking, time management, seeking social instrumental support, seeking emotional support, time off work, avoidance/escapism of stressful event and leaving the organization for another

(Continued)

Table 8.1 (Continued)

Author and Year	Context	Stressors/Strains	Coping Mechanisms
Nwokeoma et al. (2019)	Policing	High workloads and poor salary, dysfunctional feelings and irrational thoughts, organizational stressors due to: change of policy and routine at work, supervision. Operational stressors such as: arresting criminals, witnessing brutality due to community clashes and killings, repeated killings of police officers.	Rational emotive occupational health coaching through techniques such as: relaxation training, self-regulation skills training, time management, and setting realistic goals.

9 Increasing Work-Related Stress in the Netherlands and Belgium
How Do These Countries Cope?

Irene L.D. Houtman, Christophe Vanroelen, and Karolus O. Kraan

Introduction

The majority of people living with a common mental disorder are employed, but many are at greater risk of job loss and permanent labor market exclusion than colleagues without these problems (OECD – Organization for Economic Co-operation and Development, 2012). In addition, the costs of mental ill-health for society are large, reaching 3–4.5% of GDP across a range of selected OECD countries in 2010 (OECD – Organization for Economic Co-operation and Development, 2012). It is shown that in particular, mental illness is responsible for a significant loss of potential labor supply, high rates of unemployment, a high incidence of sickness absence, reduced productivity at work, and a large burden of disease (Eaton et al., 2008; Goetzel et al., 2004; OECD – Organization for Economic Cooperation and Development, 2012; Wittchen, Jacobi, & Rehm, 2011). Matrix Insight (2013) estimated that the total costs of work-related depression in the European Union are nearly €620 billion per year. The major impact is suffered by employers (44%), followed by the economy in terms of lost output (39%), the health care systems due to treatment costs (10%), and the social welfare systems due to disability benefit payments (€40 billion). Given the high costs for individuals, employers, and society at large, investing in mental health awareness, psychosocial risk management, mental ill-health prevention, and stimulating return to work after having left work because of mental health problems are urgently needed.

In this chapter, we focus on the management of mental health in the Netherlands and Belgium – two neighboring countries that were both founding members of the European Union. Both countries adhere to European directives, including the European Working Conditions Act,[1] which puts acting on risks to tackle work-related health problems at their source as a priority. Taking this into account, we will notice that in this chapter, both countries deal with the challenges of tackling work-related mental health problems at their source differently.

In the first paragraph, we will first focus on national trends in mental health and work-related mental health in particular. Subsequently, trends in their related occupational risk factors – often denoted as psychosocial risks – are discussed in reference to the traditional Job Demands-Control model (JDC-model: Karasek, 1979; Karasek & Theorell, 1990) and the more recent and related Job Demands-Resources Model (JDR-model; Bakker & Demerouti, 2007). These trends will mainly be described based on European Union data – more specifically, data from the European Working Conditions Survey (EWCS) collected by Eurofound (Eurofound, 2017). The EWCS data enable international comparative analyses. Subsequently, we will focus on psychosocial risk management in enterprises using the European Survey of Enterprises on New and Emerging Risks (ESENER-2). Next, we will discuss how prevention infrastructure in both countries deals with psychosocial and other work-related mental health risks in terms of policy. In the final chapter, we will derive conclusions from these analyses and interpretations in two national contexts and complete them with the lessons learned.

The Prevalence and Development of Work-Related Mental Health in the Netherlands and Belgium

At present, there is not much evidence on the comparative indicators of work-related mental health in the Netherlands and Belgium, let alone in Europe, apart from the EWCS which included one item of the burnout exhaustion scale in its sixth wave (Eurofound, 2017: this item is phrased as "I feel exhausted at the end of the working day"). Although this item only refers to one of three commonly recognized burnout dimensions, Schaufeli 2018 shows that this item behaves well as an approximation of burnout within Europe and in combination with other relevant concepts. Therefore, we consider it interesting to present the prevalence of exhaustion at the country-level derived from the EWCS-2015 here below (Figure 9.1 and some methodological information on the EWCS and this burnout item are presented in Appendix A). The most often used definition of burnout comes from Maslach, Jackson, and Leiter, (1996; p. 20) who describe it as "… a state of exhaustion in which one is cynical about the value of one's occupation and doubtful of one's capacity to perform". More specifically, the core dimension of burnout—exhaus-exhaustion—refers to serious and persistent fatigue, and to feeling emotionally drained and worn out. The second dimension—cyni-cynicism—also includes loss of interest and enthusiasm and doubting the significance and meaning of one's job. The final dimension of burnou-t—lack of professional efficacy—refers to feelings of incompetence and ineffectiveness and reduced personal accomplishment at work. In other words, burnout is a multidimensional construct that includes a stress reaction (exhaustion), a mental distancing response (cynicism), and a negative belief (lack of professional efficacy). For an overview of burnout, its measurement, antecedents, consequences, and explanations, see Maslach, Schaufeli, and Leiter (2001) and Schaufeli, Leiter, and

Increasing Work-Related Stress 169

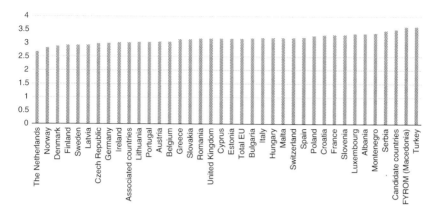

Figure 9.1 Mean Levels of Burnout in Europe (scale 1–5)5.
Source: 6th EWCS – 2015 (Eurofound).

Maslach (2009). Figure 9.1 shows the variation within Europe on this EWCS item on emotional exhaustion.

Figure 9.1 shows that the workforce in the Netherlands (2.68) reports the lowest of all mean exhaustion levels; whereas, the workforce of Belgium (3.06) rates only just below the European Union mean of 3.10. Both countries are "on the safe side" European-wise, but still quite irregular within the European spectrum. Traditionally, the work and health situation in the Netherlands is considered a bit comparable to the Scandinavian situation regarding welfare and social security systems (Esping-Andersen, 2013).

It is interesting to further consider what the trend has been – both in this outcome indicator as well as in its causes – to better place the national settings and the way in which these problems are dealt with in these settings.

The Work-Related Drivers - Psychosocial Risks At Work: The Netherlands versus Belgium, and the Rest of Europe

As determinants of work-related mental health risks, we consider different psychosocial demands as well as opportunities for control as our core indicators. First, we will consider the comparison of demands and opportunities for control among workers in the Netherlands and Belgium based on the EWCS. Both the prevalence – expressed as the percentage of high scores – and the trends in prevalence are compared in Table 9.1.

In the period considered, many of the trends in job demands, as well as opportunities for control, have been developing differently in Belgium and the Netherlands. As for quantitative demands, workers in Belgium

Table 9.1 Trends in Different Demands and Control Indicators (Percentages for High Risk) for Belgium and the Netherlands

Job Demands	Belgium 1995	2000	2005	2010	2015	The Netherlands 1995	2000	2005	2010	2015	Interaction of Time by Country $\Delta B\ (\Delta\beta)\ p$
High quantitative job demands (working at very high speed/very tight deadlines) [% half of the time or more]	29.7% ▼	33.1% ▼	39.8%	42.0% ▲	45.5% ▲	44.0%	50.0% ▲	39.3%	42.0%	39.3%	−5,8% (−0,083) ▼. Belgium shows a significant increase; whereas the Netherlands does not and even tends to decrease.
Does your job involve being in situations that are emotionally disturbing for you? [% around 1/4 of the time or more]	–	–	–	–	29.2%	–	–	–	–	21.3%	–
Does your job involve complex tasks? [% yes]	30.3% ▼	39.6% ▲	23.6% ▼	44.9% ▲	35.5%	39.6%	43.5%	45.2% ▲	37.7%	31.7% ▼	−3,7% (−0,055) ▼. Complex tasks are rising until 2015 in Belgium; in the Netherlands, complex tasks have declined significantly in

(Continued)

Table 9.1 (Continued)

Job Demands	Belgium 1995	2000	2005	2010	2015	The Netherlands 1995	2000	2005	2010	2015	Interaction of Time by Country $\Delta B\ (\Delta \beta)\ p$
Negative social interactions (last month at work, subjected to verbal abuse and/or unwanted sexual attention and/or past 12 months physical violence and/or sexual harassment and/or bullying/harassment? [% yes]	–	–	–	18.8%	17.6%	–	–	–	14.6%▼	27.0%▲	+14% (+0.086)▲. Negative social interactions appear to be stable in Belgium; whereas, these are increasing in the Netherlands –resulting in higher percentages in 2015.
Opportunities for control	43.1%	52.0%▲	43.3%	46.9%	44.1%	36.2%▼	35.3%▼	44.6%	45.4%▲	43.8%	2015, but the decline seems to have started already in 2010 – although not significantly.

(Continued)

Table 9.1 (Continued)

Job Demands	Belgium 1995	2000	2005	2010	2015	The Netherlands 1995	2000	2005	2010	2015	Interaction of Time by Country ΔB ($\Delta \beta$) p
Job autonomy (choose order/ methods/ speed) [% low]											+2.9% (+0.041)△. Low job control tends to be significantly more frequent in Belgium; whereas, there is no difference with the Netherlands anymore in 2010 and 2015.
Skill discretion (meeting precise quality standards/ assessing quality own work/solving unforeseen problems/learning new things) [% low]	55.4%	59.5%▲	55.2%	52.0%	51.0%	39.9%▼	43.5%	49.2%	45.9%	53.4%▲	+4.6% (+0.065)▲. Low skill discretion is significantly more frequent in Belgium; whereas, it is not different from the Netherlands anymore in 2015. In the Netherlands, skill discretion has

(Continued)

Table 9.1 (Continued)

Job Demands	Belgium 1995	2000	2005	2010	2015	The Netherlands 1995	2000	2005	2010	2015	Interaction of Time by Country $\Delta B\ (\Delta\beta)\ p$
											been developing quite unfavorably over the last 20 years.
Colleague help and support [% Sometimes/ rarely/ never]	–	–	–	30.0%▲	22.9%▼	–	–	–	23.9%	23.6%	+6.7% (+0.039)△. Low co-worker support in Belgium tends to be decreasing towards the level of the Netherlands in the last five years.
Manager help and support [% sometimes/ rarely/ never]	–	–	–	43.9%▲	35.2%▼	–	–	–	38.1%	41.0%	+12% (+0.060)▲. Low management support in Belgium is decreasing; whereas, this tends to be increasing in the Netherlands.

(Continued)

Table 9.1 (Continued)

Job Demands	Belgium					The Netherlands					Interaction of Time by Country
	1995	2000	2005	2010	2015	1995	2000	2005	2010	2015	ΔB (Δβ) p
Participation (consulted before objectives set / involved in improving work organization/ processes / say in choice of colleagues / apply own ideas in work / can influence important decisions) [% low]	–	–	–	54.1% ▲	46.1% ▼	–	–	–	35.6%	35.4%	+7.9% (+0.040) Δ. Low participation is more frequent in Belgium as compared to the Netherlands. Low participation is decreasing in Belgium.

Source: EWCS 1995–2015, Eurofound.

Note

Percentages indicate one side of the dichotomy (e.g., low versus high) and are tested with the Pearson χ^2-test (horizontal comparisons: low versus high). Means are tested with the t-test. The contrast is a subgroup versus "rest" (weighted deviation contrast). ▲ and ▼: $p < 0.05$, significant-high (low) percentages, and Cohen's d is at least 0.10. Open arrows Δ and ∇: also significant, but Cohen's d is smaller than 0.10. Trend-analysis: B = unstandardized linear regression coefficient = average increase/decrease per interval (β = standardized linear regression coefficient) p = significance. Interaction: Test on linear interaction between "year of the survey" and "Belgium versus the Netherlands" on each (category of each) row variable (= test whether B1=B2).

used to rate these demands as much less taxing in 1995 as compared to 2015. Quantitative demands have continuously risen over this period of 20 years. In the Netherlands, quantitative job demands appeared to have been rising until the year 2000 and have stabilized since, resulting in a quite comparable level of quantitative job demands to be reported by Belgian and Dutch workers. The fact that quantitative job demands rose until the end of the last century and have leveled off since is corroborated by the national monitor data in the Netherlands (e.g., Houtman, 1997; Houtman & van den Bossche, 2010). Workers in Belgium also report that their jobs increasingly involve complex tasks. Workers in the Netherlands did so too until the year 2005, but this was also reduced in the following decade. Demands imposed upon workers with violence and harassment have been measured quite differently over the years. However, In the fifth and sixth EWCS, it was measured as "negative social interactions." This indicator of violence and harassment appeared to be stable at the level of about 18% for workers in Belgium, whereas it rose according to Dutch workers, resulting in 27% confirming that they had experienced negative social interactions in 2015.

Opportunities for control – like job autonomy, skill discretion, as well as social support by colleagues and managers – used to be better or more favorable, as reported by Dutch workers and as compared to Belgian workers. However, more recent surveys showed a deterioration of particularly job autonomy and skill discretion as reported by Dutch workers, resulting in an almost comparable position on job autonomy and skill discretion in Belgian and Dutch workers. Although the information on social support does not have a long history, in 2015, the differences are not significantly high for social support of colleagues in both the Netherlands and Belgium but have become better for social support by the managers. This latter positive development in the last five years is not reported by Dutch workers. Finally, the level of participation of employees in decision-making organizational processes is better in the Netherlands, as reported by Dutch workers, although it is improving, as reported by Belgian workers.

Summarizing the trends in demands and control as reported by workers in Belgium and the Netherlands, the workers in Belgium report increasing quantitative and qualitative demands, except for negative social interactions. For the Dutch workers, this is the other way around. They reported high and increasing quantitative demands around 20 years ago, which actually leveled off after the turn of the century. Since the rest of the European Union workers still rose on quantitative demands after the turn of the century, the Dutch worker has turned to be more average on quantitative demands as compared to other European Union workers. However, negative social demands are on the rise in the Netherlands and are also more prominent in 2015 as compared to Belgian workers. This is paralleled by a decrease in job autonomy and skill discretion of Dutch workers over the last 20 years, resulting in a comparable situation as reported by Dutch and Belgian workers in 2015. Particularly, social support by colleagues and participation in decision-making processes appear to be stable and more favorable, as reported by Dutch workers and as compared to Belgian workers.

In Figure 9.2 we have compared the position of workers in the Netherlands and Belgium to that of the average of the rest of the European Union (EU-26), where the European Union average is taken as the middle line, and the differences (after calculating z-scores from the scale or item ratings) are positioned as differing in either a positive or negative way. Figure 9.2 shows that, on average, workers in both the Netherlands and Belgium report to have lower demands (e.g., quantitative, emotional, and complexity demands) and higher levels of resources at work (e.g., job control/autonomy, participation, and social

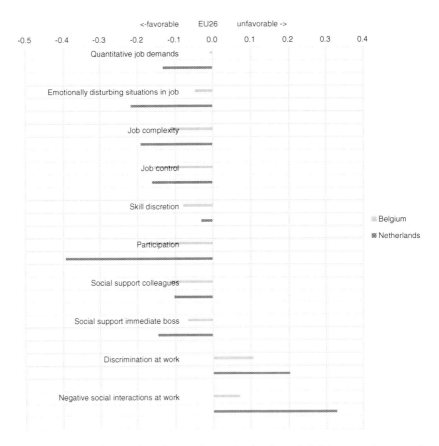

Figure 9.2 Psychosocial Risks in the Netherlands and Belgium as Compared to the Rest of Europe.
Source: EWCS 2015 (Eurofound).

support) than the European Union average. Only the social interactions at work, as well as discrimination at work, are reported to be more negative as compared to the workers in the rest of the European Union. On almost all scales, except for skill discretion, the ratings by the Dutch workers are more extreme as compared to the Belgium workers.

Political Urgency Is Often Based on the National Level and has Recently Increased Both in the Netherlands and Belgium for Slightly Different Reasons

Trend information on the emotional exhaustion scale as the core of the burnout scale is only available based on national data. For the Netherlands, these data are based on the Netherlands Working Conditions Survey (NWCS; the Dutch acronym is NEA; Hooftman et al., 2019) by TNO together with Statistics Netherlands. For emotional exhaustion, the same five-item scale has also been monitored for some years by Statistics Netherlands in their Living Situation Survey. These data show a split trend for the emotional exhaustion scale – a new way of sampling the data. Recently, a consistent increase in this exhaustion indicator is seen since 2013 – at least a net increase of 1% per year since 2013 (see Figure 9.3). This recent increase sets off several national alarm bells and recently made the State Secretary of the Netherlands promise the Parliament that the Ministry would start a project to better understand this trend and its causes and to identify the most important risk groups.[2] Unfortunately, information on the promised research is not available yet. However, it shows that these trend data do have an impact on the national policy level and may make room for new policy action. In the Netherlands, the trend is to act on primary prevention first.

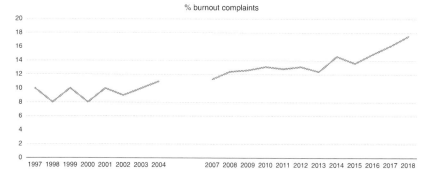

Figure 9.3 Trends in Burnout Complaints Among a Representative Sample of Dutch Employees.
Source: POLS[3] 1995–2004 (CBS); NEA 2007–2018 (TNO/CBS 2007–2018).

Despite the fact that burnout per definition is a work-related mental health outcome, there is no clear increase in psychosocial risk factors at work which could explain this increase in burnout complaints (see the EWCS trends presented in the previous paragraph, which also parallels the trends in the NWCS; Houtman, de Vroome, van der Ploeg, & Ramaekers, 2019; Houtman, Bakhuys Roozeboom, Kraan, & van den Bossche, 2017). The psychosocial risks that have been changing in the Netherlands are job autonomy and negative social interactions. Job autonomy has been decreasing since the start of the economic crisis in the Netherlands and has been leveling off since economic recovery. However, the reduction in autonomy has been quite specific in certain groups of workers with nonpermanent jobs and particularly in younger employees (Houtman & de Vroome, 2015; Houtman et al., 2019). These are not specifically the groups with high ratings of burnout or emotional exhaustion. An increase in negative social interactions, as shown in Dutch workers, can be strongly related to burnout complaints. However, this trend is not found in the way violence and harassment have been operationalized in the NWCS (Houtman et al., 2019; Houtman et al., 2017).

For Belgium, no reliable trend data on self-reported burnout or one of its components are available, as it is still impossible to create trend analyses with the EWCS data. However, a similar "state of alarm" was created by the official figures on disability and, more specifically, disability related to psychiatric problems. As is shown in Figure 9.4, the number of disabled workers had a steep increase between 1999 and 2018 – with 124% for all possible causes and 177% specifically for psychiatric causes. This represented an absolute number of about 400,000 and 150,000 workers respectively in a total working population of about 4.8 million. Recent measures to control and reverse this increase seem to have a limited impact. Apart from causes related to the nature of the OSH system and recent reforms in different social security schemes, the assumed increasing work demands and job complexity have been cited as causes of the increase in psychiatric disability. The results shown above are, to a degree, confirmed by the results from a regional workability survey conducted periodically in the region of Flanders (Bourdeaud'hui et al., 2017). In this survey, an item set on "psychological fatigue" is also included. This is probably the best available proxy for burnout. The figures show an increase in "problematic fatigue" of about 3% between 2013 and 2016 (Bourdeaud'hui et al., 2017) – see Table 9.2.

Do Organizations Acknowledge and Manage these Risks?

The European Survey of Enterprises on New and Emerging Risks (ESENER) was held for the second time in 2014[4] and inventories

Increasing Work-Related Stress 179

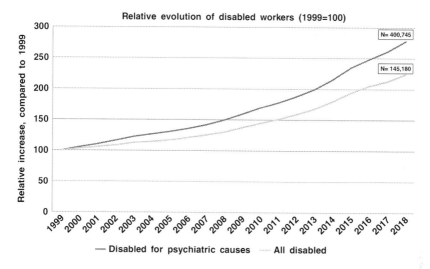

Figure 9.4 Relative Evolution of Disabled Workers in Belgium (1999–2018).
Source: Riziv, 2019 https://www.inami.fgov.be/fr/statistiques/indemnites/Pages/default.aspx#.XYst3S2B1TY).

the acknowledgment of risks at work – including psychosocial risks at work, as well as procedures and measures directed at the management of these risks within the organizations (EU-OSHA, 2016). The ESENER survey can be seen as the "employer's" story of risk management, as opposed to the EWCS, which is the employee's story. In ESENER-2, "the one who knows best about OSH" in the enterprise is interviewed. In SMEs this is often the owner or director of the enterprise, but in larger organizations, this may be a representative from human resources or an OSH-representative.

Regarding the acknowledgment of psychosocial risks, the "one who knows best about OSH" in enterprises in Belgium, in the Netherlands, and in the rest of the European Union (EU-26) states whether these risks are present (see Table 9.3). The questions that have been asked in ESENER-2 partly tap into different concepts as compared to the EWCS. As for issues common in both surveys, we see that organizations rate time pressure as more present in enterprises in the Netherlands and Belgium as compared to the EU-28 average. This contrasts with the findings from employees reported in Figure 9.2, showing that employees in the Netherlands and Belgium rate their "quantitative job demands as more favorable as compared to the rest of the European Union". The percentage of ESENER respondents, which indicate the number of employees in the organization who deal with difficult customers, patients, pupils, etc., is higher for Belgium but equal for the Netherlands, as compared to the EU-28. On the other hand, these

Table 9.2 Evolution in the Prevalence of "Acute Problematic" Risk Factors and Workability Outcomes Among Flemish Employees (2004–2016)

	2004	2007	2010	2013	2016
Workability risks factors					
Work pressure (quantitative demands)	12,8	12,5	12,3	11,1	16,3
Emotional demands	4,0	4,3	4,1	4,0	5,0
Autonomy	7,3	7,5	6,5	6,4	6,2
Skill discretion	11,5	10,5	10,5	10,3	10,5
Superior support	6,1	6,2	5,4	5,3	5,0
Workability outcomes					
Psychological fatigue	10,4	9,7	9,4	9,6	12,3

Source: Bourdeaud'hui et al. (2017). Vlaamse Werkbaarheidsmonitor 2016 – werknemers. Brussels.
Note: Due to different survey instruments and different methodologies, these results cannot be directly confirmed with the EWCS data.

Table 9.3 Psychosocial Risk Factors Present in Enterprises (% Establishments)

Psychosocial Risk	Netherlands	Belgium	EU-28
Time pressure	62	53	43
Having to deal with difficult customers, patients, pupils, etc.	58	65	58
Poor communication or cooperation within the organization	22	26	17
Employee's lack of influence on their work pace or work processes	18	13	13
Discrimination (for example – due to gender, age, or ethnicity)	5	4	2

Source: EU-OSHA, 2016.

respondents report that both in Belgium and in the Netherlands, the psychosocial risks related to poor communication and cooperation within the organization are more prevalent as compared to the EU-28. The data on workers for both the Netherlands and Belgium show that, in both countries, but particularly in the Netherlands, negative social interactions are much more prevalent than in the rest of the European Union. However, the latter may concern both contacts with customers, patients, clients, etc., as well as with colleagues or managers within the organization.

A somewhat contradictory finding between enterprise and worker opinion about psychosocial risk is the influence workers have on the pace of work or work processes. The respondents in the enterprises indicate that this is more of a problem in Dutch enterprises as compared to the EU-28, whereas it is equally experienced as a problem in Belgian enterprises. The EWCS showed a more favorable rating of control or autonomy and skill discretion for workers both in the Netherlands and Belgium, as compared to the rest of the EU.

In Table 9.4 we represent measures taken in enterprises in the Netherlands, Belgium, and in the EU-28 during the last three years. The overall picture is that all of the measures taken – reorganization in order to reduce job demands and work pressure, as well as confidential counseling and set-up of a conflict resolution procedure – were more often taken by enterprises in Belgium as compared to EU-28, and were less often taken by enterprises in the Netherlands as compared to EU-28.

The ESENER-2 also shows that about 37% of the enterprises in Belgium and 28% in the Netherlands as opposed to 17% in the EU-28 indicate using a psychologist or an in-house or externally contracted specialist. In addition, the "one who knows best about OSH" in the Netherlands and Belgium indicates quite often that there are plans and procedures to prevent bullying and harassment (70% and 83% respectively) and violence (72% and 65% respectively) more frequently, as compared to the EU-28 (47% on bullying and harassment, and 55% on violence). As for having an action plan and procedures, the "one who knows best about OSH" indicates that this is the case for about 27% of Dutch enterprises, about 36% of Belgian enterprises, and about 33% of EU-28 enterprises (EU-OSHA, 2016).

What is in Place to Tackle Psychosocial Risks at Work in Belgium and in the Netherlands? What are the Do's and Don't's?

In the above text, some discrepancy is shown between the development in work-related stress disorders and the trends in their work-related causes. This suggests that either non-work-related causes or societal processes may have influenced the perception of work-related mental health. Other factors like the history of prevention and previous preventive activities (not as recent as the measures taken in the last three

Table 9.4 Measures Implemented to Prevent Psychosocial Risks During the Last Three years (% Establishments)

Psychosocial Risk	*Netherlands*	*Belgium*	*EU-28*
Reorganization of work in order to reduce job demands and work pressure	28	40	38
Confidential counseling for employees	33	46	36
Set-up of a conflict resolution procedure	25	40	29

Source: EU-OSHA, 2016.

years) may also have had an impact on the "outcome" measure of burnout or other mental health outcomes.

The Netherlands was one of the first countries to pay attention to psychosocial risks in their occupational safety and health legislation, as this legislation was first introduced in 1990. This legislation explicitly paid specific attention to well-being at work. From 1990 onward, a lot of initiatives were undertaken by the government together with employer and employee representatives. These activities included raising awareness among employers and employees and supporting the risk assessment and evaluation – including psychosocial risks at work. This was done by having books published – like the "Handbook on work-related stress" (Handboek *werkstress*; Kompier & Marcelissen, 1990) and union brochures deduced from the stepwise approach as presented in this handbook – and by initiating related conferences. Best practices were initiated, subsidized by, and published with the help of the Ministry of Social Affairs (e.g., "Aan *de slag*" [i.e., "Get going"], Kompier, Gründemann, Vink, & Smulders, 1996; Preventing Stress, Improving Productivity; Kompier & Cooper, 1999). In addition, an expert approach was developed for improving well-being at work and job level, and courses were developed for professionals – "train the trainer" courses as well as courses and material for the Labor Inspectorate (e.g., Vaas, Dhondt, & Peeters, 1995). Sectoral activity directed at risk management appeared to be strongly associated with more active risk management at the organizational level (Houtman *et al.*, 1995; Houtman *et al.*, 1998). Already at the end of the previous century (1998), the Work and Health covenants marked the beginning. A covenant can be described as a gentleman's agreement between the employer and employee representatives of a sector, who – in the presence of and with the advice of the Ministry – agree on the risks to tackle, the approaches or measures to take, and the specific goals to be formulated at the sectoral level. In fact, these were large-scale OSH interventions, and since psychosocial factors at work were considered a major risk in the Netherlands, psychosocial risk management often was a core topic in these covenants (see also Taris, Van der Wal, & Kompier, 2010). In those days, the Dutch Ministry of Social Affairs and Employment actively encouraged and subsidized this sectoral approach to risk management. The overall aim was to achieve a reduction in exposure to sector-specific psychosocial and physical risks of about 10% over a period of approximately three years. The government funded part of the initiatives. The covenant program ended in 2007, and at the end of the Work and Health Covenant period, two large evaluations initiated by the Ministry of Social Affairs and Employment took place. One was mainly directed at absence and cost reduction, whereas the other was more directed at risk reduction at the national level, comparing risk change in sectors that did and did not participate in the covenants. The evaluation that considered absence and cost reduction resulted in quite a positive message – absence and related costs were reduced (Veerman et al., 2007). However, the study considering risk exposure was not so positive – no differences were found (Blatter, Van den Bossche, Van Hooff, De Vroome, & Smulders, 2008). These latter findings may have been an underestimation of the effects of exposure since, even in sectors where covenants had been agreed upon, not all organizations implemented interventions, and not all employees participated. Already, Semmer (2003) indicated that, comparing whole populations where interventions were or were not implemented, the impact of the interventions should be very high in order to show a significant effect, since parts of the population where interventions were implemented would not do anything about it. The latter might well have been the case in the sectors where the Work and Health Covenants had been agreed upon. Another explanation may be that only a post covenant comparison of sectors with and without such a covenant was possible. No national measurement, so no comparison, could be performed on risk exposure before the covenants were agreed upon. The fact that only a comparison on risk exposure could take place after the covenants were implemented and the fact that high-risk sectors were selected and approached to enter into these covenants may have caused bias on the comparison on exposure (Blatter et al., 2008).

Taris et al. (2010) performed more in-depth (qualitative and quantitative) analyses in nine, mainly public sector-level work-related stress programs. They concluded that the quality of the sector-level programs varied strongly across sectors. However, organizations in sectors with high-quality work-related stress programs at the sector-level were not necessarily more active than organizations in sectors with lower quality programs, but their programs were more effective. It was hypothesized that the sectors with high-level quality programs already had more experience and knowledge in the sector and that this may have increased the program's effectiveness. In sectors with less experience and knowledge on a different approach, involving the establishment of this knowledge and experience by having pilot projects, conducting research into the antecedents of work-related stress, and providing good practices may be more effective in motivating organizations to reduce job stress. In this way, the sector may begin to build a body of knowledge about the effects of job stress interventions. Within the scope of the differences between countries in psychosocial risk management activities, these conclusions on sector differences and their already installed infrastructural benefits may well apply to the results of EWCS and ESENER by country as well.

Since 2007 there are no Work and Health Covenants anymore. In 2007 and 2017, the Working Conditions Act was updated, and in 2007, well-being, as well as other specific risks, were skipped from the law text. One important aspect of the Dutch Working Conditions Act – in both the old as well as the more recent and updated act – is that employers are obliged to make a risk inventory and evaluation (RI&E). Under the Working Conditions Act, all employers must record the risks faced by their employees, as well as when and how they intend to reduce these risks in their working conditions policy. Psychosocial risks like violence and harassment are also included in the risks that may be prevalent in a company. In a consultation period with the employees, a plan of risk management measures has to be developed in which the management indicates how and when they plan to deal with the risks.

In the Netherlands, collective agreements are voluntary. We call them the "three-quarter law," because once accepted by the social partners, the agreement can be made obligatory for all companies in the sector by means of a general acceptance procedure by the Dutch Ministry of Social Affairs and Employment. Working conditions are mostly not included in collective agreements, but appointments can be made to establish a separate Education and Development Fund that deals with the main questions on working and employment conditions in the sector. These funds are often financed by fees from employers and employees. It is well known that several of these funds co-finance activities that are still supporting research, pilots, and best practices on psychosocial factors. One example is the large project financed by a specific project group of the Ministry of Home Affairs on violence and harassment as a risk factor for employees in the public sector (*"veilige publieke taak"*: http://www.rijksoverheid.nl/onderwerpen/agressie-en-geweld/geweld-tegen-overheidspersoneel[5]). The current OSH-catalogue policy of the Dutch government can be part of a sectoral collective agreement. The aim of the government is to cover all sectors and employees by an OSH-catalogue (https://www.arboportaal.nl/externe-bronnen/arbocatalogi). In a number of these OSH catalogs, attention has been paid to psychosocial risks and their management.

In addition, the main activity specific for psychosocial risks and risk management undertaken at the national level by the Ministry of Social Affairs and Employment of the Netherlands has been a yearly campaign since 2014. It is called "the week of work-related stress" and is aimed to shed light on these risks and their corresponding risk management. There has not been an attempt to evaluate the effectiveness of the campaign.

Belgium is a complex country in terms of institutional structure – involving many policy competences scattered over the federal and regional (Flanders, Wallonia, and Brussels) policy levels. OSH competences, however, are mainly concentrated at the federal level, leading to relatively uniform legislation and policy practices over the entire territory.

Notwithstanding, sectors and regions also have certain discretion when it comes to psychosocial risks at work.

While actions regarding psychosocial risk factors have been included in OSH legislation as early as 1996 and gradually developed more in the subsequent years, this domain has strongly been expanded with the "Act of 28 February 2014" on the prevention of psychosocial risks at work – including violence, harassment and sexual harassment at work"[6] and a series of related legislative initiatives. The Belgian OSH system puts a strong emphasis on prevention and uses a broad definition of OSH as "well-being at work,"[7] incorporating seven domains: "work safety," "protection of workers health at work," "psychosocial aspects of work," "ergonomic matters," "work hygiene," "embellishing of the workplace," and "all measures regarding the natural environment with an impact on the former points."[8] Prevention and control of psychosocial risks are therefore incorporated into the main OSH legislation and infrastructure. In the 2014 legislation, the concept of a psychosocial risk is defined as "the probability of one or more workers being at risk of or exposed to some aspect of the environment or behavior that creates an objective danger over which the employer has some control" (e.g., "stress," "violence," "bullying," and "sexual harassment").[9] Employers are deemed to control these psychosocial factors at five sub-domains of the work environment: work organization (e.g., distribution of tasks, relations of authority, management style), employment conditions (e.g., contract, work patterns), work content (e.g., the nature of work, complexity), relationships at work (e.g., relationships with co-workers and members of management), and occupational health and safety (e.g., physical efforts, harmful exposures) (FPS Employment, Labour, & Social Dialogue, 2013[10]). The Belgian OSH system gives a prominent position to the social partners in shaping and supervising OSH practices. At the company level, workers and trade union representatives have the legal right to be actively involved in the process of identifying and addressing psychosocial risks. Social partners also play a key role in setting policy initiatives at the national and sectoral levels.

At the federal policy level, the National Labour Council[11] is the first institution that plays an important role in shaping social and well-being policies. As an example, in 2018 and 2019, subventions to companies for pilot projects on the primary prevention of burnout have been launched by the National Labour Council[12]. Another important agent is the Higher Council for Prevention and Protection at Work. While composed of representatives from employees and employers' organizations and experts, this council acts as a national policy advisory body on OSH-related topics. The Federal Department Employment, Labor, and Social Dialogue plays the most important role in terms of policy execution – including research funding, application and enforcing of legislation, and dissemination of expertise.[13] For the latter purpose, the Belgian Safe

Work Information Center[14] serves as an interface for the field of practice. Moreover, for two periods in recent history (2008–2012 and 2016–2020), national strategies for the improvement of health and safety at work have been put in place in Belgium. The 2008 to 2012 strategy has been evaluated in a comprehensive study (Wlodarski, 2013) and concluded that the first plan contained insufficient accurate specifications of responsibilities of actors involved, objectives, and performance indicators to reach tangible results. The current National Strategy for Well-Being at Work 2016–2020[15] sets a total number of 13 operational objectives aimed at continuously improving well-being at work by strategically focusing on optimizing prevention, installing a prevention culture, optimizing the functioning of the main OSH actors, and strengthening inclusive labor market participation.

Some initiatives are located at the sectoral and regional levels. At the sector level, OSH initiatives have only started to emerge rather recently. These initiatives are in fact an enlargement of the competences of the so-called "sectoral funds," which already exist since 1958[16] and can be considered partially managed foundations funded through employer contributions and are aimed at enhancing social protection, training, and well-being of workers in a given sector. Recently, some sectors started to allocate part of their resources to specific workability foundations. A good example is the *"DemografieFondsDémographie"* founded in 2016 in the chemical sector.[17] The Belgian regions can take action based on their competences in the domains of labor market policy and preventive health. Only the Flemish region, however, has taken some initiatives complementary to the federal policies. Most important here are the activities that the Flemish social partners gathered in the Socio-Economic Council for Flanders (SERV). Since 2003, they have conducted a workability survey every three years, and connected to this is a policy program to promote workability – including a publicly accessible toolbox of good practices, training programs, and modest subventions to promote workability at the workplace.[18] From the perspective of health prevention, the Flemish Institute for Healthy Living (VIGO) is deploying primary prevention initiatives in the realm of healthy work and, more specifically, mental well-being at work.

Of course and also in Belgium, the main entry point to psychosocial risk prevention is employing organizations. Here, the principle of primary prevention by means of collective and participatory risk assessment procedures is the key. The collective and participatory approach toward the identification of risks involves management, workers' representatives, individual workers, HR, and OSH specialists (e.g. Mensura[19]). Based on the risk analysis, an action plan must be developed, implemented, and evaluated (FPS Employment, Labor, and Social Dialogue[20]). In this whole process, important actors are the so-called External Services for Prevention and Protection at Work. These are nonprofit organizations that are accredited by the federal authorities and are equipped to assume the multidisciplinary OSH support that is required by law. The federal government has financed action research aimed at establishing good examples of sustainable prevention strategies in practice (Lamberts & Terlinden, 2016).

At the level of secondary prevention, the 2014 law has specified a number of new measures in the case of individual problems of psychosocial nature. These innovations were partly informed by an evaluation of the performance of earlier legislation on psychosocial risk factors (Eertmans & Mertens, 2011). Currently, a trained "person of confidence" is charged with duties of information provision and first-line aid. An employee facing psychosocial well-being problems can appeal to this person of confidence and initiate an "informal intervention" in order to alleviate the problem. Employees may also appeal to a "formal psychosocial intervention." Such intervention implies a formal claim to the employer to take the necessary measures required to alleviate an individual of a problem or a collective problem of psychosocial nature. During a formal intervention, the applicant is protected against reprisals from the part of the employer or other members of management. An important characteristic of both the informal and formal procedures is the intent to provoke structural change to a stressful situation by taking collective and participatory actions. Finally and recently, efforts have been increased to reintegrate disabled workers in the labor market. New legislation came into effect from January 1, 2017.[21] This legislation is particularly significant for stress-related causes, as the cases of psychiatric disability almost tripled in number in 20 years' time (see supra). It is important to note that rising disability claims are putting the financial sustainability of the social security system under stress. The new legislation aims to make reintegration swifter than before by involving the development of a mandatory reintegration plan. The new legislation has been heavily criticized by trade unions, who accused the new law of facilitating dismissal for medical reasons. At present, no evaluation of the new legislation is available, although a first evaluation study is on its way.[22]

To conclude, for employers who are still not convinced that psychosocial risks are a problem for worker health as well as general organizational health, some figures on the impact of psychosocial risks at the employee level, as well as organizational level, may help.

Building infrastructure on OSH, or more specifically on psychosocial risk management, takes time, and time, as well as good practice, will help convince more employers and enterprises that psychosocial risks are a problem in need of risk management. Allowing employees to participate in decisions on how these risks should or could be managed is important.

188 *Irene L.D. Houtman et al.*

Active engagement of employees in the active risk management process is a *sine qua non* for effective risk management.

Notes

1 The European Union legislation that covers psychosocial risks has existed since 1989 (Directive 89/391/EEC, the European Framework Directive on Safety and Health of Workers at Work). 20 additional daughter directives include provisions in relation to psychosocial risks and mental health in the workplace. Several pieces of guidance have been produced by the European Commission since 1999. More recently, a review of policies and practices on mental health in the workplace, which included occupational health and safety legislation as well as other types of policies and initiatives, was published by the European Commission in 2014 (European Commission, 2014). This also included the publication of "Promoting mental health in the workplace: Guidance to implementing a comprehensive approach" as well as an interpretative document of the European Union legislation in relation to mental health in the workplace. See: https://osha.europa.eu/en/legislation/guidelines/interpretative-document-implementation-council-directive-89391eec-relation.
2 https://www.rijksoverheid.nl/documenten/kamerstukken/2018/06/14/kamerbrief-stand-van-zaken-psychosociale-arbeidsbelasting.
3 POLS = Permanent Onderzoek LeefSituatie/Permanent Living Conditions Survey.
4 The data of ESENER-3 will probably be published at the end of 2019.
5 Because of a renewal of the website toward one portal for all Dutch Ministries, the texts on this website are only in Dutch thus far.
6 http://www.ejustice.just.fgov.be/cgi_loi/change_lg.pl?language=nl&la=N&table_name=wet&cn=2014022821.
7 https://oshwiki.eu/wiki/OSH_system_at_national_level_-_Belgium.
8 http://www.employment.belgium.be/WorkArea/linkit.aspx?LinkIdentifier=id&ItemID=1896.
9 https://www.eurofound.europa.eu/publications/article/2014/belgium-preventing-psychosocial-risks-at-work.
10 http://www.emploi.belgique.be/publicationDefault.aspx?id=44860.
11 http://www.werk.belgie.be/defaultNews.aspx?id=48275.
12 http://www.werk.belgie.be/defaultNews.aspx?id=48275.
13 https://www.beswic.be/nl/themas/psychosociale-risicos-psr.
14 https://www.beswic.be/nl/over-beswic.
15 http://www.employment.belgium.be/WorkArea/DownloadAsset.aspx?id=45387.
16 http://www.werk.belgie.be/defaultTab.aspx?id=519.
17 https://www.demografiefondsdemographie.be/travail-faisable/travail/.
18 https://www.werkbaarwerk.be/werkbaarwerk.
19 https://www.mensura.be/en/client-portal/case-studies/2014-legislation-for-better-management-of-psychosocial-risks.
20 http://www.emploi.belgique.be/publicationDefault.aspx?id=44860.
21 http://www.werk.belgie.be/moduleTab.aspx?id=45586&idM=102.
22 http://www.werk.belgie.be/moduleDefault.aspx?id=47772.
23 http://www.eurofound.europa.eu/surveys/european-working-conditions-surveys.
24 www.esener.eu.
25 We used all NACE sectors, except for private households (NACE T) and

extraterritorial organisations (NACE U). NACE is the **European industrial activity classification as is** approved by the European Commission. The term NACE is derived from the French *Nomenclature statistique des activités économiques dans la Communauté européenne.*

References

Bakker, A. B. & Demerouti, E. (2007). The Job Demands-Resources model: State of the art. *Journal of Managerial Psychology, 22*(3), 309–328.

Blatter, B., Van den Bossche, S., Van Hooff, M., De Vroome, E. & Smulders, P. G. W. (2008). Effecten van arboconvenanten. *Economisch Statistische Berichten, 93*(4540), 471–473.

Bourdeaud'hui, R., Janssens, F. & Vanderhaeghe, S. (2017). *Vlaamse werkbaarheidsmonitor 2016 - werknemers.* Brussel.

Cohen, J. (1988). *Statistical power analysis for the behavioral sciences* (2nd ed.). Hillsdale NJ: Erlbaum.

Eaton, W. W., Martins, S. S., Nestadt, G., Bienvenu, O. J., Clarke, D. & Alexandre, P. (2008). The burden of mental disorders. *Epidemiologic Reviews, 30*, 1–14.

Eertmans, A. & Mertens, S. (2011). *Evaluatie van de wetgeving inzake de preventie van psychosociale belasting veroorzaakt door het werk, waaronder geweld, pesterijen en ongewenst seksueel gedrag op het werk.* ISW Limits. http://www.werk.belgie.be/moduleDefault.aspx?id=34508.

Esping-Andsersen, G. (2013). *The three worlds of welfare capitalism.* John Wiley and Sons.

EU-OSHA. (2016). *Second European Survey of Enterprises on New and Emerging Risks (ESENER-2). Overview report: Managing safety and health at work.* Luxembourg: Publications Office of the European Union. https://osha.europa.eu/nl/tools-and-publications/publications/second-european-survey-enterprises-new-and-emerging-risks-esener.

Eurofound. (2017). *Sixth European Working Conditions Survey – Overview report (2017 update).* Luxembourg: Publications Office of the European Union.

Goetzel, R. Z., Long, S. R., Ozminkowski, R. J., Hawkins, K., Wang, S. & Lynch, W. (2004). Health, absence, disability, and presenteeism cost estimates of certain physical and mental health conditions affecting US employers. *Journal of Occupational and Environmental Medicine, 46*, 398–412.

Hooftman, W. E., Mars, G. M. J., Janssen, B., de Vroome, E. M. M., Janssen, B. J. M., Pleijers, A. J. S. F., Ramaukers, M. M. M. J. & van den Bossche, S. N. J. (2019). *Nationale enquête arbeidsomstandigheden 2018. Methodologie en globale resultaten.* Leiden/Heerlen: TNO/CBS.

Houtman, I. L. D. (1997). *Trends in Arbeid en Gezondheid.* Amsterdam: NIA TNO.

Houtman, I. L. D. (1999). Monitor stress en lichamelijke belasting. Werkgevers en werknemers over risico's, gevolgen en maatregelen. *Gedrag & Organisatie, 12*(6), 364–383.

Houtman, I. L. D. & van den Bossche, S. N. J. (2010). Trends in arbeidsomstandigheden in Nederland en Europa. *Tijdschrift voor Arbeidsvraagstukken*, 26(4), 432–450.

Houtman, I., Bakhuys Roozeboom, M., Kraan, K. & van den Bossche, S. (2017). Trends in arbeidsomstandigheden: werknemers in Nederland en Europa vergeleken. *Tijdschrift voor Arbeidsvraagstukken*, 33(4), 404–428.

Houtman, I. L. D., Goudswaard, A., Dhondt, S., van der Grinten, M., Hildebrandt, V. H. & Kompier, M. A. J. (1995). *Evaluatie Monitor stress en lichamelijke belasting*. Den Haag: VUGA.

Houtman, I. L. D., Goudswaard, A., Dhondt, S., van der Grinten, M. P., Hildebrandt, V. H. & van der Poel, E. G. T. (1998). Dutch monitor on stress and physical load: Risks, consequences and preventive action. *Occupational and Environmental Medicine*, 55, 73–83.

Houtman, I. & de Vroome, E. (2015). Jongeren, werkstress en flexibele arbeidscontracten. Leiden, TNO, 6 November. http://www.monitorarbeid.tno.nl/publicaties/jongeren-werkstress-en-flexibele-arbeidscontracten.

Houtman, I., de Vroome, E., van der Ploeg, K. & Ramaekers, M. (2019). Kerncijfers. In Karasek, M. Douwes, W. Hooftman & S. van den Bossche (Eds.), *Arbobalans, 2018*. Leiden: TNO. https://www.monitorarbeid.tno.nl/publicaties/arbobalans-2018.

Karasek, R. A. (1979). Job demands, job decision latitude, and mental strain: Implications for job redesign. *Administrative Science Quarterly*, 24, 285–308.

Karasek, R. & Theorell, T. (1990). *Healthy Work : stress, productivity, and the reconstruction of working life*. New York: Basic Books.

Kivimaki, M., Nyberg, S. T., Pentii, J., Madsen, I., Magnussen Hanson, L., Rugulies, R., Vahtera, J. & Coggon, D. (2019). Individual and combined effects of job strain components on subsequent morbidity and mortality. *Epidemiology*, 30(4), e27-e29. 10.1097/EDE.0000000000001020.

Kompier, M. A. J. & Cooper, C. (1999). *Preventing stress, improving productivity; European case studies in the workplace*. London: Routledge.

Kompier, M. A. J., Grundemann, R. W. M., Vink, P. & Smulders, P. G. W. (Eds.). (1996). *Aan de slag! Tien praktijkvoorbeelden van succesvol verzuimmanagement [Get going! Ten examples of succesful management of absence]*. Alphen a/d Rijn: Samsom.

Kompier, M. A. J. & Marcelissen, F. H. G. (1990). *Handboek Werkstress. Systematische aanpak voor de bedrijfspraktijk [Hand book work-related stress, Systematic approach at work]*. Amsterdam: NIA.

Lamberts, M. & Terlinden, L. (2016). *De implementatie van een preventiestrategie psychosociale risico's, lessen uit 10 organisatiecases*. Leuven: HIVA. http://www.werk.belgie.be/moduleDefault.aspx?id=39779.

Maslach, C., Jackson, S. E. & Leiter, M. P. (1996). *Maslach Burnout Inventory Manual* (3rd ed.). Palo Alto, CA: Consulting Psychologists Press.

Maslach, C., Schaufeli, W. B. & Leiter, M. P. (2001). Job burnout. *Annual Review of Psychology*, 52, 397–422.

Matrix Insight. (2013). *Economic analysis of workplace mental health promotion and mental disorder prevention programmes and of their potential contribution to EU health, social and economic policy objectives*, Matrix Insight, research commissioned by the. European Agency for Health and Consumers.

OECD - Organisation for Economic Co-operation and Development. (2012).

Sick on the Job? Myths and Realities about Mental Health and Work. Paris: OECD Publishing.

Schaufeli, W. (2018). *Burnout in Europe – Relations with national economy, governance and culture.* Research Unit Occupational Psychology and Professional Learning (internal report). KU Leuven: Belgium. https://www.wilmarschaufeli.nl/publications/Schaufeli/500.pdf.

Schaufeli, W. B., Leiter, M. P. & Maslach, C. (2009). Burnout: 35 years of research and practice. *Career Development International, 14,* 204–220.

Semmer, N. K. (2003). Job stress interventions and organization of work. In Taris, J. C. Quick & L. E. Tetrick (Eds.), *Handbook of occupational health psychology.* Washington: American Psychological Association.

Taris, T. W., Van der Wal, I. & Kompier, M. A. J. (2010). Large-scale job stress interventions: The Dutch experience. In Vaas, J. Houdmont & S. Leka (Eds.), *Contemporary occupational health psychology: Global perspectives on research and practice* (vol. 1, pp. 77–97). Chichester: Wiley.

Vaas, S., Dhondt, S., Peeters, M. H. H., *et al.,* (1995). *De Weba-methode. Deel 1. weba analyse handleiding [The Weba method. Part 1. weba analysis guide].* Alphen a/d Rijn: Samsom.

Veerman, T., De Jong, P. H., De Vroom, B., Bannink, D., Mur, S., Ossewaarde, M., Veldhuis, V. & Vellekoop, N. (2007). *Convenanten in context. Aggregatie en analyse van werking en opbrengsten van het beleidsprogramma Arboconvenanten.* Den Haag: Ministerie van Sociale Zaken en Werkgelegenheid.

Wittchen, H. U., Jacobi, F., Rehm, J., *et al.,* (2011). The size and burden of mental disorders and other disorders of the brain in Europe 2010. *Eur Neuropsychopharm, 21,* 655–679.

Wlodarski, O. (2013). Stratégie nationale en matière de Bien-être au Travail 2008-2012, Evaluation. *Prevent.* (http://www.werk.belgie.be/moduleDefault.aspx?id=39435).

Appendix A

The European Working Conditions Survey (EWCS) 2015[23]

In 2015, the sixth EWCS was carried out. The objectives of the EWCS are to provide an overview of working conditions in order to:

- assess and quantify the working conditions of both employees and the self-employed across Europe on a harmonized basis;
- analyze relationships between different aspects of working conditions;
- identify groups at risk and issues of concern, as well as identify progress;
- monitor trends by providing homogeneous indicators on these issues; and
- contribute to European policy development, in particular, on quality of work and employment issues.

The scope of the survey questionnaire has widened substantially since the first

Irene L.D. Houtman et al.

edition, aiming to provide a comprehensive picture of everyday working life in Europe. Topics covered include employment status, working time duration and

EU-Countries	N	Mean	Standard Deviation
Austria	1,027	3.06	1.06
Belgium	2,561	3.06	1.10
Bulgaria	1,061	3.19	1.05
Croatia	1,001	3.31	0.95
Cyprus	1,001	3.18	0.91
Czech Republic	1,001	2.99	1.00
Denmark	1,000	2.89	0.97
Estonia	1,009	3.18	0.92
Finland	1,000	2.93	0.87
France	1,526	3.33	1.05
Germany	2,088	3.00	0.92
Greece	1,001	3.15	0.94
Hungary	1,012	3.21	1.00
Ireland	1,055	3.02	1.00
Italy	1,399	3.20	0.99
Latvia	978	2.94	1.03
Lithuania	1,002	3.04	0.99
Luxembourg	1,003	3.36	1.08
Malta	1,003	3.21	1.15
The Netherlands	1,025	2.68	1.09
Poland	1,191	3.28	1.03
Portugal	1,027	3.04	1.03
Romania	1,062	3.17	0.95
Slovakia	995	3.15	0.96
Slovenia	1,601	3.33	1.14
Spain	3,354	3.22	1.18
Sweden	1,001	2.93	0.99
United Kingdom	1,622	3.17	1.09
Candidate countries	6,036	3.51	1.05
Albania	1,002	3.36	0.99
North Macedonia	1,009	3.61	1.20
Montenegro	999	3.39	1.02
Serbia	1,028	3.47	1.08
Turkey	2,000	3.62	1.08
Associated countries	2,033	3.02	1.00
Switzerland	1,005	3.21	1.04
Norway	1,028	2.83	0.94
Total sample	43,675	3.18	1.06

organization, learning and training, safety and health, physical and psychosocial factors, and work and health.

Sample sizes, means, and standard deviations of burnout per country - 6th EWCS-2015

The second European Survey of Enterprises on New and Emerging Risks (ESENER-2) ([24])

EU-OSHA's ESENER-2 survey asked "those who know best about safety and health in the establishment" about the way safety and health risks are managed in the workplace, with a particular focus on PSRs (i.e. work-related stress, violence, and harassment). In 2014, a total of 49,320 establishments across all sectors ([25]) and with at least five employees, were surveyed in 36 countries covering the 28 European Union Member States (EU-28), as well as Albania, Iceland, Montenegro, the former Yugoslav Republic of Macedonia, Serbia, Turkey, Norway, and Switzerland. On average, the dataset included about 1,400 establishments per country. For ESENER-2, data were collected at the enterprise level by means of telephone interviews with the person 'who knows best about OSH issues'. In micro and small enterprises (MSEs), this was mostly the owner/director, but in larger enterprises, it was an OSH specialist, such as a health and safety officer, or a safety manager. The questionnaire was structured around similar topics to ESENER-1, including:

- day-to-day management of OSH risks;
- special focus on PSRs and risks of MSDs (emerging risks);
- drivers and barriers to OSH management; and
- worker involvement.

10 Occupational Stress, Coping Strategies, and the Impact of Culture in the Middle East
A Systematic Review of Evidence from Oman

Kaneez Fatima Sadriwala and Mustafa Malik

Introduction

Occupational stress is one of the recurring factors in modern society. The culture of a particular place plays a huge role in the perception and expression of stress and distress. Stress is a phenomenon that jeopardizes a person's mental and physical health. It affects their work-life balance and job performance. A detailed study through the scientific method is very much required in this field. The available literature in form of scientific studies is scant in the context of Oman; however, there have been regular discussions in various forums. Dr. Amira al Raaidan, a director for health education and awareness programs and the head of the Mental Health Department in the Ministry of Health in Oman, said that "Just like every other country, people in Oman undergo problems arising from workplace stress, and among these, some of the main problems are depression and anxiety. Both are very dangerous and need to be treated adequately and immediately to avoid complications that may arise from these two conditions". A young marketing executive Fatma al Lawati (name changed to protect identity), who works with one of Oman's leading banks believes that ageism, gender bias, bullying, and ever-increasing workloads are driving employees mad. Another article published in Times Oman quoted, "By 2020, depression will become the biggest form of mental health illness. That is a sign that things need to be done, and we need to take care of the well-being of these people who are suffering". On the other hand, an article published in Y Magazine (April 2017) by one of the leading newspapers in Oman reported that Omanis are happy at work. Oman is undergoing a demographic shift and a transition from traditional behavior to the modern lifestyle. In the wake of such situations, certainly, there would be effects on stress levels. In light of the above real-life situations, Oman is no exception to the vulnerability caused by stress. The purpose of learning about stress and the impact of culture on stress management is not to eliminate stress, because stress is inevitable, but to know the proper means and ways to recognize the stressors and to manage them to help the society to develop. Not all kinds of stress are bad. There is positive stress called Eustress, and negative stress called Distress (Tummers and Rocco, 2014), in their book 'Stress Management'. According to Al-Sinawi and Al-Adawi (2006),

> *The Omani population is undergoing a "demographic transition", with declining death rates complemented by high birth rates. This is likely to be accompanied by an increase in the number of people with psychiatric disorders. There is also an indication that the country is bracing itself for the social and economic consequences of a more youthful population, with far more job-seekers than the labor market can absorb. The traditional passage to adulthood is also changing, as youngsters are expected to marry late and to have children when they are well into their 20 s. However, the "adolescent turmoil" seen in Western societies is not evident in Omani society, which emphasizes family obedience.*

Oman and its Culture: An Overview

Located at the southeastern corner of the Arabian Peninsula, the Sultanate of Oman occupies a strategic position on the trade route between Europe and Asia. To the east of Oman lie the Gulf of Oman and the Arabian Sea, to the west are the United Arab Emirates and the Kingdom of Saudi Arabia, to the north is the Islamic Republic of Iran, and to the south is the Republic of Yemen. Oman's total population at the end of 2018 stood at 4.6 million (2.58 million nationals and 2.02 million expatriates). It occupies a land area of approximately 309,500 square kilometers with a coastline extending to almost 1,700 kilometers overlooking the Arabian Gulf, Gulf of Oman, and the Arabian Sea. With Muscat as the capital of the Sultanate of Oman, the Sultanate is divided into eleven governorates.

Culturally, Oman is steeped in the religion of Islam. While the majority of its population is Arabs, a sizable minority consists of Balochs and Swahilis. In addition, nearly half of the population consists of foreign workers. The culture of Oman is deeply rooted in Islam. Omanis in general are highly tolerant, adaptive, and accommodative by nature. The men and women follow a specific cultural dress code outside of their homes. The men wear a *dishdasha* (a simple collarless, long-sleeved, ankle-length gown that is usually of white color), a special type of headdress called *mussar* (embroidered woolen cloth woven over the tradition skull cap), and a special form of dagger called the *khanjar* which is affixed on waistbands or belts and is usually worn on formal and special occasions. Some men carry an ornamental stick called the *assa*, and most Omani men wear sandals on their feet. On the other hand, the Omani women wear a long robe called *abbaya* that covers them from the neck to the feet and this is mostly black in color. Women cover their heads with scarves all the time. Omani women also wear elaborate gold and silver jewelry around the head, neck, wrists, ankles, fingers, and toes. Most Omani women wear sandals or Western-type fashion shoes. Omani cuisine has a great variety and includes unique dishes from other Arab countries. *Kahwa* (which appears similar to coffee) is served with dates. Rice, meat, fish, and bread are the main ingredients of most Omani dishes – like *maqbous* and *aursia*. *Shuva* (whole lamb steamed with a variety of dried whole spices) is a popular festive meal in Oman. Lately, Oman has modernized itself with sound infrastructure including roads, communication systems, hospitals, and places of tourist attraction.

Literature Review

Occupational Stress in General

Occupational stress refers to stress or distress experienced at work. It arises due to the conflict between job demands and the amount of control over the situation (Rao & Chandraiah, 2012). Various studies have identified and established reasons for occupational stress and burnout, such as job demands (Bakker & Demerouti, 2014; Perrewe & Ganster, 1989), lack of control (Johnson et al., 2005; Mineka and Kelly, 1989), lower managerial support (Johnson et al., 2005; Van der Colff & Rothmann, 2009), role ambiguity (Grant & Langan-Fox, 2006; Beehr, Bowling, & Bennett, 2010), high workload (McVicar, 2003; Ilies, Dimotakis, & De Pater, 2010), bullying and harassment (Vickers, 2006; Hodgins, MacCurtain, & Mannix-McNamara, 2014), blame culture (Conti, Angelis, Cooper, Faragher, & Gill, 2006), poor working conditions (Dellve et al., 2015), and poor work-life balance (Byrne, 2005).

Work-related stress has been identified as a significant contributing factor to organizational inefficiency and lower performance (Mohammadi, 2011, Ongori & Agolla, 2008; Arnetz, 2006), high staff turnover (Rajamohan, Porock, & Chang, 2019; Kim & Barak, 2015; Avey, Luthans, & Jensen, 2009), absenteeism (Staufenbiel & König, 2010; Darr & Johns, 2008), decreased job satisfaction (Hoboubi, Choobineh, Ghanavati, Keshavarzi, & Hosseini, al., 2017; Bemana, Moradi, Ghasemi, Taghavi, & Ghayoor, et al., 2013; AbuAlRub, 2004; Flanagan & Flanagan, 2002), and employee well-being (Jamal, 1999; Avey, Luthans, Smith, & Palmer, 2010). While stress is unavoidable in a modern organizational context, it needs to be reduced.

Employees respond to stress differently and use different stress-coping strategies. According to Lazarus and Folkman (1984), stress is experienced only when situations are appraised as exceeding one's resources.

Thus, a person may interpret additional work responsibilities as a threat, whereas another may regard extra responsibilities as a challenge. Lazarus and Folkman (1984) define coping as "constantly changing cognitive and behavioral efforts made to master, tolerate, or reduce external and internal demands and conflicts among them".

Various coping strategies that are used by employees to reduce stress include the use of resources, peer support, teamwork, balancing priorities, fostering social relations, family support, etc. Outside work factors, such as family support, social and cultural norms, and religion and spirituality, play an important mediating role coping with occupational stress.

Some Conceptual Definitions

Occupational Stress

Hans Selye, the Founder of Stress Theory and the Father of Stress, defined stress as "the non-specific response of the body to any demand for change" in 1936. Seyle (1976) further expanded the definition of stress to explain that, since there are too many alternatives, the perception of imposed demand creates stress. While Lazarus and Folkman (1984) explained in their research that when internal or environmental demands exceed the available resources, a judgment must be made – which is the actual reason for stress. Skinner (1985) defined stress as "a reaction of a particular individual to a stimulus event". Later, Eliot (1988) concluded that "stress may be viewed as the body's response to any real or imagined event perceived as requiring some adaptive response and/or producing strain".

Various researchers studying stress at work and how to manage it also defined stress in various ways. For example, Steinberg and Ritzmann (1990) defined stress as "an underload or overload of matter, energy or information input to, or output from, a living system". Likewise, Humphrey (1992) argued that "stress can be considered as any factor, acting internally or externally, that makes it difficult to adapt and that induces increased effort on the part of the person to maintain a state of equilibrium both internally and with the external environment". McEwen and Mendelson (1993) explained that "stress is a term for certain types of experiences, as well as the body's responses to such experiences, and this term generally refers to the 'challenges' – real or implied, to the homeostatic regulatory process of the organism". Furthermore, Levi and Lunde-Jensen (1996) concluded that "stress is caused by a multitude of demands (stressors), such as an inadequate fit between what we need and what we are capable of, what our environment offers, and what it demands of us". Roger and Najarian (1998) described stress as a "preoccupation with the negative emotion following the event".

Coping

Coping used to be seen as an individually possessed habitual style for dealing with stressful situations. Lazarus and Folkman (1984) defined it as "the cognitive and behavioral efforts that people use to manage specific external and/or internal demands of a situation appraised as stressful". They argued that, while appraising the events, people first evaluate whether or not what is happening is relevant to their values, goal commitments, beliefs about the self and the world, and situational intentions. Next, they think about what they can do to deal with the situation – if it is perceived as stressful and threatening. If an event has been appraised as stressful, then individuals begin to engage in the coping process and try to return to their previous emotional state.

Coping strategies can be broadly categorized as a) problem-focused and b) emotion-focused (Lazarus & Folkman, 1984; Lazarus, 1993). While problem-focused coping acts directly on the environment or the individual to allow the person to readjust to the changed environment, emotion-focused coping reduces emotional distress by helping the individual to avoid things that cause the stress or by changing the meaning of what is occurring (Lazarus, 1993; Lazarus & Folkman, 1984).

Skinner, Edge, Altman, and Sherwood (2003) argued that when coping is regulated flexibly, "behavior is active and intentional, emotion is channeled, and orientation is goal-directed". On the other hand, Compas, Connor-Smith, Saltzman, Thomsen, and Wadsworth (2001) defined coping as "conscious volitional efforts to regulate emotion, cognition, behavior, physiology, and the environment in response to stressful events or circumstances". These two definitions show that stress responses can be placed along two dimensions – voluntary versus involuntary – and engagement (fight) versus disengagement (flight).

Culture and Coping

Culture plays an important role in coping with stress. According to Markus and Kitayama (1991), people from different cultures have remarkably different construals of the self and of others. For example, many Western cultures emphasize independence and uniqueness, while many Asian cultures assert that the relationships of a person to others is central. Thus, an individual's response to stress may vary upon whether he/she has an independent or interdependent self. The people with interdependent selves (i.e. people from Asian cultures) are more likely to express other-focused emotions such as sympathy and shame (Markus and Kitayama, 1991), avoid anger to promote harmony (Wang, 2001), and use more evading and compromising styles to deal with conflict (Triandis, 1995). Since interdependent selves value social constructs of belongingness and harmony, they use self-control and self-restraint to adjust with social contingencies, unlike independent selves who are more likely to motivated by self motives and autonomous desires and individual needs.

Many studies comparing coping and its effectiveness among different cultural backgrounds have confirmed the importance of cultural differences in coping with stress. For example, Sinha, Willson, and Watson (2000) found that social support was more widely used among Asians than among Americans. In a similar study, Liang and Bogat (1994) found that perceived social support played a buffering role in coping with stress among the Chinese.

Oman-Specific Studies on Occupational Stress and Burnout

While occupational stress has been a widely researched area across the world, only scant and scattered work has been done in the context of Oman. Preliminary research of the literature was done on the Oman database, *Masader* EBSCOhost, with the Boolean phrases: "occupational stress", "work-related stress", "job stress", "burnout", "coping", and "Oman". The initial result was run for 20 years, from 2000 to 2019, but there were no studies found before 2010. All of the studies included in this paper are from 2011 until 2019. The results were from ten academic journals, out of which only five were related to the subject matter. The thesaurus terms were burnout (psychology) (3), job stress (3), job satisfaction (2), quality of work life (2), career development (1), civil service (1), but unrelated papers were excluded from our study. The publications were from the Arab Journal of Psychiatry (4), the Oman Medical Journal (2), the Asian Academy of Management Journal (1), Global Business and Management Research (1), the Journal of Management and Public Policy (1), and The South Asian Journal of Management (1), among others. The geographic area covered was Oman (6), Muscat (1), and Saudi Arabia (1). The databases were Business Source Ultimate (4), Academic Search Ultimate (3), and the Arab World Research Source (3). A further search was done on Google Scholar and ResearchGate, where some more studies were found.

Most of the studies are focused on only a few sectors/industries such as the health sector (Lawati, Short, Abdulhadi, Panchatcharam, & Dennis, 2019; Al-Hashemi et al., 2019; Al-Nabhani, Sinawi, & Toubi, 2016; and Emam & Al-Lawati, 2014) and the education sector (Al-Alawi et al. 2019; Abu-Hilal, Al-Bahrani, & Al-Zedjali, 2017; Jahan et al., 2016; Aldhafri, 2016; Hans et al., 2015 and Kumar, 2015). There have also been a few articles in newspapers, magazines, and conference presentations specific to occupational stress. One such article was found in the oil sector by Al-Rubaee and Al-Maniri (2011). Nevertheless, one of the studies conducted by Al Busaidy and Borthwick (2012) studied the role of Islamic cultural values in mitigating occupational stress and highlighted its therapeutic importance.

Al-Rubaee (2011), while studying stress among employees working in the oil fields of a particular oil company, highlighted that the possibility of physical injury during work has been one of the major stressors for workers working in the oil sector. While in most of the instances the employees who encountered physical injuries were of a younger age (i.e. 25–34 years), these have been attributed generally to lack of information, lack of training, lack of supervision, lack of experience, and the lack of knowledge and skills.

Najat and Alan (2012), argue that much of occupational therapy theory in practice, even in non-Western countries such as those in the Middle East, is based on Western cultural values. Their study emphasized the importance of local cultural beliefs and values to the practice of occupational therapy. Through semi-structured interviews with actively practicing occupational therapists in Oman, the study established that occupational therapy based on Western principles may not always fit in a culturally different context – such as Oman. While "individualism" is emphasized in Western occupational therapy literature, the study by Najat and Alan (2012) in the context of Oman emphasized religion, the family structure, culture, and gender as important aspects.

Al-Hashemi et al. (2019), through a cross-sectional study among 190 primary care physicians, found that occupational burnout among healthcare professionals (i.e. physicians) was high on all three burnout symptoms of emotional exhaustion, depersonalization, and personal accomplishments. While Inadequate staff, frequent conflicts, stress in personal life, and lack of social support have been cited as the common reasons for burnout, the study established that longer working hours have been the most critical factor in burnout among primary health physicians in Oman. A similar study by Al-Nabhani et al. (2016) investigating burnout perceived stress and coping strategies among 276 practicing nurses and concluded that younger nurses (aged below 35 years) were more prone to experiencing stress rather than their older counterparts. Also, unmarried nurses perceived more stress than their married colleagues. Longer working hours have been seen as a critical stress factor, along with demanding patient care and fewer work breaks.

A cross-sectional study by Jahan et al. (2016) exploring the reception of occupational stress and coping strategies among medical students concluded that – while a higher level of stress among students is associated with poor academic performance, large content of study materials, and time constraints – the major coping strategies used by the students were better time management, seeking emotional support, talking to family and friends, and having adequate sleep time. A similar study by Al-Alawi et al. (2019) explores determinants of burnout and depression among medical students in Oman and showed that about 24.5% of medical students were found with depressive symptoms while 7.4% of cohorts endorsed the presence of burnout syndrome. Another cross-sectional study on 237 medical students by Elsheshtawy, Taha, Almazroui, Joshi, and Almazroui (2018), found that individual personality traits are helpful in reducing hospital anxiety and depression. They found that Individuals who had high neuroticism were more prone to have high perceived stress – which resulted in a higher development of depression and anxiety. Abu-Hilal et al. (2017), through an empirical study on 344 college students in Oman, concluded that religiousness (in this case, belief in Islam) is an important predictor of the sense of meaning in life for college students in Oman. Hence, religion can be employed in counseling and rehabilitation programs to reduce stress among students.

Hans et al. (2015) studied work-life quality and occupational stress among teachers of Business Management in private higher educational institutions and found that there was relatively low stress among the aforementioned teachers. In a similar study by Kumar (2015) on private higher education institutes, where he examined the relationship between burnout and job satisfaction, he found that emotional exhaustion and reduced personal accomplishment reduces job satisfaction and results in burnout, but spirituality worked as a coping strategy and had moderately affected the relationship between burnout and job satisfaction.

A study by Emam & Al-Lawati (2014) conducted among 142 female support staff from community disability centers in Oman argued that personal commitment and spirituality were modest predictors of support staff stress. The study concluded that spiritual belief, participating in religious communities, having faith, and using prayer were some important coping strategies used by respondents.

Culture and Work-Related Stress

Work-related stress is a pattern of physiological, emotional, cognitive, and behavioral reactions to some extremely taxing aspects of work content, work organization, and work environment. When people experience work-related stress, they often feel tense, distressed, and unable to cope. Due to globalization and changes in the nature of work, people in developing countries have to deal with increasing work-related stress. In industrialized countries, people are becoming more familiar with work-related stress and have developed mechanisms to manage it. However, in developing countries, this may not be the case yet. They are stressed due to the country's economic development and political environment also, other than their own personal traits and characteristics and family size and structure. Social obligations, cultural norms, and behavior impact their work environment which, in turn, results in stress (Hernandez & Blazer, 2006).

Empirical Studies on Perceived Stress in Oman

Methodology

The main objectives of conducting this research are to determine the prevailing occupational stress level among people in Oman, to list down the effects on their well-being, and to examine strategies on how do they cope with stress.

A questionnaire was prepared and had four sections. The first section was based on a precise measure of personal stress called the **Perceived Stress Scale**. The Perceived Stress Scale (PSS) is a classic stress assessment instrument. The tool, while originally developed in 1983 by Cohen, S. and is available for academic use in the public domain, remains a popular choice for helping us understand how different situations affect our feelings and our perceived stress. The questionnaire has been adapted from Mind Garden, Inc., info@mindgarden.com www.mindgarden.com. The PSS is reprinted with the permission of the American Sociological Association, from Cohen, Kamarck, and Mermelstein (1983).

The second section is based on the "ill effects on the job", "behavioral changes'", followed by "coping mechanisms".

Primary data was collected by administering the questionnaire on Google Forms. Proper care was taken so that the questionnaire was filled up by the target population – representing men and women, the government and private sectors, and nationals and expatriates in Oman. The questionnaire was converted into the local Arabic language, and it was distributed by the snowball technique through e-mails and WhatsApp. The response rate was very poor, which is again very peculiar about Oman and depicts their behavior towards research and education. Another important reason for the poor response is avoiding self-disclosure. The questionnaire was sent to more than 600 people, but overall, only (66) 10.1% of responses were received. The authors then conducted focus group discussions and one-on-one interviews. The full chapter theory is based on such group discussions and interviews.

Analysis of Data

The reliability of the first section of the questionnaire – ten questions were adopted from Cohen et al. (1983) – was checked and established by Cronbach's Alpha, which is 0.795 (Table 10.1), and Kaiser-Meyer-Olkin

Table 10.1 Reliability Statistics

Cronbach's Alpha	Cronbach's Alpha Based on Standardized Items	N of Items
.796	.795	10

(KMO), which measured the sampling adequacy for each variable in the model at 0.813, as given below in Table 10.2. (Reliability Statistics).

Table 10.2 KMO and Bartlett's Test

Kaiser-Meyer-Olkin Measure of Sampling Adequacy.		.813
Bartlett's Test of Sphericity	Approx. Chi-Square	265.420
	df	45
	Sig.	.000

Questions number 4, 5, 7, and 8 ("In the last month, how many times have you felt confident about your ability to handle your personal problems?", "How often you felt that things were going your way?", "How often have you been able to control irritations in your life?", and "How often have you felt that you were on top of things?") were reversed, and the total score was summed up. Having a total score of 13 and below was perceived to be low stress, 14 to 26 was moderately stressed, and above 27 was highly stressed. The analysis of the data (Table 10.3 and Figure 10.1) revealed that 15.4% of respondents were from the low-stress level, 10.8% were from the high-stress level, and 72.3% were ranging between 14 to 26 – which demonstrates moderate stress level. Moderate stress can be indicated as positive stress to foster individual performance and organizational climate (Hans et al., 2015).

Table 10.3 Stress Level

Grand Total N 65	Score	Percentage	Stress level
	Less than 13	15.4%	Low
	From 14 to 26	72.3%	Moderate
	More than 27	10.8%	High

Demographic Data of the Respondents

Table 10.4 shows the gender of respondents, Table 10.5 shows the education level of respondents. The highest responses were having higher diploma or bachelors degree. Oman is a country having various nationalities, in this research, maximum respondents (86.4%) were from Oman as shown in Table 10.6. Table 10.7 gives the detail about occupation of the respondents. 31.8% respondents were government employees, where is 34.8% are employed in large organizations. In response to the question, "Do you feel that your life is interesting?" (see Table 10.8), 40.9% responded said that, they found life very much interesting, 34.8% said, to some extent they found life interesting and

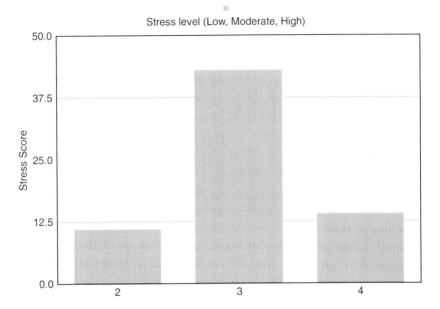

Figure 10.1 Low, Moderate, and High Stress Scores.

Table 10.4 Gender

	Frequency	Percent	Valid Percent	Cumulative Percent
	1	1.5	1.5	1.5
Female	28	42.4	42.4	43.9
Male	37	56.1	56.1	100.0
Total	66	100.0	100.0	

Table 10.5 Education

	Frequency	Percent	Valid Percent	Cumulative Percent
	1	1.5	1.5	1.5
Diploma	3	4.5	4.5	6.1
Higher Diploma/Bachelors	33	50.0	50.0	56.1
Masters	25	37.9	37.9	93.9
PhD/MPhil or above	3	4.5	4.5	98.5
Professional Certification	1	1.5	1.5	100.0
Total	66	100.0	100.0	

22.7% were of the opinion that life is not so much interesting. In response to the question, "Do you think that you have achieved the standard of living and social status that you have expected?"

Table 10.6 Nationality

	Frequency	Percent	Valid Percent	Cumulative Percent
	1	1.5	1.5	1.5
Indian	7	10.6	10.6	12.1
Jordan	1	1.5	1.5	13.6
Oman	57	86.4	86.4	100.0
Total	66	100.0	100.0	

Table 10.7 Occupation

	Frequency	Percent	Valid Percent	Cumulative Percent
	1	1.5	1.5	1.5
Government Employment	21	31.8	31.8	33.3
Large Organization (more than 50 employees)	23	34.8	34.8	68.2
Not Employed	10	15.2	15.2	83.3
Private Medium Organization (10 to 50)	2	3.0	3.0	86.4
Private Small Organization (Less than 10)	2	3.0	3.0	89.4
Self-Employed	1	1.5	1.5	90.9
Student	6	9.1	9.1	100.0
Total	66	100.0	100.0	

Table 10.8 Do you feel that your life is interesting?

	Frequency	Percent	Valid Percent	Cumulative Percent
Very much	27	40.9	41.5	41.5
To some extent	23	34.8	35.4	76.9
Not so much	15	22.7	23.1	100.0
Total	65	98.5	100.0	
System	1	1.5		
Total	66	100.0		

Table 10.9 shows the data that 42.4% respondents achieved, "To some extent," 28.8% "Very much" and 27.3% opined "Not so much," standard of living and social status has been achieved as expected. The data in Table 10.10 show the response for the question, "Do you feel that you can manage situations when they do not turn out as expected?" 95.4% respondents said that they were either very much or to some extent confident in managing situation if they did not turn out as expected. In response to the question, "Do you feel easily upset if things

Table 10.9 Do you think that you have achieved the standard of living and the social status that you have expected?

		Frequency	Percent	Valid Percent	Cumulative Percent
Valid	Very much	19	28.8	29.2	29.2
	To some extent	28	42.4	43.1	72.3
	Not so much	18	27.3	27.7	100.0
	Total	65	98.5	100.0	
Missing	System	1	1.5		
Total		66	100.0		

Table 10.10 Do you feel that you can manage situations even when they do not turn out as expected?

		Frequency	Percent	Valid Percent	Cumulative Percent
Valid	Very much	16	24.2	24.6	24.6
	To some extent	46	69.7	70.8	95.4
	Not so much	3	4.5	4.6	100.0
Total		65	98.5	100.0	
Missing	System	1	1.5		
Total		66	100.0		

Table 10.11 Do you feel easily upset if things don't turn out as expected?

		Frequency	Percent	Valid Percent	Cumulative Percent
Valid	Very much	17	25.8	26.2	26.2
	To some extent	33	50.0	50.8	76.9
	Not so much	15	22.7	23.1	100.0
	Total	65	98.5	100.0	
Missing	System	1	1.5		
Total		66	100.0		

don't don't turn out as expected?," 23.1% said they were "Not so much" upset, but 50.8% said they were "To some extent" upset if things don't turn out as expected and 26.2% were "Very much" easily upset. In response to the question, "Do you feel disturbed by the feeling of anxiety and tension?," 12.3% were not so much disturbed but 87.7% for disturbed either to some extent or very much disturbed (Table 10.12). 76.9% respondent considered family as a source of help in finding solutions to most of the problems they have, where is 23.1% do not consider family as a source of help (Table 10.13). 83.1% responded and said they worried about their health to some extent or very much, only 16.9% said they were not so much worried about their health (Table 10.14). In response to the questionare you troubled by disturbed sleep?," 26.2% of find they were very much troubled, 41.5% were trouble to some extent and 32.3% were not so much troubled by disturbed sleep (Table 10.15).

The behavioral changes (Figure 10.2) experienced by Omanis are 42.2% related to poor performance in their jobs. 32.8% are inclined to shouting at family members and 36% tend to seek help from others in performing their jobs. 23.4% sought frequent hospitalization.

People in Oman are highly religious, and the data, as in Figure 10.3,

Table 10.12 Do you feel disturbed by the feeling of anxiety and tension?

		Frequency	Percent	Valid Percent	Cumulative Percent
Valid	Very much	15	22.7	23.1	23.1
	To some extent	42	63.6	64.6	87.7
	Not so much	8	12.1	12.3	100.0
	Total	65	98.5	100.0	
Missing	System	1	1.5		
Total		66	100.0		

Table 10.13 Do you consider your family as a source of help to you in finding solutions to most of the problems you have?

		Frequency	Percent	Valid Percent	Cumulative Percent
Valid	Very much	24	36.4	36.9	36.9
	To some extent	26	39.4	40.0	76.9
	Not so much	15	22.7	23.1	100.0
	Total	65	98.5	100.0	
Missing	System	1	1.5		
Total		66	100.0		

Table 10.14 Do you sometimes worry about your health?

		Frequency	Percent	Valid Percent	Cumulative Percent
Valid	Very much	19	28.8	29.2	29.2
	To some extent	35	53.0	53.8	83.1
	Not so much	11	16.7	16.9	100.0
	Total	65	98.5	100.0	
Missing	System	1	1.5		
Total		66	100.0		

Table 10.15 Are you troubled by disturbed sleep?

		Frequency	Percent	Valid Percent	Cumulative Percent
Valid	Very much	17	25.8	26.2	26.2
	To some extent	27	40.9	41.5	67.7
	Not so much	21	31.8	32.3	100.0
	Total	65	98.5	100.0	
Missing	System	1	1.5		
Total		66	100.0		

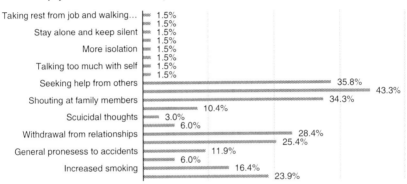

Figure 10.2 Behavioral Changes.

proves that they resort to prayers and meditation as part of their coping mechanisms. Self-positive thinking also forms a major part of their coping strategies. Yoga, travel, and playing with pets are less popular among the respondents.

Oman-Specific Cultural Behavior: How are Stress and Distress Experienced in Oman?

According to Hofstede, there are four key dimensions to any country's cultural behavior. Cultural behavior also tends to add Eustress or Distress to an individual's behavior.

1   Individualism vs. Collectivism: Hofstede states that *"Individualism means to play alone or to the extent wherein people believe that, in achieving personal success, they must work alone – which brings in more sophistication and professionalism. On the other hand, people*

Impact of Culture in the Middle East 209

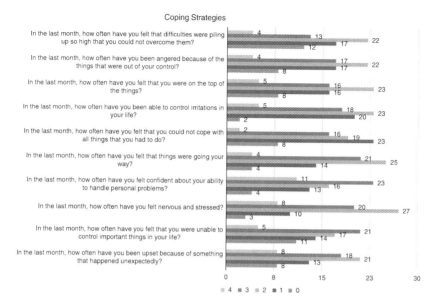

Figure 10.3 Coping Strategies.

who believe in Collectivism must work together for the mutual benefit of all in the group. This uplifts the weaker ones who are also in the group."

Collectivism and Occupational Stress

Oman falls purely in the dimension of collectivism. Omanis have tightly knit families and social groups, wherein they take great care of family members and friends. In addition to this, they will help anyone in need whether personally known or otherwise, with unquestioning loyalty. The degree of collectivism may vary from organization to organization, but in workplaces where collectivism is high, employees are friends with one another, absenteeism is low, the turnover rate is low, and even if financial benefits are less, people will still continue their jobs due to the healthy work environment. Omanis do not care much about money. Rather, they care more about their companies, companions, workplace, and, above all, their bosses or supervisors. If they are in good relations with their seniors, they continue the job. Otherwise, they quit even without having another job in hand. Students also like to work in a team. If they have something to discuss with their instructor, they come in a group. They are not confident to speak and assert their case on their own.

As noted by Al-Sinawi and Al-Adawi (2006)

The principle of unity begins with the belief in the unity of Allah: there is only one God, followed by unity of purpose of the cosmos, that is Ibadah or worship, and unity of the human community in this purpose. Worship includes any Amal-Salih or constructive work or good deed (Khan, 1986). Ashy (1999) states the major goal of Islam is unity of all aspects of personality and of society. For example, when one's neighbour does not have food or is sick, it is within this goal of unity that one is expected to help the neighbour. With modernization, the social status of Omani individuals have undergone some notable changes. These have been brought about by unprecedented prosperity, expansion of educational opportunities, and, most importantly and from the point of view of psychiatry, an increased preference for an individualistic rather than the traditional collectivistic mindset and social behavior.

2   Hofstede talks about Power Distance: "This dimension expresses the degree to which the less powerful members of a society accept and expect that power is distributed unequally. The fundamental issue here is how a society handles inequalities among people." In the case of societies with low power distance, all of the members of society are treated equally and are given equal opportunity to express their views. In Omani society, there is a high degree of power distance – the young respect the old and do not counter reply to the older members of the family. They keep their voices low and avoid eye contact with the elders. On the contrary, major decisions in the family are done through the consultation and direction of females only. Mothers are usually the decision-makers of the family.

Power Distance in Oman

In occupations, this dimension clearly marks its presence. The junior employee seldom speaks in front of the senior. Very few women occupy higher positions in offices, and male dominance is seen in almost all facets of life in Oman. Highly educated females tend to have more stress in comparison to their male counterparts. Expatriates experience more stress than Omani workers on the same hierarchy level. Power distance is observed more in family circles than in the workplace.

3   Masculinity versus Femininity: This dimension focuses on the extent to which a society stresses achievement or nurturing. Masculinity is seen to be the trait that emphasizes ambition, acquisition of wealth, and differentiated gender roles. Femininity is seen to be the trait that stresses caring and nurturing behaviors, sexuality equality, environmental awareness, and more fluid

gender roles.

From Hofstede (2001), Culture's Consequences, 2nd ed. p 297.

"Masculinity stands for a society in which social gender roles are clearly distinct: Men are supposed to be assertive, tough, and focused on material success; women are supposed to be more modest, tender, and concerned with the quality of life." "Femininity stands for a society in which social gender roles overlap: Both men and women are supposed to be modest, tender, and concerned with the quality of life." Usually, the Gulf countries are masculinity-based.

In Oman, the social norms are highly ego-oriented. Money and material things have value in society and act as a stressor, but social norms are shifting towards the quality of life and focus on people. Oman's economic growth is of high priority, but one of the major reasons for distress is the oil crisis in the last few years. The country's revenue was affected as a result of the dip in crude oil prices, which, in turn, resulted in an increase in domestic petrol and gasoline prices. Commuting has become more expensive now more than ever before, which is one of the biggest stressors for Oman. The government relaxed the population by increasing the minimum wage rate of the Omanis, but the pay remained the same for the expatriates – adding more vulnerability to their lives. Recent developments show the Oman Government's great concern for environmental protection, as they provide licenses for small and medium-sized organizations after these organizations obtain environment-protection certificates from competent authorities. Oman is highly evolving into a modern society. Thus, Oman does not fall purely into the cultural dimension of being masculinity-based.

The people of Oman are humble and kind. They are very polite. Conflicts are solved through negotiation, but religion is still the most important part of life, and only men can be priests. As far as work is considered there is a smaller or no gender wage gap, as fewer women are in management. Omanis also have a preference for higher pay for fewer working hours. They have a traditional family structure, and this clearly forms behavior and expectations from boys and girls, but failure is not considered to be a disaster. The male head is the dominant member of the family. Females usually occupy the least heard or most suppressed voice in the family. They keep their voices low and hide away from the presence of males. Omani women are expected to portray the ideal image of Muslim women – a carer of the house, of children, and of their husbands. However, women are also expected to hold a full-time job in addition to their household job. Women technically have the same rights as men but are often at a disadvantage when it comes to disputes over adultery, divorce, and child custody. In addition, many women don't report spousal and domestic abuse. Women in Oman make up the majority of the population going to universities or other places of higher learning, but also hold the highest rates of illiteracy (i.e. mainly women living in rural areas). Men and women technically have the same rights under the law; however, men often have privileges in the *Sharia* law. In the gender debate: "Are women equal to men in Oman?" 07 Mar 2018, posted by, Y Magazine, new laws, broad mindsets, and rev–amped social milieus have brought in a fresh wave of optimism in society about women's rights. Hasan al Lawati explored the gender myths and reported that women in Oman are more empowered – they have the right to vote, the right to contest elections, the right to education, the right to own property, the right to employment, the right to earn fair and equal pay, and the right to equal opportunities, but having these rights does not mean that there is no discrimination at all against women in Oman. Women lag behind. In Oman, women make 41.5% of government employees and enjoy equal pay, according to the National Statistics and Information Center as of October 2017, but women make only 24% of private-sector employees and comprise 63% of total job seekers.

A recent study by Sumaya Al Weheibi, a specialist on women and gender inequality, shows that the level of education is "significantly related to happiness" of Omani women. The higher the level of education, the higher the rate of happiness was – according to the study that targeted 1,926 Omani females from 11 governorates. Al-Wahaibi's study revealed that occupation-wise, Omani women who run their own businesses are the happiest, compared to students and employees. However, the recent study said that majority of the one-on-one interviews sample indicated that "the society is anti-women empowerment and social equality". Eight of 12 (67%) of the participants said employment status contributes to their happiness. "They expressed that obtaining a tertiary education enhanced their everyday life from different perspectives". Thus, getting a higher degree gave women the opportunity to be engaged in the workforce, and this leads them to be financially independent, and that increases their confidence and well-being positively," the researcher said. All participants indicated that the households' roles in the Omani society are highly gendered in favor of men, according to the paper. All participants indicated that the roles of the household in Omani society are highly gender-based, according to the study. The new generation, new mindset, and young Omani ladies who are empowered by the state's laws are now conquering many male-dominated fields.

4 **Uncertainty Avoidance:** Uncertainty Avoidance states tolerance towards risk. Countries with low uncertainty avoidance have more tolerance of risk (e.g., Japan has low uncertainty avoidance). Uncertainty avoidance deals with a society's tolerance for uncertainty and ambiguity; it ultimately refers to "man's search for

Truth".

It indicates to what extent a culture programs its members to feel either uncomfortable or comfortable in unstructured situations. Unstructured situations are "novel, unknown, surprising, and different from the usual". Uncertainty avoiding cultures try to minimize the possibility of such situations by strict laws and rules, safety and security measures, and, on the philosophical and religious level, by a belief in absolute Truth – "there can only be one Truth and we have it". Uncertainty Avoidance is basically how cultures adapt to changes and cope with uncertainties or the unknown future and the level of how a culture feels threatened or is anxious about ambiguity. It is not risk avoidance but rather, how one deals with uncertainty.

Oman Perspective

Oman experiences a high score on Uncertainty Avoidance. People prefer to avoid uncertainty; they avoid taking risks. For all official work, forms are available, be it opening a bank account, getting a driver's license, payment of supplies – name anything. The country follows strict rules and regulations. Safety and security measures are very high. Roads are monitored with radar, and speeding limits are regulated. This sometimes brings in frustration among commuters as they have to travel long distances to either drop off or pick up their children or reach workplaces. Road rage is also observed. However, adaption to new technologies is far higher in comparison to other countries. E-governance is of high priority in Oman. Most of the work has now been converted to electronic media. Culturally, they are a fearless and brave, ocean-exploring tribe. Oman is known for its '*Dhow*' culture, but agriculture and fishing are still the traditional economic activities in Oman. The seafaring culture – traditionally followed – brings in collectivism and a transfer of knowledge from old to young. The *dhow*-building in Oman is one of the finest in the world. Omani sailors are known for their maritime expertise and survival in adverse conditions, but knowledge transfer is from generation to generation. Uncertainty, in general, is avoided.

Culturally-Oriented Unique Distress in Omani Society

Some of the unique stressors and strains in Oman's cultural setting and some reflections on related social, cultural, and anthropological-related issues are as follows.

1   **The avoidance of self-disclosure:** The traditional value system in Oman is that of collectivism and in the event of social impropriety, like corruption, stealing, dishonesty, failure (e.g., students caught cheating during exams, name-calling in public) an individual feels

"ashamed". They like to hide their identity. Females prefer to hide their faces and turn down requests to have their pictures clicked. This behavior indicates that they are very conscious and that their feelings are controlled by how others look at them – people's perception. Their image in society is very important.

2 **Wasta, magic, the evil eye, and *hasad*:** The Omani people still greatly believe in spirit, *jinn*, and that all ill-happenings are attributed to this belief, but much attribution of this distress on external forces depends upon the level of education. In the deep desert and isolated villages, such beliefs are very high, and mental distress is treated by the traditional healers rather than doctors. Distress is communicated in a psychosomatic manner rather than psychological ways (Al-Adawi et al., 2002). If a child is hyperactive, then the family discourages the child, attributing his/her behavior to the evil eye or *hasad*. Similarly, falling ill, failure in any kind of job, or even non-performance in schools is linked to the evil eye, which means somebody thinks negatively about the individual and thus this was the result. Distress in Oman is not perceived in psychiatric parlance but rather as intra-psychic conflict.

3 **Effort-reward imbalance:** Effort-reward imbalance is possible predisposing factors leading to distress in occupational settings. Many Omani feel that their efforts are not appropriately rewarded. There are mixed feelings in both workforces in the public and private sectors. On June 24, the Times News Service revealed that around 51.8% of Omanis who are working in the private sector get a monthly salary ranging from OMR325 ($845) to OMR500 ($1,300), whereas the median household income worldwide is $9,733 (as per the World population review) http://worldpopulationreview.com/countries/median-income-by-country/The National Center for Statistics and Information (NCSI) in Oman also revealed that 13,670 (5%) of the total number of workers earn salaries of more than OMR2,000. The NCSI reported that the unemployment rate for Omanis between the ages of 25 and 29 dropped to 13.6% over the last month, but the same is not applicable to the case of expatriate workers. There is no minimum wage limit for them. Thus, this acts as a stressor for many expatriate workers. A closed focus group discussion also revealed that Omanis working in both the public and private sectors were equally stressed. For the ones working in the public sector, the lack of appreciation for good work and the lack of growth opportunities were causes of stress; whereas, for the ones working in the private sector, the employee-boss relationships and organizational politics coupled with *wasta* (i.e. informal ways and means to turn things in one's favor) were the causes of concern and stress.

4 **The perceived threat of Omanization:** Over the years, the Omani

society has depended on public sector jobs. Private sector employment is still seen as only a second choice. While the Omanization policy of the country has led to an increased focus on creating employment in the private sector, the population perceives private sector employment as more stressful and with less attractive compensation and benefits packages (Al-Lamki, 2011).

5 **Difficult topography and scattered inhabitation:** Oman is sparsely populated with a population density of 39 people per square mile. Stretched over a landmass of 309,501 square kilometers and comprised of sparsely populated valleys, deserts, and mountains, the people have to either travel hundreds of kilometers to reach their workplaces or live away from their families. This is one of the reasons why Omanis feel stressed.

6 **Dependence on expatriates:** As brought out earlier, about half of the population in Oman is comprised of foreigners. The country depends very much on the foreign workforce not only to support the organized public and private sectors, but also to uphold disorganized domestic and small family business activities. The overdependence of the Omani population on foreign workers becomes a cause of stress especially when these workers have no legal work permits. According to a report published in Times Oman on April 16, 2019, about 750 expatriate workers were deported, and another 859 were arrested in violation of Omani labor law.

7 **Strict social order, limited socializing, and less recreation:** Omani society follows an adaptive but restricted social order. Men and women follow a strict dress code while out of their homes. Socializing is restricted especially for women. Entertainment facilities are limited and whatever is available is not equally available to men and women. The restricted lifestyle, though not forced, becomes the cause of stress, especially for women.

Conclusion

The study of literature and primary data analysis, along with the in-depth interviews, focus group studies and observations reveal the deeply embedded cultural behavior of the Omani population. The dominant behavior reveals that Oman does have many cultural-specific stressors, but they are successfully able to cope with stressors. The traditional society pattern is slowly changing and education is spreading its paws all over the country. The country is gradually adapting to modernization. The Islamic religious society is in its transition phase. Modern, as well as traditional patterns, are still prevailing, but some of the areas like mental health need to addressed seriously, and awareness in this area needs to be created. The detailed literature review also revealed that there is a dearth of systematic literature on occupational stress, job-related stress, and related fields. The major studies that have been conducted are also from the last five years – from 2015 to 2019 – and those too are concentrated in two major areas: medicine and education, while all of the other industries have been left out. This depicts a major gap in the literature, and future studies should focus on these areas. The Oman government and related research communities should address this area of research. There is a high impact of culture on the stress level of people in Oman, and further studies should address that Omanis and expatriates are two different groups. However, the overall stress level among people in Oman is relatively moderate, as also identified by some of the studies. At some level, ignorance is also bliss, but some of the unique stressors in Oman should be taken due care of, and proper education and training can play an important role in mitigating superstitions and beliefs.

References

AbuAlRub, R. F. (2004). Job stress, job performance, and social support among hospital nurses. *Journal of Nursing Scholarship*, 36, 73–78.

Abu-Hilal, M., Al-Bahrani, M., & Al-Zedjali, M. (2017). Can religiosity boost meaning in life and suppress stress for Muslim college students? *Mental Health, Religion & Culture*, 20(3), 203–216.

Al-Adawi, S., Dorvlo, A. S. S., Al-Ismaily, S. S., Al-Ghafry, D. A. , Al-Noobi, B. Z., Al-Salmi, A., Burke, D. T., Shah, M. K.Ghassany, H,, & Chand, S. P. (2002). Perception of and Attitude towards mental illness in Oman. *International Journal of Social Psychiatry*, 48(4), 305–317. https://doi.org/10.1177/002076402128.

Al-Alawi, M., Al-Sinawi, H., Al-Qubtan, A., Al-Lawati, J., Al-Habsi, A., Al-Shuraiqi, M., & Panchatcharam, S. M. (2019). Prevalence and determinants of burnout syndrome and depression among medical students at Sultan Qaboos University: A cross-sectional analytical study from Oman. *Archives of environmental & occupational health*, 74(3), 130–139.

Al Busaidy, N. S. M., & Borthwick, A. (2012). Occupational therapy in Oman: The impact of cultural dissonance. *Occupational Therapy International*, 19(3), 154–164.

Aldhafri, S. (2016). Predicting pre-school teachers' burnout levels through their efficacy beliefs in the Sultanate of Oman. *Journal of Arab Children*, 17, 66.

Al-Hashemi, T., Al-Huseini, S., Al-Alawi, M., Al-Balushi, N., Al-Senawi, H., Al-Balushi, M., & Al-Adawi, S. (2019). Burnout syndrome among primary care physicians in Oman. *Oman Medical Journal*, 34(3), 205.

Al-Lamki, S. (2011). Barriers to Omanization in the private sector: The perception of Omani graduates. *The International Journal of Human Resource Management*, 9(2), 377–400.

Al-Nabhani, A. M., Sinawi, H. A., & Toubi, A. S. A. (2016). Burnout, perceived stress and coping styles among nurses at a Tertiary Care Hospital in Muscat. *Arab Journal of Psychiatry*, 27(2), 117–126.

Al-Rubaee, F. R., & Al-Maniri, A. (2011). Work related injuries in an oil field in Oman. *Oman Medical Journal*, 26(5), 315.

Al-Sinawi, H., & Al-Adawi, S. (2006). Psychiatry in the Sultanate of Oman.

International psychiatry: Bulletin of the Board of International Affairs of the Royal College of Psychiatrists, 3(4), 14–16.

Arnetz, B. B. (2006). Stress in Health and Disease. In B. B. Arnetz & R. Ekman (Eds.), Stress—Why managers should care (pp. 92–121). Weinheim, Germany: Wiley-VCH Verlag GmbH & Co. KGaA.

Ashy, M. A. (1999). Health and illness from an Islamic perspective. Journal of Religion and Health, 38(3), 241-258.

Avey, J. B., Luthans, F., & Jensen, S. M. (2009). Psychological capital: A positive resource for combating employee stress and turnover. Human Resource Management, 48, 677–693.

Avey, J. B., Luthans, F., Smith, R. M., & Palmer, N. F. (2010). Impact of positive psychological capital on employee well-being over time. Journal of Occupational Health Psychology, 15(1), 17.

Bakker, A. B., & Demerouti, E. (2014). Job demands–resources theory. In C. L. Cooper (Ed.), Wellbeing: A complete reference guide, 1–28. doi: 10.1002/9781118539415.wbwell019.

Beehr, T. A., Bowling, N. A., & Bennett, M. M. (2010). Occupational stress and failures of social support: When helping hurts. Journal of Occupational Health Psychology, 15(1), 45.

Bemana, S., Moradi, H., Ghasemi, M., Taghavi, S. M., & Ghayoor, A. H. (2013). The relationship among job stress and job satisfaction in municipality personnel in Iran. World Applied Sciences Journal, 22(2), 233–238.

Byrne, U. (2005). Work-life balance: Why are we talking about it at all? Business Information Review, 22(1), 53–59.

Cohen, S., Kamarck, T., & Mermelstein, R. (1983). A global measure of perceived stress. Journal of Health and Social Behavior, 24(4), 385–396. https://doi.org/10.2307/2136404.

Cohen, S., & Williamson, G. (1988). Perceived Stress in a Probability Sample of the United States. In S. Spacapan & S. Oskamp (Eds.), The social psychology of health. Newbury Park (24, pp. 386–396), CA: Sage, 1988. A global measure of perceived stress. Journal of Health and Social Behavior.

Compas, B. E., Connor-Smith, J. K., Saltzman, H., Thomsen, A. H., & Wadsworth, M. E. (2001). Coping with stress during childhood and adolescence: Problems, progress, and potential in theory and research. Psychological Bulletin, 127(1), 87.

Conti, R., Angelis, J., Cooper, C., Faragher, B., & Gill, C. (2006). The effects of lean production on worker job stress. International Journal of Operations & Production Management, 26(9), 1013–1038.

Darr, W., & Johns, G. (2008). Work strain, health, and absenteeism: A meta-analysis. Journal of Occupational Health Psychology, 13, 293–318.

Dellve, L., Williamsson, A., Strömgren, M., Holden, R. J., & Eriksson, A. (2015). Lean implementation at different levels in Swedish hospitals: The importance for working conditions and stress. International Journal of Human Factors and Ergonomics, 3(3–4), 235–253.

Eliot, R. S. (1988). Stress and the heart. United States.

Elsheshtawy, E., Taha, H., Almazroui, S., Joshi, K., & Almazroui, A. (2018). Personality traits as predictors of stress and depression among medical students: A cross-sectional study. *Arab Journal of Psychiatry*, 123–130. https://doi.org/10.12816/0051277.

Emam, M., & Al-Lawati, S. (2014). Spiritual experiences, personal commitment: Relationship with work stress among support staff for children with disabilities in Oman. *Journal of Disability & Religion*, 18(4), 340–360.

Flanagan, N. A., & Flanagan, T. J. (2002). An analysis of the relationship between job satisfaction and job stress in correctional nurses. *Research in Nursing & Health*, 25, 282–294.

Grant, S., & Langan-Fox, J. (2006). Occupational stress, coping and strain: The combined/interactive effect of the Big Five traits. *Personality and Individual Differences*, 41(4), 719–732.

Hans, A., Mubeen, S. A., Mishra, N., & Al-Badi, A. H. H. (2015). A study on occupational stress and quality of work life (QWL) in private colleges of Oman (Muscat). *Global Business & Management Research*, 7(3), 55–68. Retrieved from. http://elib.unizwa.edu.om:2096/login.aspx?direct=true&db=bsu&AN=113006185&site=ehost-live.

Hernandez, L. M. & Blazer, D. G. (Eds). (2006). *Institute of medicine (US) committee on assessing interactions among social, behavioral, and genetic factors in health; genes, behavior, and the social environment: Moving beyond the nature/nurture debate*. Washington (DC): National Academies Press (US); 2006. 2, The Impact of Social and Cultural Environment on Health. Available from. https://www.ncbi.nlm.nih.gov/books/NBK19924/.

Hoboubi, N., Choobineh, A., Ghanavati, F. K., Keshavarzi, S., & Hosseini, A. A. (2017). The impact of job stress and job satisfaction on workforce productivity in an Iranian petrochemical industry. *Safety and Health at Work*, 8(1), 67–71.

Hodgins, M., MacCurtain, S., & Mannix-McNamara, P. (2014). Workplace bullying and incivility: A systematic review of interventions. *International Journal of Workplace Health Management*, 7(1), 54–72.

Hofstede, G. (2001). *Culture's consequences: Comparing values, behaviors, institutions, and organizations across nations*. 2nd ed., Thousand Oaks, London: Sage Publications.

Humphrey, J. H. (1992). *Stress among women in modern society*. Charles C Thomas Pub Limited.

Ilies, R., Dimotakis, N., & De Pater, I. E. (2010). Psychological and physiological reactions to high workloads: Implications for well-being. *Personnel Psychology*, 63(2), 407–436.

Jahan, F., Siddiqui, M. A., Mitwally, M., Zubidi, A., Jasim, N. S., Zubidi, A., & Jasim, H. S. (2016). Perception of stress, anxiety, depression and coping strategies among medical students at Oman medical college. *World Family Medicine Journal: Incorporating the Middle East Journal of Family Medicine*, 99(3719), 1–8.

Jamal, M. (1999). Job stress and employee well-being: A cross-cultural empirical study. *Stress Medicine*, 15(3), 153–158.

Johnson, S., Cooper, C., Cartwright, S., Donald, I., Taylor, P., & Millet, C. (2005). The experience of work-related stress across occupations. *Journal of Managerial Psychology*, 20(2), 178–187.

Khan, M. S. (1986). *Islamic medicine*, London: Routledge.

Kim, A., & Barak, M. E. M. (2015). The mediating roles of leader–member exchange and perceived organizational support in the role stress–turnover intention relationship among child welfare workers: A longitudinal analysis. *Children and Youth Services Review, 52*, 135–143.

Kumar, Suneel (2015). Influence of spirituality on burnout and job satisfaction: A study of academic professionals in Oman. *South Asian Journal of Management, 22*(3), 137–175. http://elib.unizwa.edu.com:2096/login.aspx?.

Lawati, M. H. A., Short, S. D., Abdulhadi, N. N., Panchatcharam, S. M., & Dennis, S. (2019). Assessment of patient safety culture in primary health care in Muscat, Oman: A questionnaire-based survey. *BMC Family Practice, 20*(1), 50.

Lazarus, R. S. (1993). Coping theory and research: Past, present, and future. *Psychosomatic Medicine, 55*, 234–247.

Lazarus, R. S., & Folkman, S. (1984). *Stress, appraisal, and coping*. New York: Springer.

Levi, L., & Lunde-Jensen, P. (1996). *A model for assessing the costs of stressors at national level: Socio-economic costs of work stress in two EU member states*. Office for Official Publications of the European Communities.

Liang, B., & Bogat, G. A. (1994). Culture, control, and coping: New perspectives on social support. *American Journal of Community Psychology, 22*, 123–147.

Markus, H. R., & Kitayama, S. (1991). Culture and the self: Implications for cognition, emotion, and motivation. *Psychological Review, 98*, 224–253.

McEwen, B. S., & Mendelson, S. (1993). Effects of stress on the neurochemistry and morphology of the brain: Counterregulation versus damage. In Goldberger, L. & Breznitz, S. (Eds.), *Handbook of stress: Theoretical and clinical aspects*, pp. 101-126, Free Press.

McVicar, A. (2003). Workplace stress in nursing: A literature review. *Journal of Advanced Nursing, 44*(6), 633–642.

Milstein, G., Hybels, C. F., & Proeschold-Bell, R. J. (2019). A prospective study of clergy spiritual well-being, depressive symptoms, and occupational distress. *Psychology of Religion and Spirituality. Advance Online Publication.* https://doi.org/10.1037/rel0000252.

Mineka, S., & Kelly, K. A. (1989). The Relationship Between Anxiety, Lack of Control and Loss of Control. In Steptoe, A. & Appels, A.(Eds.), *Stress, personal control and health*, pp. 163–191, John Wiley & Sons.

Mohammadi, R. (2011). Occupational stress and organizational performance, Case study: Iran. *Procedia-Social and Behavioral Sciences, 30*, 390–394.

Ongori, H., & Agolla, J. E. (2008). Occupational stress in organizations and its effects on organizational performance. *Journal of Management Research, 8*(3), 123–135.

Perrewe, P. L., & Ganster, D. C. (1989). The impact of job demands and behavioral control on experienced job stress. *Journal of Organizational Behavior, 10*(3), 213–229.

Rajamohan, S., Porock, D., & Chang, Y. P. (2019). Understanding the relationship between staff and job satisfaction, stress, turnover, and staff outcomes in the person-centered care nursing home arena. *Journal of Nursing Scholarship, 51*(5), 560–568.

Rajasekar, James, & Renand, Franck (2013). Culture shock in a global world: Factors affecting culture shock experienced by expatriates in Oman and Omani expatriates abroad. *International Journal of Business and Management*, 8(13). Doi:10.5539/ijbm.v8n13p144.

Rao, J., & Chandraiah, K. (2012). Occupational stress, mental health and coping among informational technology professionals. *Indian Journal of Occupational & Environmental Medicine*, 16(1), 22–26.

Richardson, K. M., & Rothstein, H. R. (2008). Effects of occupational stress management intervention programs: A meta-analysis. *Journal of Occupational Health Psychology*, 13, 69–93.

Roger, D., & Najarian, B. (1998). The relationship between emotional rumination and cortisol secretion under stress. *Personality and Individual Differences*, 24(4), 531–538.

Selye, H. (1976). Stress Without Distress. In Serban, G. (Eds.), *Psychopathology of Human Adaptation*, Springer: Boston, MA. https://doi.org/10.1007/978-1-4684-2238-2_9.

Sinha, B. K., Willson, L. R., & Watson, D. C. (2000). Stress and coping among students in India and Canada. *Canadian Journal of Behavioural Science*, 32, 218–225.

Skinner, E. A., Edge, K., Altman, J., & Sherwood, H. (2003). Searching for the structure of coping: A review and critique of category systems for classifying ways of coping. *Psychological Bulletin*, 129, 216–269.

Skinner, J. E. (1985). *Psychosocial stress and sudden cardiac death: Brain mechanisms. In Stress and heart disease*. Boston, MA: Springer.

Staufenbiel, T., & König, C. J. (2010). A model for the effects of job insecurity on performance, turnover intention, and absenteeism. *Journal of Occupational and Organizational Psychology*, 83(1), 101–117.

Steinberg, A., & Ritzmann, R. F. (1990). A living systems approach to understanding the concept of stress. *Behavioral Science*, 35(2), 138–146.

Triandis, H. C. (1995). *Individualism and collectivism*. SF: Westview Press.

Tummers, L. & Rocco, P. (2014). *Policy implementation under stress: How the Affordable Care Act's frontline workers cope with the challenges of public service delivery*. APSA 2014 Annual Meeting Paper. Available at SSRN: https://ssrn.com/abstract=2452320.

Van der Colff, J. J., & Rothmann, S. (2009). Occupational stress, sense of coherence, coping, burnout and work engagement of registered nurses in South Africa. *SA Journal of Industrial Psychology*, 35(1), 1–10.

Vickers, M. H. (2006). Towards employee wellness: Rethinking bullying paradoxes and masks. *Employee Responsibilities and Rights Journal*, 18(4), 267–281.

Wang, Q. (2001). "Did you have fun?" American and Chinese mother-child conversations about shared emotional experiences. *Cognitive Development*, 16, 693–715.

Y Magazine #510. (March 8, 2018). by SABCO Press, Published on Mar. 7, 2018, Issuuissuu.com › ytabloid › docs › y_issue_510_web.

11 Occupational Stress, Health, and Well-Being Research in Portugal
A Qualitative Systematic Literature Review

Maria José Chambel, Vânia Sofia Carvalho, and Mariana Neto

Introduction

It is long-standing knowledge that a professional activity and the characteristics and conditions of the context in which it is developed influence the health and well-being of workers. In fact, it was during the nineteenth century, after the Industrial Revolution, that various aspects of the work context were seen to potentially influence the physical and mental health of workers. The dehumanization experienced in the factories during this period was not only the object of debate for sociologists and political scientists, but also for several literary writers (Chambel, 2016). However, over recent years, we have witnessed profound changes in the world of labor and enterprises which have brought consequences for the health and well-being of workers. New forms of work organization, increased pressure on professionals to work longer hours, uncertainties regarding employment security, and restructuring threats are some of the reasons that contribute not only to the persistence of the more traditional risks, but also to the emergence of new risks (Neto & André, 2016). European surveys on work conditions have referred to this adverse effect of work on the health and well-being of workers. The 2014 report indicated that over 25% of participants referred to stress as the cause of loss of well-being (Eurofound & EU-OSHA, 2014). By the same token, the 2018 report stated that 25% of participants had claimed to experience stress in the workplace during most of or throughout their working schedule, regarding this situation as having a negative impact on their health (Eurofound & EU-OSHA, 2018). In the specific case of Portugal, in the second Survey of Enterprises on New and Emerging Risks – Psychosocial Risks, it was discovered to be the country where respondents manifested most concern with stress (70% of surveyed establishments). However, no systematic review has been conducted on occupational stress, health, and well-being in Portuguese professionals. Integration of the research on this topic will contribute to further data-based knowledge and will facilitate future research by shedding light upon current gaps in the literature.

Methodology

To provide an indication of the potential size and nature of the available literature examining the occupational stress, health, and well-being of Portuguese workers, a qualitative systematic review was conducted (Paré, Trudel, Jaana, & Kitsiou, 2015). We followed the recommendations of Daudt Van Mossel, and Scott (2013) and the Preferred Reporting Items for Systematic Reviews and Meta-Analyses (PRISMA; Moher, Liberati, Tetzlaff, & Altman, 2009). The first step of the systematic review consisted of using three databases, namely ISI Web of Science, PubMed, and Scopus. Titles and abstracts were identified using three search terms. The first used the combination ["occupational stress" AND "Portugal"]. The second used the combination ["occupational health" AND "Portugal"]. Lastly, the third search term used the combination ["occupational well-being" AND "Portugal"]. A total of 401 papers were found. An initial screening was then conducted in order to remove duplicates and non-English language papers, and a total of 91 papers remained for the next step of the systematic review.

In order to eliminate papers that did not address the scope of the present review, inclusion and exclusion criteria were established (Daudt et al., 2013). The inclusion criteria were the following: (1) studies conducted with Portuguese workers, (2) studies that are empirical qualitative and quantitative, (3) studies evaluating occupational stress, health, and/or well-being, and (4) studies published in a scientific journal. As exclusion criteria, the following were not included: (1) literature reviews and meta-analyses including an indirect analysis of occupational stress, health, and/or well-being, (2) studies with a mixed sample composed not only of Portuguese workers, but also workers from other countries, and (3) studies published in congress proceedings.

Based on the inclusion and exclusion criteria, two reviewers critically and independently appraised the quality of 91 papers by assessing each paper's title and corresponding abstract. As a result of the titles and abstracts' appraisal, a total of 82 papers were considered to meet the inclusion criteria. A third reviewer then checked the remaining papers and analyzed all the 82 full-text articles. Following the full-text articles' analysis, five papers were excluded due to the fact that they did not evaluate occupational stress, health, and/or well-being, and two papers had been published in congress proceedings. Hence, 75 papers met the inclusion criteria and were used to perform the qualitative systematic review and two-step cluster analysis. In Figure 11.1, it is possible to observe the flow diagram of the systematic selection of studies undertaken in the present study.

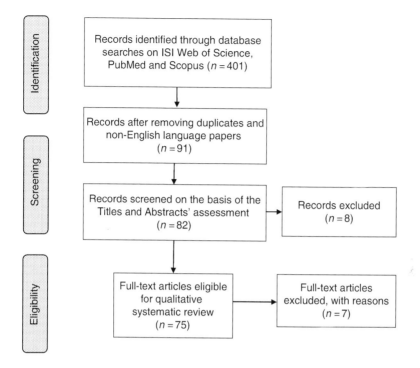

Figure 11.1 Flow Diagram of the Systematic Selection of Studies.
Adapted from: Moher, D., Liberati, A., Tetzlaff, J., Altman, D. G., The PRISMA Group (2009). Preferred Reporting Items for Systematic Reviews and Meta-Analyses: The PRISMA Statement. *PLoS Med*, 6(7): e1000097. https://doi.org/10.1371/journal.pmed1000097

Analysis

Table 11.1 summarizes the reviewed studies, providing information on: (a) authors and data, (b) periodical and area of publication (i.e., Psychology/ Social Sciences, Medicine/Health/ Mental Health, Nursing and/or other), (c) study design and data analysis (i.e., quantitative or qualitative, cross-sectional, longitudinal or intervention, descriptive, regression, structural equation model or latent profile analysis), (d) participants (i.e., sample size and occupation), (e) indicator studied and measure used (i.e., stress, health, and/or well-being), and (f) aim of the study.

In order to find similar groups of studies, a two-step cluster analysis (TSC) using a log-likelihood distance measure was performed, using SPSS Version 25 (IBM, Armonk, NY, USA). The two-step cluster analysis was used to classify groups of studies that were similar to one another in terms of sample size, work population, qualitative/quantitative

224 *Maria José Chambel et al.*

Table 11.1 Summary of Reviewed Studies

Authors (Year of Publication)	Journal (Area)	Study Design	Participants	Well-being indicator and measure used	Aim of the Study
Afonso, Fonseca, and Pires (2017)	Occupational Medicine (Medicine)	Quantitative, Cross-sectional, Descriptive	429 higher students	Anxiety and Depression – Hospital Anxiety and Depression Scale (HADS); Sleep – Pittsburgh Sleep Quality Index	To evaluate differences in sleep quality and anxiety and depression symptoms between the longer working hours group (LWHG) and regular working hours group (RWHG) and to examine factors influencing weekly working hours, sleep quality, and anxiety and depressive symptoms.
Ângelo and Chambel (2014)	European Journal of Work and Organizational Psychology (Psychology)	Quantitative, Cross-sectional, Structural Equation Model	1,487 rescue mission firefighters	Burnout- Maslach Burnout Inventory-General Version; Engagement – Utrecht Work Engagement Scale–General Version	To encourage the expansion of the Job Demands–Resources (JD-R) model with the introduction of proactive coping, in both health impairment and motivational processes.
Ângelo and Chambel (2015)	Stress & Health (Psychology, Medicine)	Quantitative, Longitudinal (two waves), Structural Equation Model	651 firefighters	Burnout – Maslach Burnout Inventory-General Version; Engagement – Utrecht Work Engagement Scale – General Version	To analyze the dynamic nature with normal and reversed causation effects between work characteristics and psychological well-being.

(*Continued*)

Table 11.1 (Continued)

Authors (Year of Publication)	Journal (Area)	Study Design	Participants	Well-being indicator and measure used	Aim of the Study
Barbosa, Nolan, Sousa, Marques, and Figueiredo, (2016)	American Journal of Alzheimer's Disease & Other Dementias (Medicine, Psychology)	Quantitative, Intervention (pretest-posttest control group design)	53 care workers	Stress – Perceived Stress Scale (PSS); Burnout – Maslach Burnout Inventory – Human Services Survey	To assess the effects of a psychoeducational intervention, designed to improve direct care workers' stress, burnout and job satisfaction, and person-centered communicative behavior in people with dementia.
Barbosa, Silva, Ferreira, and Severo. (2016)	Ata Médica Portuguesa (Medicine)	Quantitative, Longitudinal, (two waves), Regression	102 medical students	Burnout – Maslach Burnout Inventory – Student Version	To measure self-regulated learning skills and self-study across secondary-higher education transition and to explore its effect on academic burnout in the first year of medical school.
Barbosa Nolan Sousa, and Figueiredo (2014)	American Journal of Alzheimer's Disease & Other Dementias (Medicine, Psychology)	Quantitative, Intervention (pretest-posttest control group design)	56 direct care workers	Stress – Perceived Stress Scale (PSS); Burnout – Maslach Burnout Inventory – Human Services Survey	To assess the effects of a person-centered care-based psychoeducational intervention on direct care workers' stress, burnout, and job satisfaction.

(Continued)

Table 11.1 (Continued)

Authors (Year of Publication)	Journal (Area)	Study Design	Participants	Well-being indicator and measure used	Aim of the Study
Baylina, Barros, Fonte, Alves, and Rocha, (2018)	Journal of Medical Systems (Medicine)	Quantitative, Cross-sectional, Regression	361 healthcare workers	Emotional, social, psychological well-being – Mental Health Continuum- Short Form (MHC-SF)	Explore the relation of work-related risk factors and well-being among healthcare workers.
Cabeças and Mota (2014)	Advances in Intelligence Systems and Computing	Quantitative, Cross-sectional, Descriptive	906 financial services employes	Well-being- Negative Well-Being Matrix	To identify relevant occupational hazards in the financial sector workplace level and negative mental or physical well-being complaints.
Carvalho and Chambel (2014)	Social Indicators Research (Psychology)	Quantitative, Cross-sectional, Structural Equation Model	1,390 bank employees	Health – Health Perceptions; Satisfaction with Life	To examine the relationship between job demands, control and support, and work-family enrichment and, more interestingly, the work-family enrichment as a mechanism for explaining the relationship between job characteristics and employees' well-being and to, furthermore, analyze the relationship

(Continued)

Occupational Stress, Health 227

Table 11.1 (Continued)

Authors (Year of Publication)	Journal (Area)	Study Design	Participants	Well-being indicator and measure used	Aim of the Study
					of employees' perceptions of High-Performance Work System (HPWS) with job characteristics.
Carvalho and Chambel (2016a)	Journal of Career Development (Psychology)	Quantitative, Cross-sectional, Structural Equation Model	218 city council employees	Burnout – Maslach Burnout Inventory -General Version; Engagement – Utrecht Work Engagement Scale; Health Perceptions; Satisfaction with Life	To test the relationship between High-Performance Work System and workers' general well-being – tested the mediation by job characteristics and workplace well-being.
Carvalho, & Chambel (2016b)	Spanish Journal of Psychology (Psychology)	Quantitative, Cross-sectional, Latent Profile Analysis	1,885 bank employees	Burnout – Maslach Burnout Inventory -General Version; Engagement – Utrecht Work Engagement Scale; Health Perceptions; Satisfaction with Life	To analyze work-to-family conflict (WFC) and enrichment (WFE) profiles related to job characteristics and well-being at work and general well-being.
Carvalho and Chambel (2017)	Armed Forces and Society (Social Sciences)	Quantitative, Cross-sectional, Structural Equation Model	175 marine military workers	Burnout – Maslach Burnout Inventory -General Version; Engagement – Utrecht Work Engagement	To test the mediated effect of work-family conflict and the enrichment on the relationship between job characteristics and

(Continued)

Table 11.1 (Continued)

Authors (Year of Publication)	Journal (Area)	Study Design	Participants	Well-being indicator and measure used	Aim of the Study
Carvalho, Chambel, Neto, and Lopes 2018	Frontiers in Psychology (Psychology)	Quantitative, Cross-sectional, Structural Equation Model	254 services company workers	Mental health – GHQ 28 Scale; Health Perception	To examine the role of WFC as a mechanism that explains the relationship between job characteristics (i.e., those established by the Job Demands-Control-Support Model) and workers' mental health and, moreover, based on gender inequalities in work and non-work roles, to analyze gender as a moderator of this mediation.
Chambel, Carvalho, Cesário, and Lopes (2017)	Career Development International (Psychology)	Quantitative, Cross-sectional, Structural Equation Model	736 contact center workers	Burnout – Maslach Burnout Inventory -General Version; Engagement – Utrecht Work Engagement Scale; Health Perception	To compare part-time and full-time employees by analyzing the relationship between job characteristics and workplace well-being (i.e., burnout and engagement) and by the

(Continued)

Table 11.1 (Continued)

Authors (Year of Publication)	Journal (Area)	Study Design	Participants	Well-being indicator and measure used	Aim of the Study
Chambel, Lorente, Carvalho, and Martinez (2016)	Journal of Managerial Psychology (Psychology)	Quantitative, Cross-sectional, Latent Profile Analysis	2,867 workers	Engagement – Utrecht Work Engagement Scale	mediating role of the work-to-life conflict. To identify Psychological Contract profiles, differentiating between permanent and temporary agency workers (TAW), and, moreover, to analyze whether different profiles presented different levels of work engagement.
Coelho Tavares Lima, and Lourenco (2018)	International Journal of Occupational Safety and Ergonomics (Medicine; Social Sciences)	Quantitative, Longitudinal (two waves), Regression	32 field workers	Psychosocial Risks- The Copenhagen Psychosocial Questionnaire- CoPsoQ (short version)	To investigate the effect of different kinds of work on the psychosocial assessment of workers under the same management and organizational environment.
Coelho Tavares Lourenco, and Lima (2015)	Work (Medicine)	Quantitative, Cross-sectional, Descriptive	32 private administrative workers	Psychosocial Risks- The Copenhagen Psychosocial Questionnaire- CoPsoQ (short version)	To assess the association between environmental, physical, and organizational working conditions and the physical and psychosocial

(Continued)

Table 11.1 (Continued)

Authors (Year of Publication)	Journal (Area)	Study Design	Participants	Well-being indicator and measure used	Aim of the Study
					well-being of a sample of private-sector office workers.
Correia de Sousa and van Dierendonck (2014)	Journal of Organizational Change Management (Management)	Quantitative, Cross-sectional, Structural Equation Model	1,107 employees	Engagement – Utrecht Work Engagement Scale	To aim mainly at further understanding how servant leadership can affect engagement during a merger with high levels of uncertainty through the mediating role of organizational identification and psychological empowerment.
Coutinho Queirós Henriques Norton, and Alves (2019)	Work (Medicine)	Quantitative, Cross-sectional, Regression	399 employees in a public hospital	Psychosocial Risks – The Copenhagen Psychosocial Questionnaire – CoPsoQ (medium version)	To assess the main work-related determinants of high exposure to psychosocial risk factors among workers in the hospital setting.
Cruz-Mendes, Claro, & Cruz-Robazzi (2014)	La Medicina del Lavoro (Medicine)	Quantitative, Cross-sectional, Descriptive	95 nurses working in central prisons	Burnout – Maslach Burnout Inventory – General Survey	To measure the levels of burnout among nurses working in prisons and their relationship to the socio-demographic

(Continued)

Table 11.1 (Continued)

Authors (Year of Publication)	Journal (Area)	Study Design	Participants	Well-being indicator and measure used	Aim of the Study
Cumbe et al. (2017)	Revista de Psiquiatria Clínica (Medicine)	Quantitative, Cross-sectional, Regression	46 health care professional – oncology service	Burnout – Maslach Burnout Inventory – Human Services Survey	variables and type of employment contract. To assess the association between burnout, functional coping strategies, and occupational factors in a sample of oncology providers – mostly nurses.
David and Quintão (2012)	Acta Médica Portuguesa (Medicine)	Quantitative, Cross-sectional, Regression	404 teachers	Positive and Negative Affective Schedule (PANAS); Bunout – Maslach Burnout Inventory; Satisfaction with Life Scale (SWLS)	To relate burnout, personality, affectivity, coping strategies, and life satisfaction.
Duarte, and Pinto-Gouveia (2016)	International Journal of Nursing Studies (Nursing)	Quantitative, Intervention (nonrandomized, wait-list comparison design)	94 oncology nurses	Quality of Life – The professional quality of life scale, version 5 (ProQOL-5); Depression, Anxiety, Stress Scale (DASS-21); Satisfaction with Life Scale (SWLS)	To explore the effectiveness of an on-site, abbreviated, and mindfulness-based intervention for nurses.
Duarte and Pinto-Gouveia (2017)	European Journal of Oncology			Quality of Life – The Professional Quality	To clarify the relationships between several

(Continued)

Table 11.1 (Continued)

Authors (Year of Publication)	Journal (Area)	Study Design	Participants	Well-being indicator and measure used	Aim of the Study
	Nursing (Nursing)	Quantitative, Cross-sectional, Regression	221 hospital oncology nurses	of Life Scale, Version 5 (ProQOL-5)	dimensions of empathy, self-compassion, and psychological inflexibility, and positive (compassion satisfaction), and the professional quality of life.
Duarte and Pinto-Gouveia (2017)	Applied Nursing Research (Nursing)	Quantitative, Cross-sectional, Regression	298 hospital nurses	Quality of Life – The Professional Quality of Life Scale, Version 5 (ProQOL-5)	To explore the relationships between empathy, empathy-based pathogenic guilt, and professional quality of life.
Gama, Barbosa, and Vieira (2014)	European Journal of Oncology Nursing (Nursing)	Quantitative, Cross-sectional, Regression	360 nurses	Burnout – Maslach Burnout Inventory	To identify socio-demographic, professional, proximity to death, training and educational, and personal factors relevant to burnout dimensions in nurses coping with death issues.
Garrosa Rainho Moreno-Jiménez, and Monteiro (2010)	International Journal of Nursing Studies (Nursing)	Quantitative, Longitudinal (two waves), Regression	98 nurses	Burnout – Maslach Burnout Inventory; – Human Services Survey	To assess temporal and cross-sectional relationships between job stressors, hardy personalities, and coping

(Continued)

Table 11.1 (Continued)

Authors (Year of Publication)	Journal (Area)	Study Design	Participants	Well-being indicator and measure used	Aim of the Study
					resources on burnout dimensions among nurses.
Geraldes Madeira Carvalho, and Chambel (2019)	Personnel Review (Psychology)	Quantitative, Cross-sectional, Regression	2,055 contact center workers	Burnout – Maslach Burnout Inventory-General Version;	To analyze the moderating role of affective commitment in the relationship between work-personal life conflict (WPLC) and burnout.
Gomes (2014)	Interamerican Journal of Psychology (Psychology)	Quantitative, Cross-sectional, Descriptive	318 health professionals (physicians and nurses)	Stress – Stress Questionnaire for Health Professionals (SQHP); Burnout – Maslach Burnout Inventory– Human Services Survey	To analyze stress of nurses and physicians.
Gomes and Teixeira, (2016)	Stress & Health (Psychology, Medicine)	Quantitative, Cross-sectional, Confirmatory Factor Analysis	2,310 nurses	Stress -Stress Questionnaire for Health Professionals (SQHP); Psychological Well-being – GHQ 12	To analyze the psychometric properties of three instruments that focus on the professional experiences of nurses in aspects related to occupational stress,

(Continued)

Table 11.1 (Continued)

Authors (Year of Publication)	Journal (Area)	Study Design	Participants	Well-being indicator and measure used	Aim of the Study
Gomes, Cruz, and Cabanelas (2009)	Psicologia:Teoria e Pesquisa (Psychology)	Quantitative, Cross-sectional, Regression	286 nurses from hospitals and healthcare centers	Stress – Stress Questionnaire for Health Professionals (SQHP); Burnout – Maslach Burnout Inventory – Human Services Survey; Health -Physical Health Scale	To analyze occupational stress in nurses from hospitals and healthcare centers. cognitive appraisal, and mental health issues.
Gomes, Faria, and Gonçalves (2013)	Work and Stress (Psychology)	Quantitative, Cross-sectional, Structural Equation Model	333 academic teaching staff	Burnout – Maslach Burnout inventory –Educators survey	To analyze the mediating role of the cognitive appraisal on the relationship between occupational stress and burnout.
Gomes, Faria, and Lopes (2016)	Western Journal of Nursing Research (Nursing)	Quantitative, Cross-sectional, Structural Equation Model	2,302 nurses	Psychological Well-Being- GHQ 12	To test the mediating role of primary (e.g., threat and challenge perceptions) and secondary (e.g., coping potential and control perception) cognitive appraisal in the relationship between

(Continued)

Table 11.1 (Continued)

Authors (Year of Publication)	Journal (Area)	Study Design	Participants	Well-being indicator and measure used	Aim of the Study
Hernández-Marrero Pereira, and Carvalho (2016)	American Journal of Hospice and Palliative Medicine (Medicine)	Mix, Cross-sectional, Descriptive	9 palliative care teams	Burnout – Maslach Burnout Inventory – Human Services Survey; Interviews	occupational stress and psychological health. To identify the most common ethical decisions made by Portuguese palliative care teams and understand how the making of such decisions relates to burnout.
da Silva João and Saldanha Portelada (2016)	Journal of Interpersonal Violence (Psychology)	Quantitative, Cross-sectional, Descriptive	3,227 nurses	Well-being – Interpersonal Relations at Work Scale (IRWS).	To assess the existence, frequency, and intensity of mobbing within the Portuguese nurse population, as well as its impact on their well-being and interpersonal relationships
Joaquim et al. (2017)	Psychology, Health & Medicine (Psychology, Medicine)	Quantitative, Cross-sectional, Regression	118 medical residents of Oncology, Hematology, and Radiotherapy	Stress Questionnaire for Health Professionals (SQHP); Maslach's Burnout Inventory – Human Services Survey	To calculate the prevalence of burnout and stress on medical residents of Oncology, Haematology, and Radiotherapy in Portugal, as well as to determine predictors of burnout and stress.

(Continued)

Table 11.1 (Continued)

Authors (Year of Publication)	Journal (Area)	Study Design	Participants	Well-being indicator and measure used	Aim of the Study
Lapa, Carvalho, Viana, Ferreira, and Pinto-Gouveia (2016)	European Journal of Anaesthesiology (Medicine)	Quantitative, Cross-sectional, Exploratory and Confirmatory Factor Analyses	710 anesthesia specialists	Stress Questionnaire in Anaesthesiologists (SQA)	To study the validation of the Stress Questionnaire in Anaesthesiologists (SQA).
Laranjeira (2012a)	Applied Nursing Research (Nursing)	Quantitative, Cross-sectional, Descriptive and Exploratory Factorial Analysis	424 nurses	Fatigue Severity Scale (FSS)	To translate and test the reliability and validity of the Portuguese version of the FSS.
Laranjeira (2012b)	Journal of Clinical Nursing (Nursing)	Quantitative, Cross-sectional, Descriptive.	102 nurses	Stress-Perceived Stress Scale	To clarify the association between perceived stress in work and the types of coping strategies used by Portuguese nurses.
Lourenço Carnide Benavides, and Lucas (2015),	Plos One (Medicine)	Quantitative, Cross-sectional, Regression	1,761 young adults	Widespread Pain Syndrome (Fibromyalgia Survey Questionnaire); Musculoskeletal pain (Nordic Musculoskeletal Questionnaire)	To estimate the associations between psychosocial work environment and musculoskeletal outcomes (widespread pain syndrome features and regional pain) in a population-based sample of young workers.

(Continued)

Table 11.1 (Continued)

Authors (Year of Publication)	Journal (Area)	Study Design	Participants	Well-being indicator and measure used	Aim of the Study
Maia and Ribeiro (2010)	European Journal of Emergency Medicine (Medicine)	Quantitative, Cross-sectional, Regression	59 nurses and medical doctors of the National Institute of Medical Emergency	Posttraumatic Stress Disorder Scale (PTSD); Psychological Well-Being – GHQ 12	To determine the psychological impact of exposure to current death and physical injury events in the context of motor vehicle accidents among emergency personnel and to identify which variables better predict posttraumatic stress disorder.
Maroco, Maroco, Sacadura-Leite, Bastos, Vazão, & Campos (2016)	Ata Médica Portuguesa (Medicine)	Quantitative, Cross-sectional, Descriptive	1,262 nurses and 466 physicians	Burnout – Maslach Burnout Inventory – Human Services Survey	To report the incidence of burnout in healthcare professionals.
Marques-Pinto, Jesus, Mendes, Fronteira, and Roberto (2018)	Spanish Journal of Psychology (Psychology)	Quantitative, Cross-sectional, Structural Equation Model	2,235 hospital nurses	Burnout – Maslach Burnout Inventory – Human Services Survey); Engagement – The Utrecht Work Engagement Scale	To examine the predictive value of job demands and resources in the explanations of nurses' intention to leave the organization, and to test the mediating roles of professional burnout and engagement in these relationships.

(Continued)

Table 11.1 (Continued)

Authors (Year of Publication)	Journal (Area)	Study Design	Participants	Well-being indicator and measure used	Aim of the Study
Marques Alves Queiros Norton, and Henriques (2018)	Occupational Medicine (Medicine)	Quantitative, Cross-sectional, Regression	368 hospital workers	Burnout – Maslach Burnout Inventory—Human Services Survey.	To assess the prevalence of burnout in different professional groups of hospital staff, and to examine how the professional category is associated with levels of burnout.
Martinez and Ferreira (2012)	Stress and Health (Psychology, Medicine)	Quantitative, Cross-sectional, Descriptive	296 nurses at public hospitals	Presenteeism Scale (SPS-6) Health Condition Index	To analyze the predictors of presenteeism.
Martins-Pereira Teixeira Carvalho, and Hernández-Marrero (2016)	PLoS One (Medicine)	Quantitative, Cross-sectional, Regression	355 professionals from 10 intensive care units and 9 palliative care units	Maslach Burnout Inventory – Human Services Survey	To identify and compare burnout levels between professionals working in intensive care and palliative care units, and to assess which workplace experiences are associated with burnout.
Martins, Sales-Oliveira, Loureiro (2016)	International Journal of Working Conditions (Social Science)	Quantitative, Cross-sectional, Descriptive	62 university workers	Ability to Work – WorkAbility Index	To identify psychosocial indicators within the organizational context and to analyze mobbing and capacity to work in a sample of administrative

(Continued)

Table 11.1 (Continued)

Authors (Year of Publication)	Journal (Area)	Study Design	Participants	Well-being indicator and measure used	Aim of the Study
					employees of a Portuguese public university.
Martins, Andrade, Albuquerque, & Cunha. (2015)	Turkish Online Journal of Educational Technology (Education)	Quantitative, Cross-sectional, Descriptive	90 special education teachers	Burnout – Stress and Burnout Scale (CPB-R)	To assess stress and burnout in special education teachers and find out to what extent sociodemographic and psychosocial variables have a significant effect on those levels.
Mesquita, Ribeiro, and Moreira (2011)	Applied Research Quality Life (Social Science)	Quantitative, Intervention	229 male warehouse workers from a food distribution company	Health – Short Form Health Survey – SF-36	To evaluate the effect of following a 21-month exercise program on the quality of life of warehouse workers.
Monteiro and Marques-Pinto (2017)	Spanish Journal of Psychology (Psychology)	Qualitative, Content Analysis	25 journalists	Distress and Eustress Emotional Reactions – Interviews	To characterize and compare occupational stress variables perceived by journalists in their daily work and in critical scenarios.
	European Journal of			Burnout – Maslach Burnout Inventory;	

(Continued)

Table 11.1 (Continued)

Authors (Year of Publication)	Journal (Area)	Study Design	Participants	Well-being indicator and measure used	Aim of the Study
Morais Maia Azevedo Amaral, and Tavares (2006)	Anaesthesiology (Medicine)	Quantitative, Cross-sectional, Regression	263 anesthesiologists	Human Services Survey	To assess stress and burnout among Portuguese anaesthesiologists.
Alves de Moura Serranheira, and Sacadura-Leite (2016)	La Medicina del Lavoro (Medicine)	Quantitative, Cross-sectional, Regression	19 psychiatry and 20 anaesthesiology medical doctors	Psychosocial Risks – The Copenhagen Psychosocial Questionnaire – Medium Version (CoPsoQ)	To assess psychiatry and anesthesiology residents in a central and university hospital for the presence of psychosocial risks at work.
Neto, Chambel, and Carvalho, (2018)	Occupational Medicine (Medicine)	Quantitative, Cross-sectional, Regression	819 sales workers and 1,016 contact center workers	Psychological health – GHQ 12	To determine the effects of work-family life conflict on employee well-being, after controlling the effect of job demands, control, and support.
Neto, Ferreira, Martinez, and Ferreira. (2017)	Annals of Work Exposures and Health (Medicine)	Quantitative, Cross-sectional, Structural Equation Model	353 workers from a service company	Burnout – Maslach Burnout Inventory; Psychological Well-Being- GHQ 28	To examine the intervening variables of emotional exhaustion and psychological well-being in the direct and indirect relationships between workplace bullying and indicators of productivity loss due to presenteeism.

(*Continued*)

Table 11.1 (Continued)

Authors (Year of Publication)	Journal (Area)	Study Design	Participants	Well-being indicator and measure used	Aim of the Study
Neto Carvalho Chambel Manuel Pereira Miguel, and Reis (2016)	Journal of Occupational and Environmental Medicine (Medicine)	Quantitative, Longitudinal, (three waves), Structural Equation Model	713 workers of a service company	Mental health – GHQ 28	To test the reciprocal effect between work-family conflict and employee well-being using cross-lagged analyses on the basis of three waves.
Orgambídez-Ramos, Borrego-Alés & Ruiz-Frutos (2018)	Ciência & Saúde Coletiva (Medicine)	Quantitative, Cross-sectional, Regression	297 hospital nurses	Burnout – Maslach Burnout Inventory	To examine to what extent structural empowerment and vulnerability to stress can play a predictive role in the burnout.
Rodrigues, & Ferreira (2011)	Revista Latino Americana de Enfermagem (Nursing)	Quantitative, Cross-sectional, Descriptive	235 nurses	Well-being – Interpersonal Relations at Work Scale (IRWS)	To identify stressors for nurses working in intensive care units.
Pereira, Fonseca & Carvalho (2012)	International Journal of Palliative Nursing (Nursing)	Mixed, Cross-sectional, Regression	73 (quantitive) 11 (qualitative) nurses from palliative teams	Burnout – Maslach Burnout Inventory – Human Services Survey	To identify burnout levels, risk and protective factors, prevention strategies, and the emotional impact of working in palliative care among nurses in Portugal.
Pocinho and Capelo. (2009)	Educação e Pesquisa (Social Sciences)	Quantitative, Cross-sectional, Descriptive	54 teachers	Stress – Teacher Stress Questionnaire QSP	To determine teachers' vulnerability to stress, to identify the main sources of stress, to recognize

(*Continued*)

Table 11.1 (Continued)

Authors (Year of Publication)	Journal (Area)	Study Design	Participants	Well-being indicator and measure used	Aim of the Study
					teachers' main coping strategies, to analyze whether such strategies condition the presence of stress at work, and to establish whether the self-efficiency perceived can be used to predict work stress.
Queiros Carlotto Kaiseler Dias, and Pereira (2013)	Psicothema (Psychology)	Quantitative, Cross-sectional, Regression.	1,157 hospital nurses	Burnout – Maslach Burnout Inventory – Human Services Survey	To identify predictors of burnout among nurses working in hospitals.
Ramos, Serranheira, and Sousa-Uva (2018)	Revista Brasileira de Medicina do Trabalho (Medicina)	Quantitative, Cross-sectional, Descriptive	131 cash-in-transit employees	Perceived health – Age Questionaire	To establish the health and safety at work (HSW) conditions for employees, to characterize their working conditions and tasks, and to identify the aspects of their activities that influence their health and safety, as well as self-reported health problems.
	Occupational Therapy in		374 occupational therapists	Psychosocial Risks – The Copenhagen	To evaluate burnout levels and prevalence among

(*Continued*)

Occupational Stress, Health 243

Table 11.1 (Continued)

Authors (Year of Publication)	Journal (Area)	Study Design	Participants	Well-being indicator and measure used	Aim of the Study
Reis, Vale, Camacho, Estrela, and Dixe (2018)	Health Care (Medicine)	Quantitative, Cross-sectional, Descriptive		Psychosocial Questionnaire – Medium Version (CoPsoQ)	occupational therapists, as well as to relate those levels to practitioner age, gender, client age, years of professional activity, and area of practice.
Rodrigues, Paiva, Dias, Aleixo, Filipe, and Cunha (2018)	International Journal of Environmental Research and Public Health (Medicine)	Quantitative, Ambulatory Study	11 air traffic controllers	Linear Heart Rate Variability (HRV) features were extracted from ATCs Electrocardiogram (ECG) – medical clinically certified equipment (VitalJacket®).	To understand the effect of stress on cognitive performance, and to identify whether this effect is related to an autonomic response to stress.
Rodrigues, Kaiseler, Queirós, Basto-Pereira (2017)	International Journal of Emergency services (Social Sciences)	Quantitative, Diary	14 emergency response officers	Description of the Most Stressful Situation of the Working Day; Stress Intensity Lickert Scale; Open Question: What did you do to cope with the stressful situation?	To investigate stress and coping among Emergency Response Officers (EROs).
	PeerJ — Life and Environment		17 firefighters	Continuous Electrocardiogram	

(Continued)

Table 11.1 (Continued)

Authors (Year of Publication)	Journal (Area)	Study Design	Participants	Well-being indicator and measure used	Aim of the Study
Rodrigues, Paiva, Dias, and Cunha (2018)	Journal (Medicine)	Quantitative, Ambulatory Study		(ECG) and actigraphy measurement – medical clinically certified equipment (VitalJacket®).	To study the effects of stress events on physiological stress.
Roque, Veloso, Silva, and Costa (2015)	Ciência & Saúde Coletiva (Medicine)	Quantitative, Cross-sectional, Regression	305 health professionals and 392 users	Stress – Stress Questionnaire for Health Professionals (QSPS)	To examine the experience of stress in health professionals (physicians, nurses, and clinical secretaries), and to study satisfaction with the services provided by them from users.
Sá and Fleming. (2008)	Issues on Mental Health Nursing (Nursing)	Quantitative, Cross-sectional, Descriptive	107 nurses	Burnout – Maslach Burnout Inventory – Human Services Survey; General health – General Health Questionnaire (GHQ-28); Mental health – Mental Health Inventory (MHI-5)	To investigate both the prevalence of bullying in Portuguese nurses and the relationship between the symptoms of burnout and mental health in nurses who report being bullied.

(Continued)

Table 11.1 (Continued)

Authors (Year of Publication)	Journal (Area)	Study Design	Participants	Well-being indicator and measure used	Aim of the Study
Santos, Barros, and Carolino (2010)	Physiotherapy (Health Professionals)	Quantitative, Cross-sectional, Descriptive	55 hospital physiotherapists	Stress – The Occupational Stressors Inventory	To identify occupational stressors and coping resources in a group of physiotherapists, and to analyze interactions between subjective levels of stress, efficacy in stress resolution, and coping resources used by these professionals.
Satuf, Monteiro, Pereira, Esgalhado, Marina Afonso, and Loureiro (2016)	International Journal of Occupational Safety and Ergonomics (Medicine; Social Sciences)	Quantitative, Cross-sectional, Regression	971 workers from different organizations	Physical and Mental Health – MOS SF-36; Happiness – Covilhã Happiness Questionnaire (CHQ); Subjective well-being – PANAS	To study the effects of job satisfaction on mental and physical health, happiness, subjective well-being, and self-esteem.
Silva, et al. (2017)	BMC Medical Education (Medicine; Social Science)	Quantitative, Longitudinal (four waves), K-means cluster analyses. ANOVA	238 medical students	Depression – Beck Depression Inventory (BDI); Anxiety – State Trait Anxiety Inventory; Burnout – Maslach Burnout Inventory – Student Version	To determine the prevalence of depression in medical students, its developments during the course, its persistence for affected students, and to study the factors associated with

(Continued)

Table 11.1 (Continued)

Authors (Year of Publication)	Journal (Area)	Study Design	Participants	Well-being indicator and measure used	Aim of the Study
					depression and how these factors change over time.
da Fonte Sousa Gomes, dos Santos, & da Mata Almeida Carolino (2013)	Revista Latino Americana de Enfermagem (Nursing)	Quantitative, Cross-sectional, Descriptive	96 nurses of Surgery Oncology Services	Stress – Occupational Stress Inventory; Psychological Well-being (GHQ 12)	To identify sources of stress and coping strategies in nurses who work in three Head and Neck Surgery Oncology Services.
Sousa, Pereira-Machado, Greten & Coimbra, (2016)	Medical Problem of Performing Artists (Medicine)	Qualitative, Cross-sectional, Descriptive	112 professional orchestra musicians	Interviews	To describe the prevalence of the most common complaints affecting musicians in the three professional orchestras.
Teixeira, Ribeiro & Carvalho (2013)	BMC Anesthesiology (Medicine)	Quantitative, Cross-sectional, Descriptive	82 physicians and 218 nurses	Burnout – Maslach Burnout Inventory – Human Services Survey	To study the incidence and risk factors of burnout in ICUs.
Teixeira, Ribeiro, Fonseca, & Carvalho, (2014)	Journal of Medical Ethics (Medicine)	Quantitative, Cross-sectional, Regression	300 nurses and physicians	Burnout – Maslach Burnout Inventory – Human Services Survey;	To explore the ethical problems that may increase burnout levels among physicians and nurses working in intensive care units (ICUs).
			39 management consultants	Interviews	To analyze management consultants' self-

(Continued)

Table 11.1 (Continued)

Authors (Year of Publication)	Journal (Area)	Study Design	Participants	Well-being indicator and measure used	Aim of the Study
Von Humboldt, Leal, Laneiro, and Tavares (2013)	Stress & Health (Pychology, Medicine)	Qualitative, Content Analysis			perceptions of occupational stress (SPoOS), sources of stress (SoS), and stress management strategies (SMS), and to find latent constructs that can work as major determinants in consultants' conceptualization of SPoOS, SoS, and SMS.

study design, cross-sectional/longitudinal study design, data collection mode, work context, and well-being measure, but are different from the other studies. A two-step cluster analysis identifies group segmentation by first running pre-clustering and then by means of hierarchical methods (Garson, 2014). As such, it combines both approaches. This technique can detect latent relationships within and between studies with multiple distinct characteristics. The optimal cluster solution was determined using Akaike's information criterion. The quality of fit of the resulting modeled clusters was measured using the silhouette measure of cohesion and separation (Dimitriadou, Dolničar, & Weingessel, 2002). The silhouette measure contrasts the average distance among elements in the same cluster (within-cluster cohesion) with the average distance to elements in other clusters (between-cluster separation).

Results

When, Where, and What is Investigated?

The review of the articles (marked with * in the references; see also Table 11.1) revealed that publications began in 2006 but were scarce (i.e., zero, one, or three studies per year) up to 2012, while in 2016 and 2018 more published studies were observed – 16 for both years. Regarding the choice of journal publications, this review found that the vast majority (n = 70) were international had published only one paper, and the detachment occurred in Occupational Medicine (n = 3), in the Spanish Journal of Psychology (n = 3), and in Stress & Health (n = 4). As for the scientific area of these publications, the review revealed that more than one third (n = 30) had been published in Psychology and Social Sciences, more than one third (n = 29) in Medicine, Health, Mental Health, and 16% (n = 12) in Nursing and 4 in other publications[1]. The majority focused on the negative side of occupational well-being. Over half of the analyzed articles (n = 36) studied burnout; stress was analyzed in seven, anxiety and depression in nine, work engagement was investigated in only nine, and satisfaction with life in four studies.

Who was Investigated, How, and For What Purpose?

The sample size used varied from 11 to 3,227, although a significant number used samples consisting of between 51 and 300 participants (n = 34, 45.3%) or more than 300 participants (n = 32, 42.6%). Indeed, it was common to find samples with hundreds of workers (e.g., Baylina, Barros, Fonte, Alves, & Rocha, 2018; Satuf, Monteiro, Pereira, Esgalhado, Marina Afonso, and Loureiro 2016) to analyze the relationship between work-related factors and workers' well-being, to analyze the prevalence of stress – namely burnout (e.g., Marques, Alves, Queiros, Norton, and

Henriques 2018), and to validate a scale for specific professionals (e.g., Lapa, Carvalho, Viana, Ferreira, Pinto-Gouveia, 2016). However, there were also studies that presented smaller samples – focusing on the effects of stress events on physiological stress (e.g., Rodrigues, Paiva, Dias, & Cunha, 2018) or on the effects of a specific intervention (Duarte & Pinto-Gouveia, 2016). The majority (n = 40, 53.3%) of the analyzed articles used samples with healthcare professionals (only nurses: n = 22, 55%, only doctors: n = 4, 10%, both nurses and doctors: n = 5, 12.5%, and diverse professionals: n = 9, 22.5%); whereas, samples with other professionals (firefighters, police, army, or security forces: n = 6, 8%, teachers: n = 4, 5.3%, contact center or temporary workers: n = 4, 5, 3%, bank, administrative, or financial workers: n = 5, 6.7%, students: n = 2, 2.7%, and others: n = 5, 6.7%) were less frequent. Heterogeneous samples – that is, samples comprising professionals with various occupations – were used only in nine (12%) of the studies.

As far as other organizational context characteristics are concerned – namely, size and public versus private – we observed that the analyzed articles did not always contain information about the size of the organization (n = 30, 40%) or whether it was a private or public company (n = 27, 36%). However, among those that identified these characteristics, the following was observed: 22 (29.3%), 12 (16%), and 11 (14.7%) had collected data respectively from large, small to medium, and diverse organizations; while 26 (33.3%), 18 (24%), and 5 (6.7%) had collected data respectively from public, private, and diverse organizations.

The vast majority of studies were quantitative (n = 69, 92%), cross-sectional (n = 64, 85,3%), and reliant on the use of self-reported data (n = 71, 94.7%). Only three were qualitative. Six had a longitudinal design – four with two waves, one with three waves, and one with four waves. Four studies reported interventions, and four used objective or hetero-reported data.

Regarding the measures used, the vast majority of quantitative studies (65 out of 72, 90.3%) used validated international scales (e.g., burnout: Maslach Burnout Inventory (n = 36), work engagement: The Utrecht Work Engagement Scale (n = 9), health: Health Perception (n = 4), mental health: *SF-36* (n = 2), well-being: Satisfaction with Life (n = 4) and GHQ 12 or GHQ 28 (n = 9), and affects and emotions: PANAS (n = 2). However, some studies used measures developed in Portugal to analyze the stress of healthcare professionals (one used in three studies and another used in one study) and the stress of teachers and general stress and happiness (each used only in one study).

As for the aim of the studies reviewed, we observed that more than half analyzed health or well-being predictors (n = 48, 64%); four examined health or well-being indicators as mediators; four studied the consequences of health and well-being; 12 described the prevalence of stress among workgroups; three reported the validation of a health or well-being measure; and four analyzed the effects of an intervention on health or well-being. Of the studies that researched antecedents, half (n = 24) analyzed situational variables; 10 analyzed individual variables; and 14 had a mixture of situational and individual variables.

Two Main Groups of Studies Found

The cluster analysis revealed two distinct clusters. The four conditions (i.e., sample size, type of study, sample dimension, and work population) retained in the final TSC analysis had a silhouette coefficient of 0.50 – indicative of good data partitioning. The other variables (i.e., data collection mode, work context, and well-being measure) did not play an important role in clustering. The two clusters were of different sizes – with 57 studies (76%) and 18 studies (24%) respectively – and the type of study (e.g., cross-sectional, etc) was the main cluster predictor.

Cluster 1 is characterized by cross-sectional studies, smaller samples (i.e., fewer than 300 participants), exclusively quantitative approaches, and several populations of healthcare workers. Cluster 2 consists of longitudinal and mixed designs, qualitative and mixed approaches, largest sample sizes, and more diversified work population (cf., Table 11.2).

Approximately 78% (n = 14) of Cluster 2 studies had been published in the last 5 years against 56% of the studies in Cluster 1 (n = 32), and

Table 11.2 Two-Step Cluster Analysis

	Cluster 1 (n=57) Cross-Sectional n (%)	Cluster 2 (n=18) Longitudinal and Mixed n (%)
Type of study		
Cross-sectional	57 (100)	5 (28)
Longitudinal and mixed	0 (0)	13 (72)
Qualitative versus quantitative		
Qualitative	0 (0)	3 (17)
Quantitative	57 (100)	12 (66)
Mixed	0 (0)	3 (17)
Sample size[*]		
>300	23 (40)	16 (89)
<=300	34 (60)	2 (11)
Work population main categories		
Healthcare workers	34 (60)	5 (28)
Service employees	8 (14)	1 (6)
Teachers	4 (7)	0 (0)
Others	11 (19)	12 (67)

Note

[*]The variable entered the TSA as continuous.

the computer-assisted web interview data collection mode had similar proportions (28%) in both clusters. The paper-and-pencil mode recorded a higher level of use in Cluster 1 studies (67%) compared to Cluster 2 (44%).

Discussion

The aim of this chapter was to review, summarize, and evaluate the research on occupational stress, health, and well-being developed in Portugal. Along with several inclusion criteria, our review focused on 75 studies. Our qualitative systematic literature review revealed that: healthcare professionals were the most researched; quantitative and cross-sectional studies were predominant; the majority of studies sought to ascertain the causes of workers' stress, health, and/or well-being, while others pinpointed the level of stress or well-being in specific professionals; and the majority focused on the negative side of occupational stress, health, and well-being, and burnout took priority.

Professionals Studied

Health professionals, and nurses, in particular, have been recognized as professions with job and work conditions that influence their stress, health, and well-being (e.g., McVicar, 2005; Mark & Smith, 2012; O'Connor, Muller Neff, and Pitman 2018; Riahi, 2011). Our systematic review revealed that these were the most studied professionals in Portugal; thus, supporting the idea that this population is vulnerable to stress as a result of their occupational activity. However, other professionals, for example, teachers (e.g., Chambel & Ernesto, 2013), military personnel (e.g., Chambel, Castanheira, Oliveira-Cruz, & Lopes, 2015), policemen (e.g., Gomes & Afonso, 2016), airline pilots (Reis, Mestre, & Canhão, 2013), and salespeople (Castanheira & Chambel, 2010) have different work and job conditions that significantly affect their stress, health, and well-being. Therefore, future studies should be developed using samples of workers with other occupations.

The Studies' Design

Our systematic review reveals that research on occupational stress, health, and well-being in Portugal has been dominated by cross-sectional studies – with a minority representing longitudinal studies. Moreover, if we use the criteria of Kelloway and Francis (2013) that consider a longitudinal study to be one that employs three or more waves, this review will only identify two studies. Silva et al. (2017) sampled medical students and analyzed the evolution of their depression, anxiety, and burnout over time. Neto Carvalho Chambel Manuel Pereira Miguel and Reis (2016) used a sample of workers of a service company to show the reciprocal effect between work-family conflict and employee well-being for 18 months. Although this predominance of cross-sectional studies has been identified as a characteristic in occupational health literature (e.g., Häusser, Mojzisch, Niesel, & Schulz-Hardt 2010; Luchman & González-Morales, 2013; Taris & Schaufeli, 2016), it has a significant limitation. Cross-sectional studies only enable an understanding of whether the relationship between variables is significant but do not permit the establishment of unidirectional causation (e.g., De Lange, Taris, Kompier, Houtman, & Bongers, 2003; Zapf, Dormann, & Frese, 1996). Thus, a cross-sectional approach is inappropriate to show, for example, that specific personal, job-related, or organizational characteristics influence workers' stress, health, or well-being. With this design, it is also possible that reverse causation may exist, and workers' stress, health, or well-being influence their occupational situation perceptions. Of the articles included in this revision, Ângelo and Chambel (2015) sampled firefighters with a two-wave study and found that the causal direction of the relationship between job demands and burnout was reciprocal.

Future research with longitudinal designs that can address such patterns of causation (e.g., cross-lagged panel designs) would be valuable to identify the underlying processes associated with workers' stress, health, and well-being change and development. Mäkikangas, Kinnunen, Feldt, and Schaufeli's (2016) systematic review showed that changes in workers' well-being are more frequent than stability. We need more evidence on the specific features of the job and organizational context (i.e., training, human resource management practices, job insecurity, organizational change) that may influence a change in workers' stress, health, and well-being.

This systemic review also shows that intervention studies are rare in the available literature on workers' stress, health, and well-being in Portugal (Barbosa, Nolan, Sousa, Marques, & Figueiredo, 2014, 2016; Duarte & Pinto-Gouveia, 2016; Mesquita, Ribeiro, & Moreira, 2011). The intervention studies not only provide valuable information on the causal relationships, but also enable a systematic examination of the organizational actions (e.g., training, actions, and practices) and their efficacy to promote workers' health and well-being. Thus, researchers should be encouraged to employ more intervention studies in order to increase the ecological validity of organizational actions and practices and consequently increase their evidence-based nature.

Antecedents of Workers' Stress, Health, and Well-Being

Our systematic review also reveals that the majority of studies analyze the antecedents of occupational stress, health, and well-being and among these, situational factors have been underlined. This observation is in line with literature reviews (e.g., Babatunde, 2013; Nielsen, Nielsen, Ogbonnaya, Känsälä, Saari, & Isaksson 2017) that also demonstrate the relevance of job, work, and organizational factors in explaining work stress and well-being. However, in regard to situational stress, health, and well-being antecedents, this review makes it possible to distinguish different study groups. The first group includes studies that analyze different situational factors acknowledged by literature as having an influence on occupational stress, health, and well-being, without considering the specific nature of sampled professionals. The studies that used the CopSoq instrument to analyze the psychosocial risks are an example: Alves de Moura Serranheira and Sacadura-Leite (2016) sampled psychiatrists and anesthetists; Coelho Tavares Lourenco and Lima (2015) sampled private administrative workers; Coelho Tavares Lima and Lourenco (2018) sampled field workers; Coutinho Queirós Henriques Norton and Alves (2019) sampled employees in a public hospital; and Reis, Vale, Camacho, Estrela, and Dixe (2018) sampled occupational therapists. In the same group, this systematic review observed some studies that analyzed stressors underlined in literature as situational factors with detrimental effects on occupational health and well-being. As an example, da Silva João and Saldanha Portelada (2016) sampled nurses to analyze the effect of mobbing, and Neto Chambel and Carvalho (2018) sampled sales and contact center workers to analyze the effect of the work-family – life – conflict. Finally, and also included in this group, some studies performed an empirical test of a theoretical model. For example, Gomes, Faria, and Lopes (2016) conducted a study based on Lazarus and Folkman's Model (Lazarus & Folkman, 1984) and confirmed the importance of cognitive appraisal in the relationship between occupational stress and the psychological health of nurses. Ângelo and Chambel (2014) sampled firefighters by expanding the Job Demands-Resources (JD-R) model to include proactive coping in both health impairment and motivational processes and observed that proactive coping partially mediated the relationship between job demands and burnout – as well as the relationship between job resources and engagement.

The second group identified by this systematic review includes studies that analyzed some of the specific characteristics of the professional sample being studied. The assumption is that this occupation implies high stressors that contribute to the emergence of stress or illness. For example, Martins-Pereira Teixeira Carvalho, and Hernández-Marrero (2016) analyzed professionals (i.e., nurses and physicians) working in intensive and palliative care units – considering that they were at risk of developing burnout due to their provision of end-of-life care for patients – and observed that conflicts (e.g., with patients and/or families and intra and/or inter-teams) were the most significant determinant of burnout. In the same vein, Maia and Ribeiro (2010) sampled emergency personnel, considering that exposure to current death and events of physical injury in the context of motor vehicle accidents, was a high predictor of posttraumatic stress disorder (PTSD). However, the authors found that peritraumatic dissociation and distress were the only predictors of PTSD symptoms, but direct coping explained PTSD variance beyond their contribution.

This systematic review also identifies a third group which seeks to describe the participants' stress – namely, their burnout level. The assumption is that the sampled professionals are confronted with high stressors and consequently have high levels of burnout. For example, Maroco, Sacadura-Leite, Bastos, Vazão, and Campos (2016) reported the incidence of burnout in healthcare professionals (i.e., nurses and physicians); Cruz-Mendes, Claro, and Cruz-Robazzi (2014) reported the levels of burnout among nurses working in prisons; and Teixeira, Ribeiro, Fonseca and Carvalho (2013) reported levels of burnout of physicians and nurses working in intensive care units. In the same vein, the study of Marques, et al. (2018) described the levels of burnout in health professionals, comparing different professional groups of hospital staff and analyzing how the professional category is associated with levels of burnout. These studies support the idea that these professionals are vulnerable to burnout but do not contribute to explaining why and how the development of this chronic stress indicator occurs. They do not analyze the professional experiences of these workers nor bring to light the levels of stressors they encountered, or explain whether the stressors they may have encountered were related to the fact that they had these occupations. Furthermore, the studies identified in the third group of this systematic review did not use a theoretical model to ascertain the occurrence of burnout. For example, the assumptions of the Conservation of Resources Model (COR, Hobfoll, 1989) should be used. These defend that burnout occurs when a professional perceives high demands that threaten something of value to him/her, and that threat or loss taxes or exhausts the resources they have available to confront the situation. In fact, these assumptions have been supported by the meta-analysis of Lee and Ashforth (1996) - which showed that job demands were important predictors of burnout, by the meta-analysis conducted by Alarcon (2011) – which observed that higher demands and lower resources were associated with burnout, and by the systematic review of Seidler et al. (2014) which indicated that high job demands, the low possibility of exerting control, and non-supportive workplaces are important to explain the development of burnout. Thus, we suggest that future studies must analyze different situations with high demands and low resources to explain the development of burnout in Portuguese professionals.

The Consequences of Work Stress and Well-Being

There is evidence demonstrating that healthy workers perform better than non-healthy workers (Motyka, 2019) or that burnout negatively affects workers' performance (Swider & Zimmerman, 2010; Taris, 2006). Despite the fact that our literature review shows that the consequences of stress, health, and well-being are understudied, studies analyzing their effect on workers' performance support this relationship. Indeed, Martinez and Ferreira (2012) sampled nurses from a public hospital and observed that stress and health conditions predict presenteeism. Neto, Ferreira, Martinez, and Ferreira (2017) sampled workers from a service company and showed that bullying was related to well-being and exhaustion, which in turn was related to presenteeism. Lastly, Rodrigues, Paiva, Dias, Aleixo, Filipe, and Cunha (2018) showed in an ambulatory study with air traffic controllers that stress had a negative effect on cognitive performance. Furthermore, this review also reveals a study (Marques-Pinto et al., 2018) that analyzed the attitudinal consequences of workers' well-being, namely turnover intentions. Moreover, and also in line with previous studies demonstrating that burnout and engagement have consequences for health and job attitudes (Maslach, Schaufeli, & Leiter, 2001; Taris, 2006; Taris & Schaufeli, 2016), Marques-Pinto et al. (2018) sampled nurses from hospitals and showed that their decisional involvement was positively related to work engagement and negatively to burnout which, in turn, predicted their intentions to leave the hospital where they worked.

Future studies should analyze the effects of stress, health, and well-being on professionals' attitudes and behaviors and consequently help organizations to develop preventive interventions and early identification of this health condition in the work environment – contributing not only to workers' health, but also to the efficiency and effectiveness of these organizations (Salvagioni, Melanda, Mesas, González, Gabani, and De Andrade 2017).

The More Frequently Studied Negative Side

Another trend that is salient when revisiting literature on occupational stress, health, and well-being in Portugal is a prevailing negative bias of studies addressing illness rather than wellness. This is illustrated by the fact that more than half of the publications had analyzed burnout. This is not exclusive to the studies in Portugal. Indeed, Schaufeli and Salanova (2007) listed the papers published on workplace well-being in the Journal of Occupational Health Psychology between 1996 and 2005 and found that, out of 233 manuscripts, only 14 referred exclusively to positive indicators. The authors found a ratio of 14:1 in favor of papers focusing on mental illness. In the same vein, Macik-Frey, Quick, and

Nelson (2007) analyzed the literature on occupational health from 1990 to 2005 and confirmed that stress and burnout were the predominant trends. It is important to create a shift in this tendency towards illness, as failing to capture the positive aspects of work and inherent resources is inappropriate and incomplete. As argued by Turner, Barling, and Zacharatos (2002, p. 715), "... it is time to extend our research focus and explore more fully the positive sides, so as to gain a full understanding of the meaning and effects of working". Indeed, most organizations expect their workers to take responsibility and initiative, to be committed to the organization and the team, and to be involved with the job and to feel accountable for high-quality performance.

Hence, we need more studies that address the positive sides of work and the effective functioning of Portuguese professionals. Literature on stress and health has demonstrated that illness and health can be explained by different variables – the threat of loss or availability of resources; Hobfoll, 2002 - and we now have extensive evidence showing how the loss of resources is associated with feelings of illness, while the availability of resources is associated with health and well-being (Nielsen, Nielsen, Ogbonnaya, Känsälä, Saari, & Isaksson, 2017). In line with the assumption that the loss of resources explains stress and illness, for example, Joaquim et al. (2017) sampled medical residents of oncology, hematology, and radiotherapy and found that "dealing with patients" and "overwork" were important predictors of stress, and overwork was directly related to burnout. Showing that resources should prevent stress and illness in a resources loss situation, Martins-Pereira, Teixeira, Carvalho, and Hernández-Marrero (2016) sampled professionals from intensive and palliative care units and observed that higher burnout levels were significantly and positively associated with experiencing conflicts in the workplace, but having post-graduate education in intensive/palliative care was significantly but inversely associated with higher burnout levels. Confirming the role of resources in the promotion of well-being, Correia de Sousa and van Dierendonck (2014) sampled workers from two merging companies and showed that servant leadership was positively related to organizational identification and psychological empowerment which, in turn, was positively related to work engagement.

Having argued the need to increase focus on well-being and good functioning, we also believe that it is important to continue to study stress and illness. Hence, research on occupational stress, health, and well-being would benefit from more studies that are simultaneously accounting for positive and negative indicators. The very few Portuguese studies that examine both positive and negative indicators (Ângelo & Chambel, 2014, 2015; Carvalho & Chambel, 2015, 2017; Chambel, Carvalho, Cesário, & Lopes, 2017; Marques-Pinto, et al., 2018) focused on the antecedents of burnout and engagement and treated them as two independent parallel indicators. Therefore, there is still much to explore on the potential interaction effects between these two workplace well-being indicators. In line with Schaufeli and Taris (2014), the development process of engagement and the development process of burnout should not be independent. Thus, future research should deepen this research line and analyze both processes jointly – namely, the role of engagement in burnout development and vice-versa.

Conclusions

By means of the present systematic review, it was possible to elaborate on several theoretical and practical considerations. From a theoretical point of view, we noted that, to date, there is a remarkable prevalence of studies focusing on antecedents rather than the consequences of stress and these underline mental illness rather than mental wellness.

From a practical perspective, we are also able to elaborate on some final considerations. For instance, within a methodological scope, this systematic literature review has clearly highlighted a number of the limitations of previous studies that should be overcome in future research. Firstly, the predominant cross-sectional design of previous studies – which does not enable inference of the causal relationships among the variables and does not present a picture of the occupational stress, health, and well-being evolution – levels across time. Secondly, the majority of studies analyzed healthcare professionals, while other professionals that are also characterized by high stressors have either not been studied or are only studied occasionally. Finally, and still from a practical point of view, the present systematic review has allowed us to ascertain that occupational stress, health, and well-being consequences, compared to the analysis of antecedents, have received less interest from researchers. Thus, we suggest that future studies should observe the effects of occupational stress, health, and well-being. Smaller studies and cross-sectional designs may be associated with an online data collection mode and, therefore, they are easier and less expensive to perform, and are useful for academic proposals. Longitudinal designs are time-consuming, yet more robust designs are needed, along with a more diversified work population, in order to understand the specific context of Portugal. Notwithstanding, the two clusters obtained showed that an increased tendency to perform studies with large samples, and a longitudinal design has been observed in recent years – as shown in Cluster 2. These findings are of interest to national authorities that need quality information in order to plan prevention and health promotion programs, and, therefore, these types of studies should be encouraged and supported.

In short, the current work has contributed to summarize all the empirical evidence obtained to date on Portuguese workers' stress, health, and well-being, and, by doing so, it has highlighted future pathways for the research of occupational stress, health, and well-being in this country.

Note

1 When the Journal was classified with more than one area, we chose the area of work of the first author.

References

Afonso, P., Fonseca, M., & Pires, J. F. (2017). Impact of working hours on sleep and mental health. *Occupational Medicine (Oxford, England)*, 67(5), 377–382. https://doi.org/10.1093/occmed/kqx054.

Alarcon, G. M. (2011). A meta-analysis of burnout with job demands, resources, and attitudes. *Journal of Vocational Behavior*, 79(2), 549–572. https://doi.org/10.1016/j.jvb.2011.03.007.

Alves de Moura, P., Serranheira, F., & Sacadura-Leite, E. (2016). Psychosocial risks in psychiatry and anaesthesiology residents in a Portuguese General and University Hospital. *La Medicina Del Lavoro*, 107(2), 129–140.

Ângelo, R. P., & Chambel, M. J. (2014). The role of proactive coping in the job demands-resources model: A cross-section study with firefighters. *European Journal of Work and Organizational Psychology*, 23(2), 203–216. https://doi.org/10.1080/1359432X.2012.728701.

Ângelo, R. P., & Chambel, M. J. (2015). The reciprocal relationship between work characteristics and employee burnout and engagement: A longitudinal study of firefighters. *Stress and Health*, 31(2), 106–114. https://doi.org/10.1002/smi.2532.

Babatunde, A. (2013). Occupational stress: A review on conceptualisations, causes and cure. *Economic Insights-Trends & Challenges*, 65(3), 73–80.

Barbosa, A., Nolan, M., Sousa, L., & Figueiredo, D. (2014). Supporting direct care workers in dementia care: Effects of a psychoeducational intervention. *American Journal of Alzheimer's Disease and Other Dementias*, 30(2), 130–138. https://doi.org/10.1177/1533317514550331.

Barbosa, A., Nolan, M., Sousa, L., Marques, A., & Figueiredo, D. (2016). Effects of a psychoeducational intervention for direct care workers caring for people with dementia: Results from a 6-month follow-up study. *American Journal of Alzheimer's Disease and Other Dementias*, 31(2), 144–155. https://doi.org/10.1177/1533317515603500.

Barbosa, J., Silva, Á., Ferreira, M. A., & Severo, M. (2016). Transition from secondary school to medical school: The role of self-study and self-regulated learning skills in freshman burnout. *Acta Medica Portuguesa*, 29(12), 803–808. https://doi.org/10.20344/amp.8350.

Baylina, P., Barros, C., Fonte, C., Alves, S., & Rocha, Á. (2018). Healthcare workers: Occupational health promotion and patient safety. *Journal of Medical Systems*, 42(9), 2–9. https://doi.org/10.1007/s10916-018-1013-7.

Cabeças, J. M., & Mota, M. R. (2014). Employee's Perception of Occupational Hazards and Health Complaints in the Financial Sector (Portuguese Sample).

In Xu, J., Cruz-Machado, V. A., Lev, B. & Nickel, S. (Eds.), *Advances in intelligent systems and computing. Proceedings of the eighth international conference on management science and engineering management: Focused on intelligent system and management science* (Vol. 280, pp. 303–313). London: Springer. https://doi.org/10.1007/978-3-642-55182-6.

Carvalho, V. S., & Chambel, M. J. (2014). Work-to-family enrichment and employees' well-being: High performance work system and job characteristics. *Social Indicators Research, 119*(1), 373–387. https://doi.org/10.1007/s11205-013-0475-8.

Carvalho, V. S., & Chambel, M. J. (2016a). Perceived high-performance work system and subjective well-being: Work-to-family balance and well-being at work as mediators. *Journal of Career Development, 43*(2), 116–129. https://doi.org/10.1177/0894845315583113.

Carvalho, V. S., & Chambel, M. J. (2016b). Work-to-family enrichment and conflict profiles: Job characteristics and employees' well-being. *The Spanish Journal of Psychology, 19*, 1-15. https://doi.org/10.1017/sjp.2016.63.

Carvalho, V. S., & Chambel, M. J. (2017). Work–family conflict and enrichment mediates the relationship between job characteristics and well-being at work with portuguese marine corps. *Armed Forces and Society, 44*(2), 301–321. https://doi.org/10.1177/0095327X17698121.

Carvalho, V. S., Chambel, M. J., Neto, M., & Lopes, S. (2018). Does work-family conflict mediate the associations of job characteristics with employees' mental health among men and women? *Frontiers in Psychology*. https://doi.org/10.3389/fpsyg.2018.00966

Castanheira, F., & Chambel, M. J. (2010). Burnout in salespeople: A three-wave study to examine job characteristics' predictions and consequences for performance. *Economic and Industrial Democracy, 31*(4), 409–429. https://doi.org/10.1177/0143831X10365573.

Chambel, M. J. (2016). Psicologia da saúde ocupacional: Desenvolvimento e desafios [Occupational health psychology: Development and challenges]. In M. J. Chambel (Ed.), *Psicologia da Saúde ocupacional [occupational health psychology]* (pp. 3–24). Lisboa: Pactor. https://doi.org/10.5016/rlabor.v3i2.1140.

Chambel, M. J., Cesário, V., Carvalho, S., Cesário, F., & Lopes, S. (2017). The work-to-life conflict mediation between job characteristics and well-being at work: Part-time vs full-time employees. *Career Development International, 22*(2), 142–164. https://doi.org/10.1108/CDI-06-2016-0096.

Chambel, M. J., Castanheira, F., Oliveira-Cruz, F., & Lopes, S. (2015). Work context support and Portuguese soldiers' well-being: The mediating role of autonomous motivation. *Military Psychology, 27*(5), 297–310. https://doi.org/10.1037/mil0000087.

Chambel, M. J., & Ernesto, F. (2013). Job Demands in Portuguese Teachers: Lagged, Synchronous and Reverse Effects in Burnout. In S. P. Gonçalves & Neves, J. G. (Eds.), *Occupational health psychology: From burnout to well-being* (pp. 67–92). Scientific & Academic Publishing.

Chambel, M. J., Lorente, L., Carvalho, V. S., & Martinez, I. M. (2016). Psychological contract profiles among permanent and temporary agency workers. *Journal of Managerial Psychology, 31*(1), 79–94. https://doi.org/10.1108/JMP-02-2014-0070.

Coelho, D. A., Tavares, C. S. D., Lima, T. M., & Lourenco, M. L. (2018). Psychosocial and ergonomic survey of office and field jobs in a utility company. *International Journal of Occupational Safety and Ergonomics, 24*(3), 475–486. https://doi.org/10.1080/10803548.2017.1331620.

Coelho, D. A., Tavares, C. S. D., Lourenco, M. L., & Lima, T. M. (2015). Working conditions under multiple exposures: A cross-sectional study of private sector administrative workers. *Work, 51*(4), 781–789. https://doi.org/10.3233/WOR-152025.

Coutinho, H., Queirós, C., Henriques, A., Norton, P., & Alves, E. (2019). Work-related determinants of psychosocial risk factors among employees in the hospital setting. *Work, 61*(4), 551–560. https://doi.org/10.3233/WOR-182825.

Cruz-Mendes, A. M., Claro, M., & Cruz-Robazzi, M. L. C. (2014). Burnout in nurses working in Portuguese central prisons and typeof employment contract. La Medicina del Lavoro. *Work Environment, and Health, 105*(3), 214–222.

Cumbe, V. F. J., Pala, A. N., Palha, A. J. P., Gaio, A. R. P., Esteves, M. F., Mari, J., de, J., & Wainberg, M. (2017). Burnout syndrome and coping strategies in Portuguese oncology health care providers. *Revista de Psiquiatria Clinica, 44*(5), 122–126. https://doi.org/10.1590/0101-60830000000135.

da Fonte Sousa Gomes, S., dos Santos, M. M. M. C. C., & da Mata Almeida Carolino, E. T. (2013). Psycho-social risks at work: Stress and coping strategies in oncology nurses. *Revista Latino-Americana de Enfermagem, 21*(6), 1282–1289. https://doi.org/10.1590/0104-1169.2742.2365.

da Silva João, A. L., & Saldanha Portelada, A. F. (2016). Mobbing and its impact on interpersonal relationships at the workplace. *Journal of Interpersonal Violence, 34*(13), 2797–2812, 088626051666285. https://doi.org/10.1177/0886260516662850.

Daudt, H. M. L., Van Mossel, C., & Scott, S. J. (2013). Enhancing the scoping study methodology: A large, inter-professional team's experience with Arksey and O'Malley's framework. *BMC Medical Research Methodology, 13*, 48. https://doi.org/10.1186/1471-2288-13-48.

David, I. C., & Quintão, S. (2012). Burnout em professores: A sua relação com a personalidade, estratégias de coping e satisfação com a vida [Burnout in teachers: Its relationship with personality, coping strategies and life satisfaction. *Acta Medica Portuguesa, 25*(3), 145–155.

De Lange, A. H., Taris, T. W., Kompier, M. A. J., Houtman, I. L. D., & Bongers, P. M. (2003). "The Very Best of the Millennium": Longitudinal research and the demand-control-(support) model. *Journal of Occupational Health Psychology, 8*(4), 282–305. .https://doi.org/10.1037/1076-8998.8.4.282

de Sousa, M. J. C., & van Dierendonck, D. (2014). Servant leadership and engagement in a merge process under high uncertainty. *Journal of Organizational Change Management, 27*(6), 877–899. https://doi.org/10.1108/JOCM-07-2013-0133.

Dimitriadou, E., Dolničar, S., & Weingessel, A. (2002). An examination of indexes for determining the number of clusters in binary data sets. *Psychometrika, 67*(1), 137–159. https://doi.org/10.1007/BF02294713.

Duarte, J., & Pinto-Gouveia, J. (2016). Effectiveness of a mindfulness-based intervention on oncology nurses' burnout and compassion fatigue symptoms: A non-randomized study. *International Journal of Nursing Studies, 64*(1), 98–107. https://doi.org/10.1016/j.ijnurstu.2016.10.002.

Duarte, J., & Pinto-Gouveia, J. (2017). The role of psychological factors in oncology nurses' burnout and compassion fatigue symptoms. *European Journal of Oncology Nursing*, 28(1), 114–121. https://doi.org/10.1016/j.ejon.2017.04.002.

Eurofound and EU-OSHA. (2014). *Psychosocial risks in Europe prevalence and strategies for prevention*. Luxembourg: Publications Office of the European Union. Project. https://doi.org/10.2806/70971.

Eurofound and EU-OSHA. (2018). *Work on demand: Recurrence, effects and challenges*. Luxembourg: Publications Office of the European Union. Project. eurofound.link/ef18048.

Fonseca, A., Pereira, S., & Carvalho, A. S. (2012). Burnout in nurses working in Portuguese palliative care teams: A mixed methods study. *International Journal of Palliative Nursing*, 18(8), 373–381. https://doi.org/10.12968/ijpn.2012.18.8.373.

Gama, G., Barbosa, F., & Vieira, M. (2014). Personal determinants of nurses' burnout in end of life care. *European Journal of Oncology Nursing*, 18(5), 527–533. https://doi.org/10.1016/j.ejon.2014.04.005.

Garrosa, E., Rainho, C., Moreno-Jiménez, B., & Monteiro, M. J. (2010). The relationship between job stressors, hardy personality, coping resources and burnout in a sample of nurses: A correlational study at two time points. *International Journal of Nursing Studies*, 47(2), 205–215. https://doi.org/10.1016/j.ijnurstu.2009.05.014.

Garson, G. D. (2014). *Cluster Analysis*. Statistical Associates Publishing.

Geraldes, D., Madeira, E., Carvalho, V. S., & Chambel, M. J. (2019). Work-personal life conflict and burnout in contact centers. *Personnel Review*, 48(2), 400–416. https://doi.org/10.1108/pr-11-2017-0352.

Gomes, A. R., & Afonso, J. M. P. (2016). Occupational stress and coping among Portuguese military police officers. *Avances En Psicología Latinoamericana*, 34(1), 47–65. https://doi.org/10.12804/apl34.1.2016.04.

Gomes, A. R., Cruz, J. F., & Cabanelas, S. (2009). Estresse ocupacional em profissionais de saúde: Um estudo com enfermeiros portugueses. *Psicologia: Teoria e Pesquisa*, 25(3), 307–318. https://doi.org/10.1590/s0102-37722009000300004.

Gomes, A. R., Faria, S., & Gonçalves, A. M. (2013). Cognitive appraisal as a mediator in the relationship between stress and burnout. *Work and Stress*, 27(4), 351–367. https://doi.org/10.1080/02678373.2013.840341\.

Gomes, A. R., Faria, S., & Lopes, H. (2016). Stress and psychological health: Testing the mediating role of cognitive appraisal. *Western Journal of Nursing Research*, 38(11), 1448–1468. https://doi.org/10.1177/0193945916654666.

Gomes, A. R. S. (2014). Stress ocupacional em profissionais de saúde: Um estudo comparativo entre médicos e enfermeiros. *Interamerican Journal of Psychology*, 48(1), 129–141.

Gomes, A. R., & Teixeira, P. M. (2016). Stress, cognitive appraisal and psychological health: Testing instruments for health professionals. *Stress and Health*, 32(2), 167–172. https://doi.org/10.1002/smi.2583.

Gomes, S. F. S., Santos, M. M. M. C. C. dos, & Carolino, E. T. M. A. (2013). Psycho-social risks at work: Stress and coping strategies in oncology nurses. *Revista Latino-Americana de Enfermagem*, 21(6), 1282–1289. https://doi.org/10.1590/0104-1169.2742.2365.

Häusser, J. A., Mojzisch, A., Niesel, M., & Schulz-Hardt, S. (2010). Ten years on: A review of recent research on the Job Demand-Control (-Support) model and psychological well-being. *Work and Stress, 24*(1), 1–35. https://doi.org/10.1080/02678371003683747.

Hernández-Marrero, P., Pereira, S. M., & Carvalho, A. S. (2016). Ethical decisions in palliative care: Interprofessional relations as a burnout protective factor? Results from a mixed-methods multicenter study in Portugal. *American Journal of Hospice and Palliative Medicine, 33*(8), 723–732. https://doi.org/10.1177/1049909115583486.

Hobfoll, S. E. (1989). Conservation of resources. A new attempt at conceptualizing stress. *The American Psychologist, 44*(3), 513–524. https://doi.org/10.1037/0003-066X.44.3.513.

Hobfoll, S. E. (2002). Social and psychological resources and adaptation. *Review of General Psychology, 6*(4), 307–324. https://doi.org/10.1037/1089-2680.6.4.307.

IBM Inc. (n.d.). Released (2017). *IBM SPSS Statistics for Windows*. Armonk, NY: IBM Corp.

Joaquim, A., Custódio, S., Savva-Bordalo, J., Chacim, S., Carvalhais, I., Lombo, L., & Gomes, R. (2017). Burnout and occupational stress in the medical residents of oncology, haematology and radiotherapy: A prevalence and predictors study in Portugal. *Psychology, Health and Medicine, 23*(3), 317–324. https://doi.org/10.1080/13548506.2017.1344256.

Kelloway, E. K., & Francis, L. (2013). Longitudinal Research and Data Analysis. In R. R. Sinclair, M. Wang, M. Wang & L. E. Tetrick (Eds.), *Research methods in occupational health psychology. Measurement, design, and data analysis* (pp. 374–394). New York, NY: Routledge Taylor & Francis Group.

Lapa, T. A., Carvalho, S. A., Viana, J. S., Ferreira, P. L., & Pinto-Gouveia, J. (2016). Stressors in anaesthesiology: Development and validation of a new questionnaire: A cross-sectional study of Portuguese anaesthesiologists. *European Journal of Anaesthesiology, 33*(11), 807–815. https://doi.org/10.1097/EJA.0000000000000518.

Laranjeira, C. A. (2012a). The effects of perceived stress and ways of coping in a sample of Portuguese health workers. *Journal of Clinical Nursing, 21*(11–12), 1755–1762. https://doi.org/10.1111/j.1365-2702.2011.03948.x.

Laranjeira, C. A. (2012b). Translation and adaptation of the Fatigue Severity Scale for use in Portugal. *Applied Nursing Research, 25*(3), 212–217. https://doi.org/10.1016/j.apnr.2010.11.001.

Lazarus, R., & Folkman, S. (1984). *Stress, appraisal and coping*. London: Springer Publishing Company.

Lee, R. L., & Ashforth, B. E. (1996). A meta-analytic examination of the correlates of the three dimensions of job burnout. *Journal of Applied Psychology, 81*(2), 123–133. https://doi.org/10.1037/0021-9010.81.2.123.

Lourenço, S., Carnide, F., Benavides, F. G., & Lucas, R. (2015). Psychosocial work environment and musculoskeletal symptoms among 21-year-old workers: A population-based investigation (2011-2013). *PLoS ONE, 10*(6), 1–11. https://doi.org/10.1371/journal.pone.0130010.

Luchman, J. N., & González-Morales, M. G. (2013). Demands, control, and support: A meta-analytic review of work characteristics interrelationships.

Journal of Occupational Health Psychology, 18(1), 37–52. https://doi.org/10.1037/a0030541.

Macik-Frey, M., Quick, J. C., & Nelson, D. L. (2007). Advances in occupational health: From a stressful beginning to a positive future. *Journal of Management*, 33(6), 809–840. https://doi.org/10.1177/0149206307307634.

Maia, Â. C., & Ribeiro, E. (2010). The psychological impact of motor vehicle accidents on emergency service workers. *European Journal of Emergency Medicine*, 17(5), 296–301. https://doi.org/10.1097/MEJ.0b013e3283356213.

Mäkikangas, A., Kinnunen, U., Feldt, T., & Schaufeli, W. (2016). The longitudinal development of employee well-being: A systematic review. *Work and Stress*, 30(1), 46–70. https://doi.org/10.1080/02678373.2015.1126870.

Mark, G., & Smith, A. P. (2012). Occupational stress, job characteristics, coping, and the mental health of nurses. *British Journal of Health Psychology*, 17(3), 505–521. https://doi.org/10.1111/j.2044-8287.2011.02051.x.

Marôco, J., Marôco, A. L., Leite, E., Bastos, C., Vazão, M. J., & Campos, J. (2016). Burnout em profissionais da saúde Portugueses: Uma análise a nível nacional. [Burnout in Portuguese healthcare professionals: An analysis at the national level. *Acta Medica Portuguesa*, 29(1), 24–30. https://doi.org/10.20344/acta%20med%20port.v29i1.6460.

Marques-Pinto, A., Jesus, É. H., Mendes, A. M. O. C., Fronteira, I., & Roberto, M. S. (2018). Nurses' intention to leave the organization: A mediation study of professional burnout and engagement. *Spanish Journal of Psychology*, 21, E32. https://doi.org/10.1017/sjp.2018.30.

Marques, M. M., Alves, E., Queiros, C., Norton, P., & Henriques, A. (2018). The effect of profession on burnout in hospital staff. *Occupational Medicine*, 68(3), 207–210. https://doi.org/10.1093/occmed/kqy039.

Martinez, L. F., & Ferreira, A. I. (2012). Sick at work: Presenteeism among nurses in a Portuguese public hospital. *Stress and Health*, 28(4), 297–304. https://doi.org/10.1002/smi.1432.

Martins-Pereira, S., Teixeira, C. M., Carvalho, A. S., & Hernández-Marrero, P. (2016). Compared to palliative care, working in intensive care more than doubles the chances of burnout: Results from a nationwide comparative study. *PLoS ONE*, 11(9), e0162340. https://doi.org/10.1371/journal.pone.0162340.

Martins, A., Sales, C., & Joaquim, M. (2016). Assédio moral e capacidade para o trabalho. Estudo exploratório numa universidade pública Portuguesa [Mobbing and Working capacity. An exploratory study in a public university. *International Journal on Working Conditions*, 12, 36–53. ISSN 2182-9535.

Martins, A., Sales-Oliveira, C., & Loureiro, M. J. (2016). Assédio Moral e Capacidade para o Trabalho. Estudo Exploratório numaUniversidade Pública Portuguesa. *International Journal of Working Conditions*, 12, 35-53.

Martins, R., Batista, A. I., & Campos, S. (2015). Stress e burnout em professores da educação especial [Stress and burnout in teachers of special education]. *Gestão e Desenvolvimento*, 23, 193–211. Retrieved from http://www.tojet.net/.

Martins, R., Andrade, A., Albuquerque, C., & Cunha, M. (2015). Stress and burnout in special education teachers. *The Turkish Online Journal of Educational Technology, (Special Issue)*, September, 523-526.

Maslach, C., Schaufeli, W. B., & Leiter, M. P. (2001). Job burnout. *Annual Reviews in Psychology*, 52, 397–422.

McVicar, A. (2005). Workplace stress in nursing: A literature review. *Journal of Advanced Nursing*, 44(6), 633–642. https://doi.org/10.1046/j.0309-2402.2003.02853.x.

Mendes, A., Claro, M., & Robazzi, M. L. (2014). Burnout in nurses working in Portuguese central prisons and type of employment contract. *Medicina Del Lavoro*, 105(3), 214–222.

Mesquita, C. C., Ribeiro, J. C., & Moreira, P. (2011). An exercise program improves health-related quality of life of workers. *Applied Research in Quality of Life*, 7(3), 295–307. https://doi.org/10.1007/s11482-011-9161-7.

Moher, D., Liberati, A., Tetzlaff, J., & Altman, D. G. (2009). Preferred reporting items for systematic reviews and meta-analyses: The PRISMA statement. *Journal of Clinical Epidemiology*, 6(7), e1000097. https://doi.org/10.1016/j.jclinepi.2009.06.005.

Monteiro, S., & Marques-Pinto, A. (2017). Journalists' occupational stress: A comparative study between reporting critical events and domestic news. *Spanish Journal of Psychology*, 20, E34. https://doi.org/10.1017/sjp.2017.33.

Morais, A., Maia, P., Azevedo, A., Amaral, C., & Tavares, J. (2006). Stress and burnout among Portuguese anaesthesiologists. *European Journal of Anaesthesiology*, 23(5), 433–439. https://doi.org/10.1017/S0265021505001882.

Motyka, B. (2019). Employee engagement and performance: A systematic literature review. *International Journal of Management and Economics*, 54(3), 227–244. https://doi.org/10.2478/ijme-2018-0018.

Neto, M., & André, M. H. (2016). Determinantes psicossociais no trabalho e efeitos na saúde: Do reconhecimento à prevenção [Psychosocial determinants at work and health effects: From recognition to prevention]. In M. J. Chambel (Ed.), *Psicologia da Saúde Ocupacional [Occupational Health Psychology]* (pp. 25–47). Lisboa: Practor.

Neto, M., Carvalho, V. S., Chambel, M. J., Manuel, S., Pereira Miguel, J., & Reis, M. F. (2016). Work-family conflict and employee well-being over time. The loss spiral effect. *Journal of Occupational and Environmental Medicine*, 58(5), 429–435. https://doi.org/10.1097/JOM.0000000000000707.

Neto, M., Chambel, M. J., & Carvalho, V. S. (2018). Work-family life conflict and mental well-being. *Occupational Medicine*, 68(6), 364–369. https://doi.org/10.1093/OCCMED/KQY079.

Neto, M., Ferreira, A. I., Martinez, L. F., & Ferreira, P. C. (2017). Workplace bullying and presenteeism: The path through emotional exhaustion and psychological wellbeing. *Annals of Work Exposures and Health*, 61(5), 528–538. https://doi.org/10.1093/annweh/wxx022.

Nielsen, K., Nielsen, M. B., Ogbonnaya, C., Känsälä, M., Saari, E., & Isaksson, K. (2017). Workplace resources to improve both employee well-being and performance: A systematic review and meta-analysis. *Work and Stress*, 31(2), 1–20. https://doi.org/10.1080/02678373.2017.1304463.

O'Connor, K., Muller Neff, D., & Pitman, S. (2018). Burnout in mental health professionals: A systematic review and meta-analysis of prevalence and determinants. *European Psychiatry*, 53(1), 74–89. https://doi.org/10.1016/j.eurpsy.2018.06.003.

Orgambídez-Ramos, A., Borrego-Alés, Y., & Ruiz-Frutos, C. (2017). Empowerment, vulnerabilidad al estrés y burnout en enfermeros portugueses. *Ciência & Saúde Coletiva, 23*(1), 259–266. https://doi.org/10.1590/1413-81232018231.15522015.

Orgambídez-Ramos, A., Borrego-Alés, Y., & Ruiz-Frutos, C. (2018).Empowerment, vulnerabilidad al estrés y burnout en enfermeros portugueses [Empowerment, stress vulnerability and burnout among Portuguese nursing staff]. *Ciencia & Saude Coletiva, 23*(1), 259–266. https://doi.org/10.1590/1413-81232018231.15522015.

Paré, G., Trudel, M. C., Jaana, M., & Kitsiou, S. (2015). Synthesizing information systems knowledge: A typology of literature reviews. *Information and Management, 52*(2), 183–199. https://doi.org/10.1016/j.im.2014.08.008.

Pereira, S. M., Fonseca, A. M., & Carvalho, A. S. (2011). Burnout in palliative care: A systematic review. *Nursing Ethics, 18*(3). 317-326. https://doi.org/10.1177/09697330113980.

Pocinho, M., & Capelo, M. R. (2009). Vulnerabilidade ao stress, estratégias de coping e autoeficácia em professores portugueses [Stress vulnerability, coping strategies and self-efficacy in Portuguese teachers]. *Educação e Pesquisa, 35*(2), 351–367.

Queiros, C., Carlotto, M. S., Kaiseler, M., Dias, S., & Pereira, A. M. (2013). Predictores de burnout en enfermeras: Un enfoque interaccionista [Predictors of burnout in nurses: An interactionist approach]. *Psicothema, 25*(3), 330–335. https://doi.org/10.7334/psicothema2012.246.

Ramos, S., Serranheira, F., & Sousa-Uva, A. (2018). Perceived occupational hazards among cash-in-transit guards. *Revista Brasileira de Medicina do Trabalho, 16*(3), 327–335. https://doi.org/10.5327/Z1679443520180264.

Reis, C., Mestre, C., & Canhão, H. (2013). Prevalence of fatigue in a group of airline pilots. *Aviation Space and Environmental Medicine, 84*(8), 828–833. https://doi.org/10.3357/ASEM.3548.2013.

Reis, H. I. S., Vale, C., Camacho, C., Estrela, C., & Dixe, M. A. (2018). Burnout among occupational therapists in Portugal: A study of specific factors. *Occupational Therapy in Health Care, 32*(3), 275–289. https://doi.org/10.1080/07380577.2018.1497244.

Riahi, S. (2011). Role stress amongst nurses at the workplace: Concept analysis. *Journal of Nursing Management, 19*(6), 721–731. https://doi.org/10.1111/j.1365-2834.2011.01235.x.

Rodrigues, V. M., & Ferreira, A. S. (2011). Stressors in nurses working in intensive care units. *Revista latino-americana de enfermagem, 19*(4), 1025–1032. https://doi.org/10.1590/s0104-11692011000400023.

Rodrigues, S., Kaiseler, M., Queirós, C., & Basto-Pereira, M. (2017). Daily stress and coping among emergency response officers: A case study. *International Journal of Emergency Services, 6*(2), 122–133. https://doi.org/10.1108/IJES-10-2016-0019.

Rodrigues, S., Paiva, J. S., Dias, D., Aleixo, M., Filipe, R. M., & Cunha, J. P. S. (2018). Cognitive impact and psychophysiological effects of stress using a biomonitoring platform. *International Journal of Environmental Research and Public Health, 15*(6), 1080. https://doi.org/10.3390/ijerph15061080.

Rodrigues, S., Paiva, J. S., Dias, D., & Cunha, J. P. S. (2018). Stress among on-duty firefighters: An ambulatory assessment study. *PeerJ, 6*, e5967. https://doi.org/10.7717/peerj.5967.

Roque, H., Veloso, A., Silva, I., & Costa, P. (2015). Estresse ocupacional e satisfação dos usuários com os cuidados de saúde primários em Portugal [Occupational stress and user satisfaction with primary health care in Portugal]. *Ciência & Saúde Coletiva, 20*(10), 3087–3097. https://doi.org/10.1590/1413-812320152010.00832015.

Ruotsalainen, J. H., Verbeek, J. H., Mariné, A., & Consol, S. (2015). Preventing occupational stress in healthcare workers. *Cochrane Database of Systematic Reviews, 4*(11) https://doi.org/10.1002/14651858.CD002892.pub5.www.cochranelibrary.com.

Sá, L., & Fleming, M. (2008). Bullying, burnout, and mental health amongst portuguese nurses. *Issues in Mental Health Nursing, 29*(4), 411–426. https://doi.org/10.1080/01612840801904480.

Salvagioni, D. A. J., Melanda, F. N., Mesas, A. E., González, A. D., Gabani, F. L., & De Andrade, S. M. (2017). Physical, psychological and occupational consequences of job burnout: A systematic review of prospective studies. *PLoS ONE, 12*(10), e0185781. https://doi.org/10.1371/journal.pone.0185781.

Santos, M. C., Barros, L., & Carolino, E. (2010). Occupational stress and coping resources in physiotherapists: A survey of physiotherapists in three general hospitals. *Physiotherapy, 96*(4), 303–310. https://doi.org/10.1016/j.physio.2010.03.001.

Satuf, C., Monteiro, S., Pereira, H., Esgalhado, G., Marina Afonso, R., & Loureiro, M. (2016). The protective effect of job satisfaction in health, happiness, well-being and self-esteem. *International Journal of Occupational Safety and Ergonomics, 24*(2), 181–189. https://doi.org/10.1080/10803548.2016.1216365.

Schaufeli, W.B., & Salanova, M. (2007). Work Engagement: An Emerging Psychological Concept and itsIimplications for Organizations. In S. W. Gilliland, D. D. Steiner & D. P. Skarlicki (Eds.), *Research in social issues in management. Managing social and ethical issues in organizations* (Vol. 5, pp. 135–177). Greenwich, CT: Information Age Publishers.

Schaufeli, W. B., & Taris, T. W. (2014). Bridging Occupational, Organizational and Public Health. In Bauer, G. F. & Hämmig, O. (Eds.), *Bridging Occupational, Organizational and Public Health: A Transdisciplinary Approach* (pp. 117–132). Springer Netherlands. https://doi.org/10.1007/978-94-007-5640-3.

Seidler, A., Thinschmidt, M., Deckert, S., Then, F., Hegewald, J., Nieuwenhuijsen, K., & Riedel-Heller, S. G. (2014). The role of psychosocial working conditions on burnout and its core component emotional exhaustion - A systematic review. *Journal of Occupational Medicine and Toxicology, 9*(1), 10. https://doi.org/10.1186/1745-6673-9-10.

Silva, V., Costa, P., Pereira, I., Faria, R., Salgueira, A. P., Costa, M. J., & Morgado, P. (2017). Depression in medical students: Insights from a longitudinal study. *BMC Medical Education, 17*(184), 1–19. https://doi.org/10.1186/s12909-017-1006-0.

Sousa, C., Pereira Machado, J., Greten, H., & Coimbra, D. (2016). Occupational diseases of professional orchestra musicians from northen Portugal. *Medical Problems of Performing Artists, 31*(1), 8–12.

Swider, B. W., & Zimmerman, R. D. (2010). Born to burnout: A meta-analytic path model of personality, job burnout, and work outcomes. *Journal of*

Vocational Behavior, 76(2), 487–506. https://doi.org/10.1016/j.jvb.2010.01.003.
Taris, T. W. (2006). Is there a relationship between burnout and objective performance? A critical review of 16 studies. *Work and Stress*, 20(4), 316–334. https://doi.org/10.1080/02678370601065893.
Taris, T. W., & Schaufeli, W. B. (2016). The Job Demands-Resources model. In Clarke, T. S., Probst, M., Guldenmund, F. & Passmore, J. (Eds.), *The Wiley Blackwell Handbook of the Psychology of Occupational Safety and Workplace Health* (pp. 157–180). Chichester: John Wiley. https://doi.org/10.1002/9781118979013.
Teixeira, C., Ribeiro, O., Fonseca, A. M., & Carvalho, A. S. (2013). Burnout in intensive care units - a consideration of the possible prevalence and frequency of new risk factors: A descriptive correlational multicentre study. *BMC Anesthesiology*, 13(1), 38. https://doi.org/10.1186/1471-2253-13-38.
Teixeira, C., Ribeiro, O., Fonseca, A. M., & Carvalho, A. S. (2014). Ethical decision making in intensive care units: A burnout risk factor? Results from a multicentre study conducted with physicians and nurses. *Journal of Medical Ethics*, 40(2), 97–103. https://doi.org/10.1136/medethics-2012-101236.
Turner, N., Barling, J., & Zacharatos, A. (2002). Positive psychology at work. In C. R. E. Snyder & S. J. E. Lopez (Eds.), *Handbook of Positive Psychology* (pp. 715–728). New York: Oxford University Press.
Von Humboldt, S., Leal, I., Laneiro, T., & Tavares, P. (2013). Examining occupational stress, sources of stress and stress management strategies through the eyes of management consultants: A multiple correspondence analysis for latent constructs. *Stress and Health*, 29(5), 410–420. https://doi.org/10.1002/smi.2487.
Zapf, D., Dormann, C., & Frese, M. (1996). Longitudinal studies in organizational stress research: A review of the literature with reference to methodological issues. *Journal of Occupational Health Psychology*, 1(2), 145–169. https://doi.org/10.1037/1076-8998.1.2.145.

12 Organizational Stress in Russia

Natalia Ermasova, Natalia Rekhter, and Sergey Ermasov

Introduction

Work-related stress is an issue of growing concern in developing countries due to globalization and the changing nature of work. The impact of stress can be seen in many aspects of human life. It is evident in the feelings and perceptions of people when they do not have enough time, skills, or resources to effectively handle personal or professional demands (Hyde & Allen, 1996; Nichols, 2008; Selye 1956, 1974). Research has indicated that work-related stress is considered a disease or a cause of disease (Selye, 1956, 1974; Doublet, 2000; Kinman & Jones, 2005; Nguyen, Kass, Mujtaba, & Tran, 2014). Stress in the workplace not only impacts individual performance, but also the organization's effectiveness as a whole. Work-related stress may affect the organization's effectiveness due to the costs associated with increased absenteeism and staff turnover, replacement of absent workers, increased unsafe working practices, accident rates, complaints from clients/customers, and reduced productivity, performance, and profitability of organization (Nguyen et al., 2014).

The purpose of this study is to examine the level of stress in Russia. We chose Russia for several reasons. Russia is the eighth largest economy in the world by nominal value – with an estimated GDP of $2,117.8 billion in 2016 (Australian Government-Department of Foreign Affairs and Trade, 2014). According to the Russian Federation Federal State Statistical Service, Russia had a population of about 143.3 million in 2016 and is considered the largest country in the world in terms of geographic territory. Russia's labor force consists of 75.24 million workers or 52.8% of the total population.

Russia has emerged as one of the key players in the world – both politically and economically. Since the collapse of the Soviet Union, Russia has made remarkable improvements to become more open in terms of its market and global integration. With its membership in the World Trade Organization (WTO) in 2012, Russia has strengthened its position in the world economy and has opened more opportunities for its international trade. However, recently, the political and economic environment in Russia has shifted to more restricted norms. These fluctuations made Russia uniquely positioned in terms of changes in cultural norms and behaviors, peoples' motivation, and entrepreneurship (Nguyen et al., 2014). The above observations make it important to analyze the current developments in Russia. According to the Russian employment agency Unity, about 35% of managers' willful termination of employment declared that one of the main reasons for this dismissal is stress at work. In addition, there has been limited number of research examining work-related stress in Russia. This paper expands the body of knowledge of stress management and provides practical implications for managers who work with this specific population. In addition, by using a widely accepted questionnaire survey created in the United States on a Russian sample, this study further fulfills the need to validate such instrument for cross-cultural comparison purposes later on.

Literature Review

Work-Related Stress

According to Ellis (2006), stress is "a sequence of events with the presence of a concern about successful performance and fear of negative consequences resulting from performance failure, which evokes powerful negative emotions of anxiety, anger, and irritation". The more encompassing definition is provided by Nguyen, Mujtaba, and Boehmer (2012) who states that "stress can be all those feelings and perceptions in lack of time, ability, skill, or resources to effectively deal with personal or professional demands in a given time" (p.13). Stress describes the individual's perception of the psychological situation – which becomes a critical factor (Fell, Wayne, & Wallace, 1980; Folkman & Lazarus, 2015; Finn, 1997; Goldbaum, 2012; Gorelova, 2013; Halder & Mahato, 2013).

Research related to different aspects of stress is typically viewed as a subspecialization within medical sociology – a perspective that obscures commonalities with more traditional sociological areas of inquiry – especially social stratification. (Aneshensel, 1992). Pearlin (1989) suggested that stress research tends to be concerned less with the consequences of stressful life experience than with outcomes of illness – especially psychological disorders.

Various research associates stress with the multiple roles each individual plays in life. For instance, Bolino and Turnley (2005) found that the higher levels of individual initiative are associated with higher levels of employee role overload, job stress, and work-family conflict. They asserted that the relationship between individual initiative and work-family conflict is moderated by gender. Their findings suggested that the relationship between individual initiative and work-family conflict is stronger among women than among men.

There are authors who analyze occupational stress across diverse occupations. Johnson et al. (2005) compared the experience of occupational stress across a large and diverse set of occupations and found that six occupations (i.e., prison officers and the police, ambulance workers, teachers, social services, and customer services – call centers) in the United Kingdom are reporting worse than average scores on each of the factors – physical health, psychological well-being, and job satisfaction.

Some authors analyzed the differences in work overload stress perceptions of working adults in different countries. In a series of cross-cultural studies, Vietnamese working adults appeared to experience more work overload stress than their German, Dutch, Russian, and Japanese counterparts (Nguyen *et al.* 2012; Nguyen, Lee, Mujtaba, & Ruijs, 2013; Nguyen, Ermasova, Pham, & Mujtaba, 2013; Nguyen, Mujtaba, & Pham, 2013; Nguyen et al., 2014). Nguyen et al. (2012) found that German working adults appear to experience more work overload stress than Dutch working adults. However, no significant difference in stress scores was found between German and Japanese working adults (Nguyen *et al.*, 2014).

A study by Ivanova (2014) analyzed the effect of having full-time or part-time jobs on the stress level of full-time undergraduate students in Russia. The survey conducted among 2,804 such students from eight regions of Russia revealed that, among the students who had full-time or part-time jobs (54.3% of participants), 31.4% of men and 43.5% of women reported feeling stressed at work; and the same percentage of students reported feeling severely fatigued due to pressure and exhaustion of combining work with studying. An additional 10.2% of men and 15.4% of women reported feeling severely fatigued and stressed at the same time.

Shevchuk, Strebkov, and Davis (2018) suggest that "working time adversely influences satisfaction with work-life balance. The presence of extrinsic values reduces satisfaction with work-life balance, while the presence of intrinsic values improves satisfaction with work-life balance" (p. 747). It could be explained that the same job is associated "with more positive psychosocial outcomes for people who value the work itself as opposed to people who value material rewards and conditions. They are able to secure emotional rewards from the work process itself" (Shevchuk *et al.* (2018, p. 739).

Beehr, Walsh, and Taber (1976) analyzed work-related stress of 79 male and 64 female members of a white-collar union employed in drafting, mechanical, and technical-clerical jobs in a Midwestern manufacturing company. They found that some effects of role stresses on individually valued states were incompatible with their effects on three organizationally valued motivational states: involvement, an effort toward quantity, and an effort toward quality.

Stress can be positive and motivating when it is short. For example, when one needs to urgently submit reports, sometimes, the work is done more efficiently under the pressure of a deadline. Moreover, work in conditions of constant scarce resources – including time – is a mid-level stressor. Similar tension occurs when a person has: (1) difficulty in dealing with employers, (2) worries about career development, and (3) contradictory tasks. The risk of serious and chronic stress increases when there are sudden changes in working conditions or when a person is deprived of the support of colleagues, family, and leadership. Stress is formed from a combination of these factors and the inability to relax. The results of constant work-related stress are complex somatic pathology, reduced adaptive abilities of the organism, and chronic fatigue syndrome. The symptoms of work-related stress are fatigue, weakness in the morning, frequent headaches, insomnia, conflicts, or susceptibility to loneliness.

Many scholars prove a connection between chronic job stress and a host of negative outcomes among police officers (Ermasova, Cross, & Ermasova, 2020; Keinan & Malach-Pines, 2007; Kerley, 2005; Larned, 2010; Lazarus & Folkman, 1984; Lindsay, 2008). Stress can lead to depression, and depression can lead to negative coping techniques such as violence, alcohol, and substance abuse (Larned, 2010; Lazarus & Folkman, 1984; Violanti, 2001; Violanti et al, 2011). There is a longitudinal study by Gafarov, Gromova, and Panov (2019) on the impact of work-related stress on the risk of cardiovascular diseases. The study that was conducted over a 16-year period among 1,346 men and women in Siberia, Russia revealed that the risk of having cardiovascular diseases among people who are experiencing work-related stress is 3.6 times higher for men and 3.2 times higher for women, compared to individuals with no or low work-related stress. Similar results were found by Kivimäki and Kawachi (2015) in their research consisting of 232,767 respondents who demonstrated that the risk of cardiovascular diseases among people with the reported high-stress jobs was 1.26 times higher than the risk among people with low or no risk jobs.

Economic and Social Stress in Russia and Its Impact on Work-Related Stress

Yiu, Bruton, and Lu (2005) argued that the early Russian transition experience provided uniquely important insights into the historic characteristics of business groups, because it represented a case in which market failures were important; the institutional transition was in place; and business groups were young and newly formed. Since the beginning of *Perestroika* or "openness" in 1987, the business environment in Russia has been turbulent and unpredictable (Holt, Ralston, & Terpstra, 1994; Puffer, 1996). Ermasova (2013) highlighted a high level of uncertainty in economic, investment, and social aspects of life and business in Russia. In the case of Russia, Carr (2006–2007) showed that the effect of the unstable and uncertain economic environment in the country had an impact on the strategic decisions of the Russian people. Alexander Moskvin, the Scientific Director of the clinic Infoecology Social Stress Clinic, said in his interview in Gorelova (2013) that "Negative social factors have much more influence on the stress level of managers in Russia than their foreign counterparts". He highlighted the following reasons of the high-stress level of managers in Russia: (1) the general situation in the country, (2) the uncertainty, which increases negative expectations, (3) distrust of people, (4) the lack of uniform rules in business, and (5) the constant changes in accounting and legislature that do not allow managers to develop a sequence of actions.

According to Gupta, Shipp, Nash, Herrera, and Healey (2013), Russia has been a diverse and socially volatile country. Although the country is considered politically Russian, 20% of its population is comprised of ethnically non-Russian minorities. There are over 100 minority languages in various regions. A considerable body of research suggested that ethnic or racial hostility and their behavioral expressions were likely to be relatively more intense in areas where minorities comprise a smaller segment of the population than in other areas (Kleinpenning & Hagendoorn, 1993; Levin & McDevitt, 1993; Dekker, Malová, & Hoogendoorn, 2003; Gudkov, 2003).

Russia experienced economic crises in 1992, 1998, 2008, and 2016 to 2017 that led to the dramatic impoverishment of the population, social anxiety, and high levels of stress. These crises brought a lot of financial and social problems to Russia – including a high level of inflation and unemployment. Russia experienced two serious economic crises in 1992 and 1998 that were accompanied by a drop in personal income and rapid impoverishment. The start of the transition period – a "shock therapy" – occurred in 1992 after a political decision to accomplish a rapid transition to a market economy. In 1992, consumer prices grew 3.5 times faster than wages and exploded by 2,500% (Goskomstat, 1993; Klugman& Braithwaite, 1998). As a result of these dramatic changes in the economic and financial situation, the life expectancy of Russian males dropped from 63.8 to 57.7 years from 1992 to 1994. Female life expectancy dropped from 74.4 years to 71.2 years (Gavrilova, Evdokushkina, Semyonova, & Gavrilov, 2001). Gavrilova and Gavrilov (2011) suggest that "each economic crisis was associated with a rapid increase in stress-related violent mortality. On the other hand, new factors (hazards) related to the unsafety of social environment and young age mortality are becoming more and more significant" (p.18).

In addition to the decrease in the life expectancy, the economic "shock therapy" led to the increase in the so-called "social" diseases – such as depression, alcoholism, drug abuse, and suicidal attempts – which are caused by a chronic and acute state of stress and are currently afflicting the majority of the population in Russia (Shtemberg, 2014).

The 2008 economic and financial crisis in the United States of America was contingent for the Russian economy. Grima and Caruana (2017) found that "the dependency on the United States is more persistent in countries which depend on commodity prices, such as Brazil and Russia, rather than for countries whose economic growth is dependent on finished products, such as China and India" (p.729).

The World Trade Organization 2007 Report (2007, p. 1) highlighted the problem of work-related stress in Russia. Working adults in Russia are "subjected to rapid and drastic economical and social changes – where there is an increased demand for the adaptation of workers, the overriding of traditional values, the reorientation of the occupational health system, and generally poor working conditions". Psychosocial stress has increased as a result of the unprecedented changes in Russia's economic condition and the reduction of "safety net" services. During the time of transition, the population of the Russian Federation had to deal with: (1) the increased demands of learning new skills, (2) the need to adopt new ways of working, (3) the pressure of the demand for higher productivity and higher technical and computer skills, (4) the demands for increased quality of work and time pressure, (5) higher job competition, (6) increased job insecurity and fewer benefits, and (7) less time for co-workers and socializing. Moreover, the majority of people lost their life savings, were deprived of their social benefits, and experienced a higher level of corruption and criminal activities. All these changes caused an increase in the stress level among the Russian population – resulting in psychotic, stress-related disorders (Shtemberg, 2014). For instance, the number of psychotic, stress-related disorders for 1,000 adults in Russia has increased from 16.5 in 1950 to 1970 to 31.1 in 1971 to 1995 (Schepin, 1998). The number of psychotic, stress-related disorders among children from newborn to 14-year-olds was 6.3 cases for every 100,000 children in 1990 and 13.3 cases in 2000 (Gurovich, Voloshin, & Golland, 2002). According to Dmitrieva, a Director of the State Research Center of the Social and Criminal Psychiatry and also a Minister of Health of Russian Federation in 1997, 61,5% of the population of the Russian Federation requires some type of the psychotherapy, and 40% of the population suffers from the various psychological disorders – a majority of which are caused by stress (in Shtemberg, 2014).

Based on the report from the World Health Organization (WHO) (2011), the number of suicides in Russia is between 26 to 39 suicides per 100,000 of the population, depending on the source of the report. In some regions – Volgo-Vyatski, East and West Siberia, the Far East, and Ural – the number of suicides reaches 81 cases per 100,000 of the population, and in the Republics of Komi and Udmurtia, it reaches

150–180 cases per 100,000 of the population. These numbers are at least three times as high as the average rate of suicide in all other developed world countries. Half of the people who committed suicide in Russia are 30 years old or younger. Meanwhile, according to the WHO, if the number of suicides in a country exceeds 20 or more cases per 100,000 of the population, then this is a reflection of the country's deep psychological and social crises. Shtemberg (2014) asserts that the dynamic of the suicide rate in Russia from 1990 to 2000 is reflective of the Stress Theory – which describes three levels of stress and stress-related behavior. During the first phase, the increase in stress levels leads to a rapid increase in suicide rates. This phase is followed by the adaptation and the decrease in the suicide rate in the environment where stress level remains high. The third phase – exhaustion – results in another spike in the suicide rates. All three phases of the Stress Theory have presented themselves in Russia during the last three decades.

Declining health status was also closely connected to stress-induced illnesses. In a study conducted in 2018 among 1,500 respondents in the two Russian cities of Vologda and Cherepovetc, it was revealed that among respondents who reported experiencing stress often or very often, 18% reported having regular headaches, 35% had regular illnesses, 9% had a stress-related short-term disability, 7% had a stress-related long-term disability, and 34% experienced stressed-induced various chronic conditions. This is in comparison to the corresponding 9%, 16%, 2%, 2%, and 26% of the same conditions among respondents who reported seldomly experiencing stress. Among respondents who reported having regular stress, 12.7% evaluated their health as poor compared to 6.1% of respondents who reported having no or low stress in their lives (Korolenko, 2019).

Besides this, various global and local changes led to increasing demands on a growing number of workers. When workers are unable to deal with these demands, work-related stress may result. When stress persists or occurs repeatedly, it can have various negative effects on workers and the companies they work for. Psychosocial stress may manifest itself as depression, anxiety, domestic violence, an increase in smoking, work injuries, an increase in alcohol consumption, and divorce.

In Russia, managers have to spend a lot of effort on defending themselves in response to pressure from top managers; this can cause stress. Another feature of Russian corporate stress is the habit of bringing personal problems to work. Russian leaders traditionally broadcast their emotions on subordinates (Matveev, 2002).

Bokhan et al. (2018) found that the "lack of mutual understanding in the family may lead to depression, estrangement, a decline in psychological and physical health, and a decrease in the partners' ability to work" (p. 52). According to the World Population Review (2019), Russia has a significantly high level of divorces (4.7 per 1,000 of the population). Russia also has the highest rate of divorce in the world since 2011. According to the United Nations data from 2011, Russia's divorce rate was 4.8 divorces for every 1,000 residents.

Additionally and recently, Russians became one of the top users of social network sites (SNS). There is an estimated number of 73.1 million SNS users in Russia or approximately 51.9% of the entire population (comScore, 2013, The Statistical Portal, 2019). Russians also rank third in the world in terms of the number of minutes each user spends on SNSs. On average, users devote approximately 58 minutes a day interacting with various pages, groups, and events (The Statistics Portal, 2019). According to different research sources, social media can play the role of both a stressor and a stress reliever in various circumstances – including work-related stress (Harzer & Rush, 2015; Powell, 2019).

There are a plethora of positive aspects associated with the use of social media, such as, for instance, instant connectivity with like-minded people, enhanced access to a large spectrum of informational sources, rapid knowledge sharing, possibilities of crowdfunding, and the like (Brufonski, 2012; Amedie, 2015; Deen and Hendricks, 2012). However, there are also social media-associated concerns and problems. Several studies have identified a phenomenon called "Facebook depression". The phenomenon, that received its name from the most popular social media platform, describes stress caused by the pressure of staying engaged and seeking acceptance and approval of virtual friends. This type of stress is particularly persistent among teenagers, who feel the need to be perpetually engaged in texting, instant messaging, posting, liking, sharing, replying to posts, and seeking reassurance of their actions, opinions, and appearances from their peers. Often, this type of social media behavior causes anxieties, which can lead to depression and occasionally even suicidal behavior (O'Keeffe & Clarke-Pearson, 2011; Amedie, 2015).

Recently, studies have brought into discussion another stressor caused by the presence of SNS. The cause of stress is a sense of apprehension or even fear that other people might be having rewarding experiences from which one is absent. The stressor received an unofficial title of "Fear of Missing Out" (FoMO) and is associated with the feeling of fear, worries, anxieties, depression, and stress (Przybylski, Murayama, DeHaan, & Gladwell, 2013, Beyens, Frison, & Eggermont, 2016). The type of stress that can be linked to FoMO, such as, seeing Instagram, Snapchat, or Facebook pictures of events in which teenagers were not invited, receiving no likes on their posts, and other similar instances (Fox & Moreland, 2015, Beyens, et al., 2016). Studies by Chion, Lee, and Liao (2015) and Rekhter and Hossler (2019) reported that many SNS users exhibit distress when, for some reason, certain SNS were not available for them or when their smartphones went missing because of the FoMO of being socially excluded.

Social media sites – such as Instagram, Pinterest, Facebook, and blogging – provide opportunities for enhanced image perception which, consequently, leads to creating an environment of unrealistic and unachievable images of perfection (e.g., perfect surroundings, perfect food, perfect careers, perfect bodies, perfect lives, etc.). Several studies have demonstrated that this superficial imagery and struggle for virtual excellence and flawlessness can cause depressive anxiety as well as long-term emotional and psychological problems (Amedie, 2015; Fardouly, Diedrichs, Vartanian, & Hallwell, 2015).

Another problem with work-related stress is that drinking is one of the major coping mechanisms for Russians. Some researchers consider social stress as a major determinant of the sharp increase of drinking in Russia (Pridemore, 2002; Shapiro, 1997; Vlassov, 1999). Pridemore (2002) highlights that rates of alcohol consumption and homicide in Russia are among the highest in the world, and already-high levels have increased dramatically after the collapse of the Soviet Union. Russian culture is more tolerant of those who drink in excess and are more accustomed to personal and social problems that follow drinking (Pridemore, 2002). Cockerham, Hinote, & Abbott (2006) found that "females carried a much heavier burden of psychological distress than males, but this distress did not translate into greater alcohol consumption and smoking for these women or for men" (p.2381).

A specific problem of work-related stress is the presence of two workforces in many Russian firms. The first consists of older workers who have a traditional Russian mindset and resist change. The second workforce is made up of young, aggressive "New Russians" who are generally eager to adapt. Members of this group are driven by career ambitions and often have some training in business and English or a few years' experience working for a foreign firm in sales or marketing. It also appears to be a common pattern to place younger workers in charge of older ones early in their careers, thereby adding to the tension in the workplace. This indicates that Russians with different age groups may have different perceptions of work-related stress.

The study by Ermasova, Nguyen, and Bruce (2017) found that Russian working adults in this sample perceived moderate work overload stress. They did not find any significant difference in the overload of stress scores of Russian working adults based on age, gender, level of education, work experience, and management experience. Ermasova *et al.* (2017) found a significant difference in the overload stress scores of Russian working adults based on religion. Muslim practitioners had the highest scores compared to Christian and non-practicing groups. Religious minorities may feel more stressed because of how they feel about ethnic or racial hostility and their behavioral expressions.

Conclusions and Recommendations

Russian citizens lived through a unique political and economic transition in the 1990s; there were many financial and economic crises. These changes not only created new challenges, but also resulted in a high level of stress in the country – including a high level of work overload stress. It is important to be aware of the role played by Russian history and culture, as well as the unique social, political, and economic circumstances that the nation faced. According to Pietilä and Rytkönen (2008), "stress, as a concept, has emerged in a wide range of different institutional sites – such as the media and public health policy – and has become a discursive entity of contemporary social life in Russia" (p. 327).

The high level of stress is combined with unhealthy coping methods in Russia. "Many people turn to unhealthy coping methods when it comes to handling stress – such as overeating, drug or alcohol abuse, procrastinating, or sleeping too much – and, while these will offer temporary relief, in the long run, they can do more harm than good" (Jones, 2011). Russia has the highest level of alcohol consumption and divorce rate in the world.

Future studies should look into different types of work-related stress in addition to overload stress. Finally, this study only focused on Russian respondents. Future studies should examine the stress perception of people from different countries for comparative purposes, since the workforce has become more globalized and diverse now more than ever.

References

Amedie, J. (2015). The impact of social media on society (2015). *Advanced Writing: Pop Culture Intersections*. 2. Retrieved; https://scholarcommons.scu.edu/engl_176/2.

Aneshensel, C. (1992). Social stress: Theory and research. *Annual Review of Sociology, 18*, 15–38.

Australian Government-Department of Foreign Affairs and Trade. (2014). *Russian Federation*. Retrieved from http://www.dfat.gov.au/geo/fs/russ.pdf.

Beehr, T. A., Walsh, J. T., & Taber, T. D. (1976). Relationships of stress to individually and organizationally valued states: Higher order needs as a moderator. *Journal of Applied Psychology, 61*(1), 41–47.

Beyens, I., Frison, E., & Eggermont, S. (2016). "I don't want to miss a thing": Adolescents' fear of missing out and its relationship to adolescents' social needs, Facebook use, and Facebook related stress. *Computers in Human Behavior, 64*, 1–8.

Brufonski, Dedria (2012). The Global Impact of Social Media. Detroit, MI: Greenhaven Press.

Bokhan, T. G., Terekhina, O. V., Shabalovskaya, M. V., Leshchinskaia, S. B., Silaeva, A. V., Naku, E. A., & Agarkova, L. A. (2018). Spouses' psychological states and family relations in families with natural and induced pregnancies. *Psychology in Russia, 11*(4), 50–67.

Bolino, M. C., & Turnley, W. H. (2005). The personal costs of citizenship behavior: The relationship between individual initiative and role overload, job stress, and work-family conflict. *Journal of Applied Psychology*, 90(4), 740–748.

Carr, C. (2006-2007). Russian strategic investment decision practices compared to those of great Britain, Germany, the United States, and Japan. *International Studies of Management and Organization*, 36(4), 82–110.

Central Intelligence Agency. (2013). World Factbook: Russia. Retrieved from https://www.cia.gov/library/publications/the-world-factbook/geos/rs.html.

Cockerham, W. C., Hinote, B. P., & Abbott, P. (2006 Nov). Psychological distress, gender, and health lifestyles in Belarus, Kazakhstan, Russia, and Ukraine. *Social Science & Medicine*, 63(9), 2381–2394. 10.1016/j.socscimed. 2006.06.001.

comScore. (2013, April 12). Which sites capture the most screen time in Russia? Message posted to Engagement. Europe. Retrieved from http://www.comscoredatamine.com/2013/04/which-sites-capture-the-most-screen-time-in-russia/.

Chion, W.-B., Lee, C.-C., & Liao, D.-C. (2015). Acebook effect of social distress: Priming with online social networking thoughts can alter the perceived distress due to social exclusion. *Comouter in Human Behavior*, 49, 230–236. 10.1016/j.chb.2015.02.064.

Cockerham, W., Hinote, B., & Abbott, P. (2006). Psychological distress, gender, and health lifestyles in Belarus, Kazakhstan, Russia, and Ukraine. *Social Science & Medicine*, 63(9), 2381–2394.

Deen, Hana S. & Hendricks, John A. (2012). *Social media: usage and impact* (2012 Ed.). Lanham, Md.: Lexington Books, 307.

Dekker, H., Malová, D., & Hoogendoorn, S. (2003). Nationalism and its explanations. *Political Psychology*, 24(2), 345–376.

Doublet, S. (2000). *The stress myth*. Chesterfield, MO: Science & Humanities Press.

Ellis, A. P. (2006). System breakdown: The role of mental models and transactive memory in the relationship between acute stress and team performance. *Academy of Management Journal*, 49(3), 576–589.

Ermasova, N. B. (2013). *Risk management organization* (2nd Ed.). Moscow: CTI Dashkov Co.

Ermasova, N., Nguyen, L. D., & Bruce, M. (2017). Leadership and overload stress orientations of German and Russian working adults: Does government work experience make a difference? *Public Organization Review*, 17(1), 39–59.

Ermasova, N., Cross, A., & Ermasova, E. (2020). Perceived stress and coping among law enforcement officers: An empirical analysis of patrol versus non-patrol officers in Illinois, USA. *Journal of Police and Criminal Psychology*, 35, 48–63. https://doi.org/10.1007/s11896-019-09356-z.

Fardouly, J., Diedrichs, P., Vartanian, L., & Hallwell, E. (2015). Social omparison and social media: The impact of Facebook on young women's body imapge concerns and mood. *Body image*, 13, 38–25. https://doi.org/10.1016/j.bodyim.2014.12.002.

Fell, R. D., Wayne, C. R., & Wallace, W. (1980). Psychological joh stress and the police officer. *Journal of Police Science and Administration*, 8(No. 2), 139–144.

Fiedler, M. L. (n.d.). *Officer safety and wellness: An overview of the issues.* Retrieved from http://cops.usdoj.gov/pdf/OSWG/e091120401-OSWGReport.pdf.

Finn, P. (1997). Reducing stress: An organization-centered approach. *FBI - Law Enforcement Bulletin*, 66(8), 20–26.

Folkman, S., & Lazarus, R. (2015, September 23). Stress. Retrieved from stress and cognitive appraisal. https://explorable.com/stress-and-cognitive-appraisal.

Fox, J., & Moreland, J. J. (2015). The dark side of social networking sites: An exploration of the relational and psychological stressors associated with Facebook use and affordances. *Computers in Human Behavior, 45*, 168–176. 10.1016/j.chb.2014.11.083.

Gafarov, V. V., Gromova, E. A., Panov, D. O., et al., (2019). Effect of stress at work on the risk of cardiovascular diseases among the population of 25–64 years in Russia/Siberia (WHO program "MONICA-psychosocial". *Therapeutic Archive, 91*(1), 8–18. 10.26442/00403660.2019.01.000022.

Gavrilova, N., Evdokushkina, G., Semyonova, & Gavrilov, L. (2001). Economic Crises, Stress and Mortality in Russia. The Population Association of America 2001 Annual Meeting (Session 106 "Violence, Stress, and Health"). March 28–31, 2001 Washington DC., USA. Retrived from http://longevity-science.org/Gavrilova-PAA-2001.pdf.

Gavrilova, N. & Gavrilov, I. (2011). Ageing and longevity: Mortality laws and mortality forecasts for ageing populations. *Demografie, 53*(2), 109-128.

Grima, S., & Caruana, L. (2017). The effect of the financial crisis on emerging markets: A comparative analysis of the stock market situation before and after. *European Research Studies, 20*(4), 727–753.

Goldbaum, E. (2012, July 9). *Police officer stress creates significant health risks compared to general population, study finds.* Retrieved from http://www.buffalo.edu/news/releases/2012/07/13532.html.

Gorelova, E. (2013). Стресс по-русски отличается от стресса американского или скандинавского.Эксперты советуют: бороться с русским стрессом надо тоже по-иному. [Stress in Russian is different from American or Scandinavian stress. Experts advise: to fight Russian must also stress differently]. *Vedomosti.* Retrieved from http://www.vedomosti.ru/career/news/18927531/russkij-stress.

Goskomstat. (1993). Social and economic status of Russian Federation in January-March, 1993, *Economic Review No.4.* Moscow: Goskomstat. [in Russian].

Gudkov, L. (2003). Massovaia identichnost' i institutsional'noe nasilie [Mass identity and institutional violence]. *Vestnik Obshchestvennogo Mneniia, 67*, 28–44, September/October.

Gupta, N., Shipp, S., Nash, S., Herrera, J., & Healey, D. (2013). *Industrial and innovation policies in Russia, South Korea, and Brazil. Defense Analyses* (IDA) (2013) DASW01-04-C-0003 IDA Paper P-5079, 19. Retrieved from https://www.ida.org/-/media/feature/publications/i/in/innovation-policies-of-russia/ida-p-5079.ashx.

Gurovich, I. Y., Voloshin, V. M., & Golland, V. B. (2002). Actual problems of children psychological services in Russia. *Social and Clinical Psychiatry, 2*, 5–9. [In Russian].

Halder, S., & Mahato, A. (2013). Stress and psychological well being status among health care professionals. *International Journal of Occupational Safety and Health*, 3(1), 32–35.

Harzer, C., & Rush, W. (2015). The relationship of character strength with coping, work-related stress, and job satisfaction. *Frontiers and Psycology*, 6, 165–172. 10.3389/fpsyg.2015.00165.

Holt, D. H., Ralston, D. A., & Terpstra, R. H. (1994). Constraints on capitalism in Russia: The managerial psyche. *California Management Review*, 36(3), 124–141.

Hyde, D., & Allen, R. (1996). *Investigations in stress control* (4th Ed.). Boston, MA: Pearson Custom Publishing.

Ivanova, L. I. Russia's College Students. Work and Health (2014). *Russian Education and Society*, 56(1), 34–46. 10.2753/RES1060-9393560104.

Johnson, S., Cooper, C., Cartwright, S., Donald, I., Taylor, P., & Millet, C. (2005). The experience of work-related stress across occupations. *Journal of Managerial Psychology*, 20(2), 178–187.

Jones, R. (2011, September 6). *Stress and it's Dangerous Effects on the Body*. Retrieved from https://kwikblog.kwikmed.com/2011/09/06/stress-and-its-dangerous-effects-on-the-body/.

Keinan, G., & Malach-Pines, A. (2007). Stress and burnout among personnel: Outcomes, and intervention strategies. *Criminal and Behavior*, 34(No 3), 380–398.

Kerley, K. R. (2005). The costs of protecting and serving: Exploring the consequences of police officer stress. In K. Copes Edited by, *Policing and Stress*. Englewood Cliffs, NJ: Prentice Hall.

Larned, J. G. (2010). Understanding police suicide. *The Forensic Examiner*, 19(3), 64–71.

Lazarus's Theory - The Dark World of Stress. (2015, September 25). Retrieved from http://blackswanstress.weebly.com/lazarus-theory.html.

Lazarus, R. S., & Folkman, S. (1984). *Stress, appraisal, and coping*. New York, NY: Springer-Verlag.

Lindsay, V (2008). Police officers and their alcohol consumption: Should we be concerned? *Police Qarterly*, 11(1), 74–87.

Lindsay, L., & Shelley, K. (2009). Social and stress-related influences of police officers' alcohol consumption. *Journal of Police and Criminal Psychology*, 1(no. 2), 87–92.

Kinman, G., & Jones, F. (2005). Lay representations of workplace stress: What do people really mean when they say they are stressed? *Work & Stress*, 19(2), 101–120.

Kivimaki, M., Leini-Aejas, P., Luukkonen, R., Riihimaki, H., Vahtera, J., & Kirjonen, J. (2002). Work stress and risk of cardiovascular mortality: Prospective cohort study of industrial employees. *British Medical Journal*, 325(7369), 875.

Kivimäki, M. & Kawachi, I. (2015). Work stress as a risk factor for cardiovascular disease. *Current Cardiology Reports*, 17(9), 630. https://doi.org/10.1007/s11886-015-0630-8.

Kleinpenning, G., & Hagendoorn, L. (1993). Forms of racism and the cumulative dimension of ethnic attitudes. *Social Psychology Quarterly*, 56, 21–36.

Klugman, J., & Braithwaite, J. (1998). Poverty in Russia during the transition: An overview. *The World Bank Research Observer*, 13, 37–58.

Korolenko, A. V. (2019). Stress as a risk factor of public health and the spread of pernicious habits. *Health, Physical Culture and Sports*, 1(12), 3–26 (in Russian). URL. http://journal.asu.ru/index.php/zosh.

Levin, J., & McDevitt, J. (1993). *Hate crimes: The rising tide of bigotry and bloodshed*. New York: Plenum Press.

Matveev, A. V. (2002). *The perception of intercultural communication competence by American and Russian managers with experience on multicultural teams*, Dissertation, Ohio University. Ann Arbor, MI: UMI Dissertation Services.

Nguyen, L. D., Mujtaba, B. G., & Boehmer, T. (2012). Stress, task, and relationship orientations across German and Vietnamese cultures. *International Business and Management*, 5(1), 10–20.

Nguyen, L. D., Mujtaba, B. G., & Pham, L. N. T. (2013). Cross culture management: An examination on task, relationship and stress orientations of Japanese and Vietnamese. *International Journal of Strategic Change Management*, 5(1), 72–92.

Nguyen, L. D., Ermasova, N., Pham, L. N. T., & Mujtaba, B. G. (2013). Leadership and work overload stress orientations across cultures: A comparative study on Russian and Vietnamese working adults, Lahore, Pakistan, *2013 International Conference on Management Research (ICMR-2013)*, November, 21–22, 2013.

Nguyen, L. D., Kass, D., Mujtaba, B. G., & Tran, Q. H. M. (2014). Leadership and work overload stress orientations across cultures: A comparative study on German and Japanese working adults, Kamuela, Hawaii, *15th Annual Conference of the National Business and Economics Society (NBES)*, March 12–15, 2014.

Nguyen, L. D., Ermasova, N., Demin, A., & Koumbiadis, A. (2014). Work overload stress of Russian working adults: Do age, gender, education, religion, management experience and government work experience make a difference? *Academy of Business Disciplines Journal*, 6(2), 76–89.

Nguyen, L. D., Lee, K.-H., Mujtaba, B. G., & Ruijs, A. (2013). Cross culture management: An examination on task, relationship and stress orientations of Dutch and Vietnamese. *International Journal of Asian Business and Information Management*, 4(4), 1–21.

Nguyen, L. D., Lee, K.-H., Mujtaba, B. G., Ruijs, A., & Boehmer, T. (2012). Stress, task, and relationship orientations across German and Dutch cultures. *International Journal of Business and Applied Sciences*, 1(1), 30–46.

Nichols, M. (2008). *Stress and its impact on your life*. Retrieved from http://anxietypanichealth.com/2008/09/10/stress-and-its-impact-on-your-life/.

O'Keeffe, G., & Clarke-Pearson, K. (2011). The impact of social media on children, adolescents, and families. *Pediatrics*, 127(4), 800–804.

Pearlin, L. I. (1989). The sociological study of stress. *Journal of Health and Social Behavior*, 30, 241–256, September.

Pietilä, I., & Rytkönen, M. (2008). Coping with stress and by stress: Russian men and women talking about transition, stress and health. *Social Science & Medicine*, 66(2), 327–338.

Powell, M. (2019). How to tackle work stress. *Dental Nursing. 15(1)*, https://doi.org/10.12968/denn.2019.15.1.10.

Pridemore, W. (2002). Vodka and violence: Alcohol consumption and homicide rates in Russia. *American Journal of Public Health*, 92, 1921–1930.

Przybylski, A., Murayama, K., DeHaan, C., & Gladwell, V. (2013). Moticationa, emotional, and behavioral correlates of fear of missing out. *Computers in Human Behavior*, 29, 1841–1848. 10.1016/j.chb.2013.02.014.

Puffer, S. M. (1996). Women managers: A case of "too much equality"? In Sheila M. Puffer Edited by, *Business and Management in Russia* (pp. 65–78, Chapter 4). Cheltenham, UK: Edward Elgar.

Rekhter, N., & Hossler, D. (2019). Place, prestige, price, and promotion: How international students use social networks to learn about universities abroad. *The Journal of Social Media in Society*, 8(1), 124–145. Retrieved: https://www.thejsms.org/index.php/TSMRI/article/view/484/243.

Russian Federation Federal State Statistical Service (Goskomstat Russia, 2014). *Population*. Retrieved from http://www.gks.ru/bgd/regl/b13_12/IssWWW.exe/stg/d01/5-01.htm.

Selye, H. (1956). *The stress of life*. New York: McGraw-Hill.

Selye, H. (1974). *Stress without distress*. New York: Lippincott.

Schepin, I. O. (1998). Major tendencies and rules of dissemination of psychological illnesses in Russian federation. *Healthcare in Russian Federation*, 3, 41–44. [In Russian].

Shapiro, J. (1997). The hypothesis of stress as a leading explanatory variable, *In: International Population Conference/Congrès International de la Population: Beijing*, 1997 (Volume 2. 1997, pp. 529–553). Liège, Belgium: International Union for the Scientific Study of Population [IUSSP].

Shevchuk, A., Strebkov, D., & Davis, S. N. (2018). Work value orientations and worker well-being in the new economy. *The International Journal of Sociology and Social Policy*, 38(9), 736–753.

Shtemberg, A. C. (2014). Social stress and psychological condition of the population of Russia. Part 1. Social and political processes that form social stress, *Space and Time*, 1(15), 187–195. [In Russian].

Shtemberg, A. C. (2014). Social stress and psychological condition of the population of Russia. Part 2.1. Russia in transition from XX to XXI century; suicide as major indication and a consequence of the social and psychological societal crisis. *Space and Time*, 3(17), 209–219. [In Russian].

The Statistics Portal. (2017). Penetration of leading social networks in Russia as of 3rd and 4th quarter 2016. Retrieved from https://www.statista.com/statistics/284447/russia-social-network-penetration/.

The Statistical Portal (2019). Social media users. Retrieved from https://www.statista.com/study/72744/social-networks-twitter-brand-report-united-states/.

World Health Organization (WHO). (2011). *Suicide data*. Retrieved from http://www.who.int/mental_health/prevention/suicide/suicideprevent/en.

World Trade Organization (WTO). (2007). *Raising awareness of stress at work in developing countries*. Retrieved from http://www.who.int/occupational_health/publications/raisingawarenessofstress.pdf.

World Population Review (2019). *Divorce rate per country*. Retrieved from http://worldpopulationreview.com/countries/divorce-rates-by-country/.

Violanti, J. M. (2001). Coping strategies among police recruits in a high-stress training environment. *The Journal of Social Psychology, 132*, 717–729.

Violanti, J. M., Slaven, J. E., Charles, L. E., Burchfiel, C. M., Andrew, M. E., & Homish, G. G. (2011). Police and alcohol use: A descriptive analysis and associations with stress outcomes. *American Journal of Criminal Justice: AJCJ, 36*(No 4), 344–356.

Vlassov, V. (1999). The role of alcohol and social stress in Russia's mortality rate. *Journal of the American Medical Association, 281*, 321–322.

Yiu, D., Bruton, G., & Lu, Y. (2005). Understanding business group performance in an emerging economy: Acquiring resources and capabilities in order to prosper. *Journal of Management Studies, 42*(1), 183–206.

13 Occupational Stress in South Africa
From the Past to the Fourth Industrial Revolution

Claude-Hélène Mayer and Rudolf M. Oosthuizen

Introduction

The stress level in South African workplaces was already described in the 1990s as one of the highest in the world (Van Zyl, 2002). According to Nevid, Rathus, and Greene (2017), stress refers to "the strain or pressure placed on an organism to adapt or adjust". Stress is regularly described as a feeling of being overwhelmed, worried, or run-down; it can affect human beings for a long time and is frequently accompanied by an uncomfortable "emotional journey" – which triggers biochemical, physiological, and behavioral adjustments. Stress, in addition, can be described as a physiological and intellectual response to any undertaking or stimulus – which creates a disturbance or imbalance of the mind-body system (Plessis & Smith, 2013).

Almost 20 years after Van Zyl's (2002) stress research, South African organizations are still described as highly stressful contexts affecting the drastic growth of stress-related illnesses and psychological issues in and beyond workplaces (Bismilla & Gantley, 2018). This is particularly due to not only the aspects relating to the transition into the Fourth Industrial Revolution (4IR), technological adjustments, higher risk factors, and lifestyle changes in a globalized work environment, but is also due to the intrasocietal changes within the South African society, decreasing economic stability, political challenges – such as corruption and crime, and financial as well as educational downhills. South African scholars Cilliers and Flotman (2016), stated that the 21st Century world of work is known for its growing sources of stress, brought about with the aid of the demands of the Fourth Industrial Revolution, new economy, non-stop change, transformation, globalization, complexity, uncertainty, and alienation. Not being able to cope with these needs results in negative stress – or distress – manifesting among personnel as negativity, poor decision-making, emotional alienation, ineffective system and people management, and an increase in autocratic and bureaucratic leadership.

Various organizations, such as workplace health organizations and insurance companies, warn of increasing disability claims due to psychological, psychiatric, and mental disorders (Old Mutual Corporate, 2017). At the same time, selected organizations have put interventions and strategies in place to decrease stress in organizational contexts – such as applying stress evaluations to identity stressors (Ngope, 2019), increasing salutogenic functioning and sense coherence as coping mechanisms (Oosthuizen and Van Lill, 2008), and developing integrated organizational health frameworks (Hart & Cooper, 2001) and organizational strategies to combat stress at work (Adams, 2007). Stress levels have been measured in regard to their causes within and outside South African organizations over several decades to determine the causes of stress and to intervene with the appropriate interventions and tools (Van Zyl, 2002; Oosthuizen and Van Lill, 2008; Oosthuizen, 2019).

The aim of this chapter is to present an insight into selected facets of stress and its management in theory and practice within the South African occupational and organizational work context. It provides contextual information on the South African society in the past, the present, and the fourth Industrial Revolution work contexts. Conclusions and recommendations for future theory and practice are given.

Stress in South African Occupations: General Findings

As highlighted in the introduction, stress experiences and stress research have a long tradition in South African occupations and organizations (Van Zyl, 2002; Barnard, 2013; Van den Berg & Van Zyl, 2008; Van der Colff & Rothmann, 2009; De Beer, Pienaar, & Rothmann, 2016). Within the occupational and organizational stress research, South African research shows that stress experienced in the organization and at work strongly interlinks with the experience of burnout and often leads to the ill-health of employees (Van der Colff & Rothmann, 2009).

Most often, psychosocial stress at work is skilled because of challenges stemming from a challenging environment and tasks that are difficult to meet. Thus, due to the chance of failure, this evokes severe negative emotions alerting physiological responses. As indicated before, most employees in the 21st Century are threatened by psychological stress, particularly in the workplace, which has detrimental effects on the economic system of any country. An investigation was conducted in South Africa which indicated that occupational stress creates an emotional environment that can be transmitted to the home and affects the dynamics of household life. Work stress no longer affects only the employee, but also spills over and influences different human beings with whom the person interacts – such as their spouse and children. High stress levels in South Africa have further been related to various different factors – such as high divorce rates, high numbers of accidents, high drug consumption (Van Zyl, 2002) – but also to interracial conflicts and unhealthy competition at work. Nevid *et al.* (2017) note that a stressor is a supply of strain which includes mental elements – for example, examinations at university and problems in social relationships, existence adjustments such as the death of a cherished one, divorce, or career termination. Prolonged or excessive stress can overtax the coping capacity of people and cause states of emotional distress – inclusive of anxiety or despair – and bodily harm, which includes fatigue and other complications.

Work stress has been associated with out-of-workplace contexts – such as marital relationships, parenting, and psychological adjustment (Van Zyl, 2002). Oosthuizen and Koortzen (2007), indicate that the causes of stressors arising outside the work situation are characterized by marital dysfunction and divorce, limited time with family, problems with children, and lifestyle factors such as the abuse of alcohol, excessive smoking, and lack of exercise. In addition, the causes of stressors originating within the work situation manifest in terms of task characteristics, organizational functioning, physical working conditions and job equipment, career and social matters, remuneration, fringe benefits, and personnel policy. The degree of shift work, overloading, underloading, and traumatic incidents are identified as main task characteristic stressors (Oosthuizen & Koortzen, 2007). In addition, Van Zyl (2002) mentions that it appears that stress and associated health problems result in high losses within organizational contexts. Each year corporations are forced to allocate a large share of their running expenditure just to supply employee well-being benefits – resulting in greater customer costs, decreasing profits, or both (Ngope, 2019).

Coetzer and Rothmann (2007) have pointed out that high incidents of competition and rivalry between organizations, particularly in the insurance industry, lead to high-stress levels, ill-health, and decreased employee well-being. Other research contributes to the findings by highlighting that workplace incivility causes stress and, related to that, other physical illnesses – such as heart disease and migraines (Smidt, De Beer, Brink, & Leiter, 2016). Furthermore, stress in the South African workplace is caused by shame, shameful experiences, and failure experienced in the workplace (Mayer, Viviers, & Tonelli, 2017). Within the context of research on health and well-being, Barnard (2013), as well as Van den Berg and Van Zyl (2008), have highlighted that a low sense of coherence might be related to high-stress levels within the South African society. Mayer and Barnard (2015) have further pointed out that stress levels are particularly high in South African society and among women in the workplace. It can thus be assumed that members of minority groups within South African workplaces or organizations– particularly those with a low sense of coherence – might experience even higher levels of stress than members of other groups and of individuals with a high sense of coherence. Some South African researchers have highlighted that 10% of the total burden of diseases in South Africa are neuropsychiatric disorders (Lopez, Mathers, Ezzati, Jamison, & Murray, 2006), and according to Tomlinson, Grimsrud, Stein, Williams, and Myer (2009), these psychological and neuropsychiatric disorders are strongly interlinked with stress.

Other research in South Africa points out that occupational stress occurs particularly due to inadequate workplaces, which, for example, have inadequate sanitary facilities or extremely high temperatures (Venugopal et al., 2016). Nunfam, Adusei-Asante, Van Etten, Oosthuizen, and Frimpong (2018) also emphasize that employees' experiences are stressful because of heat due to climate change and a change in workers' health and safety conditions. With heat stress, employees experience social impacts, as well as heat illnesses, injuries, productive losses, inadequate social well-being, and deaths. These new work stresses need to be addressed by individual adaptation strategies, as well as by policy decisions. Other researchers, such as Chetty, Coetzee, and Ferreira (2016), have also pointed out that changes in the workplace can cause stress in South Africa. They have studied particular psychological reactions and characteristics to understand reactions to change and have highlighted that stress perception increases when job embeddedness is low and when employees are not well prepared for changes.

Van Wyk, de Beer, Pienaar, and Schaufeli (2016) look at occupational stress from a completely different point of view. They highlight that workplace boredom within the South African workplace context can also be interlinked with experienced stress. Sieberhagen, Rothmann, and Pienaar (2009) support the findings and highlight that work-related boredom and depressed moods in South African workplaces might cause stress in employees. In this context, workplace boredom is linked to experiencing a lack of job resources, which interlinks with a higher need frustration and lower motivation that must be counteracted through increased self-fulfillment, self-esteem, confidence, and lower levels of emotional exhaustion (Erasmus, 2018). In the following, and anchored in general perspectives on workplace stress, the authors will focus on stress in specific workplaces and occupational and organizational sectors to present selected findings on stress in specific societal and organizational contexts – which appear outstanding. The presentation of recent research can only provide an idea of the foci of stress research in South Africa and does not attempt to present a complete overview of the research landscape on the topic, but rather presents directions of contemporary stress research.

Stress in the South African Health Sector

According to Conradieet al. (2017), stress strongly impacts nurses across cultures and strongly influences health, well-being, and work performance in the health sector. In their research, Van der Colff and

Rothmann (2009) found that nurses in South Africa experience high levels of stress when experiencing depletion of emotional resources, feelings of depersonalization, high job demands, a lack of organizational support, and a weak sense of coherence. Stress research among nurses has gained particular interest in the past years, and research has shown that stress predicts burnout and compromises productivity and performance as well as the quality of care afforded to patients (Khamiza 2015). Khamisa, Peltzer, Ilic, and Oldenburg (2017) have, in a follow-up study, highlighted that research – particularly among nurses – needs to differentiate clearly between work stress and personal stress, since work stress relates strongly to job satisfaction and personal stress to burnout and general health.

Other research (Conradie et al., 2017) conducted in the Free State – a province in South Africa – highlighted that nurses (over 90% of which are black and female) mostly experience stress due to having to provide financially for their children and dependent minors (over 70%), caring for them (almost 40%), and fearing that they may move away (ca. 26%). However, in regard to occupational stressors, the nurses mentioned the following: high workload (66.3%), lack of decision-making by superiors (58.1%), underpayment (53.5%), endangerment of physical health (52.3%) and safety (50.0%), working hours (51.2%), pressure due to expectations from superiors (48.8%), the uncertainty of employment (48.8%), and work responsibilities (47.7%). They experienced stress regarding health issues such as hyper- and hypotension (35.3%). Because of stress, 34.5% of participants took leaves, 34.5% developed depression, and 14.3% had panic attacks.

Stern et al. (2017) emphasize that healthcare workers are often stressed when dealing with patients, and they struggle to balance maintaining their distance from patients while being professional and supportive. Their behavior might therefore express stress (e.g., shouting at patients). At the same time, the authors emphasize that patients also experience stress, anger, and helplessness. Moreover, they experience stress for certain ailments – for example, there is a stigma associated with HIV. Various studies on HIV/AIDS and stress have been conducted in the South African health context because the number of people living with HIV is relatively high, compared to the rest of the world. Research within the health context has further shown that relationship conflict in couples living with HIV increases stress and forgetfulness and that the support of the partner through caring, joking, and talking can help in a big way in reducing stress (Conroy et al., 2017).

Stress in the South African Construction, Mining, and Security Industries

In the past, stress research in the construction industry hardly focused on African contexts, and studies have only recently paid greater attention to

South Africa (Cattell, Bowen, & Edwards, 2016). The authors highlight that the experience and perception of stress relate to critical time constraints, the volume of work, and adequate compensation, as well as negatively affected work-life balance. De Beer, Rothmann, and Pienaar (2016) focus on aspects of employment, equity experiences, and affirmative action drivers in post-apartheid South Africa and point out that stress is vibrant in the construction industry.

One of the most important occupational stress factors of workers in South African mines relates to money and debt (James & Rajak, 2014). According to Jacobs and Pienaar (2016), different stressors are at play. They researched a multinational gold mining company in South Africa and found that most of the stress relates to role conflict, role ambiguity, quantitative job insecurity, coping, and safety compliance at work. The strategy used to manage stress at work is coping avoidance. Nzonzo (2016) has explored drivers of employee well-being in South Africa and has found that, particularly in the South African police force, high levels of stress occur. The author does not only ascribe these high stress levels to the apartheid history and ongoing influences of that history in the workplace, but also to contemporary trends, identity insecurities, social conditions, lifestyle, and low confidence and skills.

Stress in South African Education

The educational sector has been studied in regard to occupational stress, and findings show that teachers who suffer from workplace bullying in the South African educational system feel tired and stressed (52%) (Jacobs & de Wet, 2015). Smit and Du Plessis (2016) have supported these findings by highlighting that bullying is often an underestimated topic in workplaces – which leads to huge amounts of stress and even suicide. Vos and Kirsten's (2015) research emphasizes that workplace bullying in the educational sector and of teachers impacts strongly on the teachers' health and stress levels and is interlinked with other psychiatric conditions – such as depression, posttraumatic stress disorder, panic attacks, and a negative influence on the teaching-learning process. Within higher education institutions, Barkhuizen and Rothmann (2008) have found that occupational stressors predict ill-health and a lack of organizational commitment by academics. Stress in this occupational field relates to compensation and benefits, work overload, and work-life balance (Barkhuizen & Rothmann, 2008).

Mayer, Oosthuizen, and Surtee (2017) have pointed out that in the South African higher educational context, women leaders feel stressed by the multiple challenges they have to face daily, and the authors suggest that stress tolerance and mental health-related concepts need to be strengthened – such as salutogenesis in organizations while increasing a sense of coherence through specific interventions and tools. Parallel to studies – which focus on teachers and professionals in educational institutions – Case (2017) describes that, at the college level, young engineers-in-training are also stressed when aiming at practicing "self-authorship". Self-authorship is defined as "a synthesis of intellectual, intrapersonal, and interpersonal development" which is one goal of education and which, at the same time, can be experienced as stressful due to its complexity. Furthermore, the available research indicates that the prevalence of stress is increasing among students studying in higher education. Issues such as student retention and student progression are becoming increasingly important for all universities (Robotham & Julian 2006; Robotham, 2008).

Transformation in higher education remains slow due to low access for previously disadvantaged groups. The poor socioeconomic background of the majority of tertiary learners who come from the previously disadvantaged group is a stressor and barrier for accessing tertiary education. "Without appropriate and adequate financial funding, students who come from financially challenged households in South Africa might never be able to achieve academic success, change the negative cycle of poverty, or contribute towards changing the race and gender profile of South African academe" (Machika & Johnson, 2014). Evidence shows that, on average, 70% of the families of the higher education dropouts in South Africa were in the category of "low economic status" – the majority of which come from previously disadvantaged groups (Letseka & Maile, 2008). The Fees Must Fall movement during 2015 and 2016 – a student protest for free education – resulted in massive disruptions at universities, with students vowing to shut down universities until the government heeded their call. Despite commitments by the government to fund disadvantaged students, there is concern that free education is not sustainable in the current economic environment (Manda and Dhaou, 2019; South Africa, 2017). The entire movement seems to be accompanied by high stress levels for all parties involved.

Stress from Different Cultural Perspectives in South Africa

International research has highlighted that culture moderates the relation between perceived stress, social support, and mental and physical health (Shavitt et al., 2016). Although there seems to be various research on culture, race, and stress in the US-American context (Hunter, Case, Joseph, Mekaawi, & Bokhari, 2017), there seems to be a void in the South African context of research on culture, race, and stress. In the 1990s, Van Zyl (2002) started with research on stress levels in different South African sociocultural and racial groups. The research found that stress levels in different groups are extremely high: coloreds at 34,7%, whites at 38,1%, and 35% among black South Africans. In comparison, stress levels in the United States and Europe were between 10 and 22% (Van Zyl, 2002).

Mayer (2005) has highlighted that distress can easily occur in South Africa due to belonging to a certain cultural, ethnic, or racial community. In her study, for example, one colored interviewee emphasized that he is distressed about being part of and belonging to the colored community is stressed about "having to share the 'low self-esteem' of the 'Colored Community'" (Mayer, 2005, p. 323). A more recent study from 2017 (Jaga, Arabandi, Bagraim, & Mdlongwa, 2018), points out that the negotiation of racial affiliation, gender, race, work, and family is extremely stressful for black South African women. Based on the intersectionality theories, the authors explore how difficult it is for black women to advance at work and how stressed they feel about the expectations for them to manage the different areas in their lives. Another recent study by Marteleto, Cavanagh, Prickett, and Clark (2016) has emphasized that instability in parent-child co-residence can cause stress for children – particularly in colored and black communities. While these racial groups have historically often been exposed to a fluid household environment due to labor migration, child-fostering concepts, and non-marital fertility, HIV/AIDS adds a source of instability in these groups particularly.

Stress can occur due to racial affiliation, educational status, sociocultural background, a sense of religious-ideological obligation, threats to personal safety, feelings of inferiority and lack of self-esteem, authoritarian decision-making, as well as identity conflicts (Mayer, 2005). A white priest emphasizes that he believes that affirmative action procedures cause particular stress for whites. Additionally, interracial relationships can cause stress for the partners, as reported in a research study in 2005 – 11 years after the end of apartheid, since they fear that these kinds of relationships are still not accepted in broader society (Mayer, 2005). After having presented stress research in selected societal and organizational contexts, we will continue by focusing on the characteristics of occupational stress in South Africa.

Characteristics of Occupational Stress

South African researchers, such as Robbins, Judge, Odendaal, and Roodt (2009) and Oosthuizen (2019) distinguish between individual and organizational stress characteristics, as explained in the following section.

Individual Stress Characteristics in the Fourth Industrial Revolution in South Africa

The average employee works about 40 to 50 hours per week, but the experiences and problems with which employees are confronted with when not at work can spill over to their work. This encompasses elements in the employee's private life – primarily family issues, personal financial problems, and inherent personality characteristics. Stress signs expressed at work may additionally simply stem from the person's persona (Robbins et al., 2009).

Furthermore, employees experience the pressures of the Fourth Industrial Revolution personally in terms of the following demands (Oosthuizen, 2019):

- Flexibility: Escalating virtual work makes employees time and place-independent. Work-task rotation further necessitates employees to be flexible in their job responsibilities.
- Uncertainty tolerance: This involves enduring change, especially work-related changes due to work-task rotation or reconfigurations.
- Continuous learning: Frequent work-related transformation makes it compulsory for employees to be willing to continue to learn.
- Ability to work under pressure: Employees involved in innovation processes must be able to cope with increased pressure due to shorter product life cycles and reduced marketing time.
- Sustainable mindset: As representatives of their organizations, employees need to support sustainability initiatives.
- Compliance: This involves stricter rules regarding information technology security, working with machines, or working hours (Hecklaua et al., 2016).
- Resilience: This involves the capacity of the employee to cope in spite of Smart Technology, Artificial Intelligence, Robotics, and Algorithms (STARA), barriers, or limited resources. Resilient employees are willing and able to overcome the fears and stress of STARA by tapping into their emotional strength.

Besides personal stress characteristics, employees are impacted by organizational stress characteristics, as presented in the following section.

Organizational Stress Characteristics in the Fourth Industrial Revolution in South Africa

According to Robbins et al. (2009) and Oosthuizen (2019), organizational stress characteristics primarily include six different types of demands, which are explained in the following: task, role, STARA knowledge, and methodological, interpersonal, and societal competency demands.

Task demands encompass the format of the employees' job (e.g., autonomy, assignment variety, degree of automation), working prerequisites, and physical work layout. For example, working in an overcrowded room or in an open office where interruptions are constant can increase anxiety levels and stress. Furthermore, employees must be able to deal efficiently with a large amount of data (i.e., big data) (Huber & Kaiser, 2015). In addition, they have to acquire the necessary skills to be equipped for the increase in virtual work (Hecklaua et al., 2016; Stock-Homburg, 2013).

Role demands relate to pressures placed on an individual as a feature of the particular position they play in an organization. Role conflicts create expectations that may also be tough to reconcile or satisfy. Role overload is experienced when the worker is expected to perform more functions than time permits. Role ambiguity is created when function expectations are no longer honestly understood, and employees are no longer sure what they are supposed to do (Ngope, 2019).

STARA knowledge demands are becoming increasingly significant owing to cumulative task accountability. Employees may experience high stress levels due to the demands presented by the Fourth Industrial Revolution:

- Specialized competencies: All-inclusive and specialized competencies are required to change from operational to more strategic functions.
- Process comprehension: Advanced process intricacy demands a wider and deeper process comprehension.
- Media abilities: Accumulative virtual work requires that employees be able to use smart technology and media – for example: smart glasses.
- Programming abilities: The intensification of algorithms and digitized processes initiates an advanced demand for employees with programming abilities.
- Understanding information technology security: Virtual functions on servers or platforms compel employees to be aware of cybersecurity (Hecklaua et al., 2016; Oosthuizen, 2019).

Methodological demands in the landscape of the Fourth Industrial Revolution could also contribute to the high stress levels of employees in terms of the following (Hecklaua et al., 2016):

- Creativity: The need for more smart technology and innovative products, as well as for internal enhancements, calls for creativity.
- Innovative thinking: Every employee with more accountable and strategic functions has to act as an innovator.
- Problem-solving: Employees must be able to identify the sources of mistakes and be able to improve processes and procedures.
- Conflict-solving: An advanced service emphasis increases customer associations; conflicts need to be resolved.
- Decision-making: Since employees will have higher process accountability, they will have to make their own decisions.
- Diagnostic abilities: Constructing and scrutinizing significant amounts of information and multifaceted processes becomes compulsory.

- Research competencies: Employees have to be able to use reliable sources for continuous learning in fluctuating environments of Artificial Intelligence.
- Proficiency assimilation: Multifarious quandaries need to be elucidated more proficiently – for example: examining increasing quantities of algorithmic data (Hecklaua et al., 2016; Oosthuizen, 2019).

Interpersonal demands are pressures created by other employees. Lack of social support from colleagues and negative interpersonal relationships can cause extensive stress, especially among employees with excessive social needs. The nature and variety of social desires differ among people. The organizational structure defines the degree of differentiation in the organization, the degree of policies and regulations, as well as the point where decisions are made. Excessive guidelines and lack of participation in decisions that affect employees are examples of structural variables that could possibly cause stress. Organizational leadership refers to the managerial style of the organization's senior executives; some executives might also create a subculture characterized by tension, concern, and anxiety. In addition, some may even set up unrealistic pressures to perform in a short space of time, impose excessively tight controls, and automatically dismiss employees who cannot meet requirements. Just as environmental uncertainty influences the design of an organization's structure, it also influences stress levels among employees in any organization. Changes in the organization cycle create economic uncertainties. Political uncertainties may also have an effect on market stability, which will affect not only personnel directly involved, but also their families (Ngope, 2019).

The Fourth Industrial Revolution also demands societal competencies from employees, which could contribute to stress, namely:

- Intercultural abilities: Employees are required to have an understanding of different cultures – especially different work practices – when working internationally.
- Language abilities: Employees must be able to understand and converse with international associates and customers.
- Communication abilities: Service inclination demands good listening and presentation abilities from employees; whereas, increasing virtual work requires sufficient virtual communication abilities.
- Networking abilities: Working in a highly globalized and interconnected value chain requires knowledge networks from employees.
- Teamwork abilities: Increasing teamwork and collective work on platforms demand an ability from employees to respect team rules (Oosthuizen, 2019).

The Fourth Industrial Revolution requires developing countries such as South Africa to rise to the challenges brought by their sociohistoric, socioeconomic, and economic contexts. Developing countries need to develop models or strategies that are responsive and relevant to their context instead of blindly adopting so-called "exemplary models" that have worked in contexts that are different from the developing country adopting them. There is also a greater need to develop strategies that bring social benefits instead of focusing primarily on economic prospects brought by the Fourth Industrial Revolution. Strategies should also look into innovative ways of addressing socioeconomic stressors such as potential job losses, widening wage gaps, and skills redundancy. In demonstrating the benefits of the Fourth Industrial Revolution, the government should also explain how social innovations in Industry 4.0 could address some of society's stressors and improve the quality of life and social well-being of citizens (Manda and Ben Dhaou, 2019).

Managing Stress in South African Occupations and Organizations

After having presented the causes and impacts of stress on South African workplaces and organizations, the question arises how stress can be managed in this specific context and which interventions and tools can be used to reduce occupational stress to improve health and well-being (Sieberhagen, Pienaar, & Els, 2011; Sieberhagen *et al.* 2009). It is suggested that stress management needs to take place on different levels, namely on the individual (micro) level, on the organizational (meso) level, and on the societal (macro) level. In the following section, the authors refer to these different levels and corresponding possible stress management options.

The Micro-Level of Stress Management in South Africa

Researchers (e.g., Nunfam et al., 2018; Chetty *et al.* 2016) have pointed out that, on the individual level, employees need to develop adaptation strategies to workplaces – in particular, to workplace changes due to global, societal, organizational, or individual changes. The empowering and strengthening of individual strategies and focusing on concepts such as a sense of coherence (Mayer, 2005), self-fulfillment, confidence, and other positive psychology constructs (Erasmus, 2018) can support the reduction of stress.

The Meso-Level of Stress Management in South Africa

On the organizational level, stress needs to be reduced through organizational strategies and impact. Coetzee and Rothmann (2005) have emphasized that organizational commitment moderates the effect of work stress in organizations – impacting positively on well-being, organizational growth, stability, and the decrease of stress. This means that South African organizations need to increase organizational commitment through, for example, care for employees, specific benefits, influential training, and support of employees' professional and personal development. In this context, organizations should focus on the high embeddedness of employees at work to reduce work stress, adjust policies, and prepare their employees for (potential) changes and implement those changes through programs (Chetty *et al.* 2016). It has further been pointed out (Stern et al., 2017) that organizations should engage more in community work to cooperate with the South African healthcare system and thereby aim at reducing stress of healthcare professionals and their patients.

Previous research has also suggested that, in order to reduce stress levels in organizations, trained mental health professionals and counselors must be employed in organizations to foster the well-being of employees and to reduce the experience of workplace stress (Cooper & Bevan, 2014; Katushabe, et al., 2015; Salanova, Del Líbano, Llorens, & Schaufeli, 2014). As for international contexts (Khoury, Sharma, Rush, & Fournier, 2015), mindfulness-based training to reduce stress in individuals has been suggested for South African contexts (Mayer & Walach, 2018) to increase health and well-being and decrease stress.

The Macro-Level of Stress Management in South Africa

On the macro level and in regard to the entire South African society, the government needs to address the burning issues within the society – such as crime and safety, unemployment, Black Economic Empowerment and Affirmative Action strategies, poverty, access to education, and healthcare. However, racial tensions and the late effects of the apartheid and the historical separation of race groups also need to be addressed to deal with stress that occurs in workplaces and across society. If the burning issues of society were to be addressed by the government, the stress levels in organizations and workplaces would decrease as well. In regard to the Fourth Industrial Revolution, the South African government needs to develop a vision and proper strategies to deal appropriately with the upcoming challenges and to develop the well-being of South African society. The government and industries must cooperate to address the fears of the Fourth Industrial Revolution in the future by implementing strategies on how to address and professionally cope with the rapid global challenges.

Conclusions and Recommendations

Stress is rife in South African society. It seems to be anchored on the historical struggles of the country and the newly anticipated stressors of the rapidly occurring Fourth Industrial Revolution. The success of the Fourth Industrial Revolution will depend on leadership from all sectors working together to leverage the opportunities and address the stressors associated with the Fourth Industrial Revolution. Political leadership, for example, is responsible for developing and implementing an enabling environment for digital transformation and innovation. Business leadership is responsible for leading think tanks and the much-needed innovation in the Fourth Industrial Revolution (Manda and Ben Dhaou, 2019). Social leadership also plays an important role in preparing society for the changes and stressors brought by the Fourth Industrial Revolution. Political leadership in South Africa has recognized the Fourth Industrial Revolution and its potential to address the country's triple challenges and stressors of poverty, unemployment, and inequality. The development of policies and strategies addressing digital transformation is a sign of commitment from leadership. However, the implementation of reforms remains a stressor – as witnessed by poor policy implementation.

Manda and Dhaou (2019) stated that collaboration is critical during transformation and they associated stress with change. Collaboration between the various role-players in the Fourth Industrial Revolution is critical in ensuring the success of the Fourth Industrial Revolution that will disrupt and cause stress not only for organizations, but also the government and society. The development of policies and strategies that are responsive to the priorities of South Africa will require that the government work with business and social partners in addressing some of the stressors and in leveraging the opportunities brought by the Fourth Industrial Revolution.

References

Adams, J. (2007). *Managing people in organisations: Contemporary theory and practice*. Houndmills, UK: Parlgrave Macmillan.

Barkhuizen, N. & Rothmann, S. (2008). Occupational stress of academic staff in South African higher education institutions. *South African Journal of Psychology, 38*(2), 321–336.

Barnard, A. (2013). The role of socio-demographic variables and their interactive effect on sense of coherence. *SA Journal of Industrial Psychology, 39*(1). Doi:org/10.4102/sajip.v39i1.1073.

Bismilla, S. & Gantley, K. (2018). *The impact of stress-related illnesses and psychological issues in the workplace*. GOLEGAL Industry News and Insight, 6 June 2018. https://www.golegal.co.za/workplace-stress-impact/.

Brough, P., O'Driscoll, M. & Kalliath, T. (2009). *Workplace psychological health: Current research and practice*. Cheltenham: Edward Elgar.

Cable, D. M. & Judge, T. A. (1997). Interviewers' perceptions of person-organisation fit and organisational selection decisions. *Journal of Applied Psychology, 82*, 546–561. 10.1037/0021-9010.82.4.546.

Case, J. M. (2017). Journeys to meaning-making: A longitudinal study of self-authorship among young South African engineering graduates. *Journal of college student development*, 57(7), 863–879.

Cattell, K., Bowen, P. & Edwards, P. (2016). Stress among South African construction professionals: A job demand-control-support survey. *Construction Management and Economics*, 34(10), 700–723.

Chetty, P. J. J., Coetzee, M. & Ferreira, N. (2016). *Sources of job stress cognitive receptivity to change: The moderating role of job embeddedness*. http://uir.unisa.ac.za/bitstream/handle/10500/21845/source%20of%20job%20stress%20and%20cognitive%20receptivity.pdf?sequence=3&isAllowed=y.

Cilliers, F. & Flotman, A. P. (2016). The psychological well-being manifesting among master's students in Industrial and organisational psychology. *SA Journal of Industrial Psychology*, 42(1), 1–11.

Coetzee, S. E. & Rothmann, S. (2005). Occupational stress, organisational commitment, ill-health of employees at a higher educational institution in South Africa. *Journal of Industrial. Psychology*, 31(1), 47–54.

Coetzer, W. J. & Rothmann, S. (2007). A psychometric evaluation of measures of affective wellbeing in an insurance company. *South African Journal of Industrial Psychology*, 33(2), 7–15.

Conradie, Maria, Erwee, Danelle, Serfontein, Isabel, Visser, Maré, Calitz, Frikkie J. W. & Joubert, Gina. (2017). A profile of perceived stress factors among nursing staff working with intellectually disabled in-patients at the Free State Psychiatric Complex. *South Africa Curationis*, 40(1), 1–8. https://dx.doi.org/10.4102/curationis.v40i1.1578.

Conroy, A., Leddy, A., Johnson, M., Ngubane, T., Van Rooyen, H. & Darbes, L. (2017). "I told her this is your life": Relationship dynamics, partner support, and adherence to antiretroviral therapy among South African couples. *Culture, Health & Sexuality*, 19(11), 1239–1253.

Cooper, C. & Bevan, S. (2014). Business Benefits of a Healthy Workforce. In De Beer, A. Day, K. D. Randell, E. Kelloway & J. Hurrell Jr (Eds.), *Workplace wellbeing: How to build psychologically healthy workplaces* (1st ed.), (pp. 27–49). West Sussex: WILEY Blackwell.

De Beer, L. T., Pienaar, J. & Rothmann Jr, S. (2016). Work overload, burnout, and psychological ill-health symptoms: A three-wave mediation model of the employee health impairment process. *Anxiety, Stress & Coping*, 29(4), 387–399.

De Beer, L. T., Pienaar, J. & Rothmann, S. (2016). Job burnout, work engagement and self-reported treatment for health conditions in South Africa. *Stress Health*, 32(1), 36–46. 10.1002/smi.2576. Epub 2014 Apr 10.

Erasmus, A. (2018). *Investigating the relationships between engaging leadership, need satisfaction, work engagement and workplace boredom within the South African mining industry*. Economic and Management Sciences North-West University. https://repository.nwu.ac.za/handle/10394/30971.

French, J. R. P., Caplan, R. D. & Harrison, R. V. (1982). *The mechanisms of job stress and strain*. Chichester: Wiley.

Hadadian, Z. & Zarei, J. (2016). Relationship between toxic leadership and job stress of knowledge workers. *Studies in Business and Economics*, 11(3), 84–89.

Hart, P. M. & Cooper, C. L. (2001). Occupational Stress: Toward a More Integrated Framework. In Hecklau, N. Anderson, D. S. Ones, H. K. Sinangil & C. Viswesvaran (Eds.), *Handbook of industrial, work and organisational psychology: Vol. 2. Organisational psychology* (pp. 93–114). London: Sage.

Hecklau, F., Galeitzke, M., Flachs, S. & Kohl, H. (2016). Holistic approach for human resource management in Industry 4.0 6th CLF - 6th CIRP Conference on learning factories. *Procedia Cirp, 54*, 1–6.

Huber, D. & Kaiser, T. (2015). Wie das Internet der Dinge neue Geschäftsmodelle ermöglicht. *HMD Praxis der Wirtschaftsinformatik, 52*, 681–689.

Hunter, C. D., Case, A. D., Joseph, N., Mekaawi, Y. & Bokhari, E. (2017). The roles of shared racial fate and a sense of belonging with African Americans in black immigrants' race-related stress and depression. *Journal of Black Psychology, 43*(2), 135–158.

Jacobs, L. & de Wet, C. (2015). A quantitative exploration of the effects of workplace bullying on South African educators. *African Safety Promotion Journal, 13*(2), 32–58.

Jacobs, M. & Pienaar, J. (2016). Stress, coping and safety compliance in a multinational gold mining company. *International Journal of Occupational Safety and Ergonomics, 23*(2), 152–161.

Jaga, A., Arabandi, B., Bagraim, J. & Mdlongwa, S. (2018). Doing the 'gender dance': Black women professionals negotiating gender, race, work and family in post-apartheid South Africa, *Community, Work & Family, 21*(4), 429–444. 10.1080/13668803.2017.1311840.

James, D. & Rajak, D. (2014). Credit apartheid, migrants, mines and money. *African Studies, 73*(3), 455–476. ISSN 0002-0184 DOI 10.1080/00020184. 2014.962872.

Katushabe, S., Sumil, N. R., Sumil, M., Muhanguzi, K., Mwebesa, E. & Nakimuli, A. (2015). *Counseled and Non Counseled Employees' Psychological Well-Being in the Workplace: Revelations from Police Force, Uganda.* Oral presentation: *Bugema International Multi-Disciplinary Conference*, September 28–29.

Khamisa, N., Oldenburg, B., Peltzer, K. & Ilic, D. (2015). Work-related stress, burnout, job satisfaction and general health of nurses. *International Journal of Environmental Research and Public Health, 12*(1), 652–666.

Khamisa, N., Peltzer, K., Ilic, D. & Oldenburg, B. (2017). Effect of personal and work stress on burnout, job satisfaction and general health of hospital nurses in South Africa. *Health SA Gesondheid, 22*, a1011. https://doi.org/10.4102/hsag.v22i0.1011.

Khoury, B., Sharma, M., Rush, S. E. & Fournier, C. (2015). Mindfulness-based stress reduction for healthy individuals: A meta-analysis. *Journal of Psychosomatic Research, 78*, 519–528.

Kristof-Brown, A. L., Zimmerman, R. D. & Johnson, E. C. (2005). Consequences of individuals' fit at work: A meta-analysis of person-job, person-organization, person-group, and person-supervisor fit. *Personnel Psychology, 58*, 281–342. 10.1111/j.1744-6570.2005.00672.x.

Le Fevre, M., Matheny, J. & Kolt, G. S. (2003). Eustress, distress and interpretation in occupational stress. *Journal of Management Psychology, 18*, 726–744. 10.1108/02683940310502412.

Leka, S., Griffiths, A. & Cox, T. (2003). *Work organisation and stress: Systematic approaches for employers, managers and trade union representatives*. Geneva: World Health Organization (WHO).

Letseka, M. & Maile, S. (2008). *High university drop-out rates: A threat to South Africa's future*. HSRC Policy brief: Pretoria: HSRC.

Loo, M. K., Salmiah, M. A. & Nor, S. A. R. (2015). The sources and the impacts of occupational stress among manufacturing workers. *International Journal of Current Research and Academic Review*, 2, 166–173.

Lopez, A. D., Mathers, C. D., Ezzati, M., Jamison, D. T. & Murray, C. J. (2006). Global and regional burden of disease and risk factors, 2001: Systematic analysis of population health data. *Lancet*, 367, 1747–1757.

Machika, P. & Johnson, B. (2014). *Poor students face massive financial stress*. Mail and Guardian. [Online] Available from: http://mg.co.za/article/2014-04-08-poor-students-face-massive-financialstress. Retrieved (12/06/2015).

Manda, M. I. & Dhaou, S. B. (2019, April). *Responding to the challenges and opportunities in the 4th Industrial Revolution in developing countries*, Proceedings of the 12th International Conference on Theory and Practice of Electronic Governance (pp. 244–253). ACM.

Marteleto, L. J., Cavanagh, S., Prickett, K. & Clark, S. (2016). Instability in parent-child coresidence and adolescent development in urban South Africa. *Studies in Family Planning*, 47(1), 19–38.

Mayer, C.-H. (2005). *Artificial walls. South African narratives on conflict, difference and identity*. Stuttgart: Ibidem.

Mayer, C.-H. & Barnard, A. (2015). Balancing the Scales of Gender and Culture in Contemporary South Africa. In Mayer, S. Safdar & N. Kosakowska (Eds.), *Psychology of gender through the lens of culture. Theories and applications* (pp. 327–349). New York: Springer.

Mayer, C.-H., Oosthuizen, R. & Surtee, S. (2017). Emotional intelligence in South African women leaders in higher education. *South African Journal of Industrial and Organisational Psychology*, 43(0), a1405. https://doi.org/10.4102/sajip.v43i0.1405.

Mayer, C.-H., Viviers, R. & Tonelli, L. (2017). 'The fact that she just looked at me.' Narrations on shame in South African workplaces. *South African Journal of Industrial Psychology SA Tydskrif vir Bedryfsielkunde*, 43(0), a1385. https://doi.org/10.4102/ sajip.v43i0.1385.

Mayer, C.-H. & Walach, H. (2018). *Workplace spirituality in contemporary South Africa*. The Palgrave Handbook of Workplace spirituality.

Nevid, J. S., Rathus, S. A. & Greene, B. (2017). Stress, Psychological Factors and Health. In Ngope, J. S. Nevid, S. A. Rathus & B. Greene (Eds.). *Abnormal psychology in a changing World* (10th ed.), 141–168.

Ngope, M. M. (2019). *The relationship between emotional intelligence and occupational stress amongst firefighters in a metropolitan municipality*. Pretoria: Unpublished Dissertation, University of South Africa.

Nunfam, V. F., Adusei-Asante, K., Van Etten, E. J., Oosthuizen, J. & Frimpong, K. (2018). Social impacts of occupational heat stress and adaptation strategies of workers: A narrative synthesis of the literature. *Science of the Total Environment*, 643(1), 1542–1552.

Nzonzo, J. C. (2016). *A discourse analysis of the exogenous and endogenous drivers of employee wellbeing in South Africa.* Proceedings of the 2nd Los Angeles International Business and Social Science Research conference. North Holliwood, California, 28–30 October 2016. http://www.aabl.com.au/aablConference/public/documents/pdf/2018_03_18_09_56_16_P107-R2_FullPaper.pdf.

Old Mutual Corporate. (2017). *Biggest health risk for employees in the next three years – 64% psychological, psychiatric and mental disorders –* Fin24 – 24 November. https://www.oldmutual.co.za/news/alarming-increase-in-psychiatric-and-suicide-claims-in-sa-reports-old-mutual.

Oosthuizen, R. M. (2019). *Intelligence, Robotics, and Algorithms (STARA): Employees' perceptions and well-being of future workplaces.* In Oosthuizen, I. Potgieter, N. Ferreira. & M. Coetzee (Eds.), *Fit for the future: Theory, research and dynamics of career wellbeing. Stream 1: Critical issues in understanding career wellbeing in the emerging digital workspaces of Industry 4.0.* Springer Nature Switzerland.

Oosthuizen, R. M. & Koortzen, P. (2007). An empirical investigation of job and family stressors amongst firefighters in the South African context. *SA Journal of Industrial Psychology, 33*(1), 49–58.

Oosthuizen, J. D. & Van Lill, B. (2008). Coping with stress in the workplace. *SA Journal of Industrial Psychology, 34*(1), 64–69.

Plessis, M. B. & Smith, C. A. (2013). *Stress in South Africa.* Medical Nutritional Institute.

Robbins, S., Judge, T., Odendaal, A. & Roodt, G. (2009). *Organisational behaviour: Global and South African perspectives.* Cape Town: South Africa: Pearson Education South Africa.

Robotham, D. (2008). Stress among higher education students: Towards a research agenda. *Higher Education, 56*(6), 735–746.

Robotham, D. & Julian, C. (2006). Stress and the higher education student: A critical review of the literature. *Journal of Further and Higher Education, 30*(02), 107–117.

Salanova, M., Del Líbano, M., Llorens, S. & Schaufeli, W. B. (2014). Engaged, Workaholic, Burned-Out or Just 9-to-5? Toward a Typology of Employee Well-being, Stress and Health. *Journal of the International Society for the Investigation of Stress, 30*(1), 71–81.

Shavitt, S., Young, I. K. C., Timothy, P., Johnson, D. J., Holbrook, A. & Stavrakantonaki, M. (2016). Culture moderates the relation between perceived stress, social support, and mental and physical health. *Journal of Cross-Cultural Psychology, 47*(7), 956–980.

Sieberhagen, C., Pienaar, J. & Els, C. (2011). Management of employee wellness in South Africa: Employer, service provider and union perspectives: Original research. *SA Journal of Human Resource Management, 1*, 1.

Sieberhagen, C., Rothmann, S. & Pienaar, J. (2009). Employee health and wellness in South Africa: The role of legislation and management standards: Original research. *SA Journal of Human Resource Management, 1*, 1.

Siegrist, J. & Li, J. (2016). Associations of extrinsic and intrinsic components of work stress with health: A systematic review of evidence on the effort-reward imbalance model. *International Journal of Environmental Research and Public Health, 13*, 432. 10.3390/ijerph13040432.

Smidt, O., De Beer, L. T., Brink, L. & Leiter, M. P. (2016). The validation of a workplace incivility scale within the South African banking industry. *SA. Journal of Industrial Psychology/SA Tydskrif vir Bedryfsielkunde, 42*(1), a1316. http://dx.doi.org/10.4102/sajip.v42i1.1316.

Smit, D. M. D. & Du Plessis, J. V. D. (2016). Why should we care? Bullying in the American and South African workplace. *The International Journal of Comparative Labour Law and Industrial relations, 32*(2), 161–196.

South Africa. (2017). *National E-strategy.* Available from www.dtps.gov.za.

Stern, E., Colvin, C., Gxabagxaba, N., Schutz, C., Burton, R. & Meintjes, G. (2017). Conceptions of agency and constraint for HIV-positive patients and healthcare workers to support long-term engagement with antiretroviral therapy care in Khayelitsha, South Africa. *African Journal of Aids Research, 16*(1), 19–29.

Stock-Homburg, R. (2013). Zukunft der Arbeitswelt 2030 als Herausforderung des Personalmanagements. In Tomlinson, R. Stock-Homburg (Ed.), *Handbuch strategisches personalmanagement* (2nd ed.), (pp. 603–629). Wiesbaden: Springer Gabler.

Tomlinson, M., Grimsrud, A. T., Stein, A. J., Williams, D. R. & Myer, L. (2009). The epidemiology of major depression in South Africa: Results from the South African stress and health study. *South African Management Journal, 99*(5), 368–373.

Van der Colff, Jacoba J. & Rothmann, Sebastiaan (2009). Occupational stress, sense of coherence, coping, burnout and work engagement of registered nurses in South Africa. *SA Journal of Industrial Psychology, 35*(1), 1–10. Retrieved May 30, 2019, from. http://www.scielo.org.za/scielo.php?script=sci_arttext&pid=S2071-07632009000100001&lng=en&tlng=pt.

Van Wyk, S. M., de Beer, L. T., Pienaar, J. & Schaufeli, W. B. (2016). The psychometric proprietees of a workplace boredom scale (DUBS) within the South African context. *South African Journal of Industrial and Organisational Psychology, 41*(1) http://dx.doi.org/10.4102/sajip.v42i1.1326.

Van Zyl, E. (2002). The measurement of work stress within South African companies: A luxury or necessity? *SA Journal of Industrial Psychology, 28*(3), 26–31.

Vos, J. D. & Kirsten, G. J. C. (2015). The nature of workplace bullying experienced by teachers and the biopsychosocial health effects. *South African Journal of Education, 35*, 3.

Yada, H., Abe, H., Omori, H., Ishida, Y. & Katoh, T. (2018). Job-related stress in psychiatric assistant nurses. *Nursing Open, 5*(1), 15–20.

Van den Berg, H. S. & Van Zyl, E. S. (2008). A cross-cultural comparison of the stress experienced by high-level career women. *SA Journal of Industrial Psychology, 34*(3), 17–21.

Venugopal, V., Rekha, S., Manikandan, K., Kamalakkannan, P., Viswanathan, L., Ganesan, V. N., Kumaravel, P. & Chinnadurai, S. J. (2016). Heat stress and inadequate sanitary facilities at workplaces – an occupational health concern for women? *Global Health Action, 9*, 1. 10.3402/gha.v9.31945.

14 Organizational Stress in the United States of America Research and Practice

James Campbell Quick

Introduction

Stress as a construct in the United States was framed in 1915 by Cannon (1929) and elaborated on his notions of stress and strain in homeostasis (Cannon, 1935). Kahn et al. (1964) at the University of Michigan were the first research group that studied organizational stress. In this chapter addressing organizational stress in the United States of America, I provided an abbreviated historical backdrop before exploring the current cultural context that is being defined by several major national issues. The third major section of the chapter provides a view of the most salient concepts and measures relevant to organizational stress. This section relies on both psychological science and public health practice - the latter founded on the science of epidemiology. The fourth major section of the chapter explores the influence of the cultural context on organizational stress. The boundary between work life and non-work life is neither always sharply defined nor clear. Rather, the organizational boundary is a permeable one, through which there are impacts and spillovers between the organization and the elements in its larger environment (Nelson & Quick, 2019).

Historical Backdrop

The stress concept in America originated in medicine and physiology with the research of Walter B. Cannon, who first called it "the emergency response" (Benison, Barger, & Wolfe, 1987). Cannon (1935) and later distinguished stress from strain. The second half of the 20th century saw the proliferation of theories of organizational stress by a wide range of social psychologists, industrial engineers, sociologists, and organizational behaviorists, starting with Kahn et al. (1964). By the end of the 20th century, Cooper (1998) presents ten leading theories - several of which are American in origin. For example, the person-environment fit theory is based on Kahn's social psychological research, the burnout theory (Maslach, 1982), and the theory of preventive stress management resulted from the translation of the public health notions of prevention into an organizational stress context (Hargrove, Quick, Nelson, & Quick, 2011; Quick & Quick, 1984).

Contrary to the 1988 Business Week headline, "Stress: The Test Americans Are Failing", Americans passed the stress test when life expectancy is the operational measure throughout the 20th century. American men and women extended their average life expectancy at birth by over 50% in less than a century - from less than 50 years in 1900 to over 75 years before the mid-1980s (Vital Statistics of the United States, 1988). Further, some stress is good, and not all stress is bad. In spite of the normalcy of the stress response, stress can be the kiss of death as well as the spice of life (Levi, 2000). Stress is a direct contributing cause or an indirectly implicated one in over 50% of all human morbidity and mortality (Quick & Cooper, 2003). In the United States, the ten leading causes of death account for about 80% of all deaths. Stress is directly implicated in four causes (i.e. heart disease, strokes, injuries, and suicide and homicide) and indirectly implicated in another three (i.e. cancer, chronic liver disease, and emphysema and chronic bronchitis). These broader health statistics provide a backdrop to the current state of cultural affairs in America as related to organizational stress.

Current Cultural Context in the United States

A review of the Centers for Disease Control and Prevention's National Center for Health Statistics shows that life expectancy in the United States since the year 2000 has advanced in most years yet also shows years of decline - as in 2017 when life expectancy for the United States population declined to 78.6 years. In this section I examine the long working hours in America, ten workplace stressors resulting from business policies and practices that contribute to mortality and incremental health expenditures, health insurance and healthcare, gun violence, and the opioid epidemic of the past decade. These cultural forces have direct and indirect impacts on organizational stress and risk exposures for employees.

Long Working Hours

Worrall & Cooper (2001) found the global competition in the 1990s was pushing working hours up, especially in the United States and the United Kingdom. Interestingly at that time, the British had very long working hours as compared to their European partners. Americans appear to trump the British and other developed working cultures. Gallup's 2017 State of American Well-Being found that Americans do work hard, an average of 34.4 hours per week, which is longer than their counterparts in the world's largest economies. However, many Americans well exceed that average. Gallup found that American adults employed full-time report working an average of 47 hours per week - equating to roughly six workdays per week. Executives and senior managers can expect to work in the 50 or 60-hour range. Goh, Pfeffer, and Zenios (2016) identify long working hours as one of ten leading workplace stressors. There is no question that work carries a host of social, psychological, and economic benefits. However, work in excess becomes a harmful burden. Research has not established the optimum working hours above which the range of costs and harm exceeds the benefits accrued for the employee and for the organization.

Workplace Stressors, Mortality, and Health Expenditures

Goh *et al.* (2016) built a model to estimate the excess mortality and incremental health expenditures associated with exposure to 10 workplace stressors: unemployment, lack of health insurance, exposure to shift work, long working hours, job insecurity, work-family conflict, low job control, high job demands, low social support at work, and low organizational justice. At the core of their concern is how American business policies, practices, and workforce management practices are contributing to organizational stress and employee strain. Their epidemiological evidence links specific workplace stressors to health outcomes. However, they conclude that the aggregate contribution of these factors to overall mortality and health spending is simply unknown.

They did find over 120,000 deaths per year and approximately 5–8% of annual healthcare costs associated with, and therefore for attributable to, management practices within United States companies and the ways in which they manage their workforces. The estimates generated by their model showed that 50,000 of these excess deaths per year resulted from not having insurance. They indicate that Wilper et al. (2009) reported a number quite close (45,000), thus giving the authors confidence in their model estimates. Their research found that unemployment followed the absence of insurance closely in contributing to excess mortality. In addition, low job control was an important factor as well, contributing an estimated 31,000 excess deaths annually.

In addition to the absence of health insurance, their research found that high-demand jobs and work-family conflict were major exposures that contributed to healthcare expenditures - if not to mortality. While they found that each of the exposures contributed to healthcare expenditures, not all of them contributed to incremental deaths, at least within their model. This may be, in part, due to some of the data limitations which the authors discuss. What is especially significant about the research of Goh *et al.* (2016) is that it brings epidemiology and public health to bear the risks associated with organizational stress in the workplace.

Health Insurance and Healthcare in America

A third cultural factor, included in the Goh *et al.* (2016) research, is that of health insurance and its associated factor of healthcare in America. The United States funds its healthcare system significantly differently than virtually every other industrialized nation (Macik-Frey, Quick, & Nelson, 2007). While the United States has the best medical system in the world that can treat the sick, it does not have the best health system with an emphasis on prevention. Macik-Frey *et al.* (2007) provide two alternative models for national healthcare. One model is a national health insurance model, as used in Switzerland, where private providers are reimbursed 100% by the government for services. A second model is a National Health Service model, as used in the United Kingdom, where healthcare providers are effectively government employees. The United States follows neither model and has struggled through the Obama and Trump administrations in attempting to help tens of millions of uninsured Americans. This is a critical consequential issue in the United States, in part, due to the relationship between health insurance and mortality among adults (Wilper *et al.*, 2009). America has the most expensive system in the world with some of the worst outcomes.

The American Psychological Association (2018) has been conducting Stress in America surveys for over a decade, and the 2018 results showed a marked relationship between health insurance and stress level. Specifically, on a ten-point scale, the uninsured reported nearly 25% more stress than those who had insurance (5.6 versus 4.7). APA reported that healthcare-related stress was higher in urban areas and that higher household income did not appear to mitigate the high healthcare stress related to the cost of insurance, changes in national healthcare policy, cost of medications, and medical bills.

Gun Violence in America

Workplace violence has been a concern in America dating back to the 20th century. One FBI estimate indicated that 85% or more of workplace violence is preventable because stress often serves as the triggering event for the violence (Mack, Shannon, Quick, & Quick, 1998). However, the surge in cultural gun violence - some of which is spilling over into working environments - has reached epidemic levels in the past decades. The mass shooting in an El Paso Walmart during 2019 is one of the more dramatic and tragic examples of how gun violence in America is seriously impacting organizational stress. The cultural escalation and spread of gun violence are causing many small business owners to rethink workplace safety in order to divert the work environment from being a target (Simon & Cutter, 2019). They are using a combination of workplace changes such as security cameras and door buzzers, as well as training employees in active shooter drills that prepare them to better respond to violent and dangerous employees. While high-risk employees who can become dangerous may be a small number, likely just 1–3% of a work population, these individuals can create havoc, lead to significant loss of life, and leave traumatic aftermath that haunts the organization over an extended period of time - even years (Quick, McFadyen and Nelson, 2014).

While gun violence typically focuses on harm to others, as previously discussed, the problem also encompasses suicide by guns. This problem is less typical within most organizations but has become an escalating, even epidemic, problem within the United States military forces over the past two decades. The United States is now in the longest war, even if undeclared by the United States Congress, in its national history. The five armed services (the United States Army, the United States Navy, the United States Marine Corps, the United States Air Force, and the United States Coast Guard) are among the largest organizations in the culture. By 2008, the rising suicide rates across services, especially within the United States Army and Marine Corps, are most of those in direct contact with enemy forces in Afghanistan and Iraq, as well as the accompanying rise in post-traumatic stress disorder (PTSD) and traumatic brain injury (TBI), led then-Secretary of Defense Robert Gates to appoint 13 experts on psychological health to the Defense Board for three-year terms in 2008 to 2011. General Casey (2011) launched a comprehensive soldier fitness program aimed at raising psychological resilience in the United States Army, which, in retrospect, appears well-intended but fails to isolate and help those in the greatest need. The suicide rates in the United States military and among veterans are now well above their age-comparable civilian counterparts, while in the 1990s the case was the reverse.

The Opioid Epidemic

Suicide may be considered an act of despair - one resulting from the loss of hope. This is also true for the drug addiction problem in America. Between 2007 and 2017, "drug-use disorders" jumped from #13 to the #3 cause of premature deaths in the United States. This dramatic jump can be largely attributed to the pervasive and endemic opioid epidemic that has swept America and triggered a national response from attorney generals in many states. The State of Oklahoma won a $500 million judgment against Johnson & Johnson for their role in fueling the opioid epidemic within the state. More telling is the bankruptcy filing by Purdue Pharma, maker of OxyContin, with their proposed $10 billion settlement proposal. The scale of the opioid epidemic is daunting as are the organizational and individual effects of the epidemic - both economically and financially, as well as from a humanitarian perspective. This epidemic, as with the long war, is likely to have a long tail that will impact American culture for years to come.

Salient Concepts and Measures

What is the range of concepts and measures used in America for organizational stress research? There is no universally agreed-upon set of concepts and measures in the domain of organizational stress. Quick, Quick, Nelson, & Hurrell, (1997: p. 126) provide a comprehensive overview of 17 organizational measures and indicators, five to seven measures of modifiers of the stress response, and seven measures of individual distress or strain. In a subsequent review, Quick, Cooper, Nelson, Quick, and Gavin (2003) offer five conceptual frameworks for the study of organizational stress along with four more specific, if multifaceted, measures - for examples developed in the United States, the Job Stress Survey and the Occupational Stress Inventory - for use in organizational stress research. These are not all equally relevant nor salient in the United States culture today nor has any single organizational stress measure become the gold standard over the past 20 years. The question now is what are the most salient concepts and measures for organizational stress research and practice in contemporary America? The gap between science and practice that is noted by Goh *et al.* (2016) is the same gap in America noted by Quick and Quick (1984). What has changed in the intervening thirty years is the greater appreciation for the key roles that epidemiology and public health can play in addressing organizational stress in America (cf., Goh *et al.*, 2016).

Epidemiology and public health are less concerned with concepts and theories than they are with causal factors and surveillance systems. Preventive intervention is keyed to diagnostic information and surveillance indicators in the organization. Valid and reliable stress measurement requires multiple psychological, environmental, and medical considerations (Quick, Quick, & Gavin, 2000). Stress instruments fall into four construct categories. These are measures of (1) environmental demands and sources of stress, (2) healthy and normal stress response, (3) modifiers of the stress response, and (4) psychological, behavioral, and medical distress and strain. Goh *et al.* (2016) have isolated ten salient workplace stressors that have consequences for mortality and healthcare costs - all focusing on organization environment demands (e.g. long working hours) or modifiers of stress response (e.g. social support at work). These top ten can be used for the purpose of workplace surveillance and assessment. In addition to environmental conditions, organizational stress assessment should focus on individual responses and indicators. For the purposes of organizational stress measurement in 2019 America, we should focus on the most salient measure related to the cultural data.

Organizational surveillance and screening should include consideration of three individual strain indicators - which are anxiety, depression, and burnout. Anxiety disorders, one of the two most common presenting complaints about stress with the other being depression, affect one in every six people in the United States (Quick & Cooper, 2003). As early as 1980, NIOSH identified stress and psychological disorders in the workplace as one of the top ten occupational health hazards in America (Sauter, Murphy, & Hurrell, 1990). There is no evidence that this has changed appreciably during the intervening decades, while NIOSH and the American Psychological Association have taken constructive and cooperative actions to address the needs. Burnout is a continuing organizational stress concern within American organizations and occupations. Maslach's (2006) continuing work in educating those who need to know about this problem has been ongoing as well. One research project within the American Orthopaedic Association using the Maslach Burnout Inventory found an emergent concern with burnout among the academic leaders within the profession and offered stress management skills for mitigating the problem (Quick et al., 2006).

Individual-level measures are insufficient for organizational stress assessments when considering both research and practice. The direct costs of organizational distress and strain can be significant, running well into billions of dollars (Quick, Wright, Adkins, Nelson, & Quick, 2013). Cascio and Boudreau (2011) have done systematic research to costing employee attitudes and behaviors with organizational consequences in mind. Two key organizational indicators that they focused on are turnout and absenteeism. Turnover rates can be easily tracked and monitored by an organization as one key indicator of stress while benchmarking with industry and national averages. Cascio and Boudreau (2011) note that there are both separation costs and replacement costs associated with turnover in an organization. They suggest that the voluntary, in distinction from involuntary, turnover is what the organization should be most concerned with monitoring and managing. In fact, some turnover, and especially involuntary turnover, can be healthy for the organization - removing underperforming employees and refreshing the workplace with vital and energetic newcomers.

Absenteeism, including sick leaves, is the second key organizational indicator that Cascio and Boudreau (2011) encourage management to monitor. They estimate that 16% of absenteeism can be directly attributable to organizational stress and another 26% to family-related issues. The remaining nearly 60% may be caused by personal illness (sick leaves), personal needs, and a sense of entitlement. Accordingly, there may be hidden costs and hidden issues embedded within the absenteeism rates that management may need to explore more deeply below the indicator numbers themselves.

In addition to these two organizational indicators, which can be used both for research and for management practice, organizations might consider monitoring the workplace for high-risk employees - which are employees with the potential for acting out in damaging and destructive ways (Quick & McFadyen, 2014). Good managers, leaders, and executives throughout any organization know who these individuals are. The purpose of identifying these employees is to refer them to an organizational clinical psychologist who can triage their situation to determine if there is a need for psychological, financial, family counseling, or other stress-related needs (Klunder, 2008). The early identification and early intervention with high-risk employees in need of such services are to prevent problems and outbreaks before they occur. With the levels of gun violence and drug addiction problems in the larger culture, this category of surveillance and monitoring is well warranted.

In summary, the most salient concepts and measures for organizational stress research and practice would be:

Organizational-Level and Workplace

> Absenteeism and voluntary turnover (Cascio & Boudreau, 2011);
> Unemployment, lack of health insurance, exposure to shift work, long working
> hours, job insecurity, work–family conflict, low job control, high job demands,
> low social support at work, and low organizational justice (Goh *et al.*, 2016);

Individual-Level Screening and Assessment

> The Trait-State Anxiety Inventory (American Psychological Association, 2019a);
> Beck Depression Inventory (BDI) (American Psychological Association, 2019b);
> Maslach Burnout Inventory (MBI) (cf. Maslach, 2006).

Cultural Influences in the United States Leading to Emergent Practices

Historical and current American cultural influences lead to some of the specific practices for organizational stress management and coping mechanisms. One of the more distinctive cultural values is that of individualism - that is, respect for the autonomy and integrity of the individual. One consequence of this is that the burden of adjustment and coping with organizational stress is placed on the individual (Quick & Quick, 1984) - which stands in contrast to the more environmentally focused workplace redesign strategies prevalent in Sweden, throughout Europe, and the United Kingdom (Levi, 2000). As a result, three stress management and coping mechanisms evolved within the American culture and are primarily individually focused. These are physical fitness, positive stress, and organizational clinical psychology. In addition to these, there is an organizationally focused NIOSH-APA strategy for healthy work organizations.

Physical Fitness

A central element of the corporate wellness programs that emerged in response to the increased attention to stress in the mid-20th century in the United States was physical fitness training. Kenneth Cooper, MD was a national advocate for this movement with his research and practice in preventive medicine. Having started as a flight surgeon in the United States Air Force, Cooper put a strong emphasis on aerobic fitness and later on also emphasized flexibility and strength training (Nelson & Quick, 2019). The emphasis is on strengthening the cardiovascular system - a key system implicated in the stress response. Aerobic discipline aims to improve health and well-being, yet a key side effect of such discipline is as a stress management skill that became central to corporate wellness and fitness programs across the United States (Nelson & Quick, 2019). In addition to the cardiovascular benefit achieved in aerobic fitness, there are two other key benefits - greater longevity (i.e. fit individuals on average have five additional years of life) and improved mental health and less depression (i.e. one of the two key presenting complaints about stress) (Cooper & Cooper, 2007). Gallup's 2008–2017 national trends data show an increase in exercise from 51% to 55% - a positive and welcomed trend.

Positive Stress: Positive Organizational Behavior, Positivity, and Eustress

The primary focus in 20th-century stress and organizational stress research focused on how stress could harm, compromise, impair, cause disease and dysfunction, and/or kill (Quick *et al.*, 1997). In the late 1990s, there was a recognition that the positive aspects of stress had been downplayed and/or overlooked. The subsequent two decades have seen an emergence of sound research and practice in positive stress: positive organizational behavior (POB), positivity, and eustress. Luthans (2002) pioneered the domain of POB with an emphasis on psychological capital. His construct of psychological capital emphasizes hope, optimism, resilience, and efficacy. Evaluations of the positive impact of psychological capital on employee well-being show positive effects over time (Arvy, Luthans, Smith, & Palmer, 2010).

Fredrickson's (2009) psychological research on positivity focused on thoughts and emotions with their impact on physiology and behavior. A key aspect of her approach is the balance between the positive and the negative. Individuals who experience a roughly 1-to-1 ratio of positive to negative thoughts and emotions are difficult to spend time with due to the heavy dose of negativity; these people drain energy from others. Those individuals who have a ratio closer to 3-to-1, or maybe even 5-to-1, of positive to negative thoughts and emotions are much less stressful to be around but they are realistic about the difficulties and challenges of life. The positive extreme is comprised of individuals who experience ratios of something like 11-to-1 of positive to negative thoughts and emotions. These hyper-positive people are very difficult to engage with and have a real challenge in engaging with life's real difficulties and demands. Positivity can be contagious in a good way, just as infectious diseases can be contagious in a bad way. This aspect of positivity leads to thriving which is the flip side of harmful organizational stress. Gallup's 2008–2017 national trends data on thriving show an increase from 49% to 56% - another positive and welcomed trend greater than that of exercise.

Eustress is literally normal stress and hence, can be subsumed under positive stress. Eustress has appeared infrequently in the organizational and workplace stress literature, although that gap has begun to close over the past two decades (Nelson & Simmons, 2011). Eustress reflects the extent to which individuals appraise a situation or event as beneficial or as a potential enhancement of their well-being. Work situations elicit a mixture of both positive and negative responses from individuals. The indicators of eustress should be positive psychological states - such as attitudes or emotions that reflect an active engagement with the work environment.

Eustressed workers are actively engaged, meaning they are immersed in and pleasurably occupied by the demands of the work at hand. Workers can be engaged and perceive positive benefits even when confronted with extremely demanding stressors. Some, in fact, may wish to proactively call up this response and to prolong the experience of eustress. Nelson and Simmons (2011) refer to this process as "savoring" and offer it as a complement to what is called "coping" in response to distress. They further suggest that individuals who are likely engaged in savoring are those who are optimistic, hardy, and self-reliant, and who possess an internal locus of control and a sense of coherence. As a complement to distress prevention, we need to study eustress generation, which consists of ways that managers can help employees engender and savor the eustress response at work.

Organizational Clinical Psychology

Organizational clinical psychology is an individually focused practice that evolved within the United States. Air Force. Adkins (1999), as an organizational clinical psychologist, designed and implemented the concept of an Organizational Health Center (OHC) - a structural mechanism for enhancing health and managing stress. An OHC is one mechanism for applying behavioral science, psychology, and public health in the workplace - with an emphasis on individual prevention and intervention. Adkins' clinical psychological approach aimed to reduce stress and psychological disorders at work as proposed by NIOSH (Sauter et al., 1990). The precipitating events for Adkins to evolve this new systemic, yet individually focused, approach to organizational clinical psychology were a series of suicides in the industrial logistics depot where she was assigned. She conducted a one-year evaluation of her innovative approach and found:

1 Workers' compensation rates declined by 3.9%, following a 4.6% increase in the previous year, exceeding the management-established goal of a 3% reduction and saving over $289,000 in workers' compensation costs;
2 Healthcare utilization rates declined by 12%, yielding savings of over $150,000 in recaptured productivity alone; and
3 Deaths resulting from behavioral problems - including suicides - declined by 41%, resulting in cost savings of over $4 million.

Drawing on Adkins' (1999) innovation, Quick and Klunder (2000) applied organizational clinical psychology in the realignment and closure of the United States Air Force's largest industrial maintenance deport at Kelly Air Force Base (AFB), Texas. Triggered by the Base Realignment and Closure Commission (BRAC) recommendation in July 1995 to United States President Clinton, Kelly AFB joined the list of realigned and/or closed domestic military installations. Specifically, the San Antonio Air Logistics Center was one of the military installations on the realignment and/or closure list. The industrial restructuring process affected the largest number of federal employees in United States history. The Center at Kelly AFB was the largest industrial employer in South Texas with over 13,000 personnel (about 85% federally employed civilians and 15% military service members) and one of the largest industrial facilities in the Department of Defense. The commanding general chose to appoint an organizational clinical psychologist recommended by the United States Air Force Surgeon General's chief clinician. As an organizational clinical psychologist, one of Klunder's (2000) first actions was to identify the 1–3% of the workforce at high-risk. Over 300 individuals were identified through the screening process and triaged for the support or help that each required, being referred to professionals.

A five-year evaluation of the program ended on July 13, 2001, when the organization closed. The results were the following:

1 No fatalities: there was not a single closure-related fatality in the organization during the closure. While there was a significant decline in suicide rates throughout the Air Force, as reported by the Centers for Disease Control and Prevention for the period of 1995 to 1999, the experience at Kelly AFB is still noteworthy in this regard.
2 No incidences of workplace violence:
3 Significant cost avoidance: there were over $33,000,000 in cost savings during the six-year period based on human resource estimates of complaints that did not happen. The Air Force estimates each employee complaint at a cost of about $80,000, all costs considered. Human resources found the number of official complaints to be approximately 25% below their estimate, resulting in the significant total estimated cost savings.

Concerned organizational leadership from the commanding general all the way down was instrumental in this organizational clinical psychological intervention for organizational stress, health, and well-being. More importantly, this success did not come at the expense of organizational performance.

Healthy Work Organization: Research and Practice

Abraham Maslow called for healthy work environments as early as the 1960s. In 1998, the Workplace Health Group (WHG) was established to conduct multidisciplinary research in worker health, safety, and organizational effectiveness (Haynes et al., 2019). Their agenda aligns with the United States Centers for Disease Control and Prevention's NIOSH Total Worker Health (TWH) initiative (Hudson et al., 2019). The TWH approach integrates health protection and health promotion with a focus on changing work stressors - that is, placing some of the burdens of coping with organizational stress on the work environment rather than on the workers (Quick *et al.*, 2013). The healthy work organization approach does draw heavily on the public health notions of risk exposure, surveillance, and prevention. Within this domain, Hammer et al. (2011) bring our attention to the importance of monitoring the work-family boundary and encouraging the development of family-supportive supervisory behaviors that benefit all concerned parties.

Concluding Note: Start at the Top

Organizational stress can start at the top and have a negative cascading effect throughout the entire organization. Toxic emotions can have harmful, destructive, and contagious (Frost & Robinson, 1999) throughout an entire workplace. By the same token, good clinical intervention with a senior executive who has mastered positive stress management skills can be primary prevention and a benefit for tens, hundreds, and even thousands of workers throughout an organization. Quick and Quick (2013) identify five key threats and challenges that executives face - which are stress, burnout, social isolation, toxic effects of emotions, and traumatic events and tragedies. The American strategies of exercise, positivity, and organizational clinical psychology can enable senior leaders to confront and overcome these threats and challenges for their own benefit and for the benefit of many others in their organizations.

References

Adkins, J. A., (1999). Promoting organizational health: The evolving practice of occupational health psychology. *Professional Psychology: Research and Practice, 30,* 129–137.
American Psychological Association. (2018). *Stress in America.*Washington, DC: American Psychological Association.
American Psychological Association. (2019a). The Trait-State Anxiety Inventory. https://www.apa.org/pi/about/publications/caregivers/practice-settings/assessment/tools/trait-state (downloaded 30 September).
American Psychological Association. (2019b). Beck Depression Inventory (BDI). https://www.apa.org/depression-guideline/assessment/ (downloaded 30 September).
Arvy, J. B., Luthans, F., Smith, R. M. & Palmer, N. F., (2010). Impact of positive psychological capital on employee well-being over time. *Journal of Occupational Health Psychology, 15*(1), 17–28.
Benison, S., Barger, A. C. & Wolfe, E. L., (1987). *Walter B. Cannon: The life and times of a young scientist.* Cambridge, MA: Belknap Press.
Cannon, W. B., (1929). *Bodily changes in pain, hunger, fear and rage.* New York: Appleton. (Original work published 1915).
Cannon, W. B., (1935). Stresses and strains of homeostasis. *The American Journal of the Medical Sciences, 189,* 1–14.a.
Cascio, W. F. & Boudreau, J. W., (2011). *Investing in people: Financial impact of human resource initiatives* (2nd Ed.). Upper Saddle Ridge, NJ: Pearson Education/FT Press.
Casey, Jr. (2011). Comprehensive soldier fitness: A vision for psychological resilience in the U.S. Army. *American Psychologist, 66*(1), 1–3.
Cooper, C. L., (1998). *Theories of organizational stress.* Oxford, England: Oxford University Press.
Cooper, K. H. & Cooper, T. C., (2007). *Start Strong, Finish Strong: Prescriptions for a Lifetime of Health.* New York: NY. Avery.
Fredrickson, B., (2009). *Positivity: Groundbreaking research reveals how to embrace the hidden strength of positive emotions, overcome negativity, and thrive* New York. NY: Crown Publishers.
Frost, P. & Robinson, S., (1999). The toxic handler: Organizational hero – and casualty. *Harvard Business Review, 77,* 97–106.
Goh, J., Pfeffer, J. & Zenios, S. A., (2016). The relationship between workplace

stressors and mortality and health costs in the United States. *Management Science*, 62(2), 608–628.

Hammer, L. B., Kossek, E. E., Anger, W. K., Bodner, T. & Zimmerman, K. L., (2011). Clarifying work-family intervention processes: The roles of work-family conflict and family-supportive supervisor behaviors. *Journal of Applied Psychology*, 96(1), 134–150.

Hargrove, M. B., Quick, J. C., Nelson, D. L. & Quick, J. D., (2011). *The theory of preventive stress management: A 33-year review and evaluation. Stress and health*, 27(3), 1–11.

Haynes, N. J., Vandenberg, R. J., DeJoy, D. M., Wilson, M. G., Padilla, H. M., Zuecher, H. S. & Robertson, M. M., (2019). The workplace health group: A case study of 20 years of multidisciplinary research. *American Psychologist*, 74(3), 380–393.

Hudson, H. I., Nigam, J. A. S., Sauter, S. L., Chosewood, C., Schill, A. L. & Howard, J. (Eds.). (2019). *Total Worker Health*. Washington D.C.: American Psychological Association.

Kahn, R. L., Wolfe, R. P., Quinn, R. P., Snoek, J. D. & Rosenthal, R. A., (1964). *Organizational stress: Studies in role conflict and ambiguity*. New York: John Wiley & Sons.

Klunder, C. S., (2008). Preventive Stress Management at Work: The Case of the San Antonio Air Logistics Center, Air Force Materiel Command (AFMC), San Antonio, *Managing and Leading: SPIM Conference and Institutes*, 29 February.

Levi, L., (2000). *Guidance on work-related stress: Spice of life or kiss of death?*. Luxembourg: European Commission, Directorate-General for Employment and Social Affairs, Health & Safety at Work (100 pages).

Luthans, F., (2002). The need for and meaning of positive organizational behavior. *Journal of Organizational Behavior*, 23(6), 695–706.

Macik-Frey, M., Quick, J. C. & Nelson, D. L., (2007). Advances in occupational health: From a stressful beginning to a positive future. *Journal of Management*, 33(6), 809–840.

Mack, D. A., Shannon, C., Quick, J. D. & Quick, J. C., (1998). Chapter IV – Stress and the preventive management of workplace violence. In R. W. Griffin, A. O'Leary-Kelly & J. Collins (Eds.), *Dysfunctional behavior in organizations – Volume 1: Violent behavior in organizations* (pp. 119–141). Greenwich, CN: JAI Press.

Maslach, C., (1982). *Burnout, the cost of caring*. NJ: Prentice-Hall.

Maslach, C., (2006). *Understanding job burnout*. In A. M. Rossi, P. L. Perrewe & S. L. Sauter (Eds), *Stress and Quality of Working Life: Current Perspectives in Occupational Work* (pp. 37–51). Greenwich, CT: Information Age Publishing.

Nelson, D. L. & Quick, J. C., (2019). *ORGB: Organizational Behavior*[6]. Mason, OH: Cengage/ South-Western.

Nelson, D. L. & Simmons, B. L., (2011). Savoring eustress whole coping with distress: The holistic model of stress. In J. C. Quick & L.E. Tetrick (Eds.), *Handbook of occupational health psychology* (pp. 37–54). Washington, DC: American Psychological Association.

Quick, J. C. & Cooper, C. L., (2003). *Stress and strain* (2nd ed.). Oxford, UK: Health Press.

Quick, J. C., Cooper, C. L., Nelson, D. L., Quick, J. D. & Gavin, J. H., (2003). Stress, health, and well-being at work. In J. Greenberg (Ed.), *Organizational Behavior: The State of the Science (2/E)* (pp. 53–89). Mahwah, NJ: Lawrence Erlbaum Associates Publishers.

Quick, J. C. & Klunder, C., (2000). Preventive stress management at work: The case of the San Antonio air logistics center (AFMC), *The Proceedings of the Eleventh International Congress on Stress*, Hawaii, Hawaii, The American Institute of Stress.

Quick, J. C., McFadyen, A. & Nelson, D. L., (2014). No accident: Health, well-being, and performance at work. *Journal of Organizational Effectiveness*, 1(1), 98–119.

Quick, J. C. & Quick, J. D., (1984). *Organizational stress and preventive management.* New York: McGraw-Hill.

Quick, J. C. & Quick, J. D., (2013). Executive well-being. In A. Caza & K.S. Cameron (Eds.) Happiness and Organizations, Section VII in S. A. David, I. Boniwell & A. Conley Ayers (Eds.), *The Oxford Handbook of Happiness* (pp. 798–813). Oxford, UK: Oxford University Press.

Quick, J. C., Quick, J. D. & Gavin, J. H., (2000). Stress: Measurement. In N. Schneiderman (Ed.), *Health Psychology Section, Encyclopedia of psychology* (pp. 484–487). Washington, DC: American Psychological Association and Oxford University Press.

Quick, J. C., Quick, J. D., Nelson, D. L. & Hurrell, J. J., (1997). *Preventive stress management in organizations.* Washington, DC: American Psychological Association.

Quick, J. C., Saleh, K. J., Sime, W. E., Martin, W., Cooper, C. L., Quick, J. D. & Mont, M. A., (2006). Stress management skills for strong leadership: Is it worth dying for? *Journal of Bone & Joint Surgery*, 88(1), 217–225.

Quick, J. C., Wright, T.A., Adkins, J. A., Nelson, D. L. & Quick, J. D., (2013). *Preventive stress management in organizations* (2nd ed.). Washington, DC: American Psychological Association.

Sauter, S. L., Murphy, L. R. & Hurrell, J. J., (1990). Prevention of work-related psychological disorders: A national strategy proposed by the National Institute for Occupational Safety and Health (NIOSH). *American Psychologist*, 45(10), 1146–1158.

Simon, R. & Cutter, C., (2019). Owners rethink workplace safety. *The Wall Street Journal*, CCXXLIV(70), September 23, B6.

Vital Statistics of the United States. (1985). *Life tables*, Vol. II, Section 6 (DHHS Publication No. PHS 88-1140, January 1988), Washington, DC: US Dept. of Health and Human Services, Public Health Service, National Center for Health Statistics.

Worrall, L. & Cooper, C. L., (2001). Managing the work-life balance. *European Business Forum*, 6, 48–53.

Wilper, A. P., Woolhandler, S., Lasser, K. E., McCormick, D., Bor, D. H. & Himmelstein, D. U., (2009). Health insurance and mortality in US adults. *American Journal of Public Health*, 99(12), 2289–2295.

15 Key Issues and Future Research

Kajal A. Sharma, Cary L. Cooper, and D.M. Pestonjee

This volume reflects the current status of work stress research in various countries that are economically, socially, politically, and technologically different. Moreover, organizations in these countries have different workforce demographics, regulatory compliance, legal demands, culture and climate. However, different chapters reflect that stress is still identified and acknowledged as a significant issue in all countries. In our concluding discussion, we reflect on some of the key takeaway points arising from the discussion in different chapters and suggest future work areas.

We notice that there is consensus about some of the major sources of work stress across different countries. Stressors like work overload, work hours, lack of control, role conflict, role ambiguity, work relationships, career advancement opportunities, salary, job insecurity, organizational factors like culture and policies, and work-life balance issues are common in various national stress literature. This is not an exhaustive list, but it identifies some of the most critical stressors faced by the global workforce. However, the quality and quantity of investigations on the stress-strain relationship vary in different countries. For instance, there is extensive literature covering organizational stress issues from the United States, United Kingdom, and other European countries compared to countries like Russia, Brazil, South Africa, and many Arab and African countries. Recently, there has been an increase in research studies from India and China, as they have emerged as the hottest centers of economic growth; however, more work needs to be done.

We observe that there is considerably less research undertaken in examining the individual-difference variables - such as personality characteristics, demographic factors (i.e. age, gender, education, marital status, socioeconomic status, and ethnic or racial group), and organizational context dimensions (i.e. management styles, organizational culture, lack of communication, mutual decision-making and organization politics) - which should be investigated further and included as potential causes and/ or moderators of the work stress process. Another noticeable trend is that researchers in many developing countries have shown keen interest in analyzing the antecedents of stress as compared to examining the different consequences of stress on health. Further, moderating factors influencing the relationship between stress and ill-health - such as locus of control, gender differences, personality predispositions, and socioeconomic status - have been studied in developed countries, but such themes have not received much exposure in the literature of developing countries. More studies need to focus on the multiple consequences of stress on human health. Cooper and Quick (2017) point out that stress is directly or indirectly linked to seven of the ten leading causes of death in all developed nations, including the United States of America and the United Kingdom. These seven causes are heart disease, cancer, stroke, injuries, suicide/homicide, chronic liver disease, emphysema, and chronic bronchitis. On the other hand, according to the World Health Organization (WHO, 2007), about 75% of the world's labor force - which accounts for about 2,400 million people - lives and works in developing countries, and 20–50% of workers in industrialized countries may be subjected to hazardous exposure at work, and this rate is expected to be higher in developing and newly industrialized countries. In light of such facts, it becomes more significant for researchers to examine the link between stress and health-related outcomes and behaviors for the benefit of the global workforce.

Countries face unique climate and cultural stressors - such as heat stress, the role of the state, the role of national culture, the proportion and state of workers in the non-regulatory sector, weak legislation to protect worker rights, power harassment (i.e. managerial abuse of power), the presence of social media, and the role of religion. The influence of such factors on work and work organizations in different countries has been discussed in this book. Further research needs to be undertaken on these unique stressors, as they are responsible for the changing nature and forms of jobs as well as new and different work settings. Further research on such aspects will benefit organizations to understand the internal and external environment of their businesses, their unique challenges, effectively plan work for the workforce, and devise all-inclusive stress interventions accordingly. Cultural aspects especially may need significant attention when dealing with work-related stress in developing countries. Features such as spirituality, religion, tradition, the collectivist approach, and societal expectations and dynamics are integral to the cultural fabric of these countries. These characteristics make them different from most of the developed countries that have individualistic cultural traits. Thus, researchers need to investigate the environment in which stress occurs and focus on context-based research - which is also suggested by Cooper, Dewe, and O'Driscoll (2001), as the environment can influence the nature of strain being experienced by the individual.

Research presented in different chapters acknowledges the contribution made by present models, theories and measures developed to study stress. However, the discussion highlights the need for developing more culture-specific models and theories. This issue is critical for developing a context-based understanding of organizational stress. Most stress models and frameworks have their roots in Western cultures where they seem to fit in the internal and external environments of organizations. Nonetheless, researchers from various countries like India, China, Brazil, South Africa, Nigeria, Russia, and Japan have been using the same models to examine stress phenomena in their cultures. Considering the uniqueness of different local and national cultures, these models might not be fit for purpose and need to be customized or modified. There should also be attempts to develop new models considering the changing work and work environment in such countries. The issue of the effectiveness of psychological instruments designed based on Western theories and models used for research in other cultures is also been debated. Researchers like Laungani (2007); Spector et al. (2004); Burke (2010); Bhagat et al. (2010) have raised the issue of Western imitation in the context of cross-cultural research on stress and discussed problems associated with the use of such models, theories, and measures. Cooper et al. (2001) suggest that, in light of social and economic changes over the past two decades, the existing measures used for capturing data on stress and coping should be evaluated in terms of (a) the content of items, (b) the scoring of responses, and (c) the process of establishing internal reliability.

International research collaborations can play a critical role in helping researchers develop new models. However, for such initiatives to be successful, researchers must respect the traditions, beliefs, and values of different cultures and learn from them while developing theories and models to explain phenomena like stress-strain-coping (Palsane, Bhavsar, Goswami, & Evans, 1999). The development of indigenous models and measures might offer further clarity on how the work and work environment might be perceived differently by employees with different cultural backgrounds. Considering that the contemporary work organizations have a diversified workforce, this knowledge can be useful for organizations to understand the cultural values endorsed by their employees and how they influence employees' work attitudes and behaviors.

A prominent view found across national literature is that stress is harmful, so there has been an extensive examination of the negative side of stress compared to the positive effects of stress on the workforce. As there is a bias towards identifying the negative effects of stress, research has focused on finding the causes for it and developing coping mechanisms to deal with stress (Nelson & Simmons, 2003). Illness rather than wellness is associated as a by-product of stress and there is extensive literature to support this. Myers (2000) highlighted that the number of publications on negative states exceeds that of positive states by a ratio of 14:1, which was also supported by Avey, Luthans, and Jensen (2009). Schaufeli and Salanova (2007) suggested that failing to capture the positive effects of stress offers an inappropriate and incomplete description of this phenomenon. In his book, Selye (1956) spoke about two types of stresses - eustress and distress - found in the workplace - a concept that has been supported by much research in the following years. However, there has been extensive focus on distress compared to eustress - which highlights that researchers have focused more on treating stress symptoms rather than examining factors that can prevent distress at work. It has also been observed (Le Fevre, Matheny, & Kolt 2003) that some popular theories in the field - like control theory (Spector, 1998), P-E fit theory (Edwards, Caplan, & Van Harrison, 1998), and the Cybernetic theory (Cummings & Cooper, 1998) do not differentiate between both kinds of stresses. Most of the stress theories and models on stress have discussed how stress is generated and have supported the identification and weakening of stress-generating factors in the work environment to manage stress effectively. However, these models have failed to discuss the identification of factors that could act as buffers against stress. Nonetheless, researchers like Quick and Quick (1979) have investigated the ways to combat stress at work with their theory on preventive stress management. There has been a surge in studies focusing on positive psychology and its influence on work recently, but, before that, very few studies focussed on these aspects (e.g. Pestonjee, 1992; Lazarus, 1993; Luthans, 2002; Peterson, 2006; Avey et al., 2009; Seligman, 2012; Rahimnia, Mazidi, & Mohammadzadeh,2013; De Sousa & van Dierendonck, 2014; Abbas & Raja, 2015; Chambel, Carvalho, Cesário, & Lopes, 2017; Marques-Pinto, Jesus, Mendes, Fronteira, & Roberto, 2018; Celik, 2018). Although, more remains to be explored on the factors and mechanisms preventing stress at work. Hence, it is important to focus on positive psychology and offer a thorough examination of the positive influence of stress on work - which is also endorsed by other researchers. As suggested by Turner, Barling, and Zacharatos (2002), it is time to expand our research and focus on exploring the positive effects of stress on work fully so that we can develop a complete understanding of the meaning and effects of working.

We witness that there is a dominance of cross-sectional research in stress literature and a need for more longitudinal studies. Many researchers suggest that longitudinal research designs offer stronger conclusions on the causal relationship of different independent and dependent variables as compared to cross-sectional research designs (Fried, Rolland, & Ferris, 1984; Cooper et al., 2001; Skakon, Nielsen, Borg, & Guzman, 2010; Kelloway and Francis, 2013; Mäkikangas, Kinnunen, Feldt, & Schaufeli, 2016). They also provide an opportunity to study the influence of time factors on the dynamics of the stress-strain-coping process. Thus, such studies can help provide us with a better understanding of the causal processes. This approach can provide greater opportunity for generalization of research findings but also demands a longer-term commitment to generate effective longitudinal research. Researchers also need to be aware of the challenges of undertaking longitudinal studies - like time lag, sample size, changes during the study, and the stability of measures and a need to work around these (Ter Doest & De Jonge, 2006). Laungani (1999) also highlighted that researchers especially from developing countries face constraints like the lack of funding, the lack of informational and technological support, poor industry and academic interaction, and the lack of international collaborations - which, to our understanding, not only influence but also limit the quality and quantity of research output. The popularity of longitudinal designs has grown over the last couple of decades, yet there is still a lot of ground to cover - an observation which is echoed by other researchers like Taris and Kompier (2003); Cooper et al. (2001); Skakon et al. (2010); Pandey, Gaur, and Pestonjee (2013) and Mäkikangas et al. (2016).

We also spot that quantitative methodologies are more popular compared to qualitative methodologies in studying stress. This has also been reflected in different reviews (e.g. Jex & Beehr, 1991; Kristensen, 1996; Cooper et al., 2001; Lin, 2003; Mazzola, Schonfeld, & Spector, 2011). Quantitative studies are important in exploring the stress-strain-coping relationship and considered more time and cost-effective from the researcher's point of view. However, this method has limitations that can be overcome by examining the stress-strain-coping dynamics through a qualitative lens. Qualitative research does not limit the stressors, strains, and coping methods used by employees (Schonfeld & Farrell, 2010). Hence, as these studies do not follow any preconceived notions, they are found to be very useful in exploring and providing insights on the latent factors related to stress in different groups in different situations. This kind of research is person and organization-focused offering valuable insights on current issues and assisting the discovery of new person and situation-centric stress characteristics that can help design specific and effective interventions. Many researchers have endorsed qualitative methodologies and their importance in stress research (O'Driscoll and Cooper, 1996; Richards, Oman, Hedberg, Thoresen, & Bowden, 2006; Randall, Cox, & Griffiths, 2007; Schonfeld & Farrell, 2010; Schonfeld & Mazzola, 2013). However, researchers should also consider the limitations of the qualitative approach. Given there are limitations in both quantitative and qualitative designs, some researchers have suggested the application of a more "balanced approach". This balanced approach endorses adopting a "mixed method" design wherein the strengths of both qualitative and quantitative methods are capitalized on. We observe this as a growing trend in most of the developed countries, and studies undertaken in cross-cultural context have been especially and extensively employing triangulation methodology (Narayanan, Menon, & Spector, 1999; Cooper et al., 2001; Östlund, Kidd, Wengström, & Rowa-Dewar, 2011; Liu, Spector, & Shi, 2008; Tummala-Narra, Inman, & Ettigi, 2011; Singh, Cross, Munro, & Jackson, 2020). We suggest that more studies should adopt triangulation methodology, as it supports researchers in integrating qualitative and quantitative research outcomes and helps them clarify their theoretical propositions, as well as the foundations of their results. This method also offers an opportunity by which researchers can establish more clear links between theory and empirical findings, challenge theoretical assumptions, and develop new and perhaps culture-inclusive stress theories and models.

Another important reflection is that there is a dearth of organization-based intervention studies in stress literature. Hence, knowledge of the effectiveness of different proposed stress management interventions in practice is limited. Different researchers across countries have identified similar trends (Havermans et al., 2016; Giga, Cooper, & Faragher, 2003; Duarte & Pinto-Gouveia, 2016, Li et al., 2017; Ugwoke et al., 2018). Generally, across literature, interventions are of two kinds: person-centric and organizations-centric. Some researchers (Montano, Hoven, & Siegrist, 2014) have suggested that organization-wide interventions yield beneficial results for the organizations, as they generally lead to systemic changes to organizational practices that target all employees or a particular group of employees. On the other hand, it has been argued that in practice, organization-wise interventions to manage stress are less frequent as they incur costs and are complex in application and measurement. Hence, researchers have also been examining individual interventions that help employees to develop skills to manage, cope, and reduce their work stress. They are considered a more cost and time-effective way of countering stress, and, therefore, have also received attention from employers and employees (Tetrick & Winslow, 2015). However, evidence shows that their duration is short; hence, their effectiveness may be limited (Bhui et al., 2016). Chapters from different countries have offered some insights into popular intervention practices prevalent in those countries. We can conclude that there is an increasing trend of organization-wide interventions in developed countries; however, organizations in developing countries expect employees to take ownership of managing and coping with work stress. To create healthy organizations, it is essential to strike a balance between different kinds of interventions. Depending on the work, workgroup, and work setting, different interventions - like primary interventions (aiming to prevent exposure to known risk factors and to increase the resilience of the workforce), secondary interventions (aimed at reversing a progression), and tertiary interventions (aimed at reducing severity) - can benefit organizations (Leka & Jain, 2017). Hence researchers like Robertson and Cooper (2011) and Weinberg and Cooper (2012) have suggested that all kinds of organizations should consider a range of all such interventions to deal which work stress. Intervention-based studies not only expand understanding of causal relationships, but they also enable systematic assessment of the organization's various stress prevention management and treatment strategies and the effects of such strategies in maintaining and promoting employee's overall health and well-being at work. Therefore, more researchers should undertake intervention studies based on organizational evidence validating the organization's actions and practices and developing further knowledge on the implementation and effectiveness of various kinds of interventions. An understanding developed through such studies can also help improve general management practices in various kinds of organizations.

Today we see different types of organizations around us from big and global corporate businesses to small and medium-sized businesses who employ formal and/or informal workforces, operate in different cultures, and face exceptional challenges - like the current global pandemic caused by Covid-19. Covid-19 has once again put the critical issue of work stress management and employee health to the forefront. The role of the state, work organizations, and other stakeholders in identifying the causes of stress, taking proactive measures, analyzing the impact of stress on different groups, identifying suitable interventions, implementing identified interventions in the necessary time frame, and evaluating the helpfulness of applied interventions is seen to be critical in dealing with stress effectively within organizations and community at large during this pandemic. We have discussed stress as a global phenomenon in our first chapter, however, considering our observations from literature, we endorse that the strategies devised to eliminate stress and create healthy organizations have to include local, national flavors to be successful. Important stakeholders like governments, social partners, unions, private and public organizations, employees, and researchers together need to devise effective strategies to prevent, manage, and treat stress in the organizational space. This can be done most effectively by sharing information, resources, expertise, and experience to develop best management practices at workplaces. Researchers can also play a significant role by expanding knowledge on the best practices by undertaking more cross-cultural and interdisciplinary research. Our understanding is that implementing such quality management practices will make organizations and the workforce thrive in most cultures around the globe and help them persevere during extraordinary circumstances, like the current Covid-19 crisis. However, more research should be undertaken globally to gain a comprehensive insight on the full impact of the current pandemic on workforce and organizations to identify and to rapidly adapt to new, integrated, and sustainable interventions that make contemporary work organizations more resistant to any similar situation in the future.

References

Abbas, M. & Raja, U. (2015). Impact of psychological capital on innovative performance and job stress. *Canadian Journal of Administrative Sciences/ Revue Canadienne des Sciences del'Administration, 32*(2), 128–138.

Avey, J. B., Luthans, F. & Jensen, S. M. (2009). Psychological capital: A positive resource for combating employee stress and turnover. *Human Resource Management, 48*(5), 677–693.

Bhagat, R., Krishnan, B., Nelson, T. A., Leonard, K. M., Ford, D. L. & Billing, T. K. (2010). Organizational stress, psychological strain, and work outcomes in six national contexts: A closer look at the moderating influences of coping styles and decision latitude. *Cross-CulturalManagement: An International Journal, 17*(1), 10–29.

Bhui, K., Dinos, S., Galant-Miecznikowska, M., de Jongh, B. & Stansfeld, S. (2016). Perceptions of work stress causes and effective interventions in employees working in public, private and non-governmental organisations: A qualitative study. *BJPsych Bulletin, 40*(6), 318–325.

Burke, R. (2010). Workplace stress and well-being across cultures: Research and practice. *Crosscultural Management: An international Journal, 17*(1), 5–9.

Caulfield, N., Chang, D., Dollard, M. F. & Elshaug, C. (2004). A Review of Occupational Stress Interventions in Australia. *International Journal of Stress Management, 11*(2), 149.

Celik, M. (2018). The Effect of Psychological Capital Level of Employees on Workplace Stress and Employee Turnover Intention. *Innovar, 28*(68), 67–75.

Chambel, M. J., Carvalho, V. S., Cesário, F. & Lopes, S. (2017). The work-to-life conflict mediation between job characteristics and well-being at work. Career Development International.

Cooper, C. L., Dewe, P. J. & O'Driscoll, M. P. (2001). *Organizational stress: A review and critique of theory, research, and applications*. Thousand Oaks: SAGE.

Cooper, C. & Quick, J. C. (Eds.). (2017). *The handbook of stress and health: A guide to research and practice*. John Wiley & Sons.

Cummings, T. G. & Cooper, C. L. (1998). A cybernetic theory of organizational stress. In De Sousa, C.L. Cooper (Ed.), *Theories of organizational stress* (pp. 101–121). New York: Oxford University Press.

De Sousa, M. J. C. & van Dierendonck, D. (2014). Servant leadership and engagement in a merge process under high uncertainty. *Journal of Organisational Change Management, 27*, 877–899.

Duarte, J. & Pinto-Gouveia, J. (2016). Effectiveness of a mindfulness-based intervention on oncology nurses' burnout and compassion fatigue symptoms: A non-randomized study. *International Journal of Nursing Studies, 64*, 98–107.

Edwards, J. R., Caplan, R. D. & Van Harrison, R. (1998). Person-environment fit theory: Conceptual foundations, empirical evidence, and directions for future research. In Fried, C.L. Cooper (Ed.), *Theories of organizational stress* (pp. 28–67). New York: Oxford University Press.

Fried, M., Rolland, K. M. & Ferris, G. R. (1984). The physiological measurement of work stress: A critique. *Personnel Psychology, 37,* 583–615.

Giga, S. I., Cooper, C. L. & Faragher, B. (2003). The development of a framework for a comprehensive approach to stress management interventions at work. *International Journal of Stress Management, 10*(4), 280.

Havermans, B. M., Schelvis, R. M. C., Boot, C. R. L., Brouwers, E. P. M., Anema, J. R. & Beek, A. J. (2016). Process variables in organizational stress management intervention evaluation research: A systematic review. *Scandinavian Journal of Work, Environment & Health, 42,* 371–381.

Houtman, I, Jettinghoff, K & Cedillo, L. (2007). *Raising awareness of stress in developing countries: A modern hazard in a traditional working environment.* Protecting Workers' Health Series no. 6, Geneva: WHO.

International Labour Organization. (2016). Workplace stress: A collective challenge. https://www.ilo.org/wcmsp5/groups/public/---ed_protect/---protrav/---safework/documents/publication/wcms_466547.pdf.

Jex, S. M. & Beehr, T. A. (1991). Emerging theoretical and methodological issues in the study of work-related stress. *Research in Personnel and Human Resources Management, 9*(31), 1–365.

Kelloway, E. K. & Francis, L. (2013). Longitudinal research and data analysis. In Kristensen, R. R. Sinclair, M. Wang & L. E. Tetrick (Eds.), *Research methods in occupational health psychology: Measurement, design, and data analysis* (pp. 374–394). New York, NY: Taylor & Francis.

Kristensen, T. S. (1996). Job stress and cardiovascular disease: A theoretic critical review. *Journal of Occupational Health Psychology, 1*(3), 246.

Lazarus, R. S. (1993). From psychological stress to the emotions: A history of changing outlooks. *Annual Review of Psychology, 44*(1), 1–22.

Laungani, P. (1999). Stress in India and England. In Laungani, D.M. Pestonjee, U. Pareek & R. Agrawal (Eds.), *Studies in Stress and Its Management* (pp. 17–43). New Delhi: Oxford & IBH.

Laungani, P.D. (2007). *Understanding cross-cultural psychology.* New Delhi: SAGE (South Asia).

Leka, S. & Jain, A. (2017). *Mental Health in the Workplace in Europe - Consensus Paper,* EU Compass for Action on Mental Health and Well-being. Funded by the European Union in the fame of the 3e (2014–2020) EU Health Program. European Commission.

Le Fevre, M., Matheny, J. & Kolt, G. S. (2003). Eustress, distress, and interpretation in occupational stress. *Journal of Managerial Psychology, 18*(7), 726–744.

Li, J., Riedel, N., Barrech, A., Herr, R. M., Aust, B., Mörtl, K. & Angerer, P. (2017). *Long-Term Effectiveness of a Stress Management Intervention at Work: A 9-Year Follow-Up Study Based on a Randomized Wait-List Controlled Trial in Male Managers.* (Volume 2017). BioMed research international.

Lin, S. (2003). Occupational stress research: A review. *Psychological Science-Shanghai, 26*(143), 494–497.

Liu, C., Spector, P. E. & Shi, L. (2008). Use of both qualitative and quantitative approaches to study job stress in different gender and occupational groups. *Journal of Occupational Health Psychology, 13*, 357–370.

Luthans, F. (2002). The need for and meaning of positive organizational behavior. *Journal of Organizational Behavior: The International Journal of Industrial, Occupational and Organizational Psychology and Behavior, 23*(6), 695–706.

Mazzola, J. J., Schonfeld, I. S. & Spector, P. E. (2011). What qualitative research has taught us about occupational stress. *Stress and Health, 27*(2), 93–110.

Mäkikangas, A., Kinnunen, U., Feldt, T. & Schaufeli, W. (2016). The longitudinal development of employee well-being: A systematic review. *Work & Stress, 30*(1), 46–70.

Marques-Pinto, A., Jesus, É. H., Mendes, A. M. O. C., Fronteira, I. & Roberto, M. S. (2018). Nurses' intention to leave the organization: A mediation study of professional Burnout and Engagement. *The Spanish journal of psychology, 21*, E32.

Montano, D., Hoven, H. & Siegrist, J. (2014). Effects of organisational-level interventions at work on employees' health: A systematic review. *BMC Public Health, 14*(1), 135.

Myers, D. G. (2000). The funds, friends, and faith of happy people. *American Psychologist, 55*(1), 56.

Naghieh, A., Montgomery, P., Bonell, C. P., Thompson, M. & Aber, J. L. (2015). Organisational interventions for improving wellbeing and reducing work-related stress in teachers. *Cochrane Database of Systematic Reviews*, (4), CD010306.

Narayanan, L., Menon, S. & Spector, P. E. (1999). Stress in the workplace: A comparison of gender and occupations. *Journal of Organizational Behavior: The International Journal of Industrial, Occupational and Organizational Psychology and Behavior, 20*(1), 63–73.

Nelson, D. L. & Simmons, B. L. (2003). "Health psychology and work stress: A more positive approach". In Östlund, J.C. Quick & L. Tetrick (Eds.), *Handbook of Occupational Health Psychology*. Washington, DC: APA.

Östlund, U., Kidd, L., Wengström, Y. & Rowa-Dewar, N. (2011). Combining qualitative and quantitative research within mixed method research designs: A methodological review. *International Journal of Nursing Studies, 48*(3), 369–383.

O'Driscoll, M. P. & Cooper, C. L. (1996). A critical incident analysis of stress-coping behaviors at work. *Stress Medicine, 12*, 123–128.

Pandey, S., Gaur, S. P. & Pestonjee, D.M. (2013). Methodological Issues in Stress Research: Challenges, Concerns, and Directions. Stress and Work: Perspectives on Understanding and Managing Stress, 323.

Palsane, M. N., Bhavsar, S. N., Goswami, R. P. & Evans, G. W. (1999). The concept of stress in the Indian tradition. In Pestonjee, D.M. Pestonjee, U. Pareek & R. Agrawal (Eds.), *Studies in stress and its management* (pp. 1–15). New Delhi: Oxford & IBH.

Pestonjee, D.M. (1992). *Stress and coping: The Indian experience*. New Delhi: Sage Publications.

Peterson, C. (2006). *A primer in positive psychology*. Oxford university press.

Quick, J. C. & Quick, J. D. (1979). Reducing stress through preventive management. *Human Resource Management(pre-1986)*, 18(3), 15.

Randall, R., Cox, T. & Griffiths, A. (2007). Participants' accounts of a stress management intervention. *Human Relations*, 60(8), 1181–1209.

Rahimnia, F., Mazidi, A. K. & Mohammadzadeh, Z. (2013). Emotional mediators of psychological capital on well-being: The role of stress, anxiety, and depression. *Management Science Letters*, 3(3), 913–926.

Richards, T. A., Oman, D., Hedberg, Thoresen, C. E. & Bowden, J. (2006). A qualitative examination of a spiritually-based intervention and self-management in the workplace. *Nursing Science Quarterly*, 19(3), 231–239.

Robertson, I. & Cooper, C. (2011). *Well-being: Productivity and happiness at work*. Palgrave Macmillan.

Schaufeli, W., Salanova, M. (2007). Work engagement: An emerging psychological concept and its implications for organizations, In Schonfeld, S. W., Gilliland, D. P., Skarlicki & D. D., Steiner (Eds.), *Research in social issues in management (Volume 5): Managing social and ethical issues in organizations* (pp. 135–177). Greenwich, CT: Information Age Publishers.

Schonfeld, I. S. & Farrell, E. (2010). Qualitative methods can enrich quantitative research on occupational stress: An example from one occupational group. *New Developments in Theoretical and Conceptual Approaches to Job Stress Research in Occupational Stress and Wellbeing*, 8, 137–197.

Schonfeld, I. S. & Mazzola, J. J. (2013). Strengths and limitations of qualitative approaches to research in occupational health psychology. In Selye, L. Tetrick, R. Sinclair & M. Wang (Eds.), *Research Methods in Occupational Health Psychology: State of the art in measurement, design, and data analysis*. London, UK: Routledge.

Selye, H. (1956). *The Stress of Life*. New York: McGraw-Hill.

Seligman, M. E. (2012). *Flourish: A visionary new understanding of happiness and well-being*. Simon and Schuster.

Singh, C., Cross, W., Munro, I. & Jackson, D. (2020). Occupational stress facing nurse academics—A mixed-methods systematic review. *Journal of Clinical Nursing*, 29(5-6), 720–735.

Skakon, J., Nielsen, K., Borg, V. & Guzman, J. (2010). Are leaders' well-being, behaviours and style associated with the affective well-being of their employees? A systematic review of three decades of research. *Work & Stress*, 24(2), 107–139.

Spector, P.E. (1998). A control theory of the job stress process. In Spector, C.L. Cooper (Ed.), *Theories of organizational stress* (pp. 153–166). New York: Oxford University Press.

Spector, P. E., Cooper, C. L., Poelmans, S., Allen, T. D., O'Driscoll, M., Sanchez, J. I., et al., (2004). A cross-national comparative study of work/family stressors, working hours, and wellbeing: China and Latin America vs. the Anglo world. *Personnel Psychology*, 57, 119–142.

Taris, T. W. & Kompier, M. (2003). *Challenges in longitudinal designs in occupational health psychology*. Scandinavian Journal of Work, Environment & Health, 29, 1–4.

Tetrick, L. E. & Winslow, C. J. (2015). Workplace stress management interventions and health promotion. *Annual Review of Organizational Psychology and Organizational Behavior*, 2(1), 583–603.

Ter Doest, L. & De Jonge, J. (2006). Testing causal models of job characteristics and employee well-being: A replication study using cross-lagged structural equation modelling. *Journal of Occupational and Organizational Psychology*, 79(3), 499–507.

Turner, N., Barling, J. & Zacharatos, A. (2002). Positive psychology at work. *Handbook of positive psychology*, 52, 715–728.

Tummala-Narra, P., Inman, A. G. & Ettigi, S. P. (2011). Asian Indians' responses to discrimination: A mixed-method examination of identity, coping, and self-esteem. *Asian American Journal of Psychology*, 2(3), 205.

Ugwoke, S. C., Eseadi, C., Onuigbo, L. N., Aye, E. N., Akaneme, I. N., Oboegbulem, A. I. & Ene, A. (2018). A rational-emotive stress management intervention for reducing job burnout and dysfunctional distress among special education teachers: An effect study. *Medicine*, 97(17), 1–8.

Weinberg, A. & Cooper, C. (2012). The nature of stress in turbulent times. In *Stress in Turbulent Times* (pp. 39–61). London: Palgrave Macmillan.

WHO (2007). *Raising Awareness of Stress at Work in Developing Countries Protecting Workers' Health* Series No. 6. Geneva, Switzerland: WHO Press.

Index

Note: *Italicized* page numbers refer to figures, **bold** page numbers refer to tables.

abbaya 196
absenteeism: in Australia 7; in India 81, 92; in Japan 92, 138; in Malaysia 2; in Oman 209; in Russia 209; in United States 309
Abu-Hilal, M. 201
Act of Promoting Measures to Prevent Death and Injury from Overwork (Japan) 129
Adesola, A.O. 145
Adkins, J.A. 312–13
Adusei-Asante, K. 287
Afsharian, A. 12
ageism 194
Aguiar, O.B. 33
Ahmed, N. 93
Akintayo, I. 153
Akinyele, F.E. 145
Akinyele, S.T. 145
Al Busaidy, N.S.M. 199
Al-Adawi, S. 194, 210
Al-Alawi, M. 200
Alarcon, G.M. 254
Albania **192**, 193
alcohol use 276
Aleixo, M. 255
Alfrey, K.L. 14
algorithms 292–3
Al-Hashemi, T. 200
Allah 210
Al-Lawati, S. 201
Al-Maniri, A. 199
Almazroui, A. 201
Al-Nabhani, A.M. 198, 200
Al-Rubaee, F.R. 199, 200
Al-Sinawi, H. 194

Al-Sinawi, H. 210
Altman, J. 198
Alves, E. 253
Alves de Moura, P. 253
amal-salih 210
American Orthopaedic Association 309
American Psychological Association 306
American Sociological Association 202
An Organizational Stress Screening Tool (ASSET) 51
Anagnostopoulos, A. 74
Anene, O.P. 147
Ângelo, R.P. 253
Anil Kumar, V. 90
animal professionals 16
Anosike, N.M. 147
Antoniou, A.S. 67, 71
anxiety disorders 309
Apostolopoulou 69
artificial intelligence (AI) 292–3
arubaito (fringe workers). 132
Asano, Hirokatsu 133
Ashforth, B.E. 254
Ashy, M.A. 210
Asia Pacific Academy for Psychosocial Factors at Work 16
assa 195
aursia 196
Australia 2; causes of occupational stress 8; GDP 7, 15; landmass 7; occupational stress in 7–17; population 7
Australia, occupational stress in 8–13;

bullying 12–13; dangerous wildlife 15–16; distance 13–14; heat 14–15; incivility 12–13; job demands 9–11; job resources 9–11; occupations with highest stress levels 8; psychosocial safety climate 11–12; stressor appraisals 9–11
Austria **192**
Auton, J.C. 11
Avey, J.B. 321
Azuh, D.E. 147

Babajide, E.O. 153
Balochs 195
BAME employees 3
Banerjee, S. 90
banking sector, Nigerian 151–2
Barbour, J. 8
Barkhuizen, N. 289
Barley, S.R. 94
Barling, J. 256, 321
Barnard, A. 286
Baron, R.A. 145
Bartlett's Test 203
Base Realignment and Closure Commission (BRAC) 313
Bastos, C. 254
Baynes-Rock, M. 16
Beck Depression Inventory (BDI) 310
Beehr, T.A. 270
Beijing 46–51
Belgian Safe Work Information Center 185–6
Belgium **192**
Belgium, work-related stress in 167–88; acknowledgement of risks 178–81; burnout 168–9, *169*, *177*, 178; colleague help and support **173**; handbooks for 182; job autonomy **172**, 175–6; job demands 170–4; manager help and support **173**; negative social interactions **171**; opportunities for control **171**, 175; overview 167–8; participation **174**; prevalence of 168–9; psychosocial risks 169–77; quantitative job demands **170**, 175; risk management **181**, 181–7; skill discretion **172**; trend data *179*
Bhagat, R. 320
Bhatt, S. 89
Bi, P. 15
Biggs, A. 8, 10

blogs 276
Boase, A. 10
Boehmer, T. 269
Bokhan, T.G. 274
Bolino, M.C. 269
Bond, S.A. 12
Borg, V. 94
Borthwick, A. 199
Boudreau, J.W. 309
Braganza, D. 89
Brazil, work stress in 23–36; coding scheme 24–5; Demand-Control-Social Support Model 26; Effort-Reward Imbalance model 26; geographical characteristics 26–8; inclusions 24, *25*; methodological characteristics 26–8; partial distribution by knowledge area *27*; reactions to work stress 28–9; stressors 28–9; surveys 24, *25*; temporal characteristics 26–8, *27*; worker characterizations **28**
Brazilian Burnout Inventory 33
Brief Job Stress Questionnaire (BJSQ) 137
Brough, Paula 8, 8–9, 9–10
Bruce, M. 276
Bruton, G. 271
Bulgaria **192**
bullying 12–13
Burke, R.J. 43, 94, 320
Burman, R. 94
burnout 3, 89, 168–9, *169*, 177, 199–201, 254, 255, 309
Burnout Inventory 86

Calais, S.L. 33
Camacho, C. 253
Campos, J. 254
Cannon, Walter B. 303
cardiovascular diseases, work-related 271
Cardoso, H.F. 33
Carlotto, M.S. 33
Carr, C. 272
Cartwright, S. 3
Caruana, L. 273
Carvalho, A.S. 253, 254, 256
Carvalho, V.S. 251, 253
Cascio, W.F. 309
Case, J.M. 290
Casey, G. 307
Cavanagh, S. 291

Certified Health and Productivity Management Organization Recognition Program (Japan) 138
Chambel, M.J. 251, 253
Chand, P. 91
Chandramouleeswaran, S. 89
Chaturvedi, S.K. 93
Chen, P.Y. 12
Chetty, P.J.J. 287
China (Mainland) 44, 56
Chitra, T. 91
Chrisopoulos, S. 12
Cilliers, F. 284
Clark, S. 291
Claro, M. 254
climate change 15
Clinton, Bill 313
Coelho, D.A. 253
Coetzee, M. 287
Coetzee, S.E. 295
Coetzer, W.J. 286
Cohen, R. 69
Cohen, S. 202–3
collectivism: versus individualism 208; and occupational stress 209–10
communicaiton abilities 294
Compas, B.E. 198
compliance 292
conflict-solving 293
Connor-Smith, J.K. 198
Conradie, Maria 287
Conservation of Resources (COR) model 254
Considine, R. 14
construction industry 154, 288–9
continuous learning 292
control theory 321
Cooper, C.L. 3, 33, 43, 67, 68, 70, 94, 148, 308, 319, 322, 324
Cooper, Kenneth 311
coping mechanisms 154–5, **162–6**, 209; and culture 198–9; emotion-focused 198; problem-focused 198
coping methods/styles 89–90
Coping Strategies Scale 84
Copper, C.L. 305
correctional officers 10
counterproductive work behaviors (CWBs) 150
Coutinho, H. 253
Covid-19 3–4, 323
creativity 293
Croatia **192**

Cronbach's Alpha 202
cross-cultural studies 44–5, 270
cross-sectional studies 251–2
Cruz-Mendes, A.M. 254
Cruz-Robazzi, M. 254
culture 44; and coping 198–9; and work-related stress 201
Cunha, J.P.S. 255
cybernetic theory 321
Cyprus 64, **192**
Czech Republic 64, **192**

da Silva João, A.L. 253
daily workers 132
Dalcin, L. 33
Damásio, B.F. 33
Daudt, H.M.I. 222
Davey, A. 90
David, A. 153
De Beer, L.T. 289
De Beer, L.T. 287
deaths 313, 319
decision-making 293
Demand-Control-Social Support Model 26, 31, 34
Demerouti, E. 74
DemografieFondsDemographie 186
Denmark **192**
Denyer, D. 82
Department of Defense 313
depression 194, 274, 309
descriptive analysis 83–6
Deshmukh, M. 91
Dewe, P.J. 33, 94, 319
Dhaou, S.B. 297
dhow culture 213
diagnostic abilities 293
Dias, D. 255
disability claims 285
dishdasha 195
dispersion modeling 12
distance 13–14
distress 195, 208
divorce 274–5
Dixe, M.A. 253
Doble, N. 93
Dollard, M.F. 12
Doraiswamy, I.R. 91
Dormann, C. 12
downsizing 67
Drosos, N. 71
drought 15
Du Plessis, J.V.D. 289

dual-earner families 56

EBSCO 82
economic stress 271–6
Edge, K. 198
education sector: Nigeria 149–50; South Africa 289–90
Edwin, N. 89
effort-reward imbalance 214
Effort-Reward Imbalance model 26, 32, 34, 86
Effort-Reward Imbalance Questionnaire (ERIQ) 29
El Paso Walmart mass shooting (2019) 306–7
Eliot, R.S. 197
Elsevier 82
Elsheshtawy, E. 201
Emam, M. 201
Emerald 82
emergency workers 132
emotional intelligence 90
emotional resources 10–11
emotion-focused coping 198
Employee's Compensation Act of 2010 (Nigeria) 156
entrusted workers 132
e-payment 152
Epetimehin, S. 145
epidemiology 308
Ermasova, N.B. 276
Estonia **192**
Estrela, C. 253
European Foundation for the Improvement of Living and Working Conditions 63–4
European Survey of Enterprises on New and Emerging Risks (ESENER) 168–9, 169, 175, 178–9, 179–81, 181, **192**, 193
European Union 62
European Union (EU-28) 180–2
European Working Conditions Survey (EWCS) 168, 191, **192**
Eurozone 62
eustress 195, 208, 311–12
evil eye 214
expatriate workers 214
External Services for Prevention and Protection at Work (Belgium) 186
Ezenwaji, I.O. 151

Facebook 275, 276

Fanaras, D.L. 69
Faria, S. 253
Fees Must Fall Movement 290
femininity 210–11
Ferreira, A.I. 255
Ferreira, N. 287
Filipe, R.M. 255
Finland **192**
firefighters 10–11
Flemish Institute for Healthy Living (VIGO) 186
flexibility 292
Flotman, A.P. 284
fly-in fly-out (FIFO) workers 14
Folkman, S. 196–7, 198
Fonseca, A.M. 254
Fonseca, M.J.M. 33
Fotinatos-Ventouratos, R.S.J. 68, 70
Fourth Industrial Revolution 284, 291–5
France 62, **192**
Francis, L. 251
Frank, J. 86, 90
Freitas, C.P.P. 33
Freitas, G.R. 33
Frimpong, K. 287
Fujimura, Masanori 131
Fujioka, Yosei 132
Fukazawa, Kenji 132
Fukui, Satoe 132

Gafarov, V.V. 271
Gandhi, S. 93
Gandi, J.C. 150
Gardner, B. 14
Garg, N. 91
Gates, Robert 307
Gaur, S.P. 93, 322
Gavrilov, I. 272
Gavrilova, N. 272
GDP 1; Australia 7; Nigeria 147; Russia 268
gender bias 194
gender inequality 211–12
General Health Questionnaire 85–6
generic job resources 10
Germany 62, **192**; work-related stress in 64
Goh, J. 305, 306
Gomes, A.R. 253
Google Scholar 82
Gorelova, E. 272
Goswami, T.G. 90

334 *Index*

Gowardman, J. 16
Greater China job stressors 43–57; descriptive statistics **49**; dual-earner families 56; fit statistics **51**; *guanxi* (relationship) 56; intercorrelation of Chinese stressors **50**; intercorrelation of main variables **53**; interpersonal conflict 55; job insecurity 56; job satisfaction 51; measures of 51–2; open-ended interviews **47**; open-ended qualitative methodology 46; organizational politics 55; paternalistic leadership 55; power distance 55; regression analysis **54**; samples and procedures 46–51; strains 51–2; work-family conflict 56
Greece: economic crisis 64–6; exports 69; female labor participation in 70, 71; financial aid package to 65; GDP 69; gender employment gap 71; Kallikratis Reform 66; labor laws 73–4; physical and mental health in 68–9; population 62; stress, work-related in 63–4; unemployment rate 70
Greece, organizational stress in 62–79; attitudes toward women managers 71–2; causes of 64–76; coping mechanisms 72–4; downsizing 67; and economic crisis 64–6; GDP 65; health effects on employees 67; intervention strategies 72–4; job autonomy 70; job crafting for 74–5; and lack of transparency 67–8; and level of justice in organizations 67–8; nonstandard/atypical work arrangements 67–8; primary interventions 75; and restructuring of organizations 66–7; secondary interventions 75; skills mismatch 70; specific stressors 69–72; tertiary interventions 75; unemployment rate 65, 70
Greenberg, J. 145
Greene, B. 284
Grima, S. 273
Grimsrud, A.T. 287
Grodal, S. 94
Gromova, F.A. 271
guanxi (relationship) 56
gun violence 306–7

Guoswami, T.G. 94
Gupta, N. 272
Guzman, J. 94

Habigzang, L.F. 33
haken workers (dispatch workers) 132
Hans, A. 201
Hansen, A. 15
Haratani, Takashi 132
Hart, Peter 9, 9–11
hasad 214
Hashimoto, Hideki 134
Hayward, R. 10
Healey, D. 272
health expenditures 305
Health Perception 249
healthcare sector: India 287–8; Nigeria 150–1; South Africa 287–8
healthcare utilization ratges 313
healthy work organizations 314
heat 14–15
heat stress 15, 89
Hellas *see* Greece
Hellas Employee Assistance Programs (Hellas EAP) 73
Hellenic Republic *see* Greece
Henriques, A. 253
Hernández-Marrero, P. 253, 256
herpetologists 16
Herrera, J. 272
Higher Council for Prevention and Protection at Work 185
Hirst, G. 45
HIV/AIDS 288
Hofstede, G. 208, 210, 211
Hong Kong 44, 46–51, 56
Humphrey, J.H. 197
Hungary **192**
Hurrell 30–8
hypertension 153

Ibem, E.O. 147
Iceland 193
Ilic, D. 288
incivility 12–13
India, work stress in: in academic sector 88–9; in banking 88; burnout 89; consequences 92–3; coping methods/styles 89–90; cross-sectional studies 85–6; cultural influence 95; descriptive analysis 83–6; descriptive features of studies **109–27**; emotional intelligence 90;

in healthcare 87–8; heat stress 89; international literature 93–4; intervention-based studies 91–2; job performance 90; job satisfaction 90–1; in law enforcement 88; organization types 84; overview 81–2; research methods 84–5, *85*, *86*; stressors 44, 86–9, **87**; systematic review 82; unorganized sector 80; variables 89–92; work sectors 84, *85*; workforce characteristics 80; workplace spirituality 91
individualism 200; versus collectivism 208
Industrial Revolution 221
information technology security 293
innovative thinking 293
Inoue, Akiomi 134
Instagram 275, 276
insurance companies 285
intercultural abilities 294
International Labour Organization 1
International Monetary Fund (IMF) 80
interpersonal conflict 55
intervention studies 252, 323
Ireland **192**
"iron rice bowl" era 56
ISI Web of Science 222
Islam 195, 210
Italy **192**
Ito, Takahiro 133
Ivanova, L.I. 270

Jackson, S.E. 168–9
Jacob, D.K. 91
Jacobs, M. 289
Jahan, F. 200
Jain, N. 93
Japan, organizational stress in 128–39; government policies on 136–8; health and productivity management 138; *karo-jisatsu* 129–30; *karoshi* 129–30; long work hours 130–2, **131**; mental health implications 133–4; non-regular employment 132–4; overview 128; power harassment 134–5; sexual harassment 135; Stress Check Program for 137; stressors 133; work style reforms 136; workplace harassment 134–5

Jathanna, P.N.R. 89
Jegede, O.J. 148
Jeitinho Brasileiro 34
Jensen, S.M. 321
jinn 214
Joaquim, A. 256
Job Content Questionnaire (JCQ) 137
job crafting 74–5
job demands 9–11
Job Demands-Control model 168
Job Demands-Resources (JD-R) model 253
Job Demands-Resources model 86
job insecurity 56
job performance 90
job resources 9–11
job satisfaction 90–1
job stressors: appraisals 9–11; in Brazil 28–9, **29**; categories 43; cross-cultural studies 44–5; cultural factors 44; cultural factors in 44; in Greater China 43–57; in India 44, 86–9, **87**; in Japan 133; in Nigeria 147–8, **162–6**; in Oman 213–15; in United States 44; Western models 43–4
Job-Content Questionnaire (JCQ) 29
Johnson, S. 270
Johnson & Johnson 307
Joshi, K. 201
JSTOR 82
Judge, T. 291
Junior, P.L.D. 147

Kahn, R.I/ 303
kahwa 196
Kaiser-Meyer-Olkin (CMO) 202–3, **203**
Kallikratis Reform 66
Kamarck, T. 202
Kane, P.P. 93
karo-jisatsu (work-related suicide) 2, 129–30; causes of 129–30; future research 138; incidence of 129; versus *karoshi* 129
karoshi (death-from-overwork) 129–30; causes of 129–30; future research 138; incidence of 129; versus *karo-jisatsu* 129
Karunanidhi, S. 91
Kawachi, I. 271
Kawaguchi, Daiji 133
Kawakami, Norito 131, 134

Keenan, A. 45, 46
Kelloway, E.K. 251
Kelly Air Force Base 313
Khamisa, N. 288
Khan, S. 91
khanjar 195
Kirsten, G.J. 289
Kitayama, S. 198
Kivimaki, M. 271
Klunder, C. 313
Koller, S.H. 33
Komorida, Tatsuo 130
Kompier, M. 322
Koortzen, P. 286
Koshy, R.C. 91
Koukiadaki, A. 74
Koukoulaki, T. 66
Koul, H. 91
Kretsos. L. 74
Kumar, S.P. 91
Kumar, Suneel 201
Kumar, V.K. 91

Labor Inspectorate Authorities (Greece) 68
Lagos State, Nigeria 152, 156
Lahad, M. 69
Lambert, C.E. 94
Lambert, E.G. 86
Lambert, V.A. 94
language abilities 294
Latha, K.S. 89
Latvia 64, **192**
Laungani, P. 320, 322
Lawati, Hasan al 212
Lawler, J. 45
lawyers, stress management 10
Lazarus 198
Lazarus, R.S. 44, 196–7
Lazarus and Folkman's Model 253
Lee, R.L. 254
Leiter, M.P. 167–9, 168–9
Levi, L. 197
LGBT employees 3
Li, Y. 12
Liang, B. 199
Lipp's Inventory of Symptoms of Stress for Adults 29
Lithuania **192**
Liu, C. 45, 55, 94
Living Situation Survey (Netherlands) 177
longitudinal studies 251–2, 322

Lopes, H. 253
Lourenco, M.L. 253
Lu, Y. 271
Lunde-Jensen, P. 197
Luthans, F. 321
Luxembourg **192**

Ma, J. 44
Macedo, V.A. 147
Macedonia **192**, 193
Macik-Frey 306
Macik-Frey, M. 255
magic 214
Maia, A.C. 254
Mäkikangas, A. 322
Malaysia, absenteeism/presenteeism costs in 2
Malta **192**
Manda, M. 297
Manuel, S. 251
manufacturing sector, Nigerian 152–3
maqbous 196
Markus, H.R. 198
Maroco, J. 254
Marques, M.M. 254
Marteleto, L.J. 291
Martin, Angela 9
Martinez, L.G. 255
Martins-Pereira, S. 253, 256
masculinity 210–11
Maslach 169
Maslach, C. 33, 168
Maslach Burnout Inventory 29, 249, 309
Maslach Burnout Inventory (MBI) 310
Maslow, Abraham 314
Mayer, C.-H. 286, 289, 291
McEwen, B.S. 197
McLinton, S.S. 12
ME 68
medical residents 256
medical sociology 269
medical students 201
Mediterranean syndrome 73
Mehta, P. 90
Mendelson, S. 197
Menon, S. 44
mental health: Australia 7; Belgium 168–9; Brazil 23; Greece 68–9; Japan 133–4; Netherlands 133–4
Mermelstein, R. 202
Meyerson, D.E. 94
Michigan Organizational Assessment Questionnaire 51

micro and small enterprises (MSEs) 193
mining industry 289
Mirtschin, P. 16
Montenegro **192**, 193
Montibeler, J. 33
mortality rates 305
Mosaku, T.O. 147
Moskvin, Alexander 272
Mouza, A.M. 67
Mujtaba, B.G. 269
mussar 195
Myer, L. 287
Myers, D.G. 321

Najarian, B. 197
Nakata, Akinori 132
Narayanan, L. 44
Nash, S. 272
National Institute for Occupational Safety and Health (NIOSH) 309, 313
National Labour Council 185
National Strategy for Well-Being at Work 186
negative affectivity 150
Nelson, D.L. 256, 308, 312
Netherlands, work-related stress in 167–88; acknowledgement of risks 178–81; burnout 168–9, *169*, *177*; colleague help and support **173**; handbooks for 182; job autonomy **172**, 175–6; job demands **170–4**; manager help and support **173**; negative social interactions **171**; opportunities for control **171**, 175; overview 167–8; participation **174**; prevalence of 168–9; psychosocial risks *176*, **180**; quantitative job demands 169, **170**, 175; risk factors **180**; risk management **181**, 181–7; skill discretion **172**; trend data 177–8
Netherlands Working Conditions Survey (NWCS) 177
Neto, M. 251, 253
networking abilities 294
neuropsychiatric disorders 287
neuroticism 201
Nevid, J.S. 284, 286
Newton, T.J. 45, 46
Nguyen, L.D. 269, 270, 276
Nicholas, A.L. 147

Nielsen, K. 94
Nigeria, organizational stress in 145–57; in banking sector 151–2; in construction sector 153–4; coping mechanisms 154–5, **162–6**; cultural factors in 156–7; in education sector 149–50; government as culprit in 156–7; in healthcare sector 150–1; versus other countries 146–7; overview 145–6; in police force 154; socioeconomic factors 148; stressors and strains 147–8, **162–6**; and weak enforcement of labor laws 156; work content 147–8; work context 147–8
NIOSH Generic Job Stress Questionnaire 137
non-regular employment, in Japan 132–4; *arubaito* (fringe workers) 132; daily workers 132; emergency workers 132; entrusted workers 132; fair treatment of 136; *haken* workers (dispatch workers) 132; increasing 132–3; mental health implications 133–4; and organizational stress 133; *paato* (part-time workers) 132; seasonal workers 132; statistics 132–3; stressors 133; types of 132
Norton, P. 253
Norway **192**, 193
Nunfam, V.F. 287
nurses 150–1, 200, 254
Nurses' Stress Inventory 29
Nwokeoma, B.N. 145, 154

Obama, Barack 306
Obasi, N.J. 147
occupational stress, definition of 197
Occupational Stress Index 84
Occupational Stress Indicator (OSI) 44
occupational stress research: Australia 7–17; Belgium 167–88; Brazil 23–36; Greater China 43–57; Greece 62–79; India 80–95; Japan 128–39; Netherlands 167–88; Nigeria 145–57; Oman 194–216; Portugal 221–58; Russia 268–77; South Africa 284–97; United States 303–15
occupational therapy 200
Odendaal, A. 291
O'Driscoll, M.P. 33

O'Driscoll, M.P. 94
O'Driscoll, M.P. 319
Ogbari, M. 145
Ogbuanya 150
Ohya,Yukihiro 131
oil fields, stress in 200
Okebukola, P.A. 148
Okeke, M.N. 145, 152
OlaOlorun, A.D. 151
Olatona, F.A. 152, 154
Olawoyim, O. 148
Oldenburg 288
Olofin, A. 151
Olusegun, A.J. 148, 151
Oluwasayo, A.J. 148
Oman: cultural dress 195–6; dependence on expatriates 215; *dhow* culture 213; dishes 196; expatriate workers 214; gender inequality 211–12; gender myths 212; geographic location 195; income 214; land area 195, 215; limited socializing in 215; Omanization policy 215; population 195; religion 195; social norms 211; social order 215; stressors in 213–15; topography and scattered inhabitation 215; unemployment rate 214; women's rights in 211–12; women's roles in 211–12
Oman, occupational stress in 194–216, 199–201; behavioral changes 208; burnout 199–201; and collectivism 209–10; coping strategies 196–7, 198–9, 209; and culture 201; data analysis 202–3; definition of 196, 197; demographic data of respondents 203–8; distress in society 213–15; effects of 196; empirical studies on perceived stress 202–8; methodology 202; overview 196–7; and power distance 210–13; studies on 199–201
Onyishi, I.E. 149
Oosthuizen, J. 287
Oosthuizen, R.M. 286, 289, 291
open-ended method 45
opioid epidemic 307–8
organizational clinical psychology 312–13
Organizational Health Center (OHC) 313
organizational politics 55

Organizational Role Stress Scale 84
organizational stress: across diverse occupations 270; in banking sector 151–2; and cardiovascular diseases 271; causes of 64–76; in construction sector 153–4; coping mechanisms 72–4, 154–5, **162–6**; cross-cultural studies 270; cultural factors in 156–7, 304–8, 310–15; and drinking 276; economic factors 64–6, 271–6; in education sector 149–50; eustress 311–12; government as culprit in 156–7; government policies on 136–8; health effects 67, 271; in healthcare sector 150–1; intervention strategies 72–4; mental health implications 133–4; mortality rates 305; overload stress 276; physical fitness 311; positive effects 271; positive stress 311–12; power harassment 134–5; primary interventions 75; and religion 276; and restructuring of organizations 66–7; and roles in work 270; secondary interventions 75; sexual harassment 135; and social stress 271–6; socioeconomic factors 148; stressors 133, 147–8, 305; tertiary interventions 75; and use of social network sites 275–6; work style reforms 136; working conditions 271; working hours 130–2, 304–5; work-life balance 270; workplace harassment 134–5; *see also* work stress
organizational stress research: Greece 62–79; Japan 128–39; Nigeria 145–57; Russia 268–77; United States 303–15
Osibanjo, O.A. 149
Osmany, M. 93
Owolabi, A.O. 151
Owolabi, M.O. 151

paato (part-time workers) 132
Paiva, J.S. 255
Pandey, S. 94, 322
Panov, D.O. 271
park rangers 16
paternalistic leadership 55
Pathak, P. 89
Pearlin, L.I. 269
Peltzer, K. 288

Perceived Stress Scale (PSS) 84, 202
Pereira Miguel, J. 251
perestroika 271
"person of confidence" 187
personality traits 201
person-environment fit theory 303, 321
Pestonjee, D.M. 322
Petrou, P. 74
physical fitness 311
physical working conditions 153
Pienaar, J. 287, 289
Pinterest 276
Piraeus Bank Group 73
Pisaniello, D. 15
Poland **192**
police force, Nigerian 154
Porath, C. 3
Portugal, occupational stress research in 221–58; aim of study **224–47**; analysis 223, 248; antecedents of work stress 252–4; area of study **224–47**, 248; authors **224–47**; consequences of work stress 255; cross-sectional studies 251–2; flow diagram of systematic selection of studies 223; healthcare professionals 256; inclusion/exclusion criteria 223; intervention studies 252; journals **224–47**, 248; longitudinal studies 251–2; methodology 222; negative bias 255–6; organizational size 249; participants **224–47**; private vs. public organizations 249; professionals studies 251; reviewed studies **224–47**; sample sizes 248–9; study design **224–47**, 248–9, 251–2; two-step cluster analysis **250**; well-being indicator and measures **224–47**, 249; year of publication **224–47**, 248
positive organizational behavior 311–12
positive stress 311–12
positivity 311–12
posttraumatic stress disorder (PTSD) 254, 307
power distance 55, 210–13; femininity 211; masculinity 210; uncertainty avoidance 212–13
power harassment 134–5
Prabhu, S. 89
Prakash, C. 91

Prasad, K.D. 90
Preferred Reporting Items for Systematic Reviews and Meta-Analyses (PRISMA) 222
presenteeism: in Australia 2; in Malaysia 2; in Portugal 255
Prickett, K. 291
primary interventions 323
primary prevention stage 3
private universities, Nigerian 149
problem-focused coping 198
problem-solving 293
Probst, T.M. 45
process comprehension 293
proficiency assimilation 293
programming abilities 293
PSC-12 11–12
psychosocial safety climate (PSCs) 11–12
psychosocial stress 274
public health 308
public universities, Nigerian 149
PubMed 222
Purde Pharma 307

qualitative research 322
quantitative studies 322
Queirós, C. 253
Quick, J.C. 255, 308, 313, 321
Quick, J.D. 308, 321
Qureshi, H. 86

Raaidan, Amira al 194
Ramesh, B. 91
Ranta, R.S. 89, 91
Raper, M.J. 10
Rathus, S.A. 284
rational emotive behavior coaching (REBC) 155
Rebar, A.L. 14
Reis, C. 251, 253
religion 276
religous apparel, and religion 276
remote area nurses (RANs) 13–14
research competencies 293
resilience 292
Ribeiro, E. 254
Ribeiro, O. 254
Ritzmann, R.F. 197
road rage 213
Robbins, S. 291
Robertson, I. 324
robotics 292–3

Rocco, P. 194
Rodrigues, S. 255
Roger, D. 197
Romania **192**
Roodt, G. 291
Rothmann, S. 286, 287, 289, 295
Russia: alcohol use in 276; divorce in 274–5; economic crises 272; economic stress in 271; GDP 268; life expectancy 272; *perestroika* 271; population 268; psychotic, stress-related disorders in 273; safety net 273; social diseases 272–3; social network sites 275–6; social stress in 271; suicides 273–4; transition to market economy 272; worforce 268; workforce 276
Russia, organizational stress in 268–77, 270; across diverse occupations 270; and cardiovascular diseases 271; cross-cultural studies 270; and drinking 276; and economic stress 271–6; health effects 271, 274; of managers 272, 274; medical sociology 269; overload stress 276; positive effects 271; and religion 276; and roles in work 270; scarce resources 271; and social stress 271–6; symptoms 271; two workforces 276; and use of social network sites 275–6; working conditions 271; work-life balance 270; work-related stress 269–70

Sacadura-Leite, F. 253, 254
Sakurai, Keiko 134
Salami 150
Salanova, M. 255–6, 321
Saldanha Portelada, A.F. 253
Salgado, J. 44
Saltzman, H. 198
San Antonio Air Logistics Center 313
Sanchez 44
Sangeetha, G. 93
Sant'Anna, A.D. 147
Satisfaction with Life 249
Schaufeli 257
Schaufeli, W.B. 168, 255, 287, 321
Science Direct 82
Scopus 82, 222
Scott, S.J. 222
seal handlers 16
Searle, B.J. 11

seasonal workers 132
secondary interventions 323
secondary prevention stage 3
secondary schools 150
security industry 289
Self Reporting Questionnaire 29
self-authorship 290
self-disclosure, avoidance of 213–14
Selye, Hans 197
Semmer, N.K. 183
Serbia **192**, 193
Serranheira, F. 253
sexual harassment 135
Sharia law 212
Sherwood, H. 198
Shevchuk, A. 270
Shi, L. 45, 94
Shipp, S. 272
shuva 196
sick leaves 309
sickness absence 2
Sieberhagen, C. 287
Siebert, W. 74
Simmons, B.L. 312
Singh, M. 90
Sinha, B. 199
Siu, O. 44
Sivaramakrishnan, A. 91
Skakon, J. 94, 322
Skinner, E.A. 198
Skinner, J.E. 197
Sloan, S.J. 43
Slovakia **192**
Slovenia 64, **192**
small to medium-sized enterprise (SMEs) 9
Smart, P. 82
smart technology 292–3
Smit, D.M.D. 289
Snapchat 275
social network sites 275–6
social stratification 269
social stress 271–6
Socio-Economic Council for Flanders (SERV) 186
Souchamvali, D. 67
South Africa: colored community 291; Fourth Industrial Revolution 291–5; HIV/AIDS 288
South Africa, occupational stress in 284–97; black women 291; characteristics of 291–5; competition and rivalry 286;

construction industry 288–9; from different cultural perspectives 290–1; in education sector 289–90; effects of 285–6; health effects 286; health sector 287–8; high level of 285–6; mining industry 289; in minority groups 286; neuropsychiatric disorders from 286; overview 284–5; in police force 289; security industry 289; in sociocultural and racial groups 290–1; stress management 295–6; stressors 286; in women 286; workplace boredom 287
South Korea, work hours in 131
Spain **192**
special education teachers 149–50
specialized competencies 293
specific job resources 10
Spector, P.E. 45, 94, 320
Spector. P.E. 44
Spreitzer, G. 3
State of American Well-Being survey (2017) 304–5
Stein, A.J. 287
Steinberg, A. 197
Stern, E. 288
Stevenson, S. 16
strategic alignment 10
Strebkov, D. 270
stress: defined 284; definition of 63, 269; health effects 304
stress, work-related 1–4; causes of 1–2; definition of 63; effects of 2
Stress Check Program (Japan) 137
Stress Incident Record 46
stress management 295–6; macro-level 295–6; meso-level 295–6; micro-level 295
stress management interventions (SMIs) 8–9
Stress Management (Tummers/Rocco) 195
stress test 304
stressors 1–2, 319; appraisals 9–11; in Brazil 28–9, **29**; categories 43; cross-cultural studies 44–5; cultural factors 44; in Greater China 43–57; in India 44, 86–9, **87**; in Japan 133; in Nigeria 147–8, **162**–6; in Oman 213–15; in United States 44; Western models 43–4
study design **224**–47, 251–2

Stylianidis, S. 68
suicides: Australia 2; Japan 2, 129–30; Russia 273–4; United States 313; in United States armed services 307
Supriya, M.V. 93
Surtee, S. 289
Survey of Enterprises on New and Emerging Risks – Psychosocial Risks (Portugal) 221
sustainability 292
Swahilis 195
Sweden 64, **192**
Switzerland **192**, 193; national health insurance in 306

Taber, T.D. 270
Taha, H. 201
Taipe 46–51
Taiwan 56
Takahashi, Masaya 132
Tamayo, M.R. 33
Taris, T.W. 183, 257, 322
Tavares, C.S. 253
Taylor and Francis 82
teamwork abilities 294
Teixeira, C.M. 253, 254, 256
tertiary interventions 324
tertiary prevention stage 3
Theofanidis. D. 69
Thompson, G.G. 16
Thompson, S.A. 16
Thomsen, A.H. 198
Times Oman 194
Tomlinson, M. 287
Total Worker Health (TWH) initiative 314
Tozer, S. 16
Trait-State Anxiety Inventory 310
Tranfield, D. 82, 83
Transparent Reporting of Systematic Reviews and Meta-Analysis (PRISMA) 24
triangulation method 323
Tróccoli, B.T. 33
Trump, Donald 306
Tsuchiya, Masao 134
Tsutsumi, Akizumi 131
Tuckey, M.R. 10–11, 12
Tummers, L. 194
Turkey **192**, 193
Turner, N. 256, 321
Turnley, W.H. 269
turnover rates 309

Ugwoke 150
Ugwu, F.O. 149
Umege, D.C. 153
Umehara, Katsura 131
uncertainty: avoidance 212–13; tolerance 292
unemployment rate 214
United Kingdom **192**; national health service 306; work stress in 146–7; working hours 305
United States: economic and financial crises of 2008 273; gun violence in 306–7; health care in 306; health expenditures 305; health insurance in 306; opioid epidemic 307–8; stressors in 44; suicides in armed services 307; work hours in 131; work stress in 146
United States Air Force Surgeon General 313
United States Centers for Disease Control and Prevention 314
United States, organizational stress in 303–15, 307; cultural context 304–8; cultural influences 310–15; eustress 311–12; healthy work organizations 314; historical backdrop 303–4; mortality rates 305; organizational clinical psychology 312–13; physical fitness 311; positive organizational behavior 311–12; positive stress 311–12; positivity 311–12; working hours 304–5; workplace stressors 305
Unity (Russian employment agency) 269
Utrecht Work Engagement Scale 249

Vahtera, J. 67
Vaidya, R. 90
Valente, J.G. 33
Van den Berg, H.S. 286
Van Etten, E.J. 287
Van Mossel, C. 222
Van Wyk, S. 287
Van Zyl, E. 284, 286, 290
Vandelanotte, C. 14
Vazão, M.J. 254
Vos, J.D. 289

Wadsworth, M.E. 198
Walsh, J.T. 270

wasta 214
Watson, D.C. 199
Webster, V. 12
Weinberg, A. 324
wildlife 15–16
Williams, D.R. 287
Williams, J. 10
Williams, S. 43
Willson, L.R. 199
Wilper, A.P. 305
women: black 286; employees 3; managers 71–2; rights 211–12; roles 211–12; work stress in 286
Woods, M. 16
Work Health and Safety Act 2011 (Australia) 7
work hours: in developed countries **131**; in Japan 130–2, **131**; in South Korea 131; United Kingdom 305; in United States 305
work stress 1–4; in academic sector 88–9; antecedents 252–4; in banking 88; bullying 12–13; burnout 89; causes of 1–2; characteristics of 291–5; competition and rivalry 286; consequences 92–3, 255; construction industry 288–9; coping mechanisms 89–90; cross-sectional studies 85–6; cultural influence 95; dangerous wildlife 15–16; definition of 63; from different cultural perspectives 290–1; distance 13–14; in education sector 289–90; effects of 2, 285–6; health effects 286, 319; in healthcare 87–8, 287–8; heat 14–15; heat stress 89; high level of 285–6; incivility 12–13; inclusions 24; job demands 9–11; job performance 90; job resources 9–11; job satisfaction 90–1; in law enforcement 88; mining industry 289; in minority groups 286; neuropsychiatric disorders from 286; occupations with highest stress levels 8; organization types 84; in police force 289; psychosocial safety climate 11–12; security industry 289; in sociocultural and racial groups 290–1; stress management 295–6; stressor appraisals 9–11; stressors 28–9, 86–9, **87**, 286; surveys 24, 25; temporal

characteristics 26–8, 27; in women 286; work sectors 84, 85; worker characterizations 28; workplace boredom 287; workplace spirituality 91; *see also* organizational stress
work stress research: Australia 7–17; Belgium 167–88; Brazil 23–36; Greater China 43–57; Greece 62–79; India 80–95; Japan 128–39; Netherlands 167–88; Nigeria 145–57; Oman 194–216; Portugal 221–58; Russia 268–77; South Africa 284–97; United States 303–15
Work Stress Scale 29
worker's compensation: claims 7; rates 313
work-family conflict 56
Working Conditions Act (Netherlands) 183–4
working environment 2–3
work-life balance 270
workplace harassment: in Japan 134–6; power harassment 134–5; prevention of 136–7; sexual harassment 135
workplace health organizations 285
workplace spirituality 91
work-related stress: in Belgium 167–88; cross-cultural studies 270; in Netherlands 167–88
World Health Organisation (WHO) 1
World Health Organization (WHO) 319
World Trade Organization (WTO) 43, 268, 273
Worrall, L. 304
worship 210

Xanthopoulou, D. 74
Xiang, J. 15

Y Magazine 194, 212
Yiu, D. 271

Zacharatos, A. 256, 321
Zadow, A. 12
Ziaian, T. 12

Printed in the United States
By Bookmasters